The Racovian Catechism: With Notes and Illustrations, Translated from the Latin; to Which Is Prefixed a Sketch of the History of Unitarianism in Poland and the Adjacent Countries

Thomas Rees

THE

RACOVIAN CATECHISM,

WITH NOTES AND ILLUSTRATIONS,

TRANSLATED FROM THE LATIN:

TO WHICH IS PREFIXED

A SKETCH

OF THE HISTORY OF UNITARIANISM

IN POLAND AND THE ADJACENT COUNTRIES.

───────

By THOMAS REES, F.S.A.

───────

LONDON:

PRINTED FOR LONGMAN, HURST, REES, ORME, AND
BROWN, PATERNOSTER ROW.

1818.

Printed by Richard and Arthur Taylor, Shoe-Lane.

ADVERTISEMENT.

SEVERAL years have now elapsed since the following work was first promised to the public. A variety of circumstances have operated to delay its appearance; of which the principal has been a painful bodily indisposition of long continuance, whereby the translator was unfitted for the close application, and the mental exertion, which his undertaking required. A kind Providence, to whom he can never be sufficiently grateful, has at last restored to him the invaluable blessing of health, and enabled him thus to put the finishing hand to his task.

He cannot send his work forth to the world without expressing his consciousness, that it will stand in need of much indulgence. The reader of discernment and taste will not fail to discover many defects in its literary execution.

But

But the translator ventures to cherish the hope that the acute sufferings under which a great part of it was composed, will plead his apology for the principal of them, and mitigate the severity of criticism in respect to the whole.

In a publication of this nature, a laboured elegance of style would have been misplaced; and from the character of the original would have been impracticable in the translation. All that has been aimed at, has been, to exhibit the work in an English dress that would convey to the reader as correct an idea as possible, not only of the sentiments, but also of the manner of thinking, and the peculiar tone of feeling, which distinguished the authors of the Catechism. In this object, the translator is obliged to say, he has not always succeeded to his wishes; for he has, in his progress, had to encounter difficulties which he dares not flatter himself that he has in every case completely vanquished. On some of the subjects discussed in the Catechism, the authors and editors had not very distinct and clear ideas;—there is therefore necessarily a degree

degree of obscurity in the language in which they endeavour to express their thoughts. They have also occasionally embarrassed their style by the employment of scholastic terms and phrases, which, without a previous knowledge of the particular treatise or system to which their observations were meant more immediately to apply, it is not easy fully to understand. The translator confesses that he has on these accounts been sometimes considerably perplexed: and he is not without apprehension, that, in a few instances, the obscurity of the original may have been transfused into the translation, and that he has failed to express the precise shade of meaning which the authors intended to convey. He has however done his best; and it will afford him great pleasure to receive the corrections of any persons who may be more fortunate than himself in eliciting the sense of the original work.

It was the translator's first design to give, with an English version of the latest authorized edition of the Racovian Catechism, a detailed statement of all the alterations made

in

in the work by successive editors, with the view of exhibiting the changes which took place in the opinions of the Polish Unitarians, on some of the peculiar articles of their creed. But, on making the experiment, he soon found that he should, by such a proceeding, only crowd and disfigure his pages, without effecting any valuable object. This part of his plan, therefore, he immediately abandoned, except in relation to a few cases, in which he has deemed it proper to notice some remarkable deviations in the last from the first edition of the Catechism. He has added some other notes of his own, partly with the view of illustrating the text or the notes of his original, and partly for the purpose of explaining, to readers not already conversant with the subject, the chief points of difference between the sentiments of the Polish, and those of the modern English, Unitarians. These notes are included within [ ] brackets, and subscribed with the word TRANSLATOR. To these the writer does not attach much importance: they may serve, however, to prevent

persons

persons who are not better informed, from imputing to the Unitarians of the present day opinions that were held by their predecessors, but which they regard as unwarranted by the Scriptures.

To the original work the present editor has prefixed an Historical Introduction, comprising a view of the rise, progress, and vicissitudes of the Unitarian doctrine on the continent of Europe subsequently to the æra of the Reformation. The limits within which it was necessary that he should confine himself, rendered it impracticable to treat this subject at such length as its interest and importance would otherwise have demanded: nor could he, in such an abstract, enter into the critical discussion of those facts concerning which his statements vary from those of all preceding writers on this part of Church annals. He designs it merely as a rough and imperfect outline of a larger History of Unitarianism which he has for some time had in contemplation, and for which he has collected a considerable mass of valuable materials. With this

work,

work, should the subject appear to be interesting to the religious world, he now feels disposed to proceed, with all the expedition which other demands on his time, and the nature and magnitude of the undertaking, will admit. It may be thought that a larger portion of this sketch has been devoted to Transylvania than is warranted by its connexion with the following Catechism, which relates more particularly to Poland. But the writer conceived that he might be held justified, in consideration of the new light which he has been able to throw on the interesting transactions, hitherto so imperfectly detailed, relating to Francis David. Having the means in his hands, he felt it to be his duty to embrace the opportunity to wipe away from the memory of that eminent person the unfounded charge, by which he has so long been calumniated, of holding opinions little consonant with the Christian revelation. Nor is he without some expectation that his account of those proceedings may serve to weaken the accusations that have been preferred against Faustus Socinus

nus for the share he has been thought to have had in the direction of them. The Confessions of Faith inserted in the notes will be read with interest, as exhibiting the religious creed of a numerous body of Unitarians, of whom little information has thus far been communicated to the English public.

The editor has now only to consign his work to the disposal and blessing of the God of Truth. Should it at all conduce to promote the knowledge of His attributes and character, and to advance His merciful designs in the dispensation of " Grace and truth wherein he has in these last days spoken unto us by his Son," it will not have been undertaken in vain, and the writer will feel amply compensated for all his labours in the execution of it.

London, Feb. 1818.

VOTES of the PARLIAMENT touching the Book commonly called The RACOVIAN CATECHISM.

————

Mr. Millington reports from the Committee to whom the Book (entituled *Catechesis Ecclesiarum quæ in Regno Poloniæ, &c.* commonly called The Racovian Catechism) was referred, several passages in the said book which were now read.

- Resolved upon the question by the Parliament, That the book, Entituled *Catechesis Ecclesiarum quæ in Regno Poloniæ, &c.* commonly called The Racovian Catechism, doth contain matters that are blasphemous, erroneous, and scandalous.

Resolved upon the question by the Parliament, That all the printed copies of the book Entituled *Catechesis Ecclesiarum quæ in Regno Poloniæ, &c.* commonly called The Racovian Catechism, be burnt.

Resolved upon the question by the Parliament, That the Sheriffs of London and Middlesex be authorized and required to seize all the printed copies of the book Entituled *Catechesis Ecclesiarum quæ in Regno Poloniæ, &c.* commonly called The Racovian Catechism, wheresoever they shall be found, and cause the same to be burnt at the Old Exchange London, and in the New Palace at Westminster, on Tuesday and Thursday next.

————

Friday, the Second of April, 1652.

Resolved by the Parliament, That these Votes be forthwith printed and published.

Hen. Scobell, *Cleric. Parliamenti.*

————

London: Printed by William Field, Printer to the Parliament of England, 1652.

HISTORICAL INTRODUCTION. *Page* i

SECTION

CONTENTS.

HISTO-

HISTORICAL INTRODUCTION.

I~ the following pages, it is intended to exhibit a rapid sketch of the History of Unitarianism on the continent of Europe subsequent to the æra of the Reformation ; but more particularly of its rise, establishment, and vicissitudes in Poland and its dependencies, with a view to the churches of which the annexed Catechism was originally compiled.

It is not possible to ascertain the precise date to which the revival of the doctrine of the divine Unity ought to be referred. Long before Luther renounced the communion of the Church of Rome, and erected the standard of the Reformation in Germany, many individuals had declared their dissent from particular articles of its creed, and, in defiance of its authority, had formed themselves into societies for separate religious worship upon other principles and with different forms *. Among the tenets which were called in
question

---

* Such, among others, was the case of the Waldenses, who arose about the middle of the twelfth century, and who hold a very interesting place in Ecclesiastical History. They denied the supremacy of the Pope, remonstrated against indulgences, confession to a priest, prayers for the dead, and purgatory. They had bishops, presbyters and deacons. Some of them admitted the Catholic Church to be a true church, others re-

a
garded

question after men had thus ventured, in spite of their
spiritual shackles, to think for themselves, and to
bring the received opinions to the test of the Scriptures, the doctrine of the Trinity appears to have been
one of the first. In several of the writings of this
period traces incidentally occur of antitrinitarian
sentiments, which were regarded with deep horror,
and assailed in the severest terms of reprobation,
both by persons who still maintained their fidelity to
the Roman Church, and by those who had begun to
arraign the purity of its faith in other matters. It
seems probable, however, that these censures were
drawn forth by the doubts and insinuations which had

---

garded the Pope as Antichrist. According to some of their
published Confessions, they seem to have held the common
opinion on the subject of the Trinity; but the following extract
from a confession inserted in a curious old work, intituled
Histoire des Vaudois, par Jean Paul Perrin, printed at Geneva
in 1618, will furnish some ground of suspicion that on this
point all their churches were not strictly orthodox. " 1. *Nous
croyons qu'il n'est qu'vn seul Dieu qui est Esprit, createur de
toutes choses, Pere de tous, qui est sur tous, et par toutes choses,
et en nous tous, lequel on doit adorer en esprit et verité, auquel
seul attendons, et donnons gloire de nostre vie, nourriture, veste-
ment, santé, maladie, prosperité, et adversité, l'aimons comme
autheur de toute bonté, le craignons, comme celuy qui cognoit les
cœurs. 2. Nous croyons que Jesus Christ est le Fils de l'image
du Pere; qu'en luy habite toute plenitude de diuinité; par lequel
nous cognoissons le Pere, lequel est nostre Mediateur et aduo-
cat, et n'y a point d'autre nom sous le ciel donné aux hommes,
auquel il nous faille estre sauués : au nom duquel seul nous invo-
quons le Pere, et n'vsons d'autres oraisons que de celles qui sont
contenues en l'Escriture Saincte, ou concordantes a icelles en substance. 3. Nous croyons que le Sainct Esprit est nostre consolateur,
procedant du Pere et du Fils, par l'inspiration duquel nous faisons
prieres, estans par luy renouuelés, lequel fait toutes bonnes
œuures en nous, et par luy auons cognoissance de toute verité.*

in

in some cases been hinted, more or less obscurely, respecting this doctrine*, rather than by any public renunciation of it; of which no well attested instance is recorded, until after the Reformation had made some progress. As far as can be collected from the accusations of their adversaries, the persons who first openly impugned this tenet were ANABAPTISTS of Germany and Holland;—a designation under which were comprised, not only those wild and infuriate visionaries who were at one time the terror of all Europe, but likewise men of high character and reputation, distinguished by their solid learning, their rational

---

* Of the mode of impugning the popular creed which was adopted at this period, we have two remarkable examples in the persons of Bernard Ochin and Lælius Socinus. Ochin is charged with having pursued this method to bring some of the doctrines of the Catholic Church into disrepute in his public discourses, while he adhered to her communion, stating difficulties and objections, and omitting to answer them, or subjoining unsatisfactory solutions. At a later period of his life he did the same, in respect to the doctrine of the Trinity, through the press. In his celebrated Dialogues, (*Dial.* xx. et xxi. *lib.* ii. *pp.* 146 *et seqq.*) in discussing this subject, he insinuates strong objections to the popular notion, but adduces very feeble arguments in its support; and plainly shows that he has not without reason been charged with having embraced antitrinitarian sentiments. Lælius Socinus pursued the same plan during his residence in Switzerland, never, seemingly, openly avowing his own opinions, but embodying his objections and difficulties in the form of questions, which he submitted, with apparent modesty and diffidence, for the solution of the great luminaries of the Reformation. The freedom of some of these questions exposed him to the suspicion of heresy, and had nearly involved him in difficulties; and others of them drew from Calvin a very angry letter, in which he pettishly observes—*Si plura desideras aliunde petenda sunt. Vide* Bock, *Hist. Antitrin. tom.* li. *p.* 485 &c. et p. 609.

piety,

piety, and enlightened zeal for divine truth; who shared the obloquy attached to their denomination in consequence of denying to the rite of infant baptism the obligation of a Christian institution.

The person who is considered to have been the earliest public advocate of antitrinitarianism, is Martin Cellarius, a native of Stutgard. He was born in the year 1499, and educated at the university of Wittemberg, where he is said to have studied with singular success polite literature, philosophy, and theology, the Latin, Greek, Hebrew, Chaldee and Syriac languages. His learning and talents secured for him the warm friendship of Luther and Melancthon, whose principles he had embraced. Being deputed to hold a public disputation with Stubner and Stork, two of the founders of the German Anabaptists, he yielded to the arguments of his acute and learned opponents, and went over to their party; but pursuing his inquiries further than they had done, relinquished, among other tenets, the doctrine of the Trinity. His defection from the Lutheran cause, and his open avowal of antitrinitarian sentiments, exposed him to various persecutions, to escape which he removed in 1536 to Basil in Switzerland, where he remained until his death in the year 1564. On his settlement in this city he took the name of Borrhaus, being a translation of his original surname into the corresponding Greek term, and was appointed professor of rhetoric and philosophy. He is mentioned by Faustus Socinus in high terms of eulogy as the friend of his uncle Lælius; and the ministers of Tran-

sylvania

sylvania class him with Servetus and Erasmus, as ap- pointed by God to convey to mankind extraordinary information concerning himself and Jesus Christ. Andrew Althamerus, who wrote a work against Cellarius, represents him as having revived the errors of Paul of Samosata, &c. and maintained that Jesus Christ was a mere human prophet *.

Contemporary with Cellarius was Lewis Hetzer, a Dutchman by birth, who is usually classed among the anabaptists, but without sufficient evidence †. He settled at Zurich in the year 1523. Hetzer was a man of great learning, and deeply versed in the original languages of the Scriptures, of which he exhibited undeniable proof in a German translation of all the books of the prophets, which he published, in 1527, in conjunction with John Denkius. Sandius states that in his theological sentiments he was manifestly and certainly an Arian, and represents him as having taught that the Father alone was the true God; that Christ was inferior to the Father, and of a different essence; that there were not three persons in the godhead; and that God was neither essence nor person in the sense in which those terms are commonly em-

---

* Meshovii *Hist. Anabaptistica*, p. 3. This writer calls him Matthias Cellarius. Bock, *Hist. Antitrin. tom.* ii. *pp.* 223 et seqq. Sandii *Bibliotheca Antitrinitar.* p. 15, who quotes the words of the ministers of Sarmatia and Transylvania in their work *De falsa et vera cognitione Dei*: " *Luthero et Zwinglio dedit* [*Deus*] *referendos et justificationis et rei sacramentariæ fructus; Martino vero Cellario, Serveto, et Erasmo Roterodamo fructus alios præcipuos cognitionis veri Dei et Christi,* &c.

† Bock, *ubi supra, tom.* ii. *p.* 232.

ployed.

ployed*. He wrote a work against the deity of Christ, which however was never published ; the manuscript having fallen into the hands of Zwinglius was suppressed. Hetzer was put to death by the magistrates of Constance in the year 1529, but historians disagree as to the cause and the manner of his punishment. Seckendorff† affirms that he was burnt at the stake for his heretical opinions; but Sandius and others, concurring with this writer as to the reason of his condemnation, state, and, it would seem, more correctly, that he was beheaded ‡. But some, whose relation the learned Bock has followed, assert that he suffered on account of his licentious principles and conduct. This statement, however, which is grounded on the representation of enemies, ought to be received with much caution. At this period it was customary to implicate in the guilt of the most criminal of the anabaptist sect all whose dissent from the popular faith caused them to be ranked under this denomination ; and a denial of the supreme deity of Christ was sufficient to expose any individual, however exemplary in his morals, to the imputation of crimes the most abhorrent to his feelings. This consideration should incline us to believe with Sandius and Seckendorff, both most respectable authorities, that Hetzer's real offence was what the latter styles his blasphemies against God §.

---

* *Nucleus Hist. Eccles.* 4to. p. 424.   *Bibl. Antitrin.* p. 16.
† *Hist. Lutheran. lib.* ii. p. 145.
‡ *Bibl. Antitrin.* p. 17.
§ Bock, *ubi supra,* tom. ii. p. 231.

With

With the name of Hetzer is connected that of John Denkius, who has already been noticed as associated with him in his German version of the prophetical writings. Denkius, who is mentioned as a man of extensive erudition, and a profound Hebrew scholar, was a native of Nuremberg, and for some time held the situation of rector of the school of that city. He is stated to have maintained that God was the fountain of all created things; that the Spirit or power of God was the next in order; and afterwards the Word of God, which he had begotten of himself by the Spirit.

Hetzer and Denkius are represented as holding the first rank among the antitrinitarians of this age in Germany and Switzerland; and it is said that their fame, having spread into Italy, had the effect of bringing over to their opinions many individuals in that country *.

The next name that occurs in this connexion is that of John Campanus, supposed to have been a native of Juliers. He settled at Wittemberg in 1528, where he is charged with having clandestinely promulgated his opinions. Sandius states him to have been an Arian †. He wrote a work on the Trinity, wherein he maintained that the Son was begotten of the substance of the Father, before the world was created; that there was a time when he had no existence; and consequently that he was inferior to the Father, who employed him as his minister in the creation of the world, and in other affairs; and that

* Bock, *ubi supra, tom. ii. pp.* 240, 241.
† *Nucleus Hist. Eccles. p.* 427.

the

the Spirit was not a divine Person, but meant the nature and operations of the Father and the Son[*]. He is supposed to have died about 1530, previously to which he suffered some persecution for his opinions.

Another antitrinitarian of this period was Adam Pastor, a man of great learning, who had previously borne the name of Rudolphus Martin. He belonged to the anabaptists of Frisia, from whose society he was excluded about 1546, on account of his sentiments concerning the Trinity, having before held a public disputation on this subject at Goch in the duchy of Cleves, with Theodore Philips and Menon Simonis. He maintained that the Father alone was the true God; that the Son had existed before the world, but was not co-eternal with the Father, nor yet omnipotent, nor consubstantial with the Father, nor equal to him, but was one with him in will; and that the Holy Spirit was the power or operating energy of God[†].

About the year 1530, a person of the name of Claudius, called, from the province wherein he was chiefly known to the public, Claudius Allobrex, caused considerable sensation by the dissemination of antitrinitarian sentiments in Switzerland and some adjacent districts. He denied that there were three persons in the divine essence, and maintained that the Father was greater than the Son, and was the only true God.

---

[*] Sandii *Bibl. Antitrin. p.* 17. Bock, *ubi supra, tom.* ii. *pp.* 248, 249.

[†] Sandii *Bibl. Antitrin. p.* 38. *Nucleus Hist. Eccles. p.* 425.

He

He affirmed that the Scriptures were corrupted, espe-, cially the beginning of John's gospel, which, he con-. tended, ought to be read *In principio erat verbum, et verbum illud erat* Dei *.

The names of several other persons occur about this time, who are reputed to have held antitrinita-rian sentiments; but the limits prescribed to this sketch forbid the enumeration of them here, with the exception of Michael Servetus †, a man who holds a pre-eminent rank in this class, and whose celebrity, arising both from his splendid talents and his tragical fate, entitles him to particular notice. This di-stinguished person was born in 1509, at Villanueva in Arragon, where his father exercised the profession of public notary. After having passed with extra-ordinary success through the customary routine of juvenile instruction, he was sent to the university of Thoulouse to study the canon law. During the three years he passed in this celebrated seat of learning, he devoted a large portion of his time to the critical perusal of the Scriptures,—an employment to which he was probably excited by the spread of the Refor-mation, and which eventually led to his renunciation of the prevailing opinion concerning the Trinity. Ap-

---

* Bock, *ubi supra, tom.* i. *p.* 103, *tom.* ii. *p.* 298.

† His Spanish name was Servedo : sometimes he called himself Reves, a word formed by the transposition of some of the letters of his original surname. Occasionally it is found written Renes ; but this is an evident error of the press, the letter *u* being mistaken for *n*. At the latter part of his life he called himself Michael Villanovanus, or simply Villano-vanus, from the place of his birth.

a 5   prehending

prehending that in France he could not with safety
pursue his theological inquiries, or give publicity to
his own convictions, he removed, in 1530, to Basil in
Switzerland, where he obtained the esteem and
friendship of the most eminent of the reformed clergy
in that city. Having given these divines credit for
more enlarged views and a more liberal spirit than
they had imbibed, he made no scruple of avowing
to them the opinions he had been led to embrace.
But he soon discovered that they were as little disposed
as the Catholics to extend toleration to any who
pursued their speculations further than themselves;
—his friend Œcolampadius having taken occasion in
some letters which he addressed to him, to upbraid
him in no very gentle terms with the heresy of his
sentiments *. Finding himself thus under unpleasant
restraint, where he had looked for freedom, he quitted
Basil in 1530 or 1531, and went to Strasburg. In
the latter year, and shortly after his arrival in this
city, he published his first work on the Trinity under
the following title—*De Trinitatis Erroribus, Libri
septem, per Michaelem Serueto, alias Reues, ab Ara-
gonia Hispanum.* It was printed at Haguenau in
Alsace, by John Seccer for Conrad Rouse, a book-

---

* *Fingis, quasi nos humano more de filiatione Dei loquamur,
et crude faciamus filium Dei, aboleamusque honorem filii Dei:
id quod tum cum* SUMMA BLASPHEMIA *facis, deprehendo enim*
DIABOLICAS ILLAS VERSUTIAS. *Interim dum non summam patientiam præ me fero, dolens Jesum Christum filium Dei sic de-
honestari, parum Christiane tibi agere videor.* IN ALIIS MAN-
SUETUS ERO : IN BLASPHEMIIS QUÆ IN CHRISTUM, NON ITEM.
Allwoerden, *Hist. Michael. Serveti,* p. 13. Bock, *Hist. Antitrin.*
tom. ii. p. 331.

seller

seller of Strasburg, to whom Servetus had given his manuscript at Basil. The appearance of this book produced a very powerful sensation among the leaders of the Reformation, who embraced every opportunity to hold it up to public execration, as much, apparently, from the dread of being charged by their Catholic adversaries with holding the opinions of the author, as from their real abhorrence of the tenets it advocated *. Bucer, who resided at Strasburg, is stated to have declared publicly to his congregation, that the writer deserved to have his intestines torn from his body.

Servetus, not deeming himself secure at Strasburg while this storm raged, returned in the same year to Basil; but finding Œcolampadius most highly incensed against him for his recent publication, he took his departure for Lyons. On his way he passed through Haguenau, where, in 1532, he published,

---

* The following may be taken as a sample of their language on this occasion. It is an extract from a letter addressed by Œcolampadius to Bucer, and dated August 5, 1531:— *Invisi hac hebdomada Bernates, qui te et Capitonem salutant plurimum. Libellus* DE TRINITATIS ERRORIBUS *a quibusdam ex illis visus duntaxat, supra modum offendit. Vellem te scribere Luthero, quod nobis insciis liber alibi excusus sit. Impudentia etiam erat adscribere Lutheranis, justificationis rationem eos ignorare : ut de reliquis taceam. Sed* PHOTINIANUS *ille, vel nescio cujus sectæ homo, solus sapere sibi videtur. Nisi ab ecclesiæ nostræ doctoribus explodetur, pessime auditura est. Tu, præ aliis, oro vigiles: et si non alibi, certe in confutatione tua ad imperatorem ecclesias nostras excusa, utcunque* BESTIA *irrepserit. Abutitur omnibus in suum sensum, tantum ne confiteatur Filium coæternum Patri et consubstantialem, Atque hic est qui suscipit probandum, hominem Christum esse Filium Dei.* Allwoerden, *ubi supra, p. 29.* Bock, *tom. ii. p. 335.*

with

with his name as before, his second work, intituled,
*Dialogorum de Trinitate, Libri duo; De Justicia
Regni Christi, Capitula quatuor.* It is affirmed that,
in order to obtain permission to quit Basil unmo-
lested, he had promised to publish his recantation.
This promise he artfully contrived to fulfil in words,
in the preface to the latter work, in the first sentence
of which he states that he retracted all that he had
written in his seven books against the received doctrine of the Trinity,—not, however, he proceeds to
intimate, because what he had written was false, but
because it was imperfect *.

On his settlement at Lyons, Servetus, in order to
escape persecution, took the name of Villanovanus,
from his birth-place.   After a residence of three years
in this city he went to Paris, where he applied himself to the study of medicine with so much success
that he soon obtained his degree of doctor, and was
admitted one of the public lecturers at the university.
From Paris he returned to Lyons.   Here he was occupied in superintending the press of the Trechselii,
celebrated printers of that place, for whom he edited
an edition of Ptolemy's Geography, which was published in 1535, and again in 1542;—and also an edition
of Pagninus's Bible in Hebrew, with an interlined
Latin translation, which appeared in 1542.   In 1541
he removed his residence to Vienne in Dauphiny,

---

* *Quæ nuper, contra receptam de Trinitate sententiam, septem
libris scripsi, omnia nunc, candide lector, retracto.* NON QUIA
FALSA SINT, SED QUIA IMPERFECTA, ET TANQUAM A PARVULO
PARVULIS SCRIPTA.

where

where he practised as a physician, and enjoyed the friendship and patronage of the archbishop of the province, to whom he dedicated the second edition of Ptolemy's Geography.

After his settlement at Vienne, Servetus entered into a correspondence with Calvin, then residing at Geneva.   In the letters* which passed on this occasion, both the learned combatants displayed considerable warmth and acrimony of spirit in the defence of their respective theological systems ; and the freedom with which Servetus arraigned the tenets of the Reformer laid the foundation of that implacable resentment to which he ultimately owed his ruin ; for Calvin scrupled not to avow that he would be satisfied with no atonement for this attack upon his creed short of the death of his adversary, should the disposal of his life be ever in his power†.   While things were in this state, Servetus committed to the press his last and most celebrated work, intituled *Christianismi Restitutio*, or "Christianity Restored." It was printed in 1553 at Vienne, by Balthazar Arnollet, but neither the place nor the printer's name appears in the title page : nor was the author's name attached to this publication ;—the letters M. S. V., standing for Michael Servetus Villanovanus, are how-

---

* Thirty of the letters which Servetus addressed to Calvin are inserted at the end of his last work, *Christianismi Restitutio, pp.* 557 *et seqq.*,

† Calvin, writing in 1546 to Viret, minister of Lausanne, uses these words : *Servetus cupit huc venire: si venerit*, NUNQUAM PATIAR UT SALVUS EXEAT. Bock, *ubi supra, tom.* ii. *p.* 360.

ever placed at the end. Calvin was in possession of the secret that Servetus was the writer of this obnoxious book, a copy of it having been forwarded to him by the author. By means of a young man named William Trie, a native of Lyons, then residing at Geneva in consequence of having embraced the reformed religion, he procured some sheets of it to be conveyed to France, and put into the hands of the inquisitor at Lyons, with an intimation that the author was in his neighbourhood. He afterwards sent several of the letters which, in the course of a confidential correspondence, he had received from Servetus, in order to furnish additional evidence to convict him of heresy and blasphemy. On the ground of these documents Servetus was arrested at Vienne, and committed to prison; whence, however, he soon effected his escape. After his flight he was tried, convicted, and sentenced to the stake; his books were committed to the flames, and himself burnt in effigy.

Servetus escaped early in the month of June 1553. His intention was to proceed to Naples; and with this view, after wandering for some time, he went to Geneva, where he was recognised in the month of August, and at the instigation of Calvin committed to prison. Various attempts have been made by the apologists of the Reformer to remove from him the foul stigma of being the author of his adversary's arrest; but, in truth, Calvin himself never denied or disguised the fact. On the contrary, he expressly avows it in more than one of his printed works, and takes credit to himself for having thus acted towards a man whose

principles

principles he held in abhorrence, and whom, on more than one occasion, he thought fit to brand with the opprobrious epithet of DOG *.

Servetus, on being taken into custody, was deprived of the property he had about him, which was of considerable amount, and thrown, like a common malefactor, into a damp, squalid, and noisome dungeon. Proceedings were immediately instituted against him for his alleged blasphemies. The accusations were preferred by Nicholas de la Fontaine, a person residing in Calvin's house, either in a menial situation, or for the benefit of his instruction; but the real prosecutor, as was manifested in the course of the trial, was the Reformer himself. Servetus repelled

---

* Calvin, in his work *Fidel. Expos. Serveti Errorum*, thus avows the part he acted in this transaction: *Quidquid in senatu nostro actum est, mihi passim adscribitur. Nec sane dissimulo, mea opera consilioque jure in carcerem fuisse conjectum. Quia recepto civitatis hujus jure, criminis reum peragere oportuit: causam huc usque me esse prosecutum, fateor.* " All the proceedings of our senate are ascribed to me: and indeed I do not dissemble that he (Servetus) was thrown into prison through my interference and advice. As it was necessary according to the laws of the state that he should be charged with some crime, I admit that I was thus far the author of the transaction." Writing to Sultzerus, he observes, " When at last he was driven here by his evil destiny, one of the syndics, at my instigation, ordered him to be committed to prison: for I do not dissemble that I deemed it my duty to restrain as much as lay in my power a man who was worse than obstinate and ungovernable, lest the infection should spread more widely." *Tandem huc malis auspiciis appulsum, unus ex syndicis,* ME AUCTORE, *in carcerem duci jussit. Neque enim dissimulo, quin officii mei duxerim, hominem plusquam obstinatum et indomitum quoad in me erat compescere; ne longius manaret contagio.* Allwoerden, *ubi supra, pp.* 61, 62. Bock, *tom.* ii. *p.* 360.

the

the whole of the charges with great firmness, and
openly avowed himself the author of the writings that
were stated to contain the heretical opinions for which
he was arraigned.   His trial proved exceedingly te-
dious and vexatious, and lasted from the 14th of August to the 26th of October, when, a majority of his
judges having decided against him, he was condemned
to be burnt to death by a slow fire.

If Servetus cannot be commended for the temper
with which he sometimes replied to his accuser, it is
impossible to view without feelings of disgust, mingled
with deep concern, the manner in which Calvin acted
during the whole of these iniquitous proceedings ; and
particularly to observe the savage tone of exultation
with which, immediately after his conviction, he
stated to a friend the effects produced upon his victim
by the communication of his sentence. " But lest idle
scoundrels should glory in the insane obstinacy of
the man, as in a martyrdom, there appeared in his
death a beastly stupidity ; whence it might be concluded, that on the subject of religion he never was in
earnest. When the sentence of death had been passed
upon him he stood fixed now as one astounded ; now
he sighed deeply ; and now he howled like a maniac ;
and at length he just gained strength enough to bellow
out after the Spanish manner, *Misericordia ! Misericordia !"* * The truth, however, is, that Servetus bore
his

---

* *Cæterum ne male feriati nebulones, vecordi hominis pervica-
cia, quasi martyrio glorientur : in ejus morte apparuit belluina
stupiditas, unde judicium facere liceret, nihil unquam serio in
religione ipsum egisse. Ex quo mors ei denunciata est, nunc at-
tonito*

his fate at this trying season with great firmness and serenity, disturbed indeed, occasionally, by the view of the terrific apparatus which was preparing for his execution. He never wavered in his religious faith. When exhorted on the last morning by Farell, the minister of Neufchatel, and the friend of Calvin, who was appointed to attend him, to return to the doctrine of the Trinity, he calmly requested his monitor to convince him by one plain passage of Scripture, that Christ was called the Son of God before his birth of Mary.

The day following that whereon sentence had been passed upon him he was led to the stake, praying, " O God, save my soul; O thou Son of the Eternal God, have mercy on me." In order to aggravate his sufferings he was surrounded by green faggots, which, after half an hour of excruciating tortures, completed the work of death. In the same fire was burnt, attached to his body, his last book, *Christianismi Restitutio**. Thus perished Servetus at the age of forty-four,

---

tonito similis hærere, nunc alta suspiria edere, nunc instar lymphatici ejulare. *Quod postremum tandem sic invaluit, ut tantum* Hispanico more reboaret, Misericordia, Misericordia! AHwoerden, *ubi supra, p.* 113. Bock, *tom.* ii. *p.* 371.

* Bock (*Hist. Antitrin. tom.* ii. *p.* 376,) has extracted from another author the following interesting particulars of the execution of Servetus. *Ita ductus est ad struem lignorum, fasciculis quernis viridibus, adhuc frondosis, admixtis lignis taleis constructam. Impositus est Servetus, trunco ad terram posito, pedibus ad terram pertingentibus. Capiti imposita est corona, vel straminea, vel frondea, eaque sulphure conspersa : corpus palo alligatum ferrea catena, collum autem june crasso quadruplici aut quintuplici laxo, liber femori alligatus. Ipse carnificem rogavit, ne se diu torqueret. Interea carnifex ignem in ejus conspectum, et deinde in orbem admovit: Servetus viso igne horrendum*
_dum

four, in a PROTESTANT state, for exercising that right
of private judgement in the formation of his religious
opinions, which his persecutors had themselves acted
upon in dissenting from the Church of Rome!

The intolerant spirit displayed by the Reformers,
both in Germany and Switzerland, towards those
who went beyond themselves in the freedom of their
inquiries, and avowed or embraced sentiments in any
respect different from their own, especially in relation
to the orthodox doctrine of the Trinity, rendered it
necessary for all persons who came under this description, and were unwilling to conceal or abandon
their principles, to seek a safer asylum in some other
country. The state of Poland at this period, the
freedom of its constitution, and the tolerant spirit of
the reigning sovereign, Sigismund the Second, who
had permitted the open profession in his dominions
of the Reformed religion of the schools both of Wittemberg and Geneva, naturally directed their views to
that quarter. Among the persons who first emigrated

---

*dum exclamavit, et universum populum perterrefecerit. Cum diu
langueret, accesserunt ex populo, qui fasciculos confertim in eum
conjecerunt. Ipse horrenda voce clamans, Jesu, Fili Dei, miserere
mei, post dimidiæ circiter horæ cruciatum exustulatus et fumo
suffocatus, animum exspiravit.* It is asserted by some, and the
circumstance derives great probability from the rest of his
conduct in this business, that when Calvin beheld Servetus
led out to execution, he laughed immoderately, and was
obliged to conceal his face in his mantle. Bock, vol. ii. p. 377.
Allwoerden, p. 121, note. There is a very valuable memoir of
Servetus, grounded chiefly on Bock's materials, inserted in the
fifth volume of the " Monthly Repository of Theology and general Literature," a work which periodically conveys to the
public a rich store of interesting and important materials.

into

into Poland on account of their religious opinions, a considerable number appears to have consisted of anabaptists, or of those to whom this designation was applied. Many of them were men of education and learning, of sound principles and unimpeachable moral characters. It is to one of these that the introduction of Unitarianism into Poland is to be ascribed.

In the year 1546, a native of Holland, who went by the name of Spiritus, but who is supposed on good grounds to have been Adam Pastor, already noticed above, settled at Cracow. Being one day in the library of John Tricessius, a person of high celebrity in that city, distinguished for his literary acquirements, who had invited him to meet some of the most eminent men of the place, he took down by accident a book wherein he observed prayers addressed to the Father, the Son, and the Holy Spirit. He immediately exclaimed,—" What! have you then three Gods ?" The conversation to which this question led made a deep impression on the minds of all the party, but especially on that of Andrew Fricius Modrevius, the king's secretary, who shortly afterwards, in consequence of prosecuting his inquiries upon the subject, abandoned the doctrine of the Trinity, and appeared as the open advocate of Unitarianism in a work which he published under the title of *Sylvæ**. This proved an important event to the new settlers, and greatly contributed to the spread and establishment of their opinions.

About the time when Spiritus first appeared in Po-

* Sandii *Biblioth. Antitrin.* p. 36.

land,

land, a circumstance occurred in Italy which it will
be proper to notice in this place, as it conduced in
an eminent degree to the future progress of the Unitarian cause in the former country. While Luther
and Melancthon in Germany, and Zwinglius, Calvin,
and their associates in Switzerland, were prosecuting
the work of Reformation, the public attention was
drawn by their labours and writings to the corrup-
tions of the Church of Rome, in some of the Italian
states, and more particularly in that of Venice. Several persons distinguished for their rank and learning formed themselves into a society at Vicenza, a
small town in this district, for the purpose of discussing with freedom the principles of the popular creed,
and promoting the study of the Scriptures. In the
prosecution of their inquiries they renounced the doctrine of the Trinity; and they are reported to have
held that there is but one most high God, who created
all things by his mighty word, and preserves them by
his will and good providence; and that his only begotten Son, Jesus Christ, was as to his nature a man,
but not merely a man, having been conceived of the
Holy Spirit by the Virgin Mary.

The place of meeting, and the opinions of this society, having come to the knowledge of the officers of
the Inquisition, their deliberations were suddenly in-
terrupted. Three of the members were seized, of
whom one (James de Chiar) died in prison, and two
(Julius Trevisanus and Francis de Ruego) were put
to death at Venice; the rest were obliged to seek
their safety in flight. In the number of those who
escaped

escaped are commonly named Lælius Socinus, Niccola Paruta, Valentine Gentilis, Darius Socinus, Francis Niger, and John Paul Alciatus, and also, though it should seem erroneously, Bernard Ochin. Paruta, Gentilis, Darius Socinus, and Alciatus, settled in Moravia, but Lælius Socinus fixed his residence at Zurich *.

This

---

* *Narratio compendiosa &c. Auctore Andrea Wissowatio, ad calcem Sandii Biblioth. Antitrin. p.* 209. *Biblioth. Antitrin. in vita L. Socini, Nic. Parutæ, J. P. Alciati, pp.* 19, 25, & 27. Lubieniecii *Hist. Reform. Polonicæ, p.* 38.

Mosheim (Cent. xvi. sect. iii. part ii. note) professes to doubt the truth of this statement with respect to the rise of Unitarianism in Italy, and to question even the existence of this college, or society, at Vincenza : but the reasons on which he grounds his suspicions are extremely weak, and very insufficient to invalidate the general authenticity of the account. He objects, first, that "it is extremely improbable, nay, utterly incredible, that all the persons who are said to have been present at these assemblies were really so ;"—and he mentions in particular, Bernard Ochin, and Lælius Socinus. But, allowing that this were the case, an error in the enumeration of some names ought not, upon any rule of criticism, to be admitted as of itself a decisive proof of the falsehood of the whole of the story. Besides, Mosheim has by no means demonstrated, that these two celebrated individuals could not have been members of this association. It is, indeed, clear that Bernard Ochin could not have belonged to it in 1546, the year in which it is stated to have been dispersed, as he appears to have quitted Italy in 1543, and perhaps he might never have attended its deliberations. There is nothing, however, to render such a circumstance "utterly incredible," or "extremely improbable ;" for his residence in that part of Italy, and his attachment to the principles of the Reformation, while he yet officiated in the Roman church, render it, on the contrary, very likely that he might on some occasions hold private conferences with persons of congenial views and feelings. But there is certainly no good evidence of his having at this period embraced antitrinitarian sentiments. Mosheim's reasons for concluding that Lælius Socinus could not have been present at these assemblies, are extremely frivolous,—namely, that it cannot be supposed that so young a man, then only twenty-

one

This eminent person was born at Sienna in Tus-
cany, in the year 1525, and educated for the profession

---

one years of age, "would leave the place of his nativity (Sienna) and repair to Venice or Vincenza, without any other view
than that of disputing freely on certain points of religion ;" or
"that a youth of such inexperience should obtain the first rank
and supreme authority in an assembly composed of so many
eminently learned and ingenious men." To the former of these
reasons, our objector's own translator, Dr. Maclaine, has sufficiently replied—" Is such a supposition really so absurd ?
Is not a spirit of enthusiasm, or even an uncommon degree
of zeal, adequate to the production of such an effect ?" With
respect to the latter, the least consideration will show that
there was nothing so very extraordinary in his obtaining these
distinctions, if we take into account his splendid talents, his
extensive acquirements, the high rank of his family and the
influence possessed by them in that part of Italy. It may however be conceded to Mosheim, that this society was not " the
source and nursery of the whole Unitarian sect," and that the
Unitarian system of doctrine, as it was afterwards professed,
was not arranged and digested here in the manner intimated
by Lubieniecius in the passage above referred to of his History
of the Polish Reformation.

Mosheim refers, in confirmation of his own opinion on this
subject, to the German work of Fueslin, *Reformations Beträ-
gen.* A summary of the principal objections of this writer has
been given by Bock (*Hist. Antitrin. tom.* ii. *p.* 405). In addition
to those which Mosheim has himself urged, Fueslin observes,
1. that " neither Sandius, nor Wissowatius, adduces any authorities as the source of his information :" and 2. that " no
other writer makes any express mention of those persons who
are said to have perished by the hand of the executioner,
though every sect is forward to celebrate its martyrs." With
respect to the first of these objections, it ought to be recollected that one of these historians, Andrew Wissowatius, may
himself be regarded in the light of an original authority. He
held a very distinguished rank among the Unitarian body in
Poland, and was a lineal descendant, in no very remote degree,
of the family of the Socini, being the grandson of Faustus Socinus by his daughter Agnes, who had married Stanislaus
Wissowatius. He was therefore likely to have been accurately

sion of the law, in which many individuals of his family had raised themselves to the highest distinction.
Having

---

rately informed as to the circumstances which led to the expatriation of his family. Sandius must have written from the information communicated to him by the Polish Unitarians. He is, however, an historian of high respectability, who was not likely to put his credit to the hazard by such a statement, without having previously satisfied himself of the sufficiency of the evidence by which it was supported. As to the second objection, it must perhaps be admitted that, as far as appears, there is no direct mention of the persons who are said to have perished, in the work of any contemporary writer. I have failed to discover any in the numerous Italian histories and chronicles of this period which I have had the opportunity of examining; and the learned Bock, after the laborious investigation of voluminous documents relating to those times, makes the same confession. He supposes however that some light might be thrown on this subject, could a certain work of Francis Niger, one of the enumerated members of the Vincenza society, be discovered, the title of which he gives as follows— *Brevis Historia de Fanini Faventini, ac Dominici Bassanensis morte, qui nuper ob Christum in Italia Rom. Pont. jussu impie occisi sunt, a.* 1550. But, after all, there is nothing very remarkable in the silence of contemporary historians upon an execution of this nature. It is to be apprehended that many of a similar kind have occurred in Catholic countries, which have had no register or memorial beyond that of the tradition which may have been preserved and perpetuated (as might be the case in this instance) among their families and their friends. It might be mentioned as a circumstance tending to authenticate the statement of Wissowatius and Lubieniecius, that they give the names of the sufferers.

It has been judged proper to say thus much here on this subject, as it involves a material question of fact in connexion with the history of Unitarianism. Bock, a much higher authority in this case than Mosheim, devoted a large share of his attention to the investigation of this point, and has published a very satisfactory dissertation upon it, in his History of Antitrinitarianism, vol. ii. p. 395—421, which is recommended to the reader's perusal.

Mosheim refers in his note to Zeltner's *Historia Crypto-Sociniani*

Having turned his thoughts to theological subjects, and becoming dissatisfied with the established religion, he went to Vincenza, whence, after the dissolution of the society, he proceeded to Switzerland, an exile on account of his sentiments.   After his settlement at Zurich he made occasional tours to other countries, especially to those where the principles of the Reformation were admitted and professed.   In the year 1551 he made a journey to Poland, which he visited again about 1558.   On the former occasion, he became acquainted with Francis Lismanin, a Corsican monk, who at that time resided at Cracow in the capacity of confessor to Bona Sfortia, the queen of Sigismund the First.   Lismanin had already been partly gained over by the Polish Reformers; his conversation with Lælius Socinus completed his conversion to the Unitarian sentiments of his instructor, and determined him to quit his habit and withdraw from the communion of the Roman Church*.   Another very important accession was made to the Unitarian party at this period by the conversion of Gregory Paul, a divine of extensive learning and great talents, who officiated as the minister of a Reformed church in the suburbs of Cracow.

Thus far the dissemination of Unitarianism in Po-

---

cinianismi.   But the observations of that writer (p. 321, note) comprise merely an intimation that this alleged origin of Socinianism in Italy had not been sufficiently examined, and deserved to be further investigated.

* Lubieniecii *Hist. Refor. Pol.* p. 40. Bock, *ubi supra, tom.* ii. p. 594, *in Vita Lælii Socini.*

land

land seems to have been effected by means of conversation, or discussions of a more private kind, and by
occasional publications from the press. The first
person who appears to have stood forward in a public
assembly to impugn the doctrine of the Trinity was
Peter Gonezius, or Conyza, who, at a synod of the
reformed clergy held at Seceminia in 1556, asserted
the supremacy of the Father over the Son and Holy
Spirit, and contended that the Apostles' Creed ought
to be received as the sole rule of faith, denouncing the
Nicene and Athanasian Creeds as mere human compositions of no authority. The sensation produced
by this discourse on the minds and feelings of the Trinitarian clergy is described to have been very great;
and the immediate effect of it was an agreement to
reconsider the subject at a future meeting, and in the
mean time to obtain the opinion of Melancthon on
the disputed points *.

In the year 1558, at a synod held at Pinczow, then
the principal seat of the Antitrinitarians, the name of
Blandrata occurs as being present. George Blandrata was a native of Piedmont, of the medical profession. Having embraced the sentiments of Servetus, he quitted his native country and went to Poland,
where, through the interest of Lismanin, he was appointed physician to the queen, Bona Sfortia. He
after this returned to Piedmont, but soon removed
his residence to Geneva. Disagreeing here with Cal-

---

* Sandii *Biblioth. Antitrin.* p. 41. Lubieniecii *Hist. Refor.
Pol.* p. 111.

vin, and dreading his resentment and power after the recent fate of Servetus, he went a second time to Poland in the year 1558, and was appointed one of the elders of the reformed church of Cracow*. From Poland he removed to Transylvania, in connexion with which country his name will again occur in the course of this history.

At another synod held at Pinczow in 1563, we find John Valentine Gentilis holding a public disputation on the doctrine of the Trinity, maintaining that the Father alone was God, and that he had created before all worlds a mighty spirit, who afterwards became incarnate in the human body of Jesus. Gentilis was a native of the south of Italy, and joined himself, as we have seen, to the little society of Vincenza. After quitting Italy he settled in Moravia; but removing to Berne, in Switzerland, he was there arrested, tried for heresy, condemned, and beheaded in 1566†.

Up to this period all the synods held in Poland were composed indiscriminately of the members and ministers of all the reformed churches of every communion, Lutheran, Calvinistic, and Antitrinitarian. The consequences of the discordant opinions which were held by the parties forming these assemblies, were, as might be expected, continual disputations, which were frequently conducted with great warmth and violence. Several attempts were made by persons who felt scandalized by such proceedings, to pro-

---

* Sandii *Biblioth. Antitrin. p.* 28. Bock, *ubi supra, tom.* ii. *pp.* 470 *et seqq.*

† Sandii *Biblioth. Antitrin. p.* 26. Bock, *tom.* ii. *p.* 427.

mote

mote peace, and to reconcile the differences, especially between the Trinitarians and their Unitarian opponents, which were the chief causes of disunion; but all without success. The last effort of this kind was tried at a public conference held by appointment for this purpose at Petricow in the year 1565, which was attended by the chief persons of all the reformed churches. The Trinitarians finding themselves unable to silence their opponents, who were availing themselves of every opportunity to promulgate their sentiments, and perceiving that they were on this occasion the more numerous and powerful party, came to a resolution wholly to exclude them thenceforth from their public assemblies *. From this time, therefore, the Unitarians formed a separate religious body in the country, having their churches, their collegiate and other establishments, exclusively to themselves.

Notwithstanding, however, this separation of the Unitarian from the Trinitarian reformers, it is not to be understood that all the individuals comprised under the former denomination were perfectly agreed in their religious opinions. They all concurred in maintaining the supremacy of the Father: but with respect to Jesus Christ, some thought him to be a God of inferior nature, derived from the supreme Deity; others held the doctrine of Arius, conceiving him to have been the first created spirit, who became incarnate with the view of effecting the salvation of mankind; while a third party believed him to be a

---

* Lubieniecius, *ubi supra*, p. 201.

b 2

human

human being. These last were again divided into two classes; the one believing the miraculous conception of Jesus, the other considering him to have been the son of Joseph, as well as of Mary. Another point on which they differed among themselves was the worship of Jesus Christ;—some, even of those who believed in his simple humanity, maintaining that he was entitled to divine honours on account of the high rank and authority with which he had been invested after his resurrection, as the king and lord of the church; whilst others held that divine worship was to be paid to the Father alone. In relation to the Holy Spirit, it was the common opinion among them that it was not a Person, but the power or operating energy of God, displayed in the miracles which were wrought by Christ and his apostles as the evidence of their divine mission and authority. They differed, besides, upon some other points of minor importance, which cannot be enumerated in this general sketch.

Though these Antitrinitarian reformers have been occasionally styled UNITARIANS in the preceding narrative, in conformity with modern usage, it must be observed that they were not known by this designation in Poland. At the period now under review, they were called by various denominations, arising chiefly from local or temporary circumstances. They were first distinguished by the name of PINCZOVIANS, from the town of Pinczow, where they had their earliest settlement. Some of the body were afterwards called FARNOVIANS, from Stanislaus Farnovius, who held the Arian doctrine concerning the person of
Christ.

Christ. Others were styled BUDNÆANS, from Simon Budnæus, who maintained the opinion of the simple humanity of Christ, and denied his being a proper object of religious worship. But the designation by which they were afterwards most generally known was that of RACOVIANS, from the town of Racow, wh   ~~al years formed their metropolis.

          579 the celebrated Faustus Socinus,
t/   Lælius Socinus, arrived in Poland. He
            39, and had at an early age imbibed
            of his uncle, whose papers, after his
            o his hands. A conscientious attach-
            new opinions, induced him to relinquish
            lendid prospects in his native country,
            into voluntary exile, in order to be able
            e his theological studies, and promulgate
            nts with the greater facility and security.
            first to Switzerland, and fixed his resi-
            Basil. From hence he was called into
            nia by Blandrata, to assist him in refuting
            ng the dissemination of the opinion of Fran-
            d respecting the worship of Jesus Christ.
            at venerable confessor had been thrown into
            and while the proceedings against him were
            ding, Socinus, alarmed by an epidemic dis-
            which raged in the country, withdrew to Poland.
            it was understood that Socinus went further in
            ntiments than most of the leading individuals
            ng the Polish Unitarians, he was not permitted
            ɔin in communion with their churches, or to have
            voice in the direction of their affairs. His splendid
                                                    talents

talents and high character, however, soon procured
for him the friendship and patronage of persons of the
first distinction in the country. This circumstance
enabled him to give to the public, through the medium of the press, a considerable number of works,
upon theological subjects. His writings, in which he
is considered to have made liberal use of the manuscripts of his uncle, who was greatly his superior in
learning, and particularly in his knowledge of the original languages of the Scriptures, served to methodize
and fix the indeterminate, and frequently confused notions held at that time by many of the Polish Unitarians respecting the principal doctrines of Christianity, and to bring over nearly the whole body to his
own sentiments concerning the unity of God, and the
humanity of Jesus Christ *.

The Unitarians of Poland were now become a large
and powerful body, comprising in their number several of the first nobility, and eminently distinguished
by their learning, talents, and general respectability
of character. Their chief settlement was at Racow,
a city which was built in 1569 by a nobleman attached to their interest, who erected for them a
church and college-house. This collegiate establishment was on a large scale. It maintained a high

* A Memoir of the life of Faustus Socinus was written by
Przipcovius, and is inserted p. 419, &c. of his Works in folio.
An English translation of this, from the pen of John Biddle,
was published in 18mo, in 1653. Doctor Toulmin gave to the
public in 1777, an excellent life of this celebrated individual in
8vo. Bock has also inserted a memoir in the second volume
of his History of Antitrinitarianism, pp. 654 *et seqq.*

degree

degree of reputation, and was filled with scholars from every part of the continent of Europe. The number of the students amounted at one time to upwards of a thousand, of whom more than three hundred were of noble families. And credit may readily be given to the report of an historian concerning it, that those who came there Catholics, Lutherans, or Calvinists, were soon imbued with the sentiments of the professors, and went away enemies of the doctrine of the Trinity*.

The printing establishment at Racow soon acquired a degree of celebrity equal to that of the college, from the number of publications which issued from it, the seeming novelty, the variety and importance of the subjects to which they related, and the genius, learning, and talents of the writers. Besides the college and printing-house at Racow, they had others on a smaller scale in other towns. Their churches were found in all the chief cities, towns and villages of the kingdom ; but the principal were at Racow, Cracow, Pinczow, Lublin and Lubeck.

We are now arrived at what may be termed the flourishing period of the history of the Polish Unitarians. For the prosperous condition to which they had by this time attained they were indebted to the patronage of some powerful families, to the favourable disposition of several successive monarchs, and

---

* Lamy, *Histoire du Socinianisme, p.* 104. For an account of the Racovian Church and College, see Lubieniecius's History of the Polish Reformation, pp. 239 *et seqq.*

to

to what was denominated the PACTA CONVENTA, a
kind of contract between the sovereign and the people, whereby every candidate for the throne was
bound on oath, to preserve all the rights and privileges, both civil and religious, which belonged to the
subjects of the state*.

It may well be supposed that the Unitarians neither
acquired nor enjoyed this state of prosperity with
the cordial good-will of the other religious bodies,
whether Catholic or Reformed. Both these parties
viewed the wide dissemination of their tenets with
alarm, as threatening to subvert those principles
which they held in common, and which they regarded
as the grand essentials of Christianity. They, therefore exerted, without intermission, all the influence
they could acquire, and resorted to every artifice, to
obstruct their labours, and ruin their cause. With
what success they planned and prosecuted their measures will be seen in the sequel.

The first event that operated to the serious disad-
vantage of the Unitarian interest was a malicious prosecution instituted against an opulent merchant of
their body, named John Tyscovicius, who had served
the office of Questor, or Syndick, of the town of
Biesk in Podolia, where he resided. It was insinuated
by his enemies, that his accounts had not been fairly
kept, and he was required to verify them on oath.

---

* Hartnoch *de Repub. Polonica, lib.* ii. *cap.* ii. § 2. Haute-
ville, *Relation Historique de la Pologne, chap.* xviii.

To

To this he readily assented on condition of being permitted to swear by Almighty God :—but it was insisted that he should swear by the triune God, or by the image of Christ on the cross ; and for this purpose a crucifix, with the figure of the Saviour affixed to it, was placed in his hands. Indignant that his veracity should be questioned, and his religion insulted, he threw the crucifix to the ground, exclaiming that he knew of no such God as they proposed to him. For this act, which was construed into a heavy offence against the Trinity, he was immediately arrested and thrown into prison. Proceedings were forthwith instituted against him, which, after repeated appeals from one tribunal to another, ended in his condemnation. He was sentenced to have his tongue pierced, for his alleged blasphemy; to have his hands and feet cut off, for having thrown down and trodden upon the crucifix ; to be beheaded for his rebellious contumacy, in appealing from the first tribunal that had given decision against him ; and finally to be burnt at the stake for his heretical opinions. This sentence, horrible as it may appear, was, at the instigation of the Jesuits, executed in all its circumstances at Warsaw, on the 16th of November 1611 *.

The Catholics were greatly elated by their success in this cruel prosecution, and certainly not without reason, as they had been warmly opposed in the whole of the proceedings by many of the first individ-

---

* *Brevis Relatio de Johannis Tyscovicii Martyrio, ad calcem Sandii Bibl. Antitrin. p.* 203.

duals

duals among the nobility of the country. Their triumph gave a new impulse to their intolerance, and led them to seize every opportunity to prejudice the Unitarians in the public mind, and arm against them the powers of the government. Unfortunately, an occasion soon offered for the full display, and the ample gratification, of the insatiable spirit of hostility by which they were actuated.

In the year 1638, some students belonging to the college of Racow, with imprudent and childish zeal, beat down with stones a cross which had been placed near one of the entrances into the town. This was construed by the Catholics into a designed insult of their religion, and an act of impiety of the blackest description. Notwithstanding the parents of the youths, and the heads of the colleges, punished the offenders, and publicly apologized for their conduct, offering at the same time to make any further atonement which the case could justly require or admit ;—nothing could allay the fury of the people, who were led on and exasperated by their religious superiors. The cause was carried before the Diet of Warsaw in the course of the year, and was regarded with deep interest by all the distinguished persons there assembled. Eminent individuals of all communions,—of the Greek Church, of the Reformers, and even of the Catholic body itself,—interposed their influence to quash the proceedings, but all without success. For a decree was passed, enjoining that the Unitarian church at Racow should be closed, the college be
broken

broken up, the printing-house be demolished, and the ministers and professors be branded as infamous, proscribed, and banished the state*.

This decree was instantly executed in all its rigour, and proved a very heavy misfortune to the Unitarians. For besides depriving them of their chief seminary, and of their principal ecclesiastical establishment, it gave encouragement to the provincial tribunals in every part of the kingdom to persecute with the utmost severity all who openly professed Antitrinitarian sentiments, and to prevent the unfortunate individuals who had been expelled from Racow, obtaining a secure and peaceable asylum in other places†.

These misfortunes were shortly afterwards aggravated by an invasion of the Cossacs, who marked out the Unitarians as especial objects of their outrage and vengeance. In the year 1655 the peasants of Poland also, being instigated by the Catholics, rose up in arms against them in several districts, and pursued them everywhere with sanguinary ferocity, pillaging

---

* Lubieniecii *Hist. Reform. Polon.* p. 252. *Vindiciæ pro Unitariorum in Polonia Religionis Libertate, ad calcem Sandii Bibl. Antitrin.* p. 278. *Histoire du Socinianisme, 4to,* p. 114.

† Among the individuals who were at this period persecuted for their Unitarian sentiments, was Jonas Schlichtingius, one of the ablest writers belonging to the Unitarians of Poland. In 1647 he published a work intituled *Confessio Fidei Christianæ, edita Nomine Ecclesiarum quæ in Polonia unum Deum et Filium ejus unigenitum Jesum Christum, et Spiritum S. profitentur,* &c. For this he was proscribed by the Diet of Warsaw in the same year, and banished the state, and his book was ordered to be burnt by the hands of the common hangman. This work he afterwards published in 1651, with corrections and additions. The first edition I have never seen: the second, which is also very scarce, is in my collection.

their

their property, burning their houses, and putting all
to death who fell into their hands.

The Catholics having succeeded thus far in the execution of their designs against the Unitarians, resolved at last to put a closing hand to their work, by
either reducing them to complete silence, or forcing
them to depart the country. With this view, being
assured of the disposition of the sovereign, John Ca-
simir, they preferred against them, at the Diet of
Warsaw in 1658, a formal accusation, charging them,
among other offences, with aiding the king of Swe-
den in his late invasion of the kingdom, on the ground
of some families having, during his occupation of
Cracow, sought an asylum in that city against the
outrages of the peasants. The charges were readily
entertained; and a decree was passed forbidding the
public exercise of their religion, or the dissemination
of their sentiments in any way whatever, under the
penalty of death; and commanding them to quit the
kingdom of Poland and its dependencies, within three
years, unless in the mean time they joined the communion of the Church of Rome, or that of the tolerated reformed churches of the Lutherans or Calvinists. This dreadful edict,—which was confirmed by
three successive diets, in direct violation, if not of the
positive written laws of the nation, certainly of that
enlightened spirit by which the administration of
public affairs, as respected the subject of religion, had
for upwards of a century been conducted,—fell upon
the Unitarians as a calamity of the most afflicting
kind. Their body comprised several families of the
first

first distinction, both as to rank and opulence, who adhered to their communion from principle, and whose convictions and fidelity were not to be easily shaken by persecution. The alternative which remained to them, of expatriation, with the certain loss of a very large proportion of their property, and in some instances of almost inevitable and absolute penury, was, however, so appalling, that they determined to use what influence they could yet command to *rvert* the threatening storm, or obtain some mitigation of the sentence. Accordingly, in 1660, two years after the first decree had been passed, a synod was appointed, at the solicitation of some of the more powerful of their adherents, to be held at Cracow, in the month of March, which the Unitarian ministers were invited to attend, in order to hold a public conference or disputation with the Catholics and orthodox reformed on the principal controverted points of their respective theological systems. The Unitarian ministers augured no benefit from this measure, and being withal apprehensive that some snare might be intended, declined being present, with the exception of only one individual, ANDREW WISSOWATIUS, whose name stands most honourably connected with this celebrated assembly. Disdaining to have it imputed to him that he was ashamed openly to avow his religious opinions, or afraid to stand forward as their public advocate, at the hazard of his liberty or his life; and fearing also that if no minister of the party appeared to plead their cause, some individuals, whose resolution might have been shaken by their present

sufferings,

sufferings, and their dark future prospect, might make a fatal shipwreck of conscience by abandoning their faith; this intrepid confessor boldly proceeded to the place of meeting, and secured a reception suited to the splendour of his talents and the magnanimity of his spirit. In the disputation which followed, and which continued from the 11th to the 16th of March, Wissowatius, though standing alone, and unsupported, vanquished by his eloquence, and the overwhelming force of his reasoning, every adversary who appeared against him in the combat *.

This victory, however, which was evinced by the silence of his opponents, though it covered this undaunted champion with well merited honour, was productive of no advantage to the cause he had advocated. On the contrary, the Catholics, irritated

* There is a singular testimony to the triumph of Wissowatius on this occasion from a reverend Catholic. Being asked by Wiclopolski, the governor of Cracow, who presided at the discussions, what he thought of the controversy, he replied— " If all the devils from hell had been here, they could not have maintained their religion more ably than this one minister has done." *Et si omnes ex inferno prodirent, non possent fortius religionem suam tutari quam hic unus.*" "But what," rejoined the governor, "if more of these ministers had been present? and there are many of similar powers." "If such be the case," answered the monk, "I do not know in what manner we are to defend ourselves against such persons."—" Behold," writes a Catholic historian of this incident in a tone of lamentation, "the advantages which Catholic divines sometimes obtain from the conferences they are so ready to grant to heretics, before magistrates and others of the laity, who commonly understand the business of war, of courts, and of politics, better than the concerns of faith and piety!" *Epist. de Vita A. Wissowatii, ad calcem Sandii Bibl. Antitrin.* p. 252. Lamy, *Histoire du Socinianisme,* p. 121.

by

by a defeat, which was admitted even by their own
friends, became more violent than ever in their hostility, and resorted to a new act of cruelty to wreak
their vengeance on the unfortunate objects of their
hatred. Under pretence that the Unitarians had
violated the terms of the former edict, by promulgating their sentiments openly or clandestinely, they
procured a new and more rigorous decree to be
passed against them on the 20th of July 1660. In
this the clause in the former, allowing to the Unitarians the space of three years for the arrangement of
their affairs, the disposal of their property, and the
consideration of the alternative proposed to them,
was rescinded, and a new edict passed, enjoining them
instantly to leave the kingdom, or join the communions authorized by the laws,—empowering all magistrates and others, in case of their disobedience, to
bring them before the public tribunals, and even to
put them to death. This unexpected ordinance
reduced them to the greatest difficulties. Their enemies threw every impediment in the way to their
settling their affairs. Many found it wholly impossible to dispose of their property at any price;—
others were obliged to part with it for what was considerably beneath its value; so that several of the
noble and wealthy families who still adhered to the
party, were reduced nearly to a level with the poorest
among them. In these trying circumstances some
made an outward show of abandoning their faith, and
thus saved themselves from the evils of exile;—but a
very large proportion, rather than sacrifice their conscience

science at the throne of human power, submitted to
the painful condition of being separated for ever from
their native land. These undaunted confessors, comprising many thousand individuals of both sexes and
all ages, yielding to their hard destiny, took a final
leave of their country, and wandered with uncertain
steps, friendless and destitute, to seek an asylum in
some foreign clime. Of this honourable band about
four hundred proceeded to Transylvania and Hungary; many bent their steps towards Prussia, Silesia,
and Moravia; others emigrated to Holland and the
Low Countries, and some passed over to England *.
Thus was terminated the public profession of Unitarianism in the kingdom of Poland, about one hun-

---

* There is a very affecting detail of the evils and sufferings
endured by the Unitarians on account of these proceedings
against them, and their banishment from the country, given in
a letter of Samuel Przipcovius, dated Konigsberg 1663, and
inserted at the end of Lubieniecius's History of the Polish Reformation. The following passage will show the feelings with
which the unfortunate exiles contemplated their calamities.
*Postulas ut calamitatis et egestatis nostræ tibi descriptionem ex-
hibeam. Infandum tu nempe jubes renovare dolorem, ne per
vestigia luctuum iterum, et cruda adhuc et hiantia, necdum cica-
tricibus obducta retractare vulnera: horret animus ad exceptos
tot fulminum ictus, attonitus et pavens. Qui nos casus hucusque
agitaverint, quæque ipse miserrima vidi, et quorum pars quan-
tulacunque fui exponere, non mens tantum, sed manus quoque ac
calamus trepidat ac refugit. Fuimus, fuimus Troes, et vel ipsa
non multo ante, benignitate Dei, tot per annos indulta ecclesiis
nostris felicitas, acriorem sensum præsentium malorum reddit:
ut etiam recordari pigeat, quando et quomodo et quibus gradibus,
quod fuimus esse desymus. Et nisi mentes nostras causæ, ob
quam patimur bonitas, et commendare quondam a Domino hujus
generis patientiæ solatia erigerent, tanta calamitatis procella
prostratis atque obrutis pene optimum factu videbatur, quo levius
ferantur præsentia, præteritorum memoriam amittere.*

dred

dred and twenty years after its first introduction into that country, and after giving birth to a host of advocates, distinguished equally by their learning, their talents and their virtues, who were an ornament to their age and an honour to human nature.

For several years previously to its suppression in Poland, Unitarianism had obtained a firm establishment, and made considerable progress, in Transylvania. The settlement of Blandrata in Poland in 1558, has already been mentioned. In the year 1563 he went into Transylvania to attend the prince, John Sigismund the Second, who was labouring under a dangerous disorder ; and his success in effecting the cure of his royal patient, joined to his insinuating manners, soon rendered him a favourite at court. The influence which he thus acquired encouraged him to attempt the introduction of his theological opinions into this country ; and circumstances favoured his design in a degree far beyond what he could have anticipated. At the time of his arrival the reformed churches of Transylvania and Hungary, which were numerous and flourishing, were under the superintendance of Francis David, a divine of great learning and powerful eloquence, who resided at Clausenburg, or Coloswar, and whose distinguished talents and character had procured for him the esteem of the prince, and of many of the first nobility. David had originally adopted the Augsburg Confession, and had, in 1556, published a work in support of the Lutheran doctrine concerning the Eucharist. Shortly after this he embraced the Calvinistic system, which he appears

to

to have held when he became first acquainted with
Blandrata.   The unsettled state of David's opinions
at this period disposed him to attend the more readily
to Blandrata's objections to the leading articles of the
popular creed ; and the result of their conversations
on these subjects was his entire conversion to Unitarianism.

·   The joint efforts of these two eminent individuals,
after this event, to disseminate their opinions, though
at first they acted with great caution in explaining their
views of Christianity, soon attracted the notice and
excited the alarm of the ministers of the reformed communions. Peter Melius, the superintendant of the reformed churches in Hungary, preferred a formal complaint against them to the prince, whom he prevailed
upon to convoke a synod of the ministers of Transylvania and Hungary at Weissenburg (*Alba Julia*) in the
month of May 1556, for the consideration and settlement of the controverted points.   To this assembly
Blandrata and David submitted several propositions,
declaratory of their sentiments ; but they were drawn
up with so much care, and expressed in such ambiguous terms, that the synod found no cause for cen-
suring them, and contented itself with subjoining to
the several articles, its own " Limitations," or Commentary *.

·   Peter Melius seems to have been little satisfied with
the result of these deliberations.   Anxious to stop the

---

* These propositions were published at Clausenburg in
1566, with the limitations of the Hungarian ministers and the
judgement of another synod held at Vasarhelly.   Petri Bod,
Hist. Unitariorum in Transylvania, p. 12.

progress

progress of the new opinions, and with this view to
impart to others his own fears, and inspire them with
a portion of his own zeal, he assembled in the following year the ministers of his own district, to consider
the best means of effecting his object. This synod
was followed by some others, convened for the same
purpose. The public mind being greatly agitated by
these frequent public conferences, the prince, with
the design of composing the differences and restoring
tranquillity, summoned a general synod to be held at
Weissenburg on the 3d of March 1568*,—Blandrata
having promised that he would then publicly demonstrate the truth of his opinions. The proceedings
of this assembly were formally arranged beforehand,
and the discussions held at it were continued during
ten successive days, the chief speakers being Francis
David and Blandrata †, on the part of the Unitarians,

and

* The disputations at this synod were immediately published at Weissenburg, under the following title :—" *Brevis
Enarratio Disputationis Albanæ de Deo Trino et Christo du-
plici, coram Serenissimo Principe et tota Ecclesia decem Diebus
habita*, &c.

† If the report of the historian be worthy of credit, Blandrata made but an indifferent figure in these discussions.
Being pressed on the ninth day by an opponent who had undertaken to reply to some of his observations—he exclaimed
—*Quod ad me vero attinet—Ego nec scio, nec possum illud ex-
plicare, raucedine enim laboro. Neque ego sum Doctor Theo-
logiæ, sed Medicinæ.* Bod, *ubi supra*, p. 43.

This historian relates (p. 43) that in the course of this year
was confirmed a decree which had been passed at the diet of
Thorde in 1557, and afterwards sanctioned by the states of the
kingdom in 1563, securing to persons of all denominations the
free exercise of their religion. From the UNION of the Reformed

and on the side of the Trinitarians, Peter Melíus. It terminated, however, without accomplishing the object for which it was convened.

In the following year, Francis David, with the concurrence, and under the authority of the prince, convoked another synod, of the ministers of Transylvania and Hungary, which was held at the town of Waradin, on the 10th of October. On this occasion, David drew up a series of propositions for the consideration of the assembly, and comprising the sentiments of the Unitarians with respect to the unity of God, the person of Christ, and the nature of the Holy Spirit*. At this synod again, the chief speakers on the opposite sides were David and Melíus. Blandrata was present, but took no part in the public discussions, in consequence, it is thought, of his ill success at the former meeting. The deliberations of this assembly concluded, like those of all the preceding synods, without effecting any thing towards the reconciliation of the contending parties. Before their separation the ministers of the Orthodox Churches delivered in a written confession of their faith in opposition to the propositions of David, wherein, after stating thei. own sentiments, they condemn in no very

---

formed of all parties in passing this edict, an union to which they were led by weighty public reasons, they were designated UNITI, or UNITARII. This title was afterwards restricted to those persons who maintained that the Father alone was the true and eternal God, and by them read ly adopted of their own accord ;—while those who held that there were three persons in one essence, were by way of opposition styled *Trinitarii.*

* Bod, *ubi supra, p.* 57.

gentle

gentle terms, as "heretical blasphemies," the system of the Unitarians*. Not contented with this, Melius, full of zeal for the interest of his party, afterwards addressed a formal letter to the prince, wherein he labours to prejudice his mind against Blandrata and his followers. But in this object he wholly failed, the prince having continued to afford them his protection and patronage until the time of his death, which took place on the 14th of March 1571.

John Sigismund was succeeded by Stephen Bathor, who ascended the throne with a disposition to preserve to all classes of his subjects the same freedom of religious worship as they had enjoyed during the reign of his predecessor. On taking possession of his government, he declared that he was the king of the people, and not of their consciences :—that God had reserved three things to himself; To create something out of nothing, to know future events, and to rule men's consciences,—that therefore to tyrannize over conscience was the greatest wickedness, and an invasion of the prerogative of Heaven†.

In the year 1574, the prosperity of the Unitarian cause was seriously affected by an unfortunate rupture between the two individuals to whom it had chiefly owed its advancement and success. Blandrata having been guilty of a gross offence, which his accusers have veiled under the designation of *peccatum*

---

* Bod, *ubi supra, pp.* 67 *et seqq.*
† Idem, *p.* 83.

Italicum,

*Italicum**, David declined all further intercourse
with him, and took measures to destroy his influence
in the Unitarian body. This conduct naturally drew
upon him the enmity of Blandrata, and paved the way
for those proceedings which terminated in his death.

Blandrata, well knowing the high estimation in
which the venerable superintendant was held in the
country, felt it necessary to act against him with great
art and circumspection. Though liberty was granted to
all religious parties alike to conduct public worship on
their own principles, there existed at this time a law
that none of them should be allowed to promulgate
any new doctrine without previously obtaining the
permission of the national council. Blandrata learnt
that David had violated this ordinance, by maintaining in a public discourse that Christ could not with
propriety be addressed in prayer, since he was not
God by nature,—an opinion which was then gaining
ground among the Unitarians, but had formed no
part of their creed when the public profession of it had
been originally permitted. His first step, after receiving this information, was to request him to desist
from this conduct, intimating, with an appearance of
friendship, that if he persisted the Unitarians, including himself, might not be allowed to remain in the
country : and then, under pretence of clearing them-

---

* Bod, *ubi supra, pp.* 84 *et* 102. The authority for this account is a letter addressed by some of the Unitarian ministers
of Transylvania to Palæologus, who was then absent, convey-
ing to him an account of the proceedings against David. Bod
has given this important document entire.

                                        selves

selves from suspicion, and securing the interest of the party, he recommended to David to unite with him in accusing two or three ministers of this offence, and procuring their condemnation. But the pious superintendant treated this vile and insidious proposal with becoming indignation.

Blandrata had now recourse to another scheme. He wrote to Faustus Socinus, who was then residing at Basil, inviting him to come to Transylvania to aid him in controverting and suppressing the opinion of David, promising to defray all the expenses of his journey, and of his residence in that country. Socinus accordingly arrived at Coloswar about the middle of November 1578. Blandrata, the more effectually to prosecute his design, contrived that Socinus should be lodged in David's house, but, it should seem, carefully concealed from both of them the real motive of his conduct. During Socinus's residence with the venerable superintendant which lasted four months and a half, from November 1578 till April 1579*, he and his host had frequent disputations on the great point concerning which they mainly differed,—the invocation of Christ. At the conclusion of these conferences both the disputants appear to have remained just where they were at the commencement of them, except that the warmth into which they had occasionally been betrayed had excited on either side

* Lampii *Historia Ecclesiæ Reformatæ in Hungaria et Transylvania*, p. 303. Bod, *ubi supra*, p. 86.

a con-a considerable degree of irritation, and of personal dislike and animosity*.

By agreement, the arguments in this controversy were from time to time committed to writing, and the papers were regularly transmitted by Socinus to Blandrata. In making these communications, Socinus's motives have been severely arraigned by the friends of David; and he has been charged with voluntarily engaging with Blandrata in a plot to ensnare and ruin his host, while he was enjoying his confidence and friendship, and partaking of his hospitalities. But as far as can be collected from the evidence now before the public, Socinus appears to have done this with no other view than that of informing Blandrata, at whose solicitation he had engaged in this controversy, in what manner it was proceeding, and with what effect, as respected the mind of his opponent†.

The attempt to convince David of the error of his doctrine having failed, it became the next object to restrain him from the public assertion and dissemination of it. Socinus states that he frequently admonished him on this head, and advised him to silence not only from his own persuasion of the pernicious tendency of what he calls his IMPIOUS tenet, but also

---

* The English reader will find some account of the arguments adduced by the contending parties in this controversy in Mr. Lindsey's "Historical View of the State of the Unitarian Doctrine from the Reformation to our own Times," pp. 174, &c.

† Socini *Opera, tom.* ii. *p.* 710. Toulmin's Life of Socinus, p. 85.

however, that it comprises but a small proportion of the books which were published by the Unitarians in Poland. The others are indeed exceedingly scarce, most of them having been lost by the expulsion of the Unitarians and their dispersion through different provinces, or else by the bigotry of magistrates in their own and in other nations, by whom many of them were consigned to the flames. But some of them are still occasionally to be met with*. Among the most voluminous of these are the works of Volkelius and Smalcius, both persons of considerable eminence in the Unitarian body.

HAVING thus completed a rapid sketch of the History of Unitarianism on the Continent subsequently to the æra of the Reformation, it remains to give some account of the work which is here first presented to the public in an English dress.

After the Antitrinitarians had so far multiplied in Poland as to acquire the rank of a separate body, and to have churches of their own, they thought it proper, in imitation of the other Reformers, to draw up a summary of their religious creed in the form of a Confession or Catechism, as well, probably, for the information of others, as for the instruction of their own

---

* My own collection comprises of these scarcer works, not included in the *Bibliotheca Fratrum Polonorum*, as many probably as would form two volumes in folio, printed uniformly with the others. Among these are the works of Volkelius and Smalcius, and some of the rarest pieces of Schlichtingius.

members.

members. Among the earliest of these was one composed by Gregory Paul, who at that time was regarded
as one of the heads of the sect*. George Schomann,
also, in his last will, inserted in Sandius's *Bibliotheca
Antitrinitariorum*, speaks of one which he had drawn
up originally for the use of his own family †. Among
Socinus's works are inserted two unfinished treatises
of this kind:—the one intituled *Christianæ Religionis
brevissima Institutio, per Interrogationes et Respon-
siones, quam Catechismum vulgò vocant;* and the
other, *Fragmentum Catechismi Prioris, Fausti Socini Senensis, qui periit in Cracoviensi Rerum ipsius
Direptione ‡.* In the year 1574 there was printed at
Cracow by Alexander Turobinus (Turobinczyck) in
duodecimo, a small work of this description under the
following title: " Catechism, or Confession of Faith of
the Congregation assembled in Poland, in the Name
of Jesus Christ our Lord, who was crucified and raised
from the dead. Deut. vi. ' Hear, O Israel, the Lord
our God is one God.' John viii. 54. ' It is my Father,—of whom ye say that he is your God §.' " This
piece

---

* Sandius's *Biblioth. Antitrin.* p. 44.

† *Georgii Schomanni Testamentum Ultimæ Voluntatis, ad
calcem Sandii Biblioth. Antitrin.* p. 188. Bock, *ubi supra*, tom. i.
p. 826, *in Vita Georgii Schomanni.* Mosheim, Eccles. Hist.
cent. xvi. § iii. part ii. note.

‡ These pieces were first printed at Racow in 1618 in 12mo,
and are contained in the first volume of the folio edition of Socinus's Works, *pp.* 650—689.

§ *Catechesis et Confessio Fidei Cœtus per Poloniam congregati
in Nomine Jesu Christi, Domini nostri, crucifixi et resuscitati.*
Deut. vi. *Audi, Israel, Dominus Deus noster Deus unus est.* Jo-
hann. viii. *dicit Jesus: Quem vos dicitis vestrum esse Deum, est
Pater *

piece is ascribed to George Schomann by John Adam Müller, in his treatise *De Unitariorum Catechesi et Confessione*

Pater meus. Typis Alexandri Turobini, anno nati Jesu Christi, filii Dei, 1574.

We are indebted to Mosheim (cent. xvi. sect. iii. part ii. note,) for bringing us acquainted with this interesting document. I shall here insert the account which he has given of its contents, without noticing his observations upon it.

"The preface, which is composed in the name of the whole congregation, begins with the following salutation. *Omnibus salutem æternam sitientibus, gratiam ac pacem ab uno illo altissimo Deo Patre, per unigenitum ejus filium, Dominum nostrum, Jesum Christum crucifixum, ex animo precatur cœtus exiguus et afflictus per Poloniam, in nomine ejusdem Jesu Christi Nazareni baptizatus.* 'To all those who thirst after eternal salvation, the little and afflicted flock in Poland, which is baptized in the name of Jesus of Nazareth, sendeth greeting; praying most earnestly that grace and peace may be shed upon them by the one supreme God and Father, through his only begotten Son, our Lord, Jesus Christ, who was crucified.'—After this general salutation the Prefacers give an account of the reasons that engaged them to compose and publish this Confession. The principal of these reasons was, the reproaches and aspersions that were cast upon the Anabaptists, in several places; from which we learn that, at this time, the denomination of ANABAPTISTS was given to those who, in after times, were called SOCINIANS. The rest of this preface is employed in beseeching the reader to be firmly persuaded that the designs of the congregation are pious and upright, to read with attention, that he may judge with discernment, and, 'abandoning the doctrine of Babylon and the conduct and conversation of Sodom, to take refuge in the ark of Noah,' *i. e.* among the Unitarian Brethren.

"In the beginning of the Catechism itself, the whole doctrine of Christianity is reduced to six points. The first relates to the Nature of God, and his Son Jeus Christ; the second to Justification; the third to Discipline; the fourth to Prayer; the fifth to Baptism; and the sixth to the Lord's Supper. These six points are explained at length in the following manner: Each point is defined and unfolded, in general terms, in one question and answer, and is afterwards subdivided into its several branches in various questions and answers, in which its

d different

Confessione Fidei omnium prima, and supposed to be the identical Catechism mentioned by him in his will.

Which

different parts are illustrated, and confirmed by texts of Scripture." " In their definition of the nature of God, with which this Catechism begins, the authors discover immediately their sentiments concerning Jesus Christ, by declaring that he, together with all other things, is subject to the great Creator of the universe.

" Their notion concerning Jesus Christ is expressed in the following terms : *Est homo, mediator noster apud Deum, patribus olim per prophetas promissus, et ultimis tandem temporibus ex Davidis semine natus, quem Deus Pater fecit Dominum et Christum, hoc est, perfectissimum prophetam, sanctissimum sacerdotem, invictissimum regem, per quem mundum creavit, omnia restauravit, secum reconciliavit, pacificavit, et vitam æternam electis suis donavit : ut in illum, post Deum altissimum, credamus, illum adoremus, invocemus, audiamus, pro modulo nostro imitemur, et, in illo, requiem animabus nostris inveniamus.* 'Our mediator before the throne of God is a man, who was formerly promised to our fathers by the prophets, and in these latter days was born of the seed of David, and whom God, the Father, has made Lord and Christ, that is, the most perfect prophet, the most holy priest, and the most triumphant king, by whom he created the NEW world, by whom he has sent peace upon earth, restored all things, and reconciled them to himself, and by whom also he has bestowed eternal life upon his elect ; to the end that, after the supreme God, we should believe in him, adore and invoke him, hear his voice, imitate his example, and find in him rest to our souls.'

" With respect to the Holy Ghost, they plainly deny his being a divine person, and represent him as nothing more than a divine quality, or virtue, as appears from the following passage : *Spiritus Sanctus est virtus Dei, cujus plenitudinem dedit Deus Pater filio suo unigenito, Domino nostro, ut ex ejus plenitudine nos adoptivi acciperemus.* ' The Holy Ghost is the energy or perfection of God, whose fulness God the Father bestowed upon his only-begotten Son, our Lord, that we, becoming his adopted children, might receive of his fulness.'

" They express their sentiments concerning Justification in the ensuing terms : *Justificatio est ex mera gratia, per Dominum nostrum Jesum Christum, sine operibus et meritis nostris,*

omnium

of these Theses, severally, he subjoined Antitheses of his own by way of answer, and which he designed as a representation of the prevailing opinions of the Transylvanian Unitarians. This extraordinary document he committed to the press after David had been sent to prison, and when he had no means of disavowing it; and having prefixed to it an address to the members of the Diet, dated the 7th of April 1579, wherein he seems to speak in the person of the Prince, recommending it to their attention, he caused it to be circulated through the country *.

The

---

* Lampius, in his Ecclesiastical History of Hungary and Transylvania, referred to above, has given this forged production in its original form, pp. 305—311. As the subject is in a great measure new to the British public, and Lampius's work is not of common occurrence, Blandrata's letter shall be here transcribed entire. The Theses are given by Bod in his History, but without Blandrata's letter.

EXEMPLAR EPISTOLÆ CONVOCATORIÆ GEORGII BLANDRATÆ.

Gratia vobis et pax a Deo Patre, et Domino nostro Jesu Christo. Quoniam in proximis Comitiis Regni ad diem vigesimam sextam hujus mensis Tordæ indictis, in quibus causa Francisci Davidis serio agetur, ibique ut audiamus de eo sententia fieri non potest, quin de tota religionis causa tractetur, et de novatoribus diligens inquisitio et judicium simul fiat, quæ Comitia consecutura est brevi Synodus generalis, qua potissimum fidei confessio, quæ Verbo Dei et Regni legibus non adversetur, constituenda erit; visum est nobis vos horum admonere, ut ad utrumque Conventum ea quæ nobis ad Dei gloriam pertinere videbuntur, diligenter prius meditata, quatenus oportuerit afferre possitis. De universo enim statu Ecclesiæ, et singulorum qui in ea docendi munus habent, ut videtis agitur. Ut autem id commodius facere possitis, mittimus ad vos THESES de quibus in Synodo serio tractatum iri confidimus, imo credimus, quas ut unusquisque ex verbo publice detestetur, et quas illi Theses oppositas videtis amplectatur, necesse futurum putamus, nisi munere suo privari, et extorris jam fieri malit. Non autem quo vestrum alicui timorem incutiamus, hæc vos scire voluimus, ut scilicet, metu adacti, contra conscientiam vestram

c 2

tram

The Diet assembled at Thorda on the day appointed. The nobility, who were scandalized at the prosecution,

tram aliquid vel dicatis, vel faciatis, sed ut id præcaveretur, et in eo vobis prodesse officii nostri esse arbitrati fuimus, ne quis ex vobis aliquid quidpiam in tanto periculo præ oculis habeat, quem unam ipsam veritatem, cujus testimonium in corde suo coram Deo habere plane persuasus sit. Speramus Deum vobis affuturum, si ejus opem, ut quidem nos facimus, supplices implorare in hoc discrimine non intermiscritis. Ipse vero Deus et Dominus noster Jesus Christus consoletur corda vestra et sit Spiritu cum vestro, Amen. PRINCIPE STEPHANO BATHORIO.

Claudiopoli, 7 *Aprilis* 1579.

Then follow the Sixteen Theses printed in two columns, the one containing those ascribed to David, with this head—*Theses Francisci Davidis;* the other the Antitheses in reply to them, by Blandrata, with the title *Antitheses Georgii Blandratæ.* Fifteen of these propositions,—that is, all except the first,—are printed, with only some slight verbal differences, in the folio edition of Socinus's works, in the *Bibliotheca Fratrum Polonorum, tom.* ii. *p.* 801 ; and are given in English by Dr. Toulmin in his Life of Socinus, pp. 453 – 463. Prefixed is the following head —" Propositions in which is explained the opinion of Francis David concerning the character of Christ, together with the opposite propositions of the Church, drawn up by FAUSTUS SOCINUS, and presented to Christopher Bathory, the illustrious Prince of Transylvania." The reader will find some of these propositions inserted in a note, page 197 of the following Catechism, where they are ascribed to Socinus. I am now satisfied, however, that this title was not written by Socinus himself; but was drawn up and attached to this document either by the editor of the *Bibliotheca,* Andrew Wissowatius, or by some other person, who erroneously concluded, from the part Socinus had acted in the disputations with David concerning the invocation of Christ, that these Antitheses must have proceeded from his pen. Socinus seems never to have avowed himself the author:—nor is it very likely, considering Blandrata's dissatisfaction with his management of the controversy against David, that he should so soon have been employed by him to draw up such a document on the behalf of the Transylvanian Churches. It is worthy of remark, that this paper was not inserted by Socinus in his own account of the controversy with

prosecution, immediately held a private conference to deliberate upon the measures proper to be taken in so delicate

---

with David, which he published in 1595. In the *Bibliotheca* it occurs as a detached piece at the end of the account of his controversy with Franken, with which it has no connexion.

The copy in Socinus's works contains only fifteen propositions, the first in Lampius's copy being here omitted. That the original number was sixteen, and consequently that Lampius's copy is the most likely to have been the one forged and circulated by Blandrata, appears from their being always noticed as comprising this number. See particularly Bod, *Hist. Unit. p.* 98; Sandius's *Bibliotheca Antitrin. p.* 56; Bock's *Hist. Antitrin. tom.* i. *p.* 241, and also *p.* 63, where this excellent writer enumerates these Antitheses among the writings of Blandrata on the authority of Lampius. The first proposition is given by Lampius in these words,—

THESIS FRANCISCI DAVIDIS.
Homo ille Jesus Nazarênus, Mariæ Josephi uxoris filius ex ejusdem semine Josephi conceptus et natus est; quacunque tandem ratione id factum sit: credimus eum Messiam illum esse in Veteri Testamento a Deo promisso.

ANTITHESIS GEORGII BLANDRATÆ.
Homo ille Jesus Nazarenus, in Mariæ Virginis utero conceptus ex eaque natus est, Spiritu Sancto eam conceptionem citra carnalem viri alicujus congressum operante. Et quamvis ex Josephi Mariæ viri semine, nulla prorsus ratione, nec conceptus, nec natus fuerit, revera credendum tamen omnino nobis, eum Messiam illum esse a Deo in Veteri Testamento promissum.

The most criminal property of this document is, that it ascribes to David opinions which he never held, and which Blandrata must have known that he did not entertain;—opinions, too, which were sure to subject him to very general odium at the time, even among his own party, and which have had the effect of transmitting his name to posterity with the imputation of being a SEMI-JUDAIZER, and, in fact, a disbeliever in the truth and authority of the Christian Revelation. See Bod as above, *p.* 99; Zeltner's *Historia Crypto-Socinismi, p.* 201.—To these may be added even the Unitarian writers among ourselves; Dr. Toulmin in several passages of his Life

of

delicate and dangerous a business. David, who had been brought a prisoner to Thorda, hearing of their consultation, sent to entreat they would not on his account resort to violence, intimating that he was prepared to suffer all things for the truth which he had professed. Several deputations were sent to wait on the prince to urge him to quash the proceedings altogether, and thus extinguish the flame which had been kindled in his dominions and threatened the most dreadful consequences. But Blandrata, who, with Socinus* and others, had arrived at Thorda a week

previously

---

of Socinus, particularly p. 464; and Mr. Lindsey in his Historical View of the Unitarian Doctrine, in his account of David and his opinions, pp. 154 &c. We have David's own authority to prove the falsehood of the statement of his opinion on that subject, given in the proposition quoted above concerning the conception of Jesus; for in his Theses *De Filio Dei*, in answer to a work of Blandrata's, he expressly maintains that " he was conceived of the Holy Spirit," and consequently was not, as here asserted, the son of Joseph. This instance of wilful misrepresentation may serve to show what credit is to be attached to the other propositions, wherein he is made to prefer the Law of Moses to the Gospel of Christ; to assert that Christ was slain contrary to the divine purpose; and other things of a similar character. It is a sufficient answer to such calumnies, that the venerable confessor, when arraigned before the Diet, partly on this very document, disclaimed being the author of it, and charged his base and vindictive accuser with the forgery.

These few facts will serve to throw some new light on the history of Francis David, a man unquestionably of splendid talents and eminent virtue, to whose character and labours in the cause of Christian truth, it remains for some future historian to do the justice which thus far has been withheld from them.

* It is proper to notice, that this is the last time the name of Socinus occurs in these proceedings. What share he actually had in the persecutions which David had thus far endured cannot

not

previously to the assembling of the Diet, in order to arrange matters for the prosecution, successfully employed his influence with the prince, and prevailed upon him to turn a deaf ear to these remonstrances and petitions. The nobility became highly incensed by the manner in which these representations were received, and assumed a menacing tone. The prince was alarmed, and in order to prevent tumult adjourned the Diet to the first day of June following.

David was at this time suffering severely from a painful disorder, called by historians the colic, then very prevalent in the country. In consequence of this,

---

not perhaps at this time be accurately ascertained. There is no room to doubt but that he acceded to the measure of his imprisonment, as the means of restraining him from the dissemination of his opinion, until the Diet should determine what further steps it might be proper to take. Socinus certainly had no objection to the interference of the civil magistrate in certain cases to suppress opinions which he deemed antichristian — but he was averse to the punishment of heretics by death. The probability, however, is, that, whatever might have been the views and feelings of Socinus in respect to this persecution, Blandrata was the moving spring which put the whole in motion. He possessed the ear of the prince completely; and Socinus, who, it is to be recollected, was a stranger in the country, could have done nothing to oppose his proceedings had he been so inclined. The Diet, before which David was first summoned to appear, was dissolved before the end of April without coming to any decision. It did not re-assemble until the first of June following, when the prosecution closed. But previously to this, that is, in the month of May, Socinus, as I have observed above, withdrew to Poland. He is entitled to a fair hearing in his own defence; and the reader may consult the preface to his work *De Jesu Christi Invocatione, Disputatio,* &c. inserted in the *Bibliotheca Fratrum Polonorum,* and Dr. Toulmin's examination of the charges against him, in his Memoirs, pp. 82 &c.

his

his friends, apprehensive for his life, interceded with Blandrata to obtain his liberation until the next meeting of the Diet.   But he replied that he would sacrifice all he was worth rather than suffer him to be at large, and that he would lose his life, or he should not escape*.   In order to make himself the more secure of his victim, he obtained an order from the prince to remove him from the custody of the ministers, and place him under a military guard.   From this moment the confinement of David became more strict : all access to him was forbidden, excepting merely to his daughter and son-in-law, and such attendants as were necessary to assist him in removing to and from his bed.   In this wretched state he passed a whole month, before the expiration of which he was so enfeebled by his disorder, and the fainting fits attending it, that he was scarcely able to speak.

On the first of June the Diet assembled at Weissenburg (*Alba Julia*); and David was conveyed to that city, distant from his prison a journey of several days, in a state between life and death.   Almost immediately after his arrival he was summoned to appear before his judges, and notwithstanding his exhausted condition was ordered to stand.   But the prince, who presided on the occasion, when he beheld him, was struck with compassion, and commanded a seat to be provided for him.   The officer of the court having declared the charge on which David was arraigned, Blandrata arose, and stated that he had in vain endeavoured by conversation, letters, and messages, to

---

* Bod, *ubi supra, p.* 113.

restrain

restrain him from publicly avowing and maintaining his opinion against the invocation of Christ, and that he was therefore compelled, by a regard to his conscience, to resort to this prosecution in order to provide against the dangers which threatened the Church.

David was then called upon to reply to the accusation preferred against him, of having publicly declared that Christ ought not to be invoked in prayer; and that those who prayed to Christ sinned as much as if they invoked the Virgin Mary, Peter, Paul, and other dead saints. And Blandrata further required that he should answer in respect to his writings, whether he admitted himself to be the author of them?

The venerable confessor being himself too much oppressed and enfeebled by his disorder to speak so as to be heard by the assembly, obtained permission for his son-in-law, Lucas, to answer in his stead. In reference to his writings, he replied that he would not disown those that were really of his composition, neither would he defend as his, those which were the productions of another, and circulated under his name,—alluding to the Theses which Blandrata had distributed with the authority of the prince. And in respect to the charges themselves, he stated as to the first, that in preaching from the account of the marriage festival at Cana, he had argued, that no divine worship which was not prescribed or commanded in the Scriptures could be agreeable to God. The invocation of Christ was not there prescribed or commanded; —therefore it could not be agreeable to God. And as to the second, he observed, that if, quitting the

c 5   Scriptures,

Scriptures, and following human comments and our own fancies, we seek for grounds for the invocation of Christ, we may also, on the same reasons, invoke saints both living and dead *. While Lucas was pronouncing these answers, Blandrata, smiling sarcastically, exclaimed, " You are returning to Judaism !" To which David mildly replied,—" You, Doctor, also, held this very opinion a few years since !" Shortly after, and as soon as the business of the assembly permitted, Blandrata arose, and observed, " Francis states that I held the same opinion :—but I declare and protest before God, before the illustrious prince, and the whole Church, that I never held nor concurred in this sentiment. But if I have either said or written any thing to this effect, I now desire to revoke it, and declare my recantation;" adding, " and thou, Francis, do thou so likewise." To this Lucas warmly and abruptly answered, " He will not ; for it is not firmness but weakness in a man to revoke without reason, that which he has once asserted." After this interruption, Blandrata moved that the Theses he had printed and circulated under David's name should be read ; which closed the case on the part of the prosecutors.

David, with considerable difficulty, and against the warm efforts of Blandrata and his associates, obtained permission, on account of the exhausted state of his strength, to postpone his defence till the following day. On the breaking up of the Diet he was reconducted to prison, where he was instantly surrounded by his

---

* Bod, ubi supra, p. 123.

friends,

friends, who were filled with apprehension as to the result of these extraordinary proceedings, and doubtful what course they ought to pursue. In the number of these were several of the principal nobility, who were deeply anxious to save their venerable pastor from the danger which seemed to threaten him. David again implored them not to involve themselves on his account by any measures of violence, even if he were to fall—observing that the world would see and acknowledge that God was one, and was alone to be worshipped with divine honours. -

Early the next morning, David, unable any longer to stand, was carried into court by four ministers. The interval had been employed by his friends in collecting the writings, both manuscript and printed, of Blandrata and others of the prosecutors in this case, which contained the proofs, in their own words, of their having once held the same opinion as David respecting the invocation of Christ. Passages from these were read by Lucas in the defence of his father-in-law —and were most feebly met and evaded by the physician, who spoke as his opponent *. The chancellor requested that these writings should be given in to the

---

* Blandrata had by this time gained over to his party a considerable number of the Unitarian ministers, who afterwards saw too late the folly of their conduct. In proof that Blandrata had once held the same opinion as himself, David produced the following argument in his own words, and fully substantiated his charge,—*Si ulla vera adoratio et cultus Dei manifestatus fuit in Veteri Testamento, is a Christo declaratus fuit in N. Testamento. Sed solius Dei Patris adoratio et cultus declaratus a Christo. Joh.4.* Bod, *p.* 128.

court ;

court ; after which David and his supporters were ordered to withdraw while the assembly deliberated concerning their judgement.

The prince and the judges then proceeded to interrogate the accusers of David, and to demand of them on oath whether they concurred in his opinion and innovation ;—or whether they deemed it blasphemy against God? Blandrata rose first to reply, and thus expressed himself : " I, George Blandrata, profess, before Almighty God, and his Son our Lord Jesus Christ, before the holy angels and the elect of God, that I neither am nor have been in any respect a partaker in the guilt of this opinion of Francis David; and I affirm that it is a novel opinion, and, besides, a horrid blasphemy against God and his Son." The associates of Blandrata, to the number of twenty-five, having taken similar oaths, the public prosecutor, in the name of the prince, of himself, and of the Jesuits, after asserting his belief in the Trinity, condemned the opinion of David as blasphemy.

David being again brought before the Diet, to receive judgment, some of his accusers interceded with the prince to spare his life, alleging that he had been guilty of no capital offence in what he had declared, his argument being taken from the words of Christ. At the same time Blandrata went up Judas-like to his emaciated victim, and embracing him, said, in a low voice, " Do not fear—I have found favour with the prince." David indignantly replied, " Go, go—proceed as thou hast begun." Blandrata having resumed

his

his seat, his colleagues again importuned the prince to spare the life of the superintendant. But the Hungarian Trinitarian ministers opposed them in a long oration, wherein they exhorted the prince, on the ground of the command of Moses concerning false prophets, to put him to death as a blasphemer; and concluded in these words : " We this day, by virtue of our office, cite thee, O thou illustrious prince, the keeper of both tables, together with thy consort, thy children, and all thy posterity, before the tribunal of the awful judge Jesus Christ, whom this man has blasphemed, if thou suffer him to live !"

The prince, at this adjuration, changed colour; and, calling to the officer of the court, commanded him to give the following reply: " The illustrious prince has heard the orations of both parties : his highness therefore promises that he will take care to evince to all that he will not suffer such an offender to escape with impunity." Then turning to Francis David, he proceeded : " The illustrious prince has been made acquainted with the whole of this affair, in what manner, led by thine own fancy, and without the consent of the Church, thou hast fallen into this atheistical, execrable, and unheard-of blasphemy. His highness therefore will, according to thy desert, make an example of thee, because others also ought to be deterred from such fanatical innovations. In the mean time thou shalt be kept in the custody of the prince, until he shall determine further concerning thee*."

---

* Bod, p. 136.

David

David was now committed to close custody in the castle of Deva, none of his friends or relations being allowed access to him ; and here, worn down by the fatigues of his persecutions and the ravages of a painful disorder, he closed a long life on the 15th of November following, in the year 1579 *.

The proceedings against Francis David being thus brought to a conclusion, Blandrata, having now got rid of the only adversary whose influence he feared, called some general synods at Coloswar, for the purpose of arranging the affairs of the Unitarian Churches conformably to his own views and wishes. Demetrius Hunjadinus was, with some opposition, appointed the new superintendant; and the practice of baptizing infants in the name of the Father, the Son, and the Holy Spirit, and the observance of the Lord's Supper, which had been long disused by the Unitarians of Transylvania, were again introduced as part of their religious service. Only about eighteen out of two hundred and seventy ministers refused to assent to

---

† Bod, *p.* 144. Blandrata, writing to Palæologus on the 10th of January 1580, gives the following account of the case, with the view of exculpating himself. *Dominus Francis voluit calamo primum respondere Fausto; deinde Thesibus meis. Summa ejus doctrina fuit : sepeliendum esse Evangelium, et revertendum ad Mosen, ad legem, ad circumcisionem. Voluit pluries turbare regnum, et fieri novator, et rebellis regni publici mandati. Dicebat, tantum esse Jesum Christum, atque Mariam Virginem invocare in precibus, Mosem et Mosis lineam esse rectam, Christum autem Jesum et ejus doctrinam indirectam. Tanquam novator et turbator regni fuit condemnatus, et missus Devam ad carcerem, ubi 15 Novembris est mortuus. Neque credas me tam fuisse commotum contra eum propter Jesum Christum non invocandum in precibus, quam propter impias ejus appendices.*

this

this measure—the rest being gained over by the per-suasion or the threats of the wily physician *.

In a short time after these occurrences Blandrata lost his influence, and sunk into contempt with all ranks of persons in the Unitarian body. He attempt-ed to repossess himself of the power which he had once held and exercised in the direction of the eccle-siastical affairs of the kingdom, by joining himself to the party of the Jesuits :—but finding himself at last an object of universal dislike, he returned to Poland in 1580, where, two years afterwards, he was strangled by a near relation whom he had appointed to be the heir of his property †.

Hunjadinus was succeeded in the superintendence of the Transylvanian Churches by George Enjedinus, a divine of great eminence, deeply versed in the Latin and Greek languages, and who has left an imperish-able monument of his learning and talents in his cele-brated work, intituled, *Explicationes Locorum Vete-ris et Novi Testamenti, ex quibus Trinitatis Dogma stabiliri solet.*

Notwithstanding all that had been done by Blandra-ta to establish an uniformity of Faith in the Unitarian Churches of Transylvania, the ministers were far from agreeing on the point which had occasioned so much

---

* Socinus, adverting to this circumstance in his preface to his account of his dispute with David, writes,—*Jam vero, de Francisci Davidis causa, judicio peracto, quamvis, ejus asseclæ fere omnes, sententiam de Christo non invocando se abjicere pa-lam professi fuissent; tamen cognitum est postea, id non ex animo ab ipsis factum fuisse!* Socini *Opera,* tom. ii. p. 709.

† Socini *Opera,* tom. ii. p. 538.

agitation,

agitation, and ended so fatally to the venerable confessor and martyr David.   There still remained a large num- ber who objected to the invocation of Christ, and who, when they found themselves freed from the interfe- rence and persecution of Blandrata, made no scruple of openly avowing and promulgating their opinion. In order to restrain and silence such persons, it was found necessary, by successive princes, to enact against them new and severe laws, whereby at length all who refused to worship Jesus Christ were excluded from toleration.   Their faith was watched with great jea- lousy by the government, which obliged them from time to time to deliver in an authorized confession, agreeing in all respects with the form drawn up and subscribed by the general Synod convened by Blan- drata at Coloswar on the first of July 1579 *.

The

---

* The Confession of Faith then agreed upon and subscri- bed, as the standard of the doctrine authorized by law to be professed and taught in the Unitarian Churches, was as fol- lows :—

I. *Credimus et confitemur Jesum illum a Nazareth esse Fi- lium Altissimi unigenitum, dicique Deum juxta genuinum sen- sum S. Scripturæ propter has causas :—1. Quia conceptus est de Spiritu Sancto.   2. Quia unctus est Spiritu Sancto præ omnibus consortibus, et accepit Spiritum sine mensura.   3. Propter ma- jestatem et gloriam ; quam Pater in cœlo et in terra, postquam resurrexerit a mortuis, plenarie dedit.   4. Quia Deus Pater in plenitudine temporis restauravit et condidit omnia per ipsum, de- ditque illum nobis, ut per illum salvemur, et vitæ æternæ hære- ditatem accipiamus.*

II. *Hunc eundem Jesum Christum credimus colendum et ado- randum esse, quia Pater dedit omnia Filio, et præcepit ut illum audiamus, in ipsum credamus, ipsum colamus et adoremus.   Ideo omnes thesauros scientiæ et sapientiæ in eo abscondidit, ut ex plenitudine ejus et nos omnes accipiamus ; ut scilicet colentes Fi- lium,*

The severe restrictions thus imposed upon its professors operated very prejudicially in checking the progress of Unitarianism, and by degrees caused the defection of most of the noble families from the Unitarian party. Few events of any consequence occur in the subsequent history of the Unitarians in this coun-

---

lium, colamus Patrem, credentes in Filium, credamus in Patrem, qui Pater in Filio honoratur.

III. Confitemur, quod Jesus ille verus Messias dum fuit in terris, contulit, et etiam nunc confert bona spiritualia fidelibus per verbum et spiritum, ideoque invocandus est, propterea enim a Deo Patre in ipsum bona omnia collata sunt, ut illa ab ipso confidenter in nostris necessitatibus petamus et speremus. Hinc postquam exhibitus in mundum venit, ad illum multi confugerunt, dixerunt, "Jesu, Fili David, miserere mei" Matth. xv., Marc. x. Item, "Domine Jesu! suscipe spiritum meum;" Act. vii. neque tamen ut Deus ille Pater, in quo omnia, invocatur, 1 Cor. viii. neque etiam ea forma invocationis, qua Patrem invocamus dicendo, "Pater noster," &c. sed ea ratione, ut quod Deus Pater illi contulit certi simus nobis Christum id opulenter largiturum, quemadmodum ipse promisit—"Quicquid petieritis in nomine meo, ego faciam," Joh. xiv. Item, "Ego dabo vobis os et sapientiam." Luc. xxi. Item, "Vitam æternam dabo eis." Joh. x. Neque enim eo pacto Mediator noster est, ut nihil nobis conferat, aut quod ab eo nihil petendum, exspectandum, atque etiam sperandum sit; cum eo fine omnia a Deo Patre suo cælesti acceperit, ut ab ipso ea omnia in nos, tanquam membra ipsius, derivarentur.

IV. Dicimus etiam cum Sacra Scriptura, quod Jesus ille Christus, qui dicitur caput nostrum, sit nunc quoque Ecclesiarum Rex, et regat per spiritum suum fideles suos. "Domineturque super vivos et mortuos" Rom. xiv. imo, quod "regat omnia verbo potentiæ suæ" Heb. i. Nam Christum ideo Pater nobis dedit, ut in suis fidelibus nunc regnet, et illis vitam æternam conferat, et "Ipse sit solus sub cælo, in cujus nomine nos salvos fieri oportet." Act. iv. 12. Et quamvis dicatur 1 Cor. xv. tunc habiturum finem, quando Christus tradiderit regnum Deo et Patri, et cum omnia fuerint ei subjecta; non tamen ex eo consequitur Christum nostrum Deum, Regem nunc non esse, cum ibidem dicatur, oportere illum regnare, donec illi omnia subjiciantur. Bod, ubi supra, pp. 167 et seqq.

try,

try, as far as it has been transmitted to us. Among the principal may be mentioned a calamity that befel them in the year 1716, when the Imperial soldiers occupied Coloswar. These troops took from them, and transferred to the Catholics, their church, a new College-house just erected, together with the dwelling houses of the ministers and professors, their printing-house, their vineyards and their farms *. The latest accounts from this country, which however are not very recent, report that the cause is still continued, and apparently much in the state in which it had existed many years before,—the Unitarian churches being estimated at about two hundred, and the population connected with them at about sixty thousand. Coloswar is still the metropolitan seat, and here the Unitarians have a flourishing collegiate establishment †.

. Poland

---

* Bod, *ubi supra, p.* 186.

† That the Unitarians of Transylvania departed, in the course of time, from the simplicity of the doctrines held by them in the days of Francis David, may be seen from the following interesting document, for the sight and the use of which I am indebted to the kindness of my esteemed friend the Rev. Robert Aspland. It is to be regretted that it bears no date, and the last public act referred to in the notes is a rescript of 1713: it is evidently prior, probably several years, to the Confession published in 1787 by professor Markos, of Coloswar, mentioned by Mr. Adam in his Religious World Displayed, vol. ii. p. 174, and which I have thus far failed to procure. The notes and illustrations that accompany the following Confession my limits oblige me to omit. But I trust the document will shortly be given entire to the public. The four received systems of religion in Transylvania noticed at the head, were the Catholic, the Lutheran, the Calvinistic, and the Unitarian, the open profession of all of which was secured by the Laws.

CONFESSIO

Poland and Transylvania are the only two countries on the continent wherein Unitarianism has obtained

an

CONFESSIO FIDEI CHRISTIANÆ *secundum* UNITARIOS, *inter quatuor in Transylvania Religiones receptas numeratâ, Fundamentalibus Patriæ istius Legibus, Diplomatibus, variisque Rescriptis Cæsareis, Verbis Regüs, Capitulationibus Principum approbata, confirmata.*

Credimus Unum tantum esse DEUM OMNIPOTENTEM, *qui* SPIRITUS *est, Rerum cunctarum visibilium et invisibilium* CONDITOR, CONSERVATOR, *ac* RECTOR. PATER *omnium, super et per omnia, et in nobis omnibus; adorandus in spiritu et veritate. Quem agnoscimus esse* DATOREM, *cum præsentis tum futuræ vitæ. Est enim* REMUNERATOR *eorum qui per fidem accedunt ad Eum et quærunt Eum. Hunc diligimus tanquam omnis bonitatis* AUCTOREM, *et ceu Sapientiæ Fontem, cordiumque inspectorem timemus.*

JESUM CHRISTUM *Præcognitum ante jacta mundi fundamenta, exhibitum autem ultimis temporibus propter nos, conceptum ex Sancto Spiritu, natum e castissima Virgine; Credimus esse* DEI·PATRIS *unigenitum et proprium Filium,* IMAGINEMQUE *invisibilis* DEI, *in quo omnis plenitudo* DEITATIS *habitat, per quem cognoscimus* PATREM. *Is enim summi Genitoris voluntatem revelavit, et confirmavit, ut* PROPHETA *et* MEDIATOR *inter* DEUM *et humanum genus. In hujus sanctissimo nomine, tanquam maximi nostri Sacerdotis, invocamus* PATREM; *nam nullum aliud sub cœlo hominibus datum est nomen, per quod servari nos oporteat. Hunc ceu æternum* REGEM, *ac* DOMINUM *nostrum (cui a* DEO PATRE *qui Eum a mortuis excitavit, data est omnis in cœlo et in terra potestas) supplices divino cultu adoramus, et invocamus. Et ab eo salutem æternam præstolamur, ut a* JUDICE *vivorum et mortuorum. Nec enim Pater quenquam judicet, sed omne judicium* FILIO *dedit, ut omnes Filium honorent, quemadmodum Patrem honorant. Qui* FILIUM *non honorat, Patrem non honorat, qui Eum misit.*

Credimus SPIRITUM SANCTUM *a* DEO *et Filio ejus manantem,* VIM *esse Altissimi, nostrum autem* CONSOLATOREM: *cujus inspiratione precamur, et efficacia regeneramur. Is sine mensura a* DEO, *Filio ejus unigenito datus, nobis per eundem ceu* DONUM *ejus, et pignus æternæ hæreditatis communicatur; ut in nobis omnia bona opera efficiet, atque in omnem nos deducat veritatem.*

Credimus SANCTAM CHRISTIANAM ECCLESIAM, *omnium electorum*

an extensive public establishment.   Various attempts
were made by the Polish Socinians to introduce their
doctrines into other provinces by the employment of
missionaries to promulgate them from the pulpit, and
to distribute their writings : but these emissaries do
not appear to have laboured with much success, or to
have

---

torem DEI (*a constitutione ejus, ad finem usque mundi*) *congregationem, cujus caput est Dominus et Servator Jesus Christus. Norma vero, Doctrina Sanctorum ejus apostolorum. Hanc verbum* DEI *gubernat, Spiritus Sanctus ducit, in ea sinceri Christiani omnes versari tenentur.*

REGES, PRINCIPES, MAGISTRATUS, *confitemur a* DEO *esse. Ideoque pro iis ante omnia, coram ejusdem Divina Majestate, quotidiana devota fundimus vota : tanquam pro ministris ejus, quibus parendum est : Nam gladium gestant ut innocentes tueantur, et sontes puniant.   Propterea honorem eis deferre, tributaque persolvere tenemur.   Non solum supplicii metu, sed etiam propter conscientiam. Nullus autem ab hac obedientia sese eximere potest, si modo Christianus dici velit, Jesu Christi Domini et Servatoris nostri exemplum sequens; Is enim tributum persolvit ; nec jurisdictionem, dominationemve temporalem usurpavit, in statu illo humiliationis, gladium Verbi cœlestis exercens.*

Credimus AQUAM IN SANCTO BAPTISMO, *quem peragimus in nomine* PATRIS, FILII *et* SPIRITUS SANCTI, *esse signum externum et visibile, nobis repræsentans illud, quod virtus* DEI *intus in nobis operatur : nempe, spiritûs renovationem et carnis nostræ mortificationem in* CHRISTO JESU. *Per sanctum enim* BAPTISMUM *Christo initiati, ecclesiæ membra efficimur, et per eum Fidei nostræ professionem et vitæ emendationem declaramus.*

SANCTAM MENSAM *vel* CŒNAM DOMINI *nostri* JESU CHRISTI *credimus esse sacrum memoriale et gratiarum actionem, ob beneficia per Christi mortem nobis collata : in cœtu piorum, in fide, charitate, suique ipsius probatione celebrandam.   Et ita sacrum* PANEM *et* POCULUM *benedictum sumendo, Christi corpori et sanguini communicare, unitatemque nostram declarare : sicuti in Sacris Scriptis edocemur.*

Credimus et confitemur, totum humanum genus SUB PECCATO FUISSE, *et nos porro peccatis obnoxios esse, justificari autem ex* DEI (*qui omnes homines servari vult, et ad veritatis cognitionem venire :*)

have effected any lasting impressions. The expulsion
of the Unitarian body from Poland was, however, attended with beneficial consequences in this respect.
Those who obtained a settlement in Prussia and
Brandenburg were permitted to form churches for

*venire:) mera gratia et misericordia: non ex operibus legis,
multo vero minus nostris propriis, sed per fidem in sanguine Filii ejus Jesu Christi. Quæ Fides a* DEO *imputatur nobis in jus-
titiam: ita ut per eam, ex gratia Dei per Jesum Christum,* RE-
MISSIONEM PECCATORUM, *ac proinde et æternam salutem con-
sequamur. Nam Christus pro nobis et peccatis nostris mortem
cruentam passus, factus est victima et propitiatio. Exemplum
autem nobis reliquit, ut vestigia ejus sequamur, imitando ejus mo-
destiam, charitatem, patientiam, cæterasque virtutes, quæ potissimum in cruce ejus eluxerunt. Omnibus ergo qui remissionis
peccatorum et Regni cœlorum compotes fieri volunt, vera et seria
præteritorum delictorum agenda est pœnitentia fructusque ea
digni ex viva Fide manantes proferendi: Nam Fides sine operibus mortua est. Præceptis igitur* DEI *(quæ gravia non sunt)
obtemperandum est, quorum summa in eo continetur, ut* DEO *et
proximo debitam charitatem exhibeamus, Fides enim per charitatem debet esse operam. Curandum ergo, ne in cassum accipiamus
gratiam* DEI, *quæ cunctis hominibus illuxit salutifera, et erudit
eos, ut impietati, mundanisque cupiditatibus varie dicto, tempe-
ranter, juste, pieque vivant, in præsenti seculo, exspectantes spe-
ratam beatitudinem, adventumque gloriosum Magni* DEI *et Servatoris nostri Jesu Christi: Qui seipsum pro nobis dedit, ut nos
redimeret ab omni iniquitate, et purificaret sibi ipsi populum pe-
culiarem, sectatorem bonorum operum.*

Credimus et speramus fore CARNIS RESURRECTIONEM, *cum
justorum tum injustorum. Veniet enim Christus Dominus de cœlis, in Patris sui et sua gloria, et cum cunctis sanctis angelis, ut
judicet vivos et mortuos, qui omnes coram Tribunali ejus compa-
rebunt, et tunc unicuique reddet juxta facta ipsius. Impii quidem
et injusti perenni destinati supplicio, conjicientur in ignem æternum, Diabolo ejusque angelis paratum. Pii vero ac justi, mor-
talitate deposita, et glorioso corpore induti, transferentur in lo-
cum a Christo Domino eis paratum, ubi Thronus ipsius et* DEI
Patris est: ita ut DEI *faciem intuentes, sanctis angelis ejus æqua-
les facti, ineffabilis gaudii et æternæ felicitatis participes semper sint cum Domino.*

                                        Unitarian

Unitarian worship, which are yet in existence, though not in a very flourishing condition. Those who went into Flanders and Holland were not so fortunate;—the bigotry of the principal people, especially among the ecclesiastics, having defeated them in every attempt to obtain separate places of worship. They were, therefore, under the necessity of joining those tolerated communions which would admit them into fellowship. By this means, they soon lost every discriminating characteristic as a distinct religious community, and became amalgamated with the Remonstrants and the Mennonites, or the Low Arminians and Baptists of Holland.

The asylum afforded them in the Dutch states furnished them with favourable opportunities for the dissemination of their sentiments through the press. Here some of their principal literary characters, among whom must be named Andrew Wissowatius, employed themselves in collecting their scattered writings, and reprinting them in an uniform edition. Eight volumes in folio were thus in a short time given to the world,—comprising the chief works of Socinus, Crellius, Schlichtingius and Wolzogenius. Another volume was afterwards added, containing the writings of Przipcovius, with some smaller pieces by Andrew Wissowatius, the editor of the other volumes. This collection is commonly known by the title of BIBLIOTHECA FRATRUM POLONORUM *. It must be observed,

---

* To the writings here enumerated the works of Brenius are now commonly added as a tenth volume; and a set of the *Bibliotheca* is hardly deemed complete without it.

however,

on account of the personal danger he might incur by persisting in maintaining it in his public discourses and writings *. That Socinus had good reasons for urging the last consideration, is clearly proved by what afterwards occurred; and, indeed, he confesses that previously to his giving this warning, he had been apprized by Blandrata of his intention to declare himself the open enemy of David, to accuse him to the prince, and call in the aid of the civil power †.

Shortly after the breaking up of the conferences between Socinus and David, the latter having refused to conceal his opinion, and taken occasion on the first Sunday to preach against the invocation of Christ, the prince, at Blandrata's instigation, addressed a letter to the Senate of Coloswar, directing them to remove the venerable pastor from his ministerial office, and to put him in confinement. About the same time a general assembly of the States was convoked to meet at Thorda, on the festival of St. George next ensuing, (the 23d of April,) in order to take the affair into consideration.

Blandrata was fully aware that, from the high reputation of David, the increasing numbers of those who held the same opinion concerning the invocation of Christ, and the jealousy of the nobility attached to the

---

* Socini *Opera*, tom. ii. *p.* 711.

† The following are given as the words of Blandrata, to which Socinus adverts in his defence. *Oper. tom.* ii. *p.* 711. *Dices Francisco, me hactenus non declarasse coram Principe, me esse hostem ejus; sed deinceps pro eo me habeat. Fratribus vero dices, ut in injuncto ipsis negotio fervide pergant.* Bod, *Hist. Unitar. ubi supra, p.* 110.

Unitarian

Unitarian Churches, of any restrictions on the freedom of their worship,—he was likely to encounter formidable opposition in his proceedings : he deemed it expedient, therefore, to prepare the way by prejudicing as much as possible, against the superintendant, the minds of those who were to sit in judgement on his case.   His purpose might possibly have been sufficiently answered by the publication of the written statements, then in his possession, of the opinions of David, which the latter had put into Socinus's hands in the course of their disputations.   But as he was not satisfied with the manner in which Socinus had conducted the controversy, or with the answers he had returned to his acute and learned opponent, he could not consent to give these documents to the public, in an authentic form, and under the sanction of his authority *. Instead, therefore, of acting thus fairly, he had the baseness to resort to an artifice of the blackest description, whereby he but too well succeeded in his immediate object, and also in perpetuating an unfounded charge against the venerable object of his jealousy and vengeance, of holding tenets directly at variance with his real sentiments.   He drew up a series of Sixteen Theses, purporting to be written by Francis David, and to comprise a correct exposition, from under his own hands, of the articles of his religious creed.   To each

---

* The chief cause of the dissatisfaction of Blandrata and his friends with Socinus on this occasion was, that he had admitted *nullum extare expressum in Sacris Literis præceptum de Christo invocando*,—that " there was no express command in the Sacred Scriptures for the invocation of Christ."—*Socini Opera, tom.* ii. *p.* 710.

of

Which of these productions, or whether either of them, is to be regarded as the original of the RACO-

omnium præteritorum peccatorum nostrorum in viva fide remissio vitæque æternæ indubitatâ expectatio, et auxilio spiritus Dei vitæ nostræ non simulata, sed vera correctio, ad gloriam Dei Patris nostri et ædificationem proximorum nostrorum. ' Justification consists in the remission of all our past sins, through the mere grace and mercy of God, in and by our Lord Jesus Christ, without our merits and works, and in consequence of a lively faith, as also in the certain hope of life eternal, and the true and unfeigned amendment of our lives and conversations, through the assistance of the divine spirit, to the glory of God the Father, and the edification of our neighbours.'—As by this definition Justification comprehends in it amendment and obedience, so in the explanation of this point our authors break in upon the following one, which relates to discipline, and lay down a short summary of moral doctrine, which is contained in a few precepts, and expressed, for the most part, in the language of Scripture.——There is this peculiarity in their moral injunctions, that they prohibit the taking of oaths, and the repelling of injuries. As to what regards ecclesiastical discipline, they define it thus: *Disciplina ecclesiastica est officii singulorum frequens commemoratio et peccantium contra Deum vel proximum primum privata, deinde etiam publica, coram toto cœtu, commonefactio, denique pertinacium a communione sanctorum alienatio, ut pudore suffusi convertantur, aut, si id nolint, æternum damnentur.* ' Ecclesiastical discipline consists in calling frequently to the remembrance of every individual, the duties that are incumbent upon them, in admonishing, first privately, and afterwards, if this be ineffectual, in a public manner before the whole congregation, such as have sinned openly against God, or offended their neighbour; and lastly, in excluding from the communion of the Church the obstinate and impenitent, that, being thus covered with shame, they may be led to repentance, or, if they remain unconverted, may be damned eternally!'—In their further explication of this point, they treat, in the first place, concerning the government of the Church and its ministers, whom they divide into bishops, deacons, elders, and widows. After this they enumerate, at length, the duties of husbands and wives, old and young, parents and children, masters and servants, citizens

and

VIAN CATECHISM, seems thus far not to have been satisfactorily determined.   Sandius assigns this honour
to the work of Gregory Paul, which he designates,
Catechesis Racoviensis prima; but he gives no account of its contents, whereby a judgment might be
formed on this point; for he states no more than that
he considers it to be the piece mentioned by Wisno-

vius

---

and magistrates, poor and rich, and conclude with what relates to the admonishing of offenders, and their exclusion from
the communion of the Church in case of obstinate impenitence.

" Their sentiments concerning Prayer are, generally speaking, sound and rational. But in their notions of Baptism, they
differ from other Christian Churches in this, that they make it
to consist in immersion or dipping, and emersion, or rising
again out of the water; and maintain that it ought not to be administered to any but adult persons. 'Baptism,' say they, 'is
the immersion into water, and the emersion, of one who believes in the Gospel and is truly penitent, performed in the
name of the Father, Son, and Holy Ghost, or in the name of
Jesus Christ alone : by which solemn act the person baptized
publicly acknowledges that he is cleansed from all his sins,
through the mercy of God the Father, by the blood of Christ,
and the operation of the Holy Spirit ; to the end that, being in-
grafted into the body of Christ, he may mortify the old Adam,
and be transformed into the image of the new and heavenly
Adam, in the firm assurance of eternal life after the resurrection.' *Baptismus est hominis Evangelio credentis et pœnitentiam
agentis in nomine Patris, et Filii, et Spiritus Sancti, vel in nomine Jesu Christi, in aquam immersio et emersio, quâ publice
profitetur, se gratia Dei Patris, in sanguine Christi, opera Spiritus Sancti, ab omnibus peccatis ablutum esse, ut, in corpore
Christi insertus, mortificet veterem Adamum, et transformetur
in Adamum illum cœlestem, certus, se post resurrectionem conse-
quuturum esse vitam æternam.*

" The last point handled in this performance is the Lord's
Supper; of which the authors give an explication, that will be
readily adopted by those who embrace the doctrine of Zuingle
on that head.

" At the end of this curious Catechism there is a piece inti-

tuled

vius in 1575, as containing an exposition of Philipp.
ii. 6, which had given great offence*. The fragments of Socinus can hardly be deemed entitled to
this distinction; for though some of the statements of
the Unitarian doctrine contained in them bear a close
resemblance to those which are found in the Racovian
Catechism, the entire form is different; and they have
all the appearance of being imperfect sketches, which
the author had not thoroughly digested and arranged.
If therefore the Racovian Catechism was grounded on
either of the above productions, it seems most probable that it was on the Confession which has been
ascribed to Schomann, and whereof some account is
given in the preceding note from Mosheim.

Sandius states † that the task of revising or reform-
ing the first Racovian Catechism was assigned to
Faustus Socinus and Peter Statorius junior; which
agrees with what Socinus himself observes in reference

---

tuled *Œconomia Christiana, seu Pastoratus Domesticus*, which
contains a short instruction to heads of families, showing them
how they ought to proceed in order to maintain and increase,
in their houses, a spirit of piety, in which also their devotion is
assisted by forms of prayer, composed for morning, evening,
and other occasions."

An answer to this Catechism was published by Zachar. Ur-
sinus, under the following title, *Refutatio Catechismi Anabap-
tistici et Samosatenici.* Bock, *Hist. Antitrin. tom.* i. p. 826.

* Sandii *Bib. Antitrin.* p. 44.

† *Biblioth. Antitrin. pp.* 44, 78, *et* 104. It ought to be observed here that the work was never published in Latin under
the title of *Catechesis Racoviensis*; but obtained this designation either from its having been printed at Racow, or in consequence of that city being regarded as the metropolis of the
Polish Unitarians.

to

to this subject in a letter addressed to Valentine Ra-
decius, pastor of the Unitarian Church of Coloswar,
dated the 23d of November 1603 *.   They were,
however, both prevented by the hand of death from
completing their undertaking ; and it was in consequence transferred to Valentine Smalcius and Jerome
Moscorovius, with whom it would appear that Volkelius also was associated †. The work, as modelled and
completed by these eminent persons, was first published in the Polish language in duodecimo, in 1605 ‡.
Smalcius afterwards translated it into German, and
published it in 1608, under the title of *Der Kleine
Catechismus, zur Uebung der Kinder in dem Christ-
lichen Gottesdienste*, with a dedication addressed
to the University of Wittemberg.   In the following
year, 1609, a Latin version of it, executed by Jerome Moscorovius, was published at Racow under
the following title : *Catechesis Ecclesiarum quæ in
Regno Poloniæ, et magno Ducatu Lithuaniæ, et
aliis ad istud Regnum pertinentibus Provinciis, af-
firmant, neminem alium, præter Patrem Domini
nostri Jesu Christi, esse illum unum* DEUM *Israëlis:
Hominem autem illum Jesum Nazarenum, qui ex
Virgine natus est, nec alium, præter aut ante ipsum,
Dei Filium unigenitum, et agnoscunt et confitentur.
Ante annos quatuor Polonicè, nunc verò etiam La-*

---

* *Epistolæ ad Amicos*, 12mo, p. 679. *Opera, folio, tom.* i.
p. 492.

† Bock, *Hist. Antitrin. tom.* i. p. 847.

‡ This is in fact, properly speaking, the first edition of the
RACOVIAN CATECHISM ; and it is extremely scarce.

tinè

tinè edita*. "The Catechism of the Churches, which in the Kingdom of Poland and in the great Dukedom of Lithuania, and in other Provinces belonging to that Kingdom, affirm that no other Being besides the Father of our Lord Jesus Christ, is the one God of Israel; and acknowledge and confess that the Man, Jesus of Nazareth, who was born of a Virgin, and no other besides or before him, is the only-begotten Son of God," &c.—To this edition was prefixed by the translator and editor a dedication addressed to James the First of England. Another edition in German was printed in 12mo at the Racow press in 1612, under the following title, *Catechismus der gemeine derer leute, die da im Kœnigreich Polen und im Gros-Fürstenthum Litthaven, und in andern Herrschaften zu der kron Polen gehœrig, &c* †. The original work was reprinted in London in 18mo, with the imprint of *Racovia*, in the year 1651, with the Life of Socinus by Przipcovius appended to it. Prefixed was the following title:—*Catechesis Ecclesiarum quæ in Regno Poloniæ, &c. cui accedit Fausti Socini Senensis Vita, et Dissertatio Operibus suis, ab Equite Polono præmissa. Cum Catalogo Operum ejusdem Fausti Socini.* In the year following this book at-

---

* It may be mentioned here that there are two editions bearing the date of 1609. They are both in 18mo, one comprising 279 pages; the other, which is on smaller paper, extending to 317 pages. It is difficult perhaps to determine which of them proceeded from the Racow press. I am disposed to think that the former copy is the original, and that the other was printed subsequently in Holland. There is a copy of each of them in Dr. Daniel Williams's Library.

† Walchii *Bibliotheca Theologica selecta, tom.* i. *p.* 537. Vogtii *Catalog. Hist. Crit. Librorum Rariorum, p.* 183.

tracted

tracted the notice of the British Parliament, who, on the 2d of April 1652, passed a resolution, requiring the Sheriffs of London and Middlesex to seize all the copies of the Catechism, and cause them to be burnt at the London Exchange, and at Palace Yard, Westminster, on the 6th and 8th of the same month *. The life of Socinus was afterwards published separately.

An English edition of this work in 18mo was printed at Amsterdam in 1652 for Brooer Janz, under the following title: " The Racovian Catechisme; wherin you have the Substance of the Confession of those Churches, which in the Kingdom of Poland, and the great Dukedome of Lithuania, and other Provinces appertaining to that Kingdom, do affirm, that no other save the Father of our Lord Jesus Christ is that one God of Israel; and that the Man Jesus of Nazareth, who was born of the Virgin, and no other besides or before him, is the only-begotten Sonne of God." Dr. Toulmin conjectures that this translation was executed by John Biddle †, and the date of its appearance renders this extremely probable. The translator has omitted the dedication to James the First, and substituted a preface of his own. It must be observed that this work is, in many parts, rather a paraphrase than a version of the original; and that occasionally the translator has introduced whole clauses to express his

---

* See the original VOTES in another part of this volume. This edition is exceedingly scarce :—it is mentioned in no foreign work relating to the Racovian Catechism; and the only copy I have seen is in the British Museum. Sandius and Walchius notice the circumstance of its being burnt by order of the Parliament, but both mistake the date.

† Life of Socinus, p. 260.

own

own opinion, though at variance with the sentiments of the compilers of the Catechism. One instance of this interpretation, relating to the Holy Spirit, is noticed in the present work *.

After the expulsion of the Unitarians from Poland, Jonas Schlichtingius prepared an edition of this work for the press, considerably altered and enlarged from the Latin edition of 1609, which was afterwards printed under the following title: *Catechesis Ecclesiarum Polonicarum, unum Deum Patrem, illiusque Filium unigenitum, una cum Spiritu Sancto, ex S. Scriptura confitentium, anno 1609 in lucem primum emissa, et post per Viros aliquot in eodem Regno correcta: Iterumque interpositis compluribus annis à Johanne Crellio, Franco, ac nunc tandem a Jona Schlichtingio à Bucoweic recognita, ac dimidia amplius parte aucta. Irenopoli sumptibus Frederici Theophili post annum Domini* 1659. " Catechism of the Polish Churches, which confess, according to the Holy Scriptures, one God the Father, his only begotten Son, and the Holy Spirit :—first published in the year 1609, and afterwards corrected by some Persons in the same kingdom. Again, after an interval of some years, first by John Crellius, and now at length by Jonas Schlichtingius, revised and enlarged more than half."—Irenopolis stands in the title-page for Amsterdam; and Sandius intimates that the date of the publication, here expressed by *post annum Domini* 1659, was about 1665 †. To this edition are appended some notes and emendations by Martin

---

* See page 75.   † *Biblioth. Antitrin. p.* 130.

Ruarus,

Ruarus, with occasional observations upon them, by way of reply, from the pen of Schlichtingius; and prefixed to it is an admirable address to the reader on the rights of private judgment in religious matters, the joint production of Andrew Wissowatius and Joachim Stegman the younger.

This edition was translated into Dutch by John Cornelius, commonly called Knoll; but as he made considerable alterations in it, and omitted the chapters on Baptism and the Lord's Supper, his version was never admitted by the Unitarians. In consequence of which they published a complete edition in the same language in quarto, in 1666 *.

In the year 1680 this Catechism was republished in quarto under the following title: *Catechcsis Ecclesiarum Polonicarum, unum Deum Patrem, illiusque Filium unigenitum Jesum Christum, una cum Spiritu Sancto, ex S. Scriptura confitentium. Primum anno 1609 in lucem emissa; et post earundem Ecclesiarum jussu correcta ac dimidia amplius parte aucta; atque per Viros in his cœtibus inclytos, Johannem Crellium, Francum, hinc Jonam Schlichtingium à Bukoweic, ut et Martinum Ruarum, ac tandem Andream Wissowatium recognita atque emendata; Notisque cùm horum, tum et aliorum illustrata, nunquam antehac hoc modo edita.* " Catechism of the Churches of Poland, which confess, according to the Holy Scriptures, one God the Father, his only begotten Son Jesus Christ, and the Holy

---

* Sandii *Bib. Ant. p.* 101.   Walchii *Biblioth. Theol. Select. ubi supra, p.* 539.

Spirit.

Spirit. First published in the year 1609, and since, by order of the same Churches, corrected, and enlarged more than half, and revised and improved by Men eminent in those congregations,—John Crellius of Franconia, Jonas Schlichtingius of Buckoweic, and Martin Ruarus, and at last by Andrew Wissowatius. Illustrated with Notes both by them and by other Persons ; never before published in this form. Stauropolis, by Eulogetus Philalethes.'' This edition was printed at Amsterdam by Christopher Pezold, and first appeared appended to Crellius's *Ethica Aristotelica*, which was published in quarto in 1681. Wissowatius revised the text, and introduced into it most of the emendations suggested by Ruarus in his notes to the preceding edition: but the alterations are not very material, being confined, with the exception of one or two instances, to verbal corrections. He added however some valuable notes of his own. Besides these, several other notes from the pen of his learned nephew Benedict Wissowatius are likewise inserted here, and two bearing the initials F. C., which stand for Florian Crusius *, a physician of considerable eminence, who was married to the sister of Wolzogenius. There is reason to suspect that the last editor of this edition was Benedict Wissowatius, from the manner in which the labours of Andrew Wissowatius in the revision of the text are noticed in the prefatory remarks, and also from the notes of Benedict Wissowatius being designated merely as those of B.W. This edition was followed

---

* Bock, *ubi supra, tom.* i. *p.* 1029. Walchius, *ut supra, tom.* i. *p.* 541.

by

by another in small octavo in 1684, intituled *Catechesis Ecclesiarum Polonicarum, unum Deum Patrem, illiusque Filium Jesum Christum, una cum Spiritu Sancto, ex Sacra Scriptura confitentium. Primum anno 1609 in lucem emissa; et post earundem Ecclesiarum jussu correcta ac dimidio amplius parte aucta, atque per Viros in his cœtibus inclytos, Johannem Crellium, Francum, hinc Jonam Schlichtingium a Bukoweik; ut et Martinum Ruarum, ac tandem Andream Wissowatium, Benedictum Wissowatium, nec non anonymum quendam F. C. recognita atque emendata. Notisque horum, tum et aliorum illustrata. Editio novissima. Stauropoli, per Eulogetum Philalethem.* "The Catechism of the Churches of Poland, which confess, according to the Holy Scriptures, one God, the Father, and his only-begotten Son, Jesus Christ, with the Holy Spirit. First published in the year 1609; and since, by order of the same Churches, corrected, and enlarged more than half; and revised and improved by Men eminent in those congregations,— John Crellius of Franconia, Jonas Schlichtingius of Bukoweic, Martin Ruarus, Andrew Wissowatius, Benedict Wissowatius, and also a certain anonymous person F.C. Illustrated with the Notes of those and of other Persons. The last edition. Stauropolis, by Eulogetus Philalethes, CIƆIƆCLXXXIV."

This edition, though purporting in the title-page to be the last of this Catechism in the Latin language, is, in fact, as far as respects the text and body of the work, the identical edition of Schlichtingius printed "after 1659," or about 1665. It has the
same

same mistakes, and the same table of errata at the end. It would appear that the publisher had a stock remaining on hand, and that he thought he might promote the sale of them by printing, as an appendix, the notes inserted in the quarto edition of 1680, and prefixing to the whole a new title-page, such as has been copied above, declaratory of the contents of the book. The quarto edition of 1680 must therefore be regarded as in reality the latest, and is in every respect the most valuable. The text is the most correct, and the notes are inserted in the places to which they properly belong : and it also exhibits the most recent view of the theological system of the Polish Unitarians. On these accounts a decided preference was given to it, after a careful collation with the other editions, for the present work,—and the translation has in every instance been made after the text as here amended.

Besides the editions of this Catechism above enumerated, which were published by the Unitarians themselves, there are a few others extant, which were printed by their adversaries, with the view of adding their own observations upon its doctrines by way of refutation. The first of these is contained in a work of Nicolaus Arnoldus, intituled *Religio Sociniana, seu Catechesis Racoviana Major, publicis Disputationibus, inserto ubique formali ipsius Catecheseos contextu, refutata. Amstelodami apud Joannem Janssonium, 4to, 1654.* Walchius speaks of this book as not being held in much estimation [*]. The author seems at first to have used

---

[*] *Biblioth. Theolog. Selecta, ubi supra, tom.* i. *p.* 545.

the

the German translation of the Catechism, and to have given in his work his own Latin version; as the language, in the earlier part, differs materially from that of Moscorovius's Latin edition of 1609, which, however, he afterwards transcribes throughout.   At a subsequent period, Joachim Langius printed the edition of Schlichtingius of 1664 or 1665, omitting the annotations upon it *: and at a still later date Oeder published an edition in a work bearing this title: *Catechesis Racoviensis, seu Liber Socinianorum primorum, ad fidem editionis anno* 1609 *recensuit, Socinianam vero Impietatem, et hoc libro traditam et a recentioribus assumtam adcurate profligavit Georg. Lud. Oederus. Francof. et Lipsiæ,* 1739, 8*vo.*

Moscorovius's Latin edition of the Racovian Catechism printed in 1609, as intimated in the title-page, is here given entire, and to this work the commentary and the answer of Oeder are chiefly applied.   Occasionally, however, he transcribes passages from the later editions, with the notes upon them, and subjoins his animadversions upon those also.   Mosheim † speaks of Oeder's work as comprising " a solid refutation" of the doctrines of the original Catechism, and this judgment has been adopted with implicit faith by more recent writers. To Mosheim himself, and those who agree with him in their theological sentiments, it might appear in this light ; but it will give little satisfaction to persons who dissent from the popular creed. The author certainly displays a very respect-

---

* Walchius, *ubi supra, tom.* i. *p.* 541.

† Eccles. Hist. cent. xvi. sect. iii. part ii. par. xix. note.

able

able share of learning and talents; but, like many others of the same class of controversial writers, is too fond of substituting exclamations and abuse for argument and demonstration.

Several other works in reply to the Racovian Catechism were published on the continent, and some in our own country. Wolfgangus Franzius printed at Wittemberg in 1620 a book with this design, under the following title : *Augustanæ Confessionis Articuli Fidei* xxi. *et Articuli Abusuum* vii. *Disputationibus* xxxiv. *in tres libellos distributis, adversus Pontificios, Calvinianos ac cumprimis Antitrinitarios, seu Photinianos hodiernos, breviter explicati et ex Verbo divino confirmati, cum Adpendice trium Commentationum de tribus Personis Divinitatis, in quibus' monstratur, qua methodo Antitrinitarii hodierni potenter et feliciter sint confutandi et reprimendi.* To this work Valent. Smalcius published a reply from the Racow press in 1614, with this title: *Refutatio Thesium Frantzii de præcipuis Religionis Christianæ Capitibus:* and to this Frantzius published a rejoinder in 1621, intituled, *Vindiciæ Disputationum theologicarum pro Augustana Confessione, adversus Valent. Smalcium.*

In 1613 Geor. Rostius published an answer in German, which is spoken of as a performance of no great merit [*]. By the appointment of the University of Wittemberg, who seem to have taken high offence at the dedication of the Catechism to them, Frederick Baldwin drew up an elaborate answer to it, which was

---

[*] Walchius, *ubi supra, tom.* i. *p.* 543.

published

published in German, but without the author's name, in 1619. A Latin translation of this work was printed the year after, under the following title : *Solida Refutatio Catechismi Ariani, qui Racoviæ in Polonia anno* 1608 *excussus &c.* To this writer is assigned the first rank among those who have undertaken to refute the doctrines of the Racovian Catechism *.

Other replies were published by Christopher Sonntagius in his *Pseudocatechismus Racoviensis explosus. Altorf.* 1705, 4*to*, and Henric. Alstedius in his *Theologia Polemica*, which was translated into Dutch by John Greyde, and printed in 1651. To which may be added a work by Matthew Wren, intituled, *Increptatio Barjesu, sive Polemicæ Adsertiones Locorum aliquot S. Scripturæ ab Imposturis Perversionum in Catechesi Racoviana, &c. Londini* 1660, *et Lugdun. Batav.* 1668†.

Mosheim remarks‡ that " it must be carefully observed, that the Catechism of Racow, which most people look upon as the great standard of Socinianism, and as an accurate summary of the doctrine of that sect, is, in reality, no more than a collection of the popular tenets of the Socinians, and by no means

---

* Walchius, *ubi supra*, tom. i. *p.* 543.

. † For further information concerning the Racovian Catechism the reader may be referred to the following works : Placcii *Theatr. Anonymor. p.* 89. Schmidii *Programmat. de Catechismo Racoviensi, Helmstadt.* 1707, 4*to*. Wolfii *Not. ad Casauboniana, p.* 213. Fabricii *Histor. Bibliothec. par.* vi. *p.* 468. Rambachii *Einleitung in die religionstreitigkeiten mitdden Socinianern, part* i. *p.*294. *Novis Literar.* Hamburg 1708. Koecheri *Biblioth. Symbol. p.* 656. *Vide* Walchii *Biblioth. Theol. Selecta,* tom. i. *pp.* 535 *et seqq. et p.* 545 *nota* ** *ad calcem.*

‡ Eccles. Hist. cent. xvi. sect. iii. part ii. par. xix.

                                a just

a just representation of the secret opinions and sentiments of their doctors. The writings therefore of these learned men must be perused with attention, in order to our knowing the hidden reasons and true principles from whence the doctrines of the Catechism are derived. It is observable, besides, that, in this Catechism, many Socinian tenets and institutions, which might have contributed to render the sect still more odious, and to expose its internal constitution too much to public view, are entirely omitted; so that it seems to have been less composed for the use of the Socinians themselves, than to impose upon strangers, and to mitigate the indignation which the tenets of this community had excited in the minds of many."

These are grave insinuations and charges to be deliberately preferred by the learned chancellor of an university, in an historical work professedly designed to convey to the pupils under his immediate superintendance, and to the world at large, a correct representation of the state of opinion among Christians in various times and countries: and it would have been well if he had condescended to verify his accusations by something in the form of evidence. How came HE to know the SECRET OPINIONS and SENTIMENTS of the Socinian doctors? By the attentive perusal of the writings of these learned men? But if in their WRITINGS they may be discovered, he might have vouchsafed to inform his readers, how they could still remain SECRET; and in what manner those REASONS and PRINCIPLES could continue HIDDEN and FICTITIOUS, which are avowed and published to the world

in

in printed compositions accessible to all men? Why, moreover, has not our author, as became a faithful historian, stated what those "secret opinions and sentiments" of the Socinians were, of which he speaks? What the "hidden reasons and true principles from whence the doctrines of the Catechism were derived?" Why has he not explained the nature of those "Socinian tenets and institutions" which he declares to be "entirely omitted" in this Catechism, and which in his judgment "might have contributed to render the sect still more odious, and have exposed its internal constitution TOO MUCH to public view?" Had he been pleased to have added such facts and elucidations to his work, the world might have been prepared to acknowledge the JUSTICE as well as the LIBERALITY of the charge he thus solemnly denounces against a whole community of "learned men," of wilfully "IMPOSING UPON STRANGERS," with the view of "mitigating the indignation which their tenets had excited in the minds of many!"

It is painful to observe a writer, on many accounts so highly respectable, thus forgetting what is due to the dignity and truth of History, and indulging the feelings of a low and bigoted controversialist, by dealing out foul aspersions and dark unfounded insinuations against his theological adversaries.

The Polish Socinians always designed their Catechism to be an "accurate summary" and a "just representation" of their religious opinions. And a careful comparison of it with the published writings of the leading persons in their community will show,

　　　　　　　　　　　　　　　　　that

that it is justly entitled to be regarded in this light. It omits no material article of their creed; and comprises those very "tenets and institutions" which had excited against them most "odium" and most "indignation" in the minds of religious professors of other parties. It is true, indeed, that individuals among the Unitarians dissented from some of the articles maintained in this Catechism; but their objections are openly stated in their writings; and their integrity will on examination be found to be above suspicion, and their characters were exemplary and irreproachable.

Mosheim objects further to this Catechism, that " it never obtained among the Socinians the authority of a public confession or rule of faith;" and that " hence the doctors of that sect were authorized to correct and contradict it, or to substitute another form of doctrine in its place." It would appear that this writer had no idea of a public confession of faith, except as a general rule of religious belief, carrying with it the AUTHORITY of law, and to which all men through successive generations, and in the face of increasing light and knowledge, were to be compelled by civil penalties to conform in every the minutest particular :—a notion which was natural enough in the chancellor of a Lutheran university, who was himself bound by the Confession of Augsburg, which he was not " authorized to correct or contradict," and in the place of which he could not, without forfeiting his situation, " substitute another form of doctrine." But the Polish Unitarians had other thoughts on this head, and far more enlightened views of Christian freedom.

freedom. To adopt the judicious remarks of a late venerable and esteemed friend*,—"it would have been inconsistent with the liberty of prophesying, for which we see they argue in the preface [to the Catechism], to have limited their religious inquiries to this standard; and to have treated it as a Rule of Faith, would have been a violation of their declarations, that they dictated to no one, and assumed no authority. And the alterations their sentiments underwent, were the consequence of their avowed principles, and the result of the free inquiry they allowed. The [last] edition of the Catechism was different from a preceding publication of that kind, being in some places altered, and in some instances enlarged. This they own; and their plea is not only a justification of those alterations, but a caveat against any censure of any future changes in their religious system; and furnishes an answer to the eminent historian. 'We think,' say they, 'there is no reason to be ashamed of it, if our Church improve in some respects. We are not in every instance to cry out——I believe—I stand in my rank—here I fix my foot, and will not be removed the least from this place.—This is like the Stoics, obstinately to support every thing, and stiffly to persevere in our opinion. It is the duty of the Christian philosopher, or of the candidate for the wisdom that comes from above, to be ευπειθην, not αυθαδην; easy to be persuaded, not pertinaciously pleasing himself; but ready to give up his opinions, when any other offers supported by stronger evidence †.'"

---

* Dr. Toulmin;—Life of Socinus, p. 270.
† *Præfat. ad Catechismum Pol. Eccl.*

CATECHISM

OF

THE CHURCHES OF POLAND,

Which confess, according to the Scriptures, one God,
the Father, his only begotten Son, Jesus
Christ, and the Holy Spirit.

First published in 1609; and since, by order of the same
Churches, corrected, and more than one half enlarged;
revised also and improved by Men eminent in
those Congregations,—

JOHN CRELLIUS, JONAS SCHLICHTINGIUS, MARTIN
RUARUS, ANDREW WISSOWATIUS, BENEDICT
WISSOWATIUS, and an anonymous Writer
F. C.

Illustrated with their Notes.

Regula fidei una omnino est, sola immobilis et irreformabilis, cre-
dendi scilicet in unicum Deum omnipotentem, mundi conditorem: et
Filium ejus Jesum Christum, natum ex Virgine Maria, crucifixum sub
Pontio Pilato, tertia die resuscitatum à mortuis, receptum in cœlis, se-
dentem nunc ad dextram Patris, venturum judicare vivos et mortuos,
per carnis resurrectionem: Hac lege fidei manente, cætera jam disci-
plinæ et conversationis, admittunt novitatem correctionis, operante sci-
licet et proficiente usque in finem, gratia Dei.
TERTULLIAN. *Lib. de Virg. Veland. cap.* i.

STAUROPOLIS:

BY EULOGETUS PHILALETHES, CIƆIƆCLXXX.

of discord, ensigns of immortal enmities and factions among men. The reason of this is, that those Confessions and Catechisms are proposed in such a manner that the conscience is bound by them, that a yoke is imposed upon Christians to swear to the words and opinions of men; and that they are established as a Rule of Faith, from which, every one who deviates in the least is immediately assailed by the thunderbolt of an anathema, is treated as a heretic, as a most vile and mischievous person, is excluded from heaven, consigned to hell, and doomed to be tormented with infernal fires.

Far be from us this disposition, or rather this madness. Whilst we compose a Catechism, we prescribe nothing to any man: whilst we declare our own opinions, we oppress no one. Let every person enjoy the freedom of his own judgment in religion; only let it be permitted to us also to exhibit our view of divine things, without injuring and calumniating others. For this is the golden Liberty of Prophesying which the sacred books of the New Testament so earnestly recommend to us, and wherein we are instructed by the example of the primitive apostolic church. "Quench not the spirit," says the apostle (1 Thess. v. 19, 20); "Despise not prophesying; prove all things, hold fast that which is good."

How deaf is the Christian world, split as it is into so many sects, become at this day to that most sacred admonition of the apostle!—And who are you, base mortals, who strive to smother and extinguish the fire of the Holy Spirit in those in whom God has thought fit to kindle it? Is not this pertinaciously to strive against God? "Do ye provoke the Lord? Are ye stronger than He?" (1 Cor. x. 22.) Who are you that despise or envy in others the gift of Prophecy, which surpasses almost all other divine gifts? Why do you not rather imitate Moses, that great Mediator of the Old Covenant, than whom no man was more meek ; and say with him (Numb. xi. 29.) " Would God, that all the Lord's people were prophets ?" Who are you that permit not men to prove either your own opinions or the opinions of others, that what is good might be retained, and what is bad rejected ;—but would have your sentiments adopted without examination or inquiry, and worshipped with servile submission, and the sentiments of others rejected and condemned without trial ? " What ? came the word of God out from you ? or came it unto you only ?" (1 Cor. xiv. 36.) Do you alone carry the key of knowledge, so that from you nothing in the Sacred Scriptures is locked up, nothing sealed ; and so that no one can open what you close, or close what you open ? Why do you not remember that one alone is our master, to whom these prerogatives pertain,—even CHRIST : but that we all are brethren, to no one of whom is given authority and dominion over the conscience of another ? For although some of the brethren may excel others in spiritual gifts, yet in respect to freedom, and the right of sonship, all are equal.

But whilst, with the apostle, we contend, that the spirit should not be quenched, nor prophesyings be despised, it must not be thought that we are advocating the cause of enthusiasts, and arrogating to ourselves divine miraculous inspirations, or prophetical authority. We acknowledge that now there exist no longer such miraculous gifts as the divine goodness, at the first rise of the Church, poured out by Christ, in a full and, so to speak, a threefold measure, in order that the novelty of the Christian religion might, as by a pillar, be supported by them. Nevertheless, no one, we apprehend, will assert that the arm of the Lord is shortened, or deny that the Holy Spirit is even yet given to believers in Christ. For although those

rivers of living water do not now flow from the belly
of believers,—that is, though the Holy Spirit be not
given in such abundance as before ; though it do not
now display itself in so conspicuous a manner ; though
it have not, as formerly, such efficacy as to create and
produce new properties in men;—it suffices, that such
a divine influence may nevertheless be at this day
hoped for by all who invoke Christ with a pure heart,
as may improve the powers which they possess by
nature, or have acquired by art and study ; and, with
due care and industry, render the mind acute and pe-
netrating in seeking the sense of the Holy Scriptures.
We admit, also, that no prophets are now sent whose
words are to be regarded as divine oracles which it is
unlawful to reject.   We do not, therefore, by any
means assume such an authority for ourselves :—nay,
this is the very thing which we reprobate in those
persons who place their Confessions and Catechisms
almost on an equality with the writings of prophets
and apostles, so that it is not permitted to us even to
open our lips against them. We believe, however, that
there exists at present such a gift of prophecy, whereby
the most hidden meanings of the sacred Scriptures
may be penetrated, and the mind of the Holy Spirit,
by whose authority they were written, be everywhere
happily and correctly discerned :—which gift, although it be very important, is nevertheless far inferior in dignity and excellence to the gift of prophecy
by which the times of the apostles were distinguished.
For to the latter very little of human talent and exertion was added ;—but the former requires a great
deal.   They who are endowed with the one cannot
mistake, in what they declare in the name of God,—
those who possess the other are never exempt from the
danger of erring. The reason is, that the persons who
possess the latter are not themselves the principal
cause   the things they utter, but the Holy Spirit,

which dictates to them the matter, and sometimes even the very words; so that they are nothing but the instruments of the Holy Spirit, and serve for its mouth and tongue:—whilst those who possess the former are the first cause of their declarations, the Holy Spirit being only the second and assisting cause. Hence it follows that the authority of the one gift can by no means be equal to that of the other. But as the one gift was not bestowed upon all men, as the apostle plainly intimates, in explaining the diversity of gifts existing in the Church (1 Cor. xii. 10—29), so also, in respect to the other, although all men, if they earnestly strive for it, may perhaps obtain, yet all do not acquire it, because all do not seek it with equal diligence and application. And as the one was given in an unequal measure, both as to quality and quantity, so it is certain that the other also is, in like manner, conferred upon some in a greater, and upon others in a less quantity, or, so to speak, in a less dose. On this account besides, no one who has not this gift ought to arrogate it to himself; nor should he who has a little attribute to himself more than he possesses; as the apostle also admonishes in reference to all divine gifts in general (Rom. xii. 3, 4, 5) " I say through the grace given unto me, to every man that is among you, not to think of himself more highly than he ought to think; but to think soberly, according as God hath dealt to every man the measure of faith. For as we have many members in the same body, and all the members have not the same office, so we, being many, are one body in Christ, and every one members one of another." That is to say, just as the whole human body is not the tongue only, or the eye, —for, as the same apostle writes (1 Cor. xii. 17), " If the whole body were an eye, where were the hearing ? if the whole were hearing, where were the smelling ?"— so the body of the Church of Christ is not made up of teachers and prophets alone. And as again in the human body, the eyes do not usurp the office of hearing, which pertains to the ears, nor the ears the office of seeing, which belongs to the eyes, nor the feet the office of speaking, which belongs to the tongue, nor the hands the office of walking, which pertains to the feet; but every member rests satisfied with the peculiar faculty with which it has been invested, and does not encroach upon the offices of the other members; so also in the Church of God, there are divers faculties, divers gifts of God, and divers offices; and therefore every one ought to rate himself according to his measure, and keep within his proper bounds, lest he should trench upon districts he ought not to touch, and put his sickle into what may be called the harvest of another. Occasion will otherwise be given for a complaint similar to that of Horace (*Lib.* ii. *Epist.* 1.)

> *Navem agere ignarus navis timet : abrotonum ægro*
> *Non audet, nisi qui dïdicit, dare : quod medicorum est,*
> *Promittunt medici : tractant fabrilia fabri :*
> *Scribimus indocti doctique poemata passim.*

> A pilot only dares a vessel steer;
> A doubtful drug unlicens'd doctors fear;
> Musicians are to sounds alone confin'd,
> And each mechanic hath his trade assign'd :
> But every desperate blockhead dares to write;
> Verse is the trade of every living wight.   FRANCIS.

For in this manner did Jerome justly complain of old, in his Epistle to Paulinus, that all men claimed for themselves the art of publicly interpreting the Scriptures. "This," he observes, "the prating old woman, the silly dotard, the wordy sophist, and all universally, assume, abuse, and teach, before they have learnt it. Some, led by pride, and studying lofty expressions, philosophize concerning the Holy Scriptures, among weak women : Others—oh shame! learn from women, what they should teach to men ;—and lest this should be too little, publish to others, with a certain facility, nay, audacity of speech, what they do not themselves understand." This writer of sainted name does not reprove this practice, because women, and old persons generally, read, and endeavoured to understand, the sacred writings;—in which sense the popish writers are wont commonly to adduce his words, and to draw off the laity from the perusal and study of the Scriptures ;—but he censures it, and indeed justly, because most of them arrogated to themselves what they did not possess; because persons who were not endowed with gifts proper for teaching wished to be the instructors and masters of others, and who therefore ought to have remembered the maxim *Ne sutor ultra crepidam*, " Cobler, stick to your last." For he well shows before that integrity of life, joined with diligence in prayer, is not alone sufficient for the office of a teacher or prophet in the Church. " Because," he states, " a holy simplicity alone availed himself; and in the proportion in which he edified by the merit of his life, he did injury if he did not resist the destroyers." Hence also, the apostle (1 Tim. iii. 2; Titus i. 9,) would have a bishop elected, who, besides possessing a good life, was " apt to teach." But who would deny that he who is expert in speech, who is familiar with the liberal arts, who has a clear and cultivated judgment, who also has a flowing style of teaching, teeming with a rich store of ideas and words,—is commonly and ordinarily more " apt to teach," than he who is destitute of all these things ? We say that he is ORDINARILY more apt ;— for we speak not now of what can and may be done by God in an extraordinary case.

Thus, therefore, courteous reader, thou perceivest, that although we contend for the liberty of prophesying, and would not have the mouth of any person in the Church closed by force and violence, we neverthe-

less claim it for those alone who have the gift of prophecy. We do not for prophesying require at this
time a divine mission, either direct or indirect; nor a
succession continued from the days of the apostles;
nor an indelible character; nor the other qualifications
which the human imagination has dreamed of in the
darkness of ignorance; but with sufficient reason we
require for prophesying, the gift of prophesying. For
this, indeed, is as it were the soul of prophecy :—
and as the body without the soul is dead, so prophecy
without this gift is vain, senseless, and dead. We wish,
indeed, that all the people would prophesy :—but at
the same time would not have the person prophesy
who knows not how. The apostle would have
him alone speak in the Church (1 Cor. xiv. 30) to
whom something has been revealed; that is, who is
able to advance something for the edification of the
Church. But he who cannot do this should hold his
peace. "Every one of you," saith the apostle,
(ver. 26,) "hath a psalm, hath a doctrine, hath a
tongue, hath a revelation, hath an interpretation,"
(for the thing itself shows that these are to be understood thus disjunctively,) "let all things be done
unto edifying." But how ridiculous, may we not
ask, and how absurd would it be, if any one ignorant
of the art of music, and unskilled in the modulation
of his voice, were yet to desire, with a discordant
and rude noise, to sing, or rather to bray, in the
church? Or if any one in Poland, ignorant of the
Polish language, or in Belgium, ignorant of the Belgic
language, were to wish to speak to the people in
public, would not he excite laughter, rather than
promote the edification of the Church?—But not less
absurd is it, that he who is uninstructed for its duties
should wish to execute the office of a teacher.

The liberty, therefore, for which we plead, is that
which lies in the middle way, between licentiousness

and usurpation : and in order that it may not degenerate into licentiousness, we would have it fenced in by the bounds of equity and right reason. And first, we conceive that in religious matters, a distinction ought to be observed, so that the things necessary to salvation, and those which are most nearly connected with them, and are of the highest utility, should be accurately discriminated from those which are not necessary, nor so useful. Those things that are necessary it is unlawful for any one to remove from their place, or to impugn ; nor can any person dissent from them without the loss of salvation ;—and where there is not an agreement in these points, there can be no brotherly affection. But these necessary things are very few, and written in the Holy Scriptures so clearly and explicitly, and as it were with a sun-beam, that they cannot fail of being easily discerned by those who have a sane mind in a sound body. As to those things which are not so clear, we deny that they are to be regarded as necessary. And here we also say with Hilary, that they are happy who in things necessary to salvation, at least as far as respects belief, confine themselves within the limits of that most simple creed called the Apostles'. But in other matters, which are not absolutely necessary, we require that this liberty of prophesying should be conceded.

But neither do we ask for this without limitation and restriction ; but wish it to be restrained by the reins of Piety, Charity and Prudence. Piety demands that nothing should be said or done against conscience; that nothing be uttered reproachful to God and Christ, or contrary to his glory and commands. Charity teaches us that no one should be injured, that scandal, calumnies, railing accusations against our neighbour, invidious and unfair representations of the opinions of others, should be avoided :—and on the other hand, that our equity, gentleness, and modesty should be known to all men. And lastly, it pertains to Prudence to have regard to times, places, persons, things, and other circumstances, that every thing should not be spoken, in every manner, in every place, and at every time; but that all things should be done decently and in order, and for the edification of the Church (1 Cor. xiv. 26, 40). By which rule the apostle himself restricted the liberty of prophesying in the church :—but upon these matters we have not room now to treat more at length.

There is one thing besides, of which we would apprize thee, courteous reader, in respect to this edition of our Catechism *, that we now give it to the public rather as a corrected than as a new work. For that which was published in the year 1609, and dedicated to his most serene highness James King of Great Britain, is in some respects the same; but now in many places enlarged, corrected and altered by the chief luminaries of our Church, John Crellius, Jonas Schlichtingius, and Martin Ruarus. For we do not think that we ought to be ashamed, if in some respects our Church improves. We ought not in every case to cry out, " I stand in my rank; here I fix my foot, and will not suffer myself to be in the least measure removed from hence." It belongs to the Stoics obstinately to defend every thing, and to persevere stiffly and tenaciously in their opinion :—To the Christian philosopher, and to the candidate for that wisdom which comes from above, it pertains to be ευπειθης not αυθαδης, easily to be persuaded, not pertinaciously pleasing himself; prepared to give up his opinion when another that is better offers. With this disposition do we always publish our sentiments, and now, reader, submit this Catechism to your judgment

---

[* This was written of the edition of 1665, bearing on the title page post annum Domini 1659. TRANSL.]

and examination. If you conceive that in any thing we are carried out of the path of truth, give us your friendly admonition. Be assured that when you convince us by just and solid reasons, you will not find us averse to the truth, than which nothing is more dear to us. Would that all who desire to be accounted Christians were of this disposition! the truth would then more easily triumph.

Another reason for the republication of this Catechism may be added,—that some one, not perhaps with any evil design, but otherwise assuming to himself too much of the office of a judge, has lately published it in the Belgic language, interpolated, and altered at his pleasure. On this account we testify that we do not acknowledge that as our work. From this, as we now give it by public authority, we wish to be judged concerning our views of religion. As to the rest, we beseech the God of all grace that, after having dispelled the darkness of error which overshadows the Christian world, he would, for his mercy's sake, cause us all to run with unoffending steps the course of faith and piety, and obtain the crown of eternal salvation at the glorious appearance of our Lord and Saviour Jesus Christ,—to whom, together with the Father, be praise and honour and glory for ever and ever. Amen.

———

Address to the Reader concerning this Edition *.

Behold, we publish once more the Confession of Faith of those Churches which, after the way that formerly was, as well as now is, called heresy, worship the God of their fathers. For they by no means fear, upon every proper occasion, to confess with their mouth before all the world, that which they believe in their heart. And it behoves all who aim at this ultimate

* [This address was added to the other preface in the quarto edition of 1680, from which the following translation is made. TRANSL.]

object, to render to every one a reason for those things which they believe, and hope and do, and at the same time to expose and dissipate the errors by which the way leading to this highest good is obscured and perverted.

But you must not imagine, gentle reader, that we offer you any thing that is new and unheard of. For this is the Catechism which in the year 1609, as is stated above, was dedicated in the name of these Churches to the King of Great Britain by Jerome Moscorovius. After an interval of several years, having by an order of the Churches been revised and enlarged by some of the principal persons of this communion, it was published "after the year 1659," (about 1660) at the charge of an illustrious individual, who wished to be known by the name of Fredericus Theophilus: the preface which you have above, the joint production of Andrew Wissowatius and Joachim Stegman the younger, being prefixed; and some notes and corrections of Jonas Schlichtingius and Martin Ruarus inserted at the end. This Catechism, revised, and amended agreeably to the corrections just noticed, by Andrew Wissowatius, and, with the addition of some notes by himself, we again give to the public. For he has not thought it proper to alter the text of the Catechism without the general consent of these congregations. He has not scrupled, however, to correct the mistakes with which the former edition abounded; and to illustrate its meaning by the addition of some passages of Scripture. Nothing therefore is omitted in this edition besides mere errors: but these errors furnished a strong additional motive for republishing the work. Another reason for reprinting it was the earnest entreaty of some persons, in distant countries and beyond seas, that it should again be given to the public.

Influenced by these considerations we have undertaken this task, which we hope will not be without utility. We have inserted in their proper places the notes of Schlichtingius and Ruarus, already mentioned, which were loosely scattered at the end of the book : more of the annotations of these persons, which hitherto have been allowed to remain any where, we have not been able to discover. To these we have now added the notes of Andrew Wissowatius, and also some by F. C. which we found at the end of the book, together with some others by B. W. here inserted for the first time. We do not by any means hold forth these notes as comprising the common opinion of these Churches, but freely submit them to the judgment as well of the persons who belong to these churches, as of those who belong to other communions. And we beseech all, that, laying aside for a little while their prejudices and preconceived opinions, and especially the carnal reasons which becloud the mind, they would, before they condemn any thing, weigh all by the sound understanding which God has himself bestowed ; and prove them by the word of God, as by a touchstone ;—looking back in all things and asking, according to the word of the Lord spoken by the prophet (Jer. vi. 16), in the " old paths." For as, the nearer the fountain, the more clear the water is, so also we observe that the Church is the less polluted, the nearer it is to those who received the divine wisdom with their own ears. But now we have to lament that many things are introduced into it which were not so in the beginning ; and on the contrary, that many things which formerly pertained to it, have been wholly taken away. We justly complain, therefore, with that ancient historian Egesippus (quoted by Eusebius, *lib.* iii. *c.* 32) that after the departure of the apostles and of apostolic men, the standard of sound doctrine was corrupted ; and therefore desire that that pure and undefiled virgin may be restored to us. Nor do we think that we ought altogether to despair but that that golden age may be brought back, provided only that every one would for this purpose contribute the ability which God has given him. We beseech, therefore, and exhort all men, that, moved by the love of truth, and having their loins girded about with it, they may lay for their foundation ardent love both towards God and their neighbour : and at the same time, that, abstaining from things which are unlawful, they may endure adversity with constancy, bearing always fixed in their mind those unequalled words (which are quoted by the ancients simply under the title of SCRIPTURE; see Irenæus, *lib*. iii. *c.* 37. Origen on Rom. xvi. and *Periarch. lib.* i. *c.*3) spoken by Hermas, the earliest writer after the apostles, (*lib.* ii. *mand.* 1.) " First of all," says he, " believe that there is one God who created and completed all things : and, as there was nothing before, he caused all things to be : himself containing all things, but alone contained by no one : who cannot be described by words, nor conceived by the mind. Believe therefore in him, and fear him ; and in his fear live abstemiously and virtuously ; and if thou keepest this commandment thou shalt live to God."

It behoves us to be at all times endowed with this disposition ; that thus having passed through this evil world soberly, righteously and piously, and having an immoveable hope, we may pass into that future better world ; and that every one of us, when the time of his departure is at hand, may be able to exclaim with that faithful servant of the Lord,—" I have fought a good fight, &c."   May the God of Gods, whose honour and glory we are seeking with our whole might, prosper our undertakings, and grant that we may all at length come to an unity of faith ; to which may He lead us by his word, and spirit, through Jesus Christ, his only begotten Son, through whom, and with whom, to Him be blessing and honour, glory and dominion, for ever and ever.   Amen.

THE

RACOVIAN CATECHISM.

SECTION I.

OF THE HOLY SCRIPTURES.

I wish to be informed by you what the Christian Religion is?

The Christian Religion is the way of attaining eternal life, which God has pointed out by Jesus Christ: or, in other words, It is the method of serving God, which he has himself delivered by Jesus Christ.

Where may it be learnt?

In the Holy Scriptures; especially those of the New Testament.

Are there, then, other Holy Scriptures, besides those of the New Testament?

There are: namely, the Scriptures of the Old Testament.

CHAPTER I.

OF THE AUTHENTICITY OF THE HOLY SCRIPTURES.

How may it be proved that the Scriptures, including those of the Old and of the New Testament, are authentic?

I will reply to this question, first, as it relates to

B   the

the Scriptures of the New Testament; and, afterwards, as it respects those of the Old Testament.

How do you prove the authenticity of the Scriptures of the New Testament?

By two considerations: the first, addressed to persons who believe the Christian Religion to be true;—the second, addressed to those who deny its truth.

What is the first of these considerations?

It is this :—that there is no just cause why their authenticity should be called in question.

How does this appear?

There seem to be four causes from which the truth of a book may justly be doubted, but not one of these is in this instance to be discovered.

What are those causes?

They are—first, that the author is wholly unknown:—secondly, that he is suspected:—thirdly, that it appears, from some other source, that the book is corrupted:—and fourthly, that there is sufficient evidence to weaken its credibility.

Inform me how it appears that the first of these causes has in this case no existence?

Because, from the very first rise of the Christian Religion, all its professors, though widely differing from each other in their opinions on other points, have with one consent agreed, that the books of the New Testament were written by the persons whose names they severally bear :—whoever, therefore, would invalidate the unanimous testimony of so many individuals, and of so many centuries, ought to be able to account for this fact by the most decisive reasons.

But

But were no doubts entertained by the ancients respecting some of these authors ?

There certainly were respecting some of them : but as the writings of these authors, which are but few in number, contain nothing that is at variance with the works of those concerning whom no doubt has at any time been entertained, the credibility and authority of both must be regarded as equal.

How does it appear that the second cause of doubting the truth of a work,—namely, the author being suspected,—has in this instance no existence ?

An author is deemed open to suspicion—first, when he is not thoroughly acquainted with his subject :—secondly, when his statements are at variance with his knowledge of facts :—and thirdly, when his writings exhibit any indications of doubtful veracity. But nothing of this kind is discoverable in the authors of the New Testament.

How do you prove this with respect to the first case ?

It is impossible the mind can admit any suspicion that these authors had not a perfect knowledge of the subjects upon which they wrote ; because some of them were eye and ear witnesses of what they describe and relate ; whilst the rest received from these persons the fullest information respecting the same matters, and by this means became thoroughly acquainted with them.

How do you prove the same respecting the second case ?

As the Christian Religion prohibits lying, even in the most trifling concerns, it is evident that these authors, who were not only the first Christians, but also the first teachers of Christianity, would on no account publish a falsehood ; especially in a case so important as this, which might draw the whole world into some pernicious error.

How do you prove the same respecting the third case ?

This follows of course, if the answers in the former two cases be admitted. For, if these authors were thoroughly acquainted with their subject, and had no disposition to write contrary to their knowledge of facts ; and if, in the execution of their task, they exercised all the care which persons engaged in such an undertaking would necessarily employ ;—how is it possible that any contradictions or falsehoods should exist in their works ? Moreover, men eminent for their discernment and erudition, without any inducement from external considerations, and indeed frequently in opposition to human power, have in every age adhered to these writings with unhesitating confidence ;—which they never would have done, had any such contradiction and falsehood been perceptible in them. And again, this may be clearly established by a rigid examination of all those passages wherein it is suspected that any thing of this kind may be discovered.

You have shown why two out of the four enumerated causes which are admitted to expose the truth of writings to just suspicion, have in this case no existence :

istence :—prove the same in respect to the third of those causes—namely, that it appears from some other source that the book is corrupted ?

If this cause had here any existence, it must happen that the books of the New Testament are corrupted, either entirely, or in part. But they cannot be entirely corrupted : otherwise those persons to whom they have been ascribed could not have been the authors of them. And if they have been partially corrupted, the alterations must be either in those matters which are of great, or in those which are of little, importance. But it is apparent that they have not been corrupted in things of great importance, because the corrupted part, from not corresponding with that which remained uncorrupted, could not escape detection. But if there exist in them any corruption in relation to things of less importance, this ought not to be deemed of sufficient consequence to destroy the credibility of the whole of the books.

Can you prove in any other way that these books have not been corrupted ?

Certainly : for, in the first place, it is wholly incredible that God, whose goodness and providence are infinite, should have permitted those Scriptures wherein he has revealed himself, declared his will, and the way of salvation, and which have always been received and approved by all pious men as writings of divine authority, to be in any manner corrupted. In the next place, as such a multiplicity of copies of these books were, from the very first, transcribed ; as these copies were dispersed into so many different places,

and

and translated into such a great variety of languages; it is impossible, had such a corruption of them taken place, that they should agree in one common reading. And hence it happens that the text of different copies is found to vary in those passages where even the slightest alteration has been admitted.

How does it appear that the fourth cause of doubting the veracity of writings,—namely, that there is sufficient evidence to weaken their credibility,—does not exist here ?

· This you may yourself by this time have perceived; since there are no conclusive and sufficient testimonies, from men entitled to credit, by which these writings can be disproved or invalidated.

· You have explained the first consideration whereby the authenticity of the New Testament is established; state to me now what the second is, to which you adverted ?

Although this consideration alone, that there exists no just cause why these writings should be suspected, affords a strong argument in proof of their authenticity, yet I will mention another of far greater weight, which must necessarily command for them our assent.

What is that ?

The truth of the Christian Religion: for as this is comprised in the books of the New Testament, and in no other writings except such as rest upon their authority, it is evident that these books also are, on this account, necessarily entitled to credit.

· But how do you prove that the Christian Religion is true ?

First,

First, from the divinity of its author;—and secondly, from the nature and circumstances of the Religion itself; for these all demonstrate that it is divine,
and consequently true.

Whence does it appear that Jesus Christ, the author of the Christian Religion, was divine?

From the truly divine miracles which he wrought
and also from this circumstance,—that after having
submitted to the most cruel death, on account of the
religion he had taught, God raised him again to life.

How do you know that he wrought miracles; and
that those miracles were divine?

That he wrought miracles, is proved by the acknowledgement, not only of those who believed in him,
but also of his professed enemies, the Jews. That
those miracles were divine, may easily be inferred
from hence, that otherwise they must be attributed to
the devil: but this the perfect holiness of the doctrine of Christ, established by these miracles, makes it
impossible for us to admit; as it is utterly hostile to
the counsels of the devil [a], and designed for his shame

and

---

[a] [This is one topic respecting which the Unitarians of the
present day differ in opinion from the Socinians of Poland,
namely, the existence of a real being, called the Devil, or Satan; " originally of angelic rank, but now degenerated; of inveterate malice, and unrelenting cruelty; who delights to injure mankind; and whose power of injuring them extends to
their minds and to their bodies, to this material world, and to
the future state." Most modern Unitarians have abandoned this
belief, as a vulgar error, involving the most palpable inconsis-
tencies, and wholly irreconcileable with the fundamental truths
of natural and revealed religion. The reader will find this subject most ably discussed in Mr. John Simpson's Essays on the
Language

and complete discomfiture, and for the highest glory
of God.   You will, moreover, perceive the divinity of
the miracles of Jesus, when I shall have proved that
God raised him from the dead.   For, as he asserted
that he wrought miracles by a divine power, it is evident, since God after his crucifixion restored him to
life, that what he had declared was true—namely, that
his miracles were divine.

Prove to me, then, that God raised him from the
dead ?

This appears from the two following considerations:
—first, that many persons almost immediately after his
death most positively affirmed that they had beheld
him raised from the dead ; and, on account of their
attesting this fact, exposed themselves to much persecution, and several of them to the most painful
deaths.   It hence necessarily follows, either that Jesus was actually raised from the dead ; or else, that
these men, by persisting to declare what they knew
to be false, voluntarily subjected themselves to such
heavy misfortunes, and to the most cruel deaths.   The
latter case, common sense alone would show to be
impossible :—the former must therefore be considered as demonstrated.   Secondly, a great multitude
of other persons also, who had received their information from these first witnesses, submitted, in attes-

Language of Scripture, volume i. essay ii. intituled " An attempt to explain the meaning of the words יטש, ΣΑΤΑΝ, ΣΑ-
ΤΑΝΑΣ, ΔΙΑΒΟΛΟΣ, etc." He may also consult Mr. Farmer's
excellent Essays on the Demoniacs of the New Testament, and
on Christ's Temptation.   TRANSLATOR.]

tation

tation of the same fact, to heavy calamities, and to the most horrid deaths ; which they never would have done, unless they had been convinced of its certainty by the most indisputable evidence[1].

Is

---

[1] What is asserted here, and in some answers that follow, as well as the truth of the Christian Religion generally, may, without adverting to other arguments, be in this manner clearly demonstrated : No person of sane mind will deny that some things were done antecedently to his birth, and when he could not have been a present spectator : but he can know this in no other way than by testimony and historical relation.   Now if any history be worthy of credit, certainly that of Jesus of Nazareth and his disciples may safely be considered in this light ; a history which has through so many ages been confirmed, by the constant and unanimous testimony of an uninterrupted succession of witnesses of such high respectability, existing among all the various nations of the earth, and differing widely from each other in their language and manners, and in their opinions on other points : No one, besides, during the whole of this interval, having been able to impeach the credit of the religion itself, by substantiating against it a charge of falsehood, while almost all have been labouring to extirpate it by force.   It is apparent, as will be shown in the sequel, that these witnesses could not have been instigated to give their testimony by any prospects of worldly advantage ;—and yet (and in this consists the force of the argument) an immense host of them, like a cloud, reaching from the earliest age down to our own time, may be produced.   The reader who wishes to see the truth of Christianity discussed more at length, may consult the work of Faustus Socinus on the Authority of the Holy Scriptures, Grotius's book on the Truth of the Christian Religion, Joachim Stegman junior's *Brevis Veritatis Religionis Christianæ Demonstratio* (Brief Demonstration of the Truth of the Christian Religion) inserted in the works of Brennius, and Henry More's *Magni Mysterii Pietatis Explanationes, Lib. Sept.*[b]   BENEDICT WISSOWATIUS.

[b] [Socinus's work above referred to, is not so well known to the English reader as it ought to be, considering its great merit. It contains a clear and comprehensive summary of the argu-

ments

Is there any other proof of this fact?

Yes:—for it is wholly incredible that this religion,
—which holds out to its professors none of the glory,
wealth, or pleasures of this world, but on the contrary
takes away from them all such attractions, and subjects them to many of the adversities and afflictions of
the present state,—should have been received by so
many nations, unless it had been confirmed by the
resurrection of Jesus Christ from the dead; and also
by the signal miracles wrought in his name after this
event,

---

ments in favour of the genuineness and credibility of the Scriptures, and of the truth of the Christian Religion: and its utility
has been superseded by no publication of more recent date.
The best Latin edition is that printed without the author's
name, at Steinfurt in 1611, under the editorial direction of
Vorstius, whose pious labour drew on him the heavy censures
of the bigots of the time, who did not believe, it seems, that
" any good thing could come out of RACOW." This edition is
now exceedingly scarce. An English translation of it was published in 1731, in a thin octavo volume, by Mr. Edward
Combe, a divine of the Church of England, who prefixed a dedication to the Queen. This translation is also scarce: it is
moreover of rather uncouth execution: and, on these accounts,
he would deserve well of the Christian world, who should give
the work to the English public in a more pleasing and inviting
dress.

Grotius's treatise is better known, both to the scholar and to
the mere English reader; the Latin being no unusual school
book, and several English translations being current in the
market. Dr. Smallbrook, bishop of St. David's, says of this
work, that Grotius in the composition of it " was, among several other authors, more especially assisted by the valuable
performance of a writer otherwise justly of ill fame, viz. Faustus Socinus's little book *De Auctoritate S. Scripturæ*." (Charge
to the Clergy of St. David's, 1729.) The reader will be at no
loss

event, whereby it was evinced that he was then alive, and exercised authority in heaven[c].

You have proved from its author that the Christian Religion is divine :—I wish you now to do the same from the nature of the Religion itself?

This appears from its precepts and promises; which are of so sublime a kind, and so far surpass the inventive powers of the human mind, that they could have had no author but God himself. For its precepts inculcate a celestial holiness of life, and its promises comprehend the heavenly and everlasting happiness of man.

How do you prove the same from the circumstances of this religion?

---

loss to discriminate between the verdict of the critic and the charitable denunciation of the bishop.

Stegman's treatise is an excellent little compendium. It is appended, as stated above, to Brennius's Commentary on the Scriptures of the Old and New Testament, which is often classed as a tenth volume of the *Bibliotheca Fratrum Polonorum*.

Numerous references might be here given to more modern English works on this subject : the names of a few only can however be inserted. Dr. Lardner's great work on the Credibility of the Gospel History holds a pre-eminent rank in this class. Dr. Paley's more popular View of the Evidences of Christianity, in two volumes octavo, is also a work of great and acknowledged merit. Besides these, the reader may consult with advantage Bishop Watson's Apologies in Answer to Paine and Gibbon, and Mr. Belsham's Summary View of the Evidence and practical Importance of the Christian Revelation, which comprises a concise but comprehensive abstract of the arguments in behalf of the truth and divine authority of our holy religion. TRANSL.]

[c] [The opinion of the Polish churches with respect to the nature and extent of the authority with which Christ was invested after his resurrection, will be explained hereafter. TRANSL.]

This

This can be easily shown from its rise, progress, power, and effects.

How do you prove from its rise that the Christian Religion is divine?

This you will readily perceive when you consider who the first founders of this Religion were;—men of mean birth, held in universal contempt; aided by no power or wealth, by no worldly wisdom or authority, in converting others to their doctrine.

How do you prove the same from its progress?

From this consideration:—that in a very short interval of time it spread in a manner truly astonishing; —for several nations, and an innumerable multitude of persons, learned and unlearned, of exalted rank and of mean condition, and of both sexes, relinquishing the religious systems which they had derived from their parents and ancestors, allured by no prospect of worldly advantage, and intimidated by none of the heavy sufferings which usually befell its professors,— embraced the religion of Christ; exhibiting a change which nothing but the heavenly origin and the divine power of this Religion could have effected.

How do you prove the same from its power and effects?

First, because it could be suppressed by no human wisdom, or craft, or force, or authority. Secondly, because it did away all the old religious systems, excepting the Jewish, which it acknowledged to be of divine authority, though it was to flourish only until the advent of Christ, the author of so much more perfect a religion.

You

You have now shown me how authentic and credible the Scriptures of the New Testament are ;—prove to me in the next place that the Scriptures of the Old Testament are equally entitled to belief?

This, indeed, is shortly proved from hence, that the Scriptures of the New Testament bear witness to their authenticity. Since, therefore, the witnesses are, as I have already demonstrated, true and authentic, it is evident that that concerning the truth of which they testify must also be true and authentic.

CHAPTER II.

OF THE SUFFICIENCY OF THE HOLY SCRIPTURES.

YOU have proved to my satisfaction that the Scriptures of the Old and the New Testament are authentic and credible ;—I wish to know, further, whether they are of themselves sufficient,—so that in things necessary to salvation they alone are to be depended upon ?

They are in this respect amply sufficient; because Faith that "worketh by Love," which alone, the apostle Paul asserts (Gal. v. 6.), " availeth anything in Christ Jesus," is in them sufficiently inculcated and explained.

How do you prove that Faith is sufficiently inculcated and explained in the Holy Scriptures?

From hence :—because Faith, which is directed to God and Christ, is nothing else than the belief " that God is, and that he is the rewarder of them that seek him." (Heb. xi. 6.)   And this Faith is most fully inculcated in the Scriptures.

How

How do you prove the same in respect to Love ?

This appears from hence, that the duties of Love, whether towards God, or Christ, or our neighbour, are so fully explained, either in general or in particular precepts, as to place it beyond doubt, that he who practically observes them is endued with perfect love : and the same may also be asserted of the other duties of piety.

Have you any other reasons to prove this perfection of the Holy Scriptures ?

There are, indeed, several other reasons; but I shall content myself on the present occasion with noticing only two.   The first is, that every thing which, in addition to the Law delivered by Moses, it is necessary to believe under the Gospel, in order to salvation, has been declared by the authors of the Evangelical History.   For Christ, as he himself testifies, taught all these things : and whatever he taught as necessary to be known, it was the express object of these writers faithfully to record.   And Luke asserts in respect to himself (Acts i. 1, 2, compared with his Gospel, chap. i. 3, 4.) that he had declared " all that Jesus began both to do and teach, until the day in which he was taken up." So also John xx. 31 ; " But these are written, that ye might believe that Jesus is the Christ the Son of God; and that believing ye might have life through his name."

What is the second of these reasons ?

It is this :—that it is wholly incredible, that in so large a body of sacred literature, which God caused to be written and preserved with the express view of furnishing

nishing men with the knowledge of saving truths, those few particulars with which it is necessary for every person, even the most ignorant, to be acquainted, in order to his salvation, should not all have been included: and that, while a great number of things are written, the knowledge of which is not essential to salvation,—any one of those particulars should have have been omitted, without which all the rest are of no avail.

Of what use then is right reason, if it be of any, in those matters which relate to salvation?

It is, indeed, of great service, since without it we could neither perceive with certainty the authority of the sacred writings, understand their contents, discriminate one thing from another, nor apply them to any practical purpose. When therefore I stated that the Holy Scriptures were sufficient for our salvation, so far from excluding right reason, I certainly assumed its presence.

If then such be the state of the case, what need is there of Traditions, which, by the Church of Rome, are pronounced to be necessary to salvation, and which it denominates the unwritten word of God?

You rightly perceive, that they are not necessary to salvation.

What then is to be thought concerning them?

That some of them are not to be reckoned under the name of traditions, in the sense in which the Papists employ the term;—but that many of them were not only invented, without just reason, but are also productive of great injury to the Christian Faith.

What

What are the traditions of the former class?

They are those whose origin may be deduced from historical writings, or other authentic testimonies and sources of information, independent of the authority of the Church, and of the spirit, by which it is itself continually directed. For there is a certain medium between sacred scripture and what they call tradition.

What are the injury and danger resulting from the traditions of the latter class?

That they furnish occasion to draw men from divine truth to falsehood, and to fables of human device.

But the Papists appear to maintain these traditions on the authority of the Scriptures?

Some of the testimonies which they adduce from the Scriptures, in support of their traditions, do indeed demonstrate, that several things were said and done by Christ and his apostles which are not included in the sacred volume: but they by no means prove that those things are essential to salvation; much less, that they are the identical matters which the Church of Rome obtrudes upon our belief. Some of those testimonies, as evidently appears from several passages of Scripture, do not refer to traditions which were never committed to writing; but to such as were not written with an exclusive view to particular persons and seasons; but which, nevertheless, might have been written by the same individuals or by others, in respect of other times, and of other, or even of the same, persons. Moreover, though some traditions were to be admitted, those ought on no account to be received

which

which are repugnant to the written word of God, or to sound reason;—of which kind are not a few maintained by the Roman Church.

CHAPTER III.

OF THE PERSPICUITY OF THE HOLY SCRIPTURES.

YOU have now shown that the Holy Scriptures are both authentic and sufficient;—what is your opinion as to their perspicuity?

Although some difficulties do certainly occur in them; nevertheless, those things which are necessary to salvation, as well as many others, are so plainly declared in different passages, that every one may understand them; especially if he be earnestly seeking after truth and piety, and implore divine assistance.

How will you prove this?

By the following considerations:—first, that since it was the design of God, when it pleased him to give the Holy Scriptures to mankind, that they should from them acquaint themselves with his will; it is not to be believed that the writings he would furnish them with for this purpose, should be of so defective a kind, that his will could not be perceived and understood from them by all. Secondly, that the apostles, even at the very first promulgation of the Christian Religion, addressed their epistles, which comprise the chief mysteries of Christianity, to men of plain understandings.

Whence then arise such differences in ascertaining the sense of the Scriptures?

These differences, so far as they relate to the parts of Sacred Writ which are necessary to salvation, are

not

not very numerous; though the contrary is commonly
supposed.   And where differences do really exist, although some of them may arise from the obscurity of
particular texts, yet the greatest number must be
charged to men's own fault.   For either they read the
Scriptures with negligence, or bring not with them a
sincere heart, disengaged from all corrupt desires; or
have their minds warped by prejudice; or seek not
divine assistance with becoming earnestness; or else,
finally, are perplexed by their ignorance of the languages in which the Scriptures were written.   This
last circumstance, however, can hardly exist in reference to those particulars which are essential to
salvation : for, if some of these be conveyed in more
obscure, the rest are delivered in the plainest, declarations of Scripture.

By what means may the more obscure passages of
Scripture be understood ?

By carefully ascertaining, in the first instance, the
scope, and other circumstances, of those passages, in
the way which ought to be pursued in the interpretation of the language of all other written compositions.
Secondly, by an attentive comparison of them with si-
similar phrases and sentences of less ambiguous meaning.   Thirdly, by submitting our interpretation of the
more obscure passages to the test of the doctrines
which are most clearly inculcated in the Scriptures, as
to certain first principles; and admitting nothing that
disagrees with these.   And lastly, by rejecting every
interpretation which is repugnant to right reason, or
involves a contradiction.

Are

Are the same rules of interpretation to be applied to the predictions of the Prophets ?

Not altogether : for the meaning of the more obscure prophecies cannot be ascertained without the immediate aid of the divine spirit, unless men divinely inspired have furnished us with their proper explanation, or communicated to us the information by which we may be enabled to understand them ;—or unless their true interpretation have been shown in their accomplishment.   This is what the apostle meant to assert, when he observed (2 Peter i. 20,) that " no prophecy of the Scripture is of any private interpretation."

If the proper mode of interpreting the Scriptures be such as you have stated, of what service are religious teachers ?

To propose and inculcate those things which are necessary to salvation, notwithstanding they may be already plainly declared in the Scriptures ;—since all' men are not able, or, if able, are not of their own accord disposed, to peruse them ; and since it will be easier to acquire a clear apprehension of these things after the detached passages relating to them, which are dispersed throughout the sacred volume, have been collected by such teachers into one view.   Further, to excite men to maintain, and reduce to practice, the knowledge they have once acquired : and lastly, to assist them to understand those matters which are more difficult.

SECTION

SECTION II.

CONCERNING THE WAY OF SALVATION.

CHAPTER I.

THE REASONS OF THE REVELATION OF THE WAY OF SALVATION.

I ACKNOWLEDGE myself satisfied by you in respect to the Holy Scriptures : but, as you stated at the commencement, that the way which leads to immortality was pointed out by God, I wish to know why you made this assertion ?

Because man is not only obnoxious to death ; but could not of himself discover a way to avoid it, and that should infallibly conduct to immortality.

But wherefore is man obnoxious to death ?

On two accounts :—whereof the first is, that he was originally created mortal ;—that is, was so constituted that he was not only by nature capable of dying, but also, if left to himself, could not but die ; though he might, through the divine goodness, be for ever preserved alive.

How does this appear ?

First, because he was formed out of the earth :— secondly, because, as soon as he was created, he had need of food : and thirdly, because he was destined by God to beget children :—neither of which circumstances can be affirmed of an immortal nature. Besides, if Adam had been created immortal, it would have

have availed nothing to grant him the tree of life, whose fruit had the power of perpetuating existence. And lastly, who can doubt that his nature was such that he might have been stabbed, or suffocated, or burnt, or crushed to pieces, or in many other ways destroyed?

But how can this be reconciled to those passages of Scripture wherein it is asserted, that "God made man in his own image, and after his own likeness" (Gen. i. 26); that "he was created to be immortal," (Wisdom of Sol. ii. 23).; and that "death entered into the world by sin" (Rom. v. 12)?

With respect to the first passage, wherein it is declared that man was made in the image of God, it is to be remarked, that the "image of God" does not signify immortality; as is hence apparent, that the Scriptures, even after man had been made subject to death, still acknowledge this image in him: thus Genesis ix. 6; "Whoso sheddeth man's blood, by man shall his blood be shed—for in the image of God made he man." And James iii. 9; "Therewith (the tongue) bless we God, even the Father; and therewith curse we men, which are made after the similitude of God."—The phrase properly imports the authority of man, and his dominion over all inferior creatures, which result from the reason and judgement communicated to him; as may clearly be perceived from the very passage itself in which it is first employed, Genesis i. 26; "Let us make man, in our own image, after our likeness: and let them have dominion over the fish of the sea, and over the fowl of the air, and
over

over the cattle, and over all the earth, and over every creeping thing that creepeth upon the earth."

What think you of the second testimony adduced in this case?

I observe, first, that the passage is taken from an apocryphal book, and therefore cannot be admitted to furnish any decisive proof. Secondly, it is one thing to assert that man was created immortal, but a far different thing to say that he was created for immortality. The former indicates his natural condition; the latter only declares the end for which he was created. Indeed, if man was created with the intent that he should ultimately become immortal, how could he have been created immortal? Lastly, the word αφθαρσια, (incorruptibility,) which the author employs in this place, is not here opposed to every kind of corruption or death, but to that only which truly deserves the name—that which involves the utter destruction of man. This he intimates, among other reasons, by describing the just as exempt from this corruption and death; though he asserts not only that they naturally die, but also that they often close their lives in torments. See Wisdom, chap. i. 12; and chap. iii. 1, &c.

What answer do you make to the third testimony adduced in this case, from Rom. v. 12,—that death entered into the world by sin?

The apostle does not in this passage speak of mortality, but of death itself; and, indeed, of eternal death: but mortality differs widely from these; since a person may be mortal, and yet never die; much
less

less necessarily remain for ever under the power of death.

What is the second cause of man's being obnoxious to death ?

That the first man transgressed an express command of God, to which the denunciation of death was annexed.   Hence, also, it has come to pass, that he has brought the whole of his posterity under the same ordinance of death as himself; the personal offences of all of riper years being, however, taken into account, the guilt of which has been aggravated through the declared law of God, which men have violated. This you may perceive from the comparison which the apostle institutes, in the fifth chapter of his epistle to the Romans, between Christ and Adam, and from what he there observes concerning the effect of the introduction of the law in multiplying offences.

I perceive that man is obnoxious to death :—how do you prove that he could not of himself discover the way by which he might avoid death, and which would infallibly conduct him to immortality ?

This may be seen from hence,—that so glorious a recompense, and the sure means of obtaining it, must wholly depend on the will and counsel of God. But this will and counsel, what human being can explore, and clearly ascertain, unless they be revealed by God himself ?   The difficulty of discovering them is, besides, increased, in proportion to the degree in which they differed from the thoughts of the " natural man."   And that the things which relate to our salvation are of this kind, the apostle shows in the second

cond

cond chapter of his first Epistle to the Corinthians, where he treats at large upon this subject.

CHAPTER II.

CONCERNING THOSE THINGS WHICH CONSTITUTE THE WAY OF SALVATION.

I PERCEIVE that the way of salvation has been discovered to us by God:—I wish now to be informed what it is ?

It consists of the knowledge of God and of Christ, as the Lord Jesus has himself declared (John xvii. 3), " This is life eternal, that they might know thee, the only true God, and Jesus Christ whom thou hast sent."

What kind of knowledge do you mean ?

By this knowledge I do not understand any merely barren and speculative acquaintance with God and Christ, but accompanied with its proper effects; that is, with a lively or efficacious faith, and a suitable and exemplary conduct. For this alone do the Scriptures acknowledge as the true and saving knowledge of God, as the apostle John testifies (1 John ii. 3, 4), when he states, " Hereby we know that we know him, if we keep his commandments. He that saith I know him, and keepeth not his commandments, is a liar, and the truth is not in him." To this might be added other declarations of a similar kind from the writings of the same apostle, and of some other sacred authors. (See particularly John iii. 6. 3 John ii. Titus i. 16.)

SECTION

SECTION III.

OF THE KNOWLEDGE OF GOD.

———

CHAPTER I.

OF THE NATURE OF GOD.

WHAT do you understand by the term GOD?

The supreme Lord of all things.

And whom do you denominate Supreme?

Him, who, in his own right, has dominion over all things, and is dependent upon no other being in the administration of his government.

What does this dominion comprise?

A right and supreme authority to determine whatever he may choose (and he cannot choose what is in its own nature evil and unjust) in respect to us and to all other things, and also in respect to those matters which no other authority can reach; such as are our thoughts, though concealed in the inmost recesses of our hearts;—for which he can at pleasure ordain laws, and appoint rewards and punishments.

State to me wherein consists the knowledge of God?

In an acquaintance with his NATURE and his WILL.

What things relating to his NATURE are to be known?

They are of two kinds: the one comprising those things which are necessary to be known in order to salvation; and the other, those, whereof the knowledge eminently conduces to our salvation.

What

What are the things relating to the nature of God, the knowledge of which is necessary to salvation?

They are the following :—first, That God is; secondly, That he is one only; thirdly, That he is eternal; and fourthly, That he is perfectly just, wise, and powerful[2].

What is it to know that GOD IS?

It is to know, and be firmly convinced, that there actually exists a Being who possesses supreme dominion over all things[3].

What is it to know that God is ONE ONLY?

This you may of yourself easily understand—that there cannot be more beings than one who possess supreme dominion over all things.

But do not the Scriptures teach that there are " many Gods?"

---

[2] "Perfectly happy," ought, I think, to be added here : for it is necessary this should be believed concerning God by those who hope for perfect happiness from him hereafter.   M. RUARUS.

[3] The existence of God ought to be treated of here : but this our Catechism presupposes.   If any person should desire to see the proofs on this subject stated, he may consult Crellius's work " *De Deo et ejus Attributis.*"   And also the " *Institutiones Theologicæ*" of Episcopius and Curcellæus[d].—BEN. WISSOWATIUS.

[d] [Crellius's learned treatise on God and his Attributes, above referred to, may be found among his collected works in the *Bibliotheca Fratrum Polonorum*: and the Institutions of Episcopius and Curcellæus, severally in the folio editions of their works. The English reader may consult on this topic, Dr. Sam. Clarke's " Demonstration of the Being and Attributes of God:" and also " The Being and Attributes of God Demonstrated," by Henry Knight, A.M.   This excellent work was published after the author's death, and ushered into the world under the powerful recommendation of Drs. Benson, Lardner, and John Taylor.   TRANSL.]

Though

Though they do indeed assert this, yet it is not in that sense in which they proclaim and declare that there is one only God,—namely, he who possesses supreme dominion, derived from no other being, and consequently circumscribed by no limits. But by GODS they mean to designate those who received what divinity they had from that one God, upon whom, as their head, they depended: thus in the following passages, Psalm lxxxii. 1. and 6: " God standeth in the congregation of the mighty; he judgeth among the Gods." " I have said ye are Gods, and all of you are children of the Most High." John x. 34, 35 : " Is it not written in your law, I said ye are Gods ? If he called them Gods unto whom the word of God came," &c. For nothing forbids but that the one God may communicate, and may have communicated, of his dominion and authority to others, notwithstanding the Scriptures assert that he is the only potentate and king. 1 Tim. vi. 15.

But why do the Scriptures thus speak ?

Because that he alone has dominion of himself, and is the head of all things ; while all other beings are dependent upon him, and exercise their derived dominion solely through his kindness : on which accounts, also, it is stated that he is the " only wise God," " who alone hath immortality," and that " there is none good but he." Rom. xvi. 27. Jude 25. 1 Tim. vi. 16. Matt. xix. 17.

What is it to know that God is Eternal ?

That he is without either beginning or end ; that he always has been, and always will be ; in so much

c 2   that

that he cannot but be and exist perpetually. Hence it is that in the Scriptures he is styled INCORRUPTIBLE and IMMORTAL.

What is it to know that God is perfectly Just ?

That in all his measures he pursues rectitude; that he is the furthest possible removed from all wickedness, and therefore from every kind of injustice. Truth and faithfulness form also properties of his justice.

What is it to know that God is perfectly Wise ?

That he not only, in a general way, knows all things, but is also intimately acquainted with every single thing, even the most secret; that he understands likewise how to order his counsels, proceedings and works in the fittest possible manner, and to apply them to the accomplishment of his pleasure.

What is it to know that God is supremely Powerful?

That he is able to perform whatever he may will.

Is God then able to perform only those things which he wills ?

I do not say which he WILLS, but which he MAY WILL, that is, whatever he CAN WILL. For the power of God extends to all things whatsoever, or that do not involve what is termed a contradiction.

Wherefore is the knowledge of all these things necessary to salvation ?

Because, without an acquaintance with them we should not be able to enter upon the way of salvation ; or, at least, not to persevere in it to the end. By this consideration, principally, it is, that the necessity of this knowledge is to be estimated.

Show

Show me how this appears with respect to each of them separately ?

In relation to the first—who does not perceive that it is necessary to salvation to believe in the existence of God ? for unless we do this, we cannot believe that there is any way of salvation, or any religion at all. Hence the author of the Epistle to the Hebrews observes (chap. xi. 6) that " he that cometh to God must believe that he is."

How do you prove the second particular, that God is one, to be necessary to salvation ?

Unless we believe God to be but one, we shall be led to worship more Gods; which, as I shall show hereafter, is contrary to the way of salvation. For if God be not one only, we cannot love him with " ALL our heart, and soul, and strength." On which account the Scriptures frequently admonish us of this truth, that God is one. Thus Moses proclaims, (Deut. vi. 4.) " Hear, O Israel, The Lord our God is one Lord:"—a declaration which is repeated by our Lord, Mark xii. 29. So again, (Deut. iv. 35.) " The Lord he is God, there is none else." And Deut. xxxii. 39, " See now, that I, even I, am he, and there is no God with (or besides) me." To these testimonies may be added the following : 1 Cor. viii. 4, 5, 6, " There is none other God but one ; for though there be that are called Gods, whether in heaven or in earth (as there be Gods many and Lords many)—but to us there is but one God, the Father." 1 Tim. ii. 5 : " There is one God, and one Mediator between God and men, the Man Christ Jesus." Ephes. iv. 6 : " There is—

one

one God and Father of all." Gal. iii. 20 : " But God is one."

How is the knowledge of the Eternity of God ne- cessary to salvation ?

Unless we believe God to have been without begin- ning, we shall be led to infer that he was produced by some other Being, and be induced to worship that other Being as the supreme God. And if we do not believe that he will endure for ever, how can we hope to receive from him eternal life, to which we are con- ducted by the way of salvation ?

How does it appear that a knowledge of the Jus- tice of God is necessary to salvation ?

That to believe that God is perfectly just is neces- sary to salvation, is manifest from hence: first, in or- der to convince us that he will certainly accomplish whatever he has promised, how unworthy so ever we may be of his bounty : and, secondly, that we may be incited to bear, with unruffled minds, the trials which, after having entered on the way of salvation, we must needs encounter, together with all other adversities and disappointments ; feeling convinced that these things can be in no respect unjust since they are per- mitted by God.

How do you prove the same in respect to the per- fect Wisdom of God ?

To believe that God is perfectly wise is hence neces- sary to salvation,—that we may harbour no doubt that even our hearts, which are of all things the most dif- ficult to be scrutinized, and from which, principally, the value of our obedience will be estimated, are at all
times

times perfectly seen and known by him: and that we may be convinced that he possesses a clear knowledge of the means of providing for and securing our salvation ; and also of the reason of all the difficulties we encounter, although to our perceptions they may seem to occur without design.

How do you prove that a knowledge of the infinite Power of God is necessary to salvation ?

This does not admit of doubt :—for who could hope for eternal life from God, as its original author, unless he were convinced that his power is circumscribed by no limits or bounds ?   Or who could endure the sufferings which threaten and befal those who worship God conformably to the Christian religion, unless he were thoroughly impressed with the assurance, that all things are in the hands of God ;—that these occurrences happen not without his will ; and that there is nothing, either on earth or in heaven, that can overrule his divine power so as to prevent his accomplishing the things he has promised, and which we expect from him ?

I now fully perceive that the knowledge of these things is necessary to salvation :—But is it not, besides, requisite to know that God possesses an uncontrolled freedom of will ; that he is immense in his presence, infinitely good, and infinitely happy ?

It is, indeed, necessary to know these things concerning God :—some of them are, however, sufficiently comprehended in the particulars already discussed ; while the rest will be included in the explication of the Will of God.

Show

Show this of each of them separately;—and first, of the perfect freedom of the divine Will?

· This is evidently included in that supreme dominion, which I have already stated to be implied in the term GOD; since there can exist no dominion without freedom of will, nor supreme dominion unless that freedom be perfect. Hence, in lately describing that dominion, I have made distinct mention of WILL and CHOICE.

Show the same respecting the Immensity of God?

Immensity, in the sense in which the Scriptures attribute it to God, imports the supreme perfection of his dominion, power, and wisdom, and also of his providence, which extends to all affairs, and to all places. In so far then as it may be referred to the divine dominion, power, and wisdom, which I have stated to be all of them perfect, it has been already considered;—but as far as it relates to the Providence of God, it will be included in the observations on the Will of God.

To what do you refer the Goodness of God?

His goodness, if it be taken to mean his holiness, has been already included under his justice: but if it be understood of his mercy and benignity, as it very frequently is in the Scriptures, it is to be referred to the divine Will.

What say you as to his Happiness?

That God is happy, it is impossible for any one not to believe who admits that he is eternal, perfectly wise, and just, and powerful, and withal invested with supreme dominion over all things. For his life must necessarily be of all others the most perfect and delightful.

ful. This is to be not happy merely, but blessed in the highest degree.

You have explained to me what things are necessary to be known concerning the attributes of God, in order to salvation : state, in the next place, what those are which you deem eminently conducive to the same end?

The principal thing is to guard against falling into the common error, wherein it is maintained, with palpable contradiction, that there is in God only ONE essence, but that he has three persons [4].

Prove to me that in the one essence of God, there is but one Person?

This indeed may be seen from hence, that the essence of God is one, not in kind but in number. Wherefore it cannot, in any way, contain a plurality of persons, since a person is nothing else than an individual intelligent essence. Wherever, then, there exist three numerical persons, there must necessarily, in like manner, be reckoned three individual essences; for in the same sense in which it is affirmed that there is one numerical essence, it must be held that there is also one numerical person.

---

[4] Whether it be not necessary to salvation to know that God is one in person as well as in essence, may be easily ascertained from the testimony of our Lord, quoted a little further on, from John xvii. 3. And whether in maintaining that there is in the supreme God a plurality of persons, Christians do not involve themselves in the crime of polytheism, and consequently of idolatry, it behoves them again and again to consider. On this point, the observations of Crellius, in discussing this subject in his *Ethica Christiana*, may be consulted. *Vide lib.* iii. *cap.* 2. —BEN. WISSOWATIUS.

Who is this one divine Person?

The Father of our Lord Jesus Christ.

How do you prove this?

By most decisive testimonies of Scripture :—thus Jesus says (John xvii. 3) " This is life eternal, that they might know THEE, (the Father) THE ONLY TRUE GOD." The apostle Paul writes to the Corinthians (1 Cor. viii. 6), " To us there is but ONE GOD, THE FATHER, of whom are all things :"—and again, in addressing the Ephesians (chap. iv. 6), he says, " There is—ONE GOD AND FATHER OF ALL ; who is above all, and through all, and in you all."

How happens it, then, that Christians commonly maintain, that, with the Father,—the SON and the HOLY SPIRIT are persons in one and the same Deity?

In this they lamentably err—deducing their arguments from passages of Scripture ill understood.

What are the arguments by which they endeavour to support their opinion?

The principal are these: first, they affirm, that in the Scriptures, not only the Father, but the Son also, and the Holy Spirit, are severally called and shown to be God ; and, since the same Scriptures assert that God is only one, they infer that these three compose that one God.

How can this argument be invalidated?

I will reply to this question, first, as it respects the Son, and afterwards as it relates to the Holy Spirit.

What answer do you make in respect to the Son?

The term GOD is employed in the Scriptures chiefly in two senses. The former of these is, when it de-

signates

signates Him who so rules and presides over all things
in heaven and on earth, that he acknowledges no superior; and is in such respects the author and head of
all things, that he depends upon no other being, and
possesses power which is absolutely infinite: and in this
sense the Scriptures assert that God is One. The latter sense is, when it denotes a Being, who has received
from that one God some kind of superior authority
either in heaven, or on earth among men, or power
superior to all things human, or authority to sit in
judgement upon other men; and is thus rendered in
some sense, a partaker of the Deity of the one God.
Hence it is that in the Scriptures the one God is
styled the " God of Gods," Psalm cxxxvi. 2; and it
is in this latter sense that the Son of God is called
God in some passages of Scripture.

Whence do you prove that the Son of God is in this
latter sense called God in the Scriptures?

From those words of the Son of God himself,
(John x. 35, 36) " If he" (David) " called them
Gods, (that is, Psalm lxxxii. 6, " ye are Gods)" unto
whom the word of God came, and the Scripture cannot be broken; say ye of him, whom the Father hath
sanctified and sent into the world, Thou blasphemest,
because I said, I am the Son of God?" Christ most
clearly intimates in these words that the title GOD is
applied in the Scriptures to those who are greatly inferior to the one God; that is, to the rulers and judges
of the people: and tacitly implies that he was himself
for this reason the Son of God, that is, peculiarly,
being not inferior to any one of those persons whom

God

God had honoured with the title of Gods, but rather
greatly the superior of them all; and was on this very
account God,—that the " Father had sanctified him,
and sent him into the world:" which cause, and the
whole of this reasoning of Christ, are accommodated
to the latter, and not to the former signification of the
term GOD.

What reply do you make respecting the Holy Spirit?

The Holy Spirit is never expressly called God in
the Scriptures.   Nor is it to be inferred that it is itself God, or a person of the Divinity, because in some
places those things are attributed to it which belong
to God: but this proceeds from a very different cause,
as you shall hear in its proper place.

What is the second argument whereby it is attempted to be proved that these three persons are
united in one Deity?

This argument is drawn from those passages of
Scripture wherein the Father, Son, and Holy Spirit
are, on some account, joined together.

Which are those passages?

The first is the command of Jesus (Matthew
xxviii. 19), to baptize " in the name of the Father,
the Son, and the Holy Spirit."   The second is comprised in the address of Paul to the Corinthians
(1 Corinth. xii. 4—6), " There are diversities of gifts,
but the same Spirit : and there are differences of ad-
ministrations, but the same Lord: and there are diversities of operations, but it is the same God which
worketh all in all."   The third is found in the First
Epistle of John, chap. v. 7, " There are three that
bear

bear record in heaven, the Father, the Word, and the Holy Spirit, and these three are one."

What ought we to think of these testimonies?

I answer generally in respect to them, that they only prove the existence of the Father, Son, and Holy Spirit, and that they are associated in divine things; which I not only admit, but also constantly declare; insomuch that I pronounce that person to be no Christian who either does not know or does not believe this.   It is evident, nevertheless, that these testimonies do not prove the matter in dispute; namely, that the Father, Son, and Holy Spirit, are three persons in the one essence of God.

It does, however, seem as if it might be inferred, from the kind of union affirmed of these three in the cited passages, that they are three persons in one divine essence?

By no means. For, in respect to the first, the baptismal command, although the Father, Son, and Holy Spirit, are so associated together that we are to be baptized in their joint names, yet it cannot be hence proved that they are persons in one divine essence.   For it is not at all unusual in the Scriptures, in other cases equally with the ordinance of baptism, to join with God, in religious matters, both persons and things which in no way pertain to the divine essence.   Of PERSONS, you have an example in the First Book of Samuel (chap. xii. 18), where it is said that " all the people greatly feared the Lord, AND SAMUEL."—So also Exodus xiv. 31, " And the people
feared

feared the Lord, and believed the Lord AND HIS SER-
VANT MOSES."—Of THINGS, we have an instance
in Acts xx. 32 ; where Paul, addressing the Ephesians, says, " I commend you to God, AND TO THE
WORD OF HIS GRACE."   Things are also joined with.
Christ (Ephes. vi. 10), " Be strong in the Lord, AND
IN THE POWER OF HIS MIGHT. "And in the Book of
Revelation (chap. iii. 12), things are joined to God
and Christ : " I will write upon him the name of
my God, AND THE NAME OF THE CITY OF MY GOD,
WHICH IS NEW JERUSALEM, which cometh down out
of heaven from my God; and I will write upon him my
new name."

But it is maintained, that he must necessarily be
God, in whose name we are baptized ?

Those who hold this opinion egregiously err : for
we read (1 Cor. x. 2) that the Israelites " were all
baptized UNTO MOSES in the cloud and in the sea :"
Acts xix. 3, that some were baptized " UNTO JOHN'S
BAPTISM:" and Rom. vi. 3, that Christians are " baptized INTO THE DEATH OF CHRIST:"—though Moses
was not God, and though neither the baptism of John
nor the death of Christ, was even a person, much less
God.

But to be baptized into any one's NAME, seems to
be a very different thing from being baptized into
any person or thing ?

Not at all : for agreeably to the import of the Hebrew idiom, both phrases are well known to have the
same meaning, as may be seen in this very case. For.

what

what is stated in Acts ii. 38, of converts being "baptized in the name of Jesus Christ," is in other places (Rom. vi. 3 ; Gal. iii. 27) expressed more briefly by being " baptized into Jesus Christ."

But why does Christ speak in this manner of the Holy Spirit, if it be not a person ?

·Because he connects the Holy Spirit with the Father and himself, as a kind of celestial teacher and master, by whose inspiration and power his doctrine would be promulgated in the world.

What reply do you make to the second cited testimony, wherein the apostle Paul seems to ascribe divine operations to the Holy Spirit, equally with the Father and the Son ?

Although divine operations are here attributed to God, to the Lord, (who is Christ,) and also to the Holy Spirit, it cannot be hence proved that these three are the one God. Indeed the direct contrary is to be inferred from the passage ; since the Lord, (that is Christ,) and the Holy Spirit, are most clearly distinguished by the apostle from the one God. The Lord, (or Christ,) and the Holy Spirit, are mentioned conjointly with God on this account,—because the former is the person by whose instrumentality God operates all the effects which are there referred to ; and the latter the virtue or energy of God, by the communication of which all those operations are performed.

What answer do you make to the third testimony quoted from the First Epistle of John, respecting the three heavenly witnesses ?

I observe, first, that since it is known that these words

words are wanting in most[e] of the older Greek copies,
and also in the Syriac, Arabic, Æthiopic, and the
more ancient Latin versions, as the principal persons

---

[e] [In all the earlier editions of the Catechism this clause was
written *Cum notum sit in Græcis exemplaribus vetustioribus: ea
verba non haberi, &c.* " Since it is known that these words
are wanting in the older Greek copies," &c. The adjective
plerisque (MOST) was first inserted in the text in the edition of
1680, in consequence of the following note upon the place by
Ruarus. *Addatur plerisque: Nam Erasmus ea* [scil. VERBA "*Tres
sunt qui testantur, &c.*"] *in Britannico Codice invenit, Robertus
quoque Stephanus in aliquot Regiis.* " For Erasmus found them
(the words 'there are three, &c.') in the *Codex Britannicus*, and
also Robert Stephens in some MSS. in the King's Library." This
Codex Britannicus, which is here ranked among the more ancient Greek manuscripts of the New Testament, turns out to
be no other than the MS. in the Dublin Library, now called
Codex Dublinensis, or *Montfortius*, which is pronounced by
competent judges to have been probably written about the year
1520. It contains the disputed passage, indeed, but " translated in a bungling manner from the modern copies of the
Vulgate." It is certain that Erasmus never saw the MS. which
he notices as the *Codex Britannicus*; an extract was sent to
him containing this verse, and on this authority he was induced to insert it in the text of the third edition of his Greek
Testament, the two former having been published without it.
The other ground of introducing *plerisque*, namely Robert Stephens's manuscripts from the French king's library, proves
equally untenable. The mistake into which the learned world
has been led on this subject seems to have arisen from a typo-
graphical error. Of the manuscripts used by Robert Stephens,
seven contained the Catholic Epistles. In printing this chapter he inserted the controverted verse, but marked the words
εν τωι ουρανωι (IN HEAVEN), as wanting in his MSS. And because
he took no notice of the remainder of the passage, it has been
taken for granted that it was contained in them. As, however,
no MSS. are now found containing the verse, but omitting these
words, it is concluded that the mark of omission has been
placed by mistake after εν τωι ουρανωι (IN HEAVEN), instead of after
the words εν τηι γηι (IN EARTH). See Porson's Letters to Travis,
letter iv. page 54, &c. TRANSL.]

even

even among our adversaries have themselves shown, nothing certain can be concluded from them. There are, besides, some persons who deem the genuineness of the passage suspicious;—that is to say, Erasmus, Beza, Franc. Lucas, and the Louvain divines.   On this account Luther could not venture to admit the words; and his colleague Bugenhagius, in his Commentary on John, warned all printers against inserting them in the text.   Besides, the principal Fathers among the advocates of the doctrine of the Trinity, whose names may be seen in the editions of Louvain, of Beza, Serarius, and Pelargus, do not acknowledge them. They do not agree with the preceding context.' And Grotius asserts that they are wholly wanting in a very ancient manuscript which was transmitted by the patriarch Cyrillus to the king of Great Britain.—I observe in the next place, that even if the passage were found in the authentic Scriptures, it could not be proved from it that there are three persons in one God.   For it ought not to be inferred from the words, that all these are PERSONS, merely because they are said to bear record: for in the following verse, the very same thing is stated of the spirit, the water, and the blood.   When then it is said that they are one, or, as some copies read, in one, no other unity ought to be understood than that which is wont to exist in witnesses who agree in their testimony.   This is apparent not only from the circumstance that the writer is here speaking of witnesses, but also because he makes a similar assertion in the following verse concerning the spirit, the water, and the blood—that

THESE

This you will easily understand if you only consider
how pernicious the opinion of the adverse party is.
For, in the first place, that opinion may easily weaken
and subvert the belief in one God, while at one time
it asserts that there is but one God, and at another
declares the existence of three persons each of whom
is God; and indeed does destroy it, in so far as it denies that the person of that God, whom it calls one,
is one also. Secondly, it tarnishes the glory of the
one God, who alone is the Father of Christ, by trans-
ferring it to another, who is not the Father. Thirdly, this opinion comprises some things which are un-

---

the editors of the Improved Version of the New Testament have
given in its place a concise summary of the evidence against the
genuineness of the passage, which, as being short, and perfectly
within the comprehension of the mere English reader, shall be
here transcribed. " 1. This text concerning the heavenly witnesses is not contained in any Greek manuscript which was
written earlier than the fifteenth century. 2. Nor in any Latin
manuscript earlier than the ninth century. 3. It is not found
in any of the ancient versions. 4. It is not cited by any of the
Greek ecclesiastical writers, though to prove the doctrine of
the Trinity they have cited the words both before and after this
text. 5. It is not cited by any of the early Latin Fathers, even
when the subject upon which they treat would naturally have
led them to appeal to its authority. 6. It is first cited by Vigilius
Tapsensis, a Latin writer of no credit in the latter end of the
fifth century, and by him it is suspected to have been forged.
7. It has been omitted as spurious in many editions of the New
Testament since the Reformation: in the two first of Erasmus, in those of Aldus, Colinæus, Zwinglius, and lately of
Griesbach. 8. It was omitted by Luther in his German Version. In the old English Bibles of Henry VIII., Edward VI.,
and Elizabeth, it was printed in small types, or included in
brackets: but between the years 1566 and 1580 it began to
be printed as it now stands; by whose authority is not known."
TRANSL.]

worthy

unworthy of the one supreme God :—asserting, for instance, that the one most high God is the Son or Spirit of some other Being, and that therefore he has a father and author—that the one most high God was made man—and that a man was the one most high God ;—and other things of a similar kind. Fourthly, it renders God, the Son of God, and the Holy Spirit very different objects of mental perception and of faith, from what they really are; and the more especially since it declares the Son of God, a character to which he is truly entitled, to be (I shudder to relate it) a false God, an idol, and unworthy of divine worship, and indeed of himself undeserving of this very title. Fifthly, it is calculated in like manner to subvert in our apprehensions, the true notion of salvation, by destroying the distinction between the first and the second cause ; and prevents our knowing rightly who is the primary author of our salvation, and in what manner it is effected by God through Christ and the Holy Spirit. Lastly, this opinion presents a formidable obstacle to unbelievers to receive the Gospel, by inculcating things that are repugnant to those divine testimonies, which some of them receive, and also to right reason. Above all, if Christ be thought to be the one God, the force of his commandment, by which we are required to imitate him, is wholly destroyed, and the obedience which he yielded to God becomes a mere nullity.—Now all these consequences are avoided by that system which maintains that the person of the one God is but one.

May not this opinion concerning three persons in

one

one God, which is attended with so many inconveniences, prevent the salvation of some men ?

Although this opinion may not be considered as exposing to final condemnation any person who enter-
tains no suspicion of his being in error, and who may
have enjoyed no advantages for coming to the knowledge of the truth ;—provided he believe that Jesus
Christ was truly a man, that he really died for our sins,
and rose again for our justification; that after his resurrection he was constituted by God both Lord and
Christ, made the head of the church, and appointed to
be the judge of quick and dead ; and thus embraces a
faith in Christ which worketh by love, and becomes
a new creature; and who therefore does not perceive
the tendency of his erroneous opinion, holding it rather
according to the sound of the words than their real
sense and import, and is disposed to embrace the truth
as soon as any one convinces him of his mistake :—
Although, I say, this opinion may not be considered
as exposing to final condemnation a person of this
character; nevertheless the salvation of that man is
beyond doubt in great danger, who, when occasion
offers, does not examine into the truth of the doctrine
of the unity of God's person, or who obstinately re-
sists it, or is unwilling to acknowledge it, or, if he
acknowledge it, will not venture openly to profess it,
but, as Christ speaks, is ashamed of it, and does not
promote it as far as his opportunities would enable
him, or else shrinks from it after he has known and
embraced it; and particularly if, without any osten-
sible cause, or for some reason ill understood, or

against

against his own conscience, he condemn those who maintain it; declare them unworthy of Christian fellowship, and even of the Christian name; and above all if he harass and persecute them : or, lastly, if following the influence of his erroneous opinion, he depart from those things without which no one can obtain salvation.

Is there any thing else pertaining to the nature of God, the knowledge of which you conceive to conduce to salvation ?

Yes :—that his essence is spiritual, and invisible.

How do you prove this ?

That the essence of God is spiritual appears from those words of Christ recorded John iv. 24 ; where he declares that " God is a spirit." That God is invisible may also be inferred from this passage; and is besides asserted in several other texts of scripture. Thus Colossians i. 15, Christ is called the "image of the INVISIBLE GOD." 1 Timothy i. 17, God is styled the "king eternal, immortal, INVISIBLE." In the sixth chapter and sixteenth verse it is stated that " no man hath seen, or can see him." And John (chap. i. 18) uses a similar mode of expression—" No man hath seen God at any time."

Of what use is the knowledge of these attributes ?

First, Christ intimates its utility when he argues from God's being a spirit, that he ought to be worshiped in spirit and in truth. Secondly, it is of use to apprise us that those passages of Scripture in which bodily members are ascribed to God, are to be interpreted figuratively; and that, in consequence, we may

be

be restrained from degrading the majesty of God, as if he were like to a mortal man, and from forming, for the purpose of worship, any visible resemblance of him.

CHAPTER II.
OF THE WILL OF GOD.

You have now explained to me those things which relate to the nature of God; we must, in the next place, consider those which pertain to his will;—wherefore I wish you, first, to inform me what you understand by the terms, THE WILL OF GOD?

By the Will of God, I do not understand that faculty of willing naturally inherent in the Deity, but the effect of that faculty: though in this place those things alone ought to be considered, the knowledge of which pertains to the Christian religion.

What are these things?

Some of them were known even before the coming of Christ; and some were first revealed by him.

What are those of the former class?

These were, in part, known before the delivery of the Law, and in part declared by the Law.

What are those things which were known by mankind before the delivery of the Law?

The principal are the three following: First, the creation of heaven and earth, and of all that they contain. Secondly, the providence of God over all affairs, especially over mankind, whereby he beholds and governs all, and preserves the whole as long as to him seems proper. And thirdly, the rewarding of those who seek him, that is, who obey his commands, and the punishing of those who refuse him obedience.

This

This last head comprises some knowledge of those things which are pleasing to God, and by the observance of which he is obeyed; and it is probable that none of those particulars which were known of old and before its promulgation were omitted in the Law of Moses.

Wherefore is it necessary to believe concerning God that he created heaven and earth?

Three principal reasons may be assigned:—First, that it is God's will we should believe this, since the work of creation pertains to his highest glory. Hence it is that in the Scriptures both God himself and his ministers so frequently admonish us on this head; as you may perceive in the following passages, among others. Isaiah xliv. 24, " I am the Lord that maketh all things; that stretcheth forth the heavens alone, that spreadeth abroad the earth by myself." Genesis i. 1, " In the beginning God created the heaven and the earth." Psalm xxxiii. 6—9. " By the word of the Lord were the heavens made, and all the host of them by the breath of his mouth. He gathereth the waters of the sea together as an heap; he layeth up the depth in storehouses. Let all the earth fear the Lord; let all the inhabitants of the world stand in awe of him. For he spake and it was done; he commanded and it stood fast." Acts iv. 24, " Lord, thou art God, which hast made heaven and earth, and the sea, and all that in them is." Acts xiv. 15. " We—preach unto you, that ye should turn from these vanities unto the living God, which made heaven and earth, and the sea, and all things that are therein."

therein." Acts xvii. 24, " God that made the world,
and all things therein, seeing that he is Lord of heaven
and earth, dwelleth not in temples made with hands."
Revelation xiv. 7, " Fear God, and give glory to him
—and worship him that made heaven and earth, and
the sea, and the fountains of waters." The second
reason is, that unless we are firmly convinced that
God created heaven and earth, we shall have no foundation for believing that his Providence is such as I
have declared it to be over all affairs, and more especially over every human being: and on this account
we shall feel no inducement to yield him obedience.
And the third is, that it is from creation that God's
authority over us, out of which arises the necessity
of our obedience to him, is made manifest.

From this answer I perceive that I have no occasion
to ask, why we ought to believe in God's providential
care over all things, and especially over every human
being, or concerning his rewarding those who seek
him :—Wherefore state to me what those things are,
which were declared to mankind by the Law, and
are necessary to be known by Christians?

They are those things which are comprised in the
moral law, and principally in the Decalogue; of which
I shall speak hereafter in enumerating those things
which have been revealed by Christ.

SECTION

SECTION IV.

OF THE KNOWLEDGE OF CHRIST.

———

CHAPTER I.

OF THE PERSON OF CHRIST.

As you have stated that there are some things relating to the Will of God, which were first revealed by Jesus Christ, and also asserted, at the commencement, that the way of salvation consisted in the knowledge of him,—I now wish you to specify what those particulars are, concerning Jesus Christ, which I ought to know?

Certainly : You must be informed, then, that there are some things relating to the PERSON, or nature, of Jesus Christ, and some, to his OFFICE, with which you ought to be acquainted.

What are the things relating to his Person, which I ought to know?

This one particular alone,—that by nature he was truly a man; a mortal man while he lived on earth, but now immortal. That he was a real man the Scriptures testify in several places : Thus 1 Timothy ii. 5, "There is one God, and one mediator between God and men, the MAN Christ Jesus." 1 Corinthians xv. 21, 22, "Since by MAN came death, by MAN came also the resurrection of the dead. For as in ADAM all die, even so in CHRIST shall all be made alive." Romans v. 15, "If through the offence of one, many be

D 2   dead,

dead, much more the grace of God, and the gift by
grace, which is by one MAN, Jesus Christ, hath
abounded unto many." John viii. 40, " But now ye
seek to kill me, A MAN that hath told you the truth."
See also Hebrews v. 1, &c. Such, besides, was the
person whom God promised of old by the prophets;
and such also does the Creed called the Apostles',
which all Christians, in common with ourselves, embrace, declare him to be[o].

Was, then, the Lord Jesus a mere or common man?

By no means: because, first, though by nature he
was a man, he was nevertheless, at the same time,
and even from his earliest origin, the only begotten
Son of God. For being conceived of the Holy Spirit,

---

[o] It is on account of his being strictly a man, that he is so
frequently called in the Scriptures " The Son of Man ;" a title
which in the Syriac language, the dialect wherein it is admitted
by many that our Lord conversed, signifies properly a human
being :—For in this language even Adam, the first man, is
called the SON OF MAN, as may be seen Romans v. 12; 1 Corinthians xv. 21.[h] B. WISSOWATIUS.

[h] [This idiomatic peculiarity is not preserved in the Latin
translation which accompanies the Syriac New Testament in
Walton's Polyglott. The two passages here referred to may
be thus literally rendered from the Syriac :—Rom. v. 12. *Si-
cut per manum filii hominis intravit peccatum in mundum, et per
manum peccati mors : et ita in omnes filios hominis transiit mors,
in eo quod omnes peccaverunt.*

" As by the hand of the son of man sin entered into the
world, and death by the hand of sin; and so death passed upon
all the sons of man, for that all have sinned."

1 Cor. xv. 21. *Et quemadmodum per manum filii hominis ex-
titit mors, ita etiam per manum filii hominis est resurrectio mortuorum.*

" Since by the hand of the son of man came death, so also by
the hand of the son of man came the resurrection of the dead."
TRANSL.]

                                                          and

and born of a virgin, without the intervention of any
human being, he had properly no father besides God:
though considered in another light, simply according
to the flesh, without respect to the Holy Spirit, of
which he was conceived, and with which he was
anointed, he had David for his father, and was therefore his son. Concerning his supernatural conception,
the angel thus speaks to Mary, Luke i. 35, " The Holy Ghost shall come upon thee, and the Power of the
Highest shall overshadow thee; therefore also that
holy thing which shall be born of thee shall be called
the Son of God [7]." Secondly, because, as Christ testifies

---

[7] We do not find in the whole body of the sacred writings
any cause antecedent to this of Jesus Christ's being the Son of
God ;—a circumstance which ought to be borne in mind, in opposition to those persons who, not satisfied with this, contend that the chief cause of his filiation consisted in his being
begotten from everlasting out of the essence of the Father; or,
according to others, in his having been created or produced by
God before all creatures [i].   B. Wissowatius.

[i] [The title Son of God is understood by most English Unitarians of the present day to denote generally, any person who
is the object of the divine favour, and distinguished by peculiar religious blessings or privileges : and is thought to have
been emphatically applied to Jesus on account of the OFFICE
he sustained as the Messiah, or Christ. It is not considered as
implying any superiority of NATURE ; or as necessarily sup-
posing, agreeably to the opinion maintained in the above answer, that he was supernaturally conceived, or that he was invested after his resurrection with universal authority and dominion.   Unitarians do not regard the doctrine of the miraculous conception as at all militating against their opinion of the
proper humanity of Jesus ; for the case might be deemed analo-
gous to that of Adam, whom no one ever thought to be more
than man because he was formed out of the ordinary course of
generation. This doctrine, however, though formerly held by
Dr. Lardner, and some other eminent Unitarians, seems now
to

tifies of himself, he was sanctified and sent into the world by the Father; that is, being in a most remarkable manner separated from all other men, and, besides being distinguished by the perfect holiness of his life, endued with divine wisdom and power, was sent by the Father, with supreme authority, on an embassy to mankind. Thirdly, because, as the apostle Paul testifies, both in the Acts of the Apostles, and in his Epistle to the Romans, he was raised from the dead by God, and thus as it were begotten a second time;—particularly as by this event he became like God immortal. Fourthly, because by his dominion and supreme authority over all things, he is made to resemble, or, indeed, to equal God : on which account, " a king anointed by God," and " Son of God," are used in several passages of Scripture as phrases of the same

---

to be rejected by all the public advocates of this system, as unsupported by adequate scriptural authority. It is taught in no other portion of the received copies of the New Testament, besides the Introductory chapters of the gospels of Matthew and Luke : and the genuineness of these is either suspected or denied. Dr. Carpenter, in his " Unitarianism the Doctrine of the Gospel," while he rejects the first two chapters of Matthew as an interpolation, is disposed to retain those of Luke ; and suggests an ingenious explanation of the passage relating to the point under our consideration, to show that the language of the original does not necessarily suppose that there was any thing miraculous in the circumstance of the conception of Jesus. The English reader may consult on this subject the Improved Version of the New Testament, under Matthew, chapters i. and ii., and Luke i. and ii. Belsham's Calm Inquiry concerning the Person of Christ, (1st edit.) p. 12, 255, &c. Dr. Carpenter's work above noticed, p. 172, &c. and Appendix i. and Jones's Sequel to his Ecclesiastical Researches. TRANSL.]

import.

import.   And the sacred author of the Epistle to
the Hebrews (chap. i. ver. 5) shows from the words of
the Psalmist (Psalm ii. 7), " Thou art my Son, this
day have I begotten thee," that Christ was glorified
by God, in order that he might be made a Priest, that
is, the chief director of our religion and salvation,—in
which office are comprised his supreme authority and
dominion.   He was, however, not merely the only begotten Son of God, but also A GOD, on account of the
divine power and authority which he displayed even
while he was yet mortal: much more may he be so de-.
nominated now that he has received all power in heaven and earth, and that all things, God himself alone
excepted, have been put under his feet.—But of th<i>v</i>
you shall hear in its proper place.

But do you not acknowledge in Christ a divine, as
well as a human nature or substance?

If by the terms divine nature or substance I am to
understand the very essence of God, I do not acknowledge such a divine nature in Christ; for this were
repugnant both to right reason and to the Holy Scriptures.   But if, on the other hand, you intend by a
divine nature the Holy Spirit which dwelt in Christ,
united, by an indissoluble bond, to his human nature[*],

and

---

[*] It ought to be noticed here that in the opinion of the ancients, besides the Holy Spirit, which is the Power of God,
being given to Christ without measure, the Wisdom of God also,
as the Scriptures, indeed, intimate, or that divine energy and
ατιφοια, which seems to have been the Shechinah of the Hebrews, or the Logos of the first Christians, dwelt in the Messiah.   So the great Grotius rightly remarks, in the Fifth Book

of

and displayed in him the wonderful effects of its extraordinary presence; or if you understand the words in the sense in which Peter employs them (2 Peter i. 4), when he asserts that " we are partakers of a divine nature," that is, endued by the favour of God with divinity, or divine properties,—I certainly do so far acknowledge such a nature in Christ as to believe that next after God it belonged to no one in a higher degree.

Show me how the first mentioned opinion is repugnant to right reason?

First, on this account, That two substances endued with opposite and discordant properties, such as are God and man, cannot be ascribed to one and the same individual, much less be predicated the one of the other. For you cannot call one and the same thing first fire, and then water, and afterwards say that the fire is water, and the water fire. And such is the way in which it is usually affirmed;—first, that Christ is God, and afterwards that he is a man; and then that God is man, and that man is God.

But what ought to be replied, when it is alleged that Christ is constituted of a divine and human nature, in the same way as man is composed of a soul and body?

The cases are essentially different:—for it is stated

---

of his work on the Christian Religion, as also in several places in his Commentaries. The Chaldee Paraphrast on Isaiah xlii.1, may likewise be consulted.

These agree with the words of the apostle Paul, Coloss. ii. 3 and 9; " In whom are hid all the treasures of wisdom and knowledge." " In him dwelleth all the fullness of the godhead bodily:" and 1 Cor. i. 24, " Christ the power of God and the wisdom of God." B. WISSOWATIUS.

that

that the two natures are so united in Christ, that he is both God and man: whereas the union between the soul and body is of such a kind that the man is neither the soul nor the body.   Again, neither the soul nor the body, separately, constitutes a person: but as the divine nature, by itself, constitutes a person, so also must the human nature, by itself, constitute a person; since it is a primary or single intelligent substance.

Show me, in the next place, how it appears to be repugnant to the Scriptures, that Christ possesses the divine nature which is claimed for him?

First, because the Scriptures propose to us but one only God; whom 1 have already proved to be the Father of Christ.   And this reason is rendered the more evident from Christ's being in several passages of Scripture not only distinguished from God absolutely so called, but often also expressly from the one or only God. Thus 1 Cor. viii. 6, " There is but one God, the Father, of whom are all things, and we in him; and one Lord, Jesus Christ, by whom are all things, and we by him." And John xvii. 3, "This is life eternal, that they might know thee, the only true God, and Jesus Christ whom thou hast sent." Secondly, because the same Scriptures assert, as I have already shown, that Jesus Christ is a man; which itself deprives him of the divine nature that would render him the supreme God.   Thirdly, because the Scriptures explicitly declare that whatever of a divine nature Christ possessed, he had received as a gift from the Father; and refer it to the Holy Spirit, with which he had by the Father been anointed and filled.   Thus Phil. ii. 9, "God hath

highly

highly exalted him, and GIVEN him a name which is
above every name." 1 Cor. xv. 27, "When he saith all
things ARE PUT UNDER HIM, it is manifest that HE
is excepted which DID PUT ALL THINGS UNDER HIM."
Luke iv. 14 and 18, " Jesus returned in the power of
the Spirit into Galilee." " The spirit of the Lord is
upon me, because he hath anointed me to preach the
gospel to the poor." Matt. xxviii. 18, "All power is
GIVEN unto me in heaven and in earth." Acts x. 38,
" God anointed Jesus of Nazareth with the Holy
Ghost and with power." Isaiah xi. 2, "And the spirit of the Lord shall rest upon him, the spirit of wisdom and understanding, the spirit of counsel and
might, the spirit of knowledge and of the fear of the
Lord." John v. 19 and 36, " The Son can do nothing
of himself, but what he seeth the Father do : for what
things soever he doeth, these also doeth the son likewise." " The works which the Father hath given me
to finish, the same works that I do bear witness of me,
that the Father hath sent me." John vii. 16, " My
doctrine is not mine, but his that sent me." John
viii. 26, " He that sent me is true ; and I speak to the
world those things which I have heard of him." John
x. 25, " The works that I do in my Father's name,
they bear witness of me." And, moreover, because
the same Scriptures plainly show that Jesus Christ
was accustomed to ascribe all his divine words and
works, not to himself, nor to any divine nature which
he possessed distinct from the Holy Spirit, but to his
Father ; which renders it evident that the divine nature which some would claim for Christ must have
been

been wholly inactive and useless. Fourthly, because
Christ repeatedly prayed to the Father : whence it
is evident that he had not in himself a nature of that
kind which would have made him the supreme God.
For why should he have recourse to another person,
and supplicate of him, what he might have obtained
from himself? Fifthly, because Christ explicitly
declares, that he is not himself the ultimate object
of our Faith ; for he thus speaks, John xii. 44,
" He that believeth on me, believeth not on me,
but on Him that sent me." On this account Peter
(1st Epist. i. 21) states that it is " by Christ we do
believe in God." Sixthly, because Christ frequently
asserts that he came not of himself, but was sent by
the Father (John viii. 42). That he spoke not of
himself, but that the Father which sent him gave
him a commandment, what he should say, and what
he should speak (John xii. 49). That he came not
to do his own will, but the will of him that sent
him (John vi. 38). Neither of which could have
happened in respect to the supreme God. Seventhly, because Christ while he was yet living on
earth affirmed of himself, that he was ignorant of the
day of judgement ; and stated that the knowledge of
it was confined to the Father alone. " But of that
day and that hour knoweth no man, no, not the angels
which are in heaven, NEITHER THE SON, but the Father" (Mark xiii. 32. See also Matt. xxiv. 36). But
the supreme God could not have been wholly ignorant
of any thing. Eighthly, to omit other reasons, because Christ distinctly affirms (John xiv. 28), that his

Father

Father was greater than he—by which he intimates that he is not equal to his Father. He also, on several occasions, calls the Father his God. Matt. xxvii. 46; Mark xv. 34, " My God, my God, why hast thou forsaken me ?" John xx. 17, "I ascend unto my Father and your Father, to my God and your God." Revel. iii. 12, " Him that overcometh will I make a pillar in the temple of my God, and he shall go no more out; and I will write upon him the name of my God, and the name of the city of my God, which is New Jerusalem, which cometh down out of heaven from my God." The Father is called the God of Christ by other sacred writers, particularly by Paul: thus Ephes. i. 17, " The God of our Lord Jesus Christ, the Father of Glory," &c. And the same apostle observes (1 Cor. xi. 3), that God is the head of Christ; (1 Cor. iii. 23), that as we are Christ's, so in like manner, " Christ is God's." And (1 Cor. xv. 28), that at a certain period " the Son himself would be subject unto him, that had put all things under him :"—things which could not have been predicated of Christ, had he possessed a divine nature.

But to these arguments, and others of a similar kind, it is replied, that such things are spoken of Christ in reference to his human, and not his divine nature ?

But this is done without reason : partly because those who so assert, take for granted the very point in dispute; namely, that Christ is possessed of a divine nature;—and partly because there is no room for such

a di-

a distinction when any thing is absolutely, and without
any limitation, denied, or might be denied, concerning
Christ. For otherwise I might at one time be allowed to say, that Christ was not a man, that he did
not die, that he was not raised ; and at another, on
the contrary, that he was not the only begotten Son
of God, that he was not, as themselves pretend, the
supreme God, and that he was not possessed of this
divine nature :—because the former circumstances
would be incompatible with the divine, the latter
with human, nature. The reason of this is, that those
things which may be, and usually are, affirmed absolutely of any whole, without any limitation being expressly stated, cannot be denied absolutely of 'the
same whole, although in respect to some part those
things may not appertain to it. Thus when we affirm
absolutely that a man is tall, that he is corruptible,
that he eats and drinks, and the like ; we cannot at the
same time deny these things absolutely concerning him,
because they do not appertain to one, and that the
nobler part of him,—his soul.   Much less then ought
any thing to be denied absolutely concerning Christ,
which may be affirmed absolutely of him, although it
may not comport with his human nature, which is
infinitely inferior to the divine ; the more particularly
in those places where Christ is thought to be described and designated from his divine nature ; such
as when he is called " the Son," that is " of God."
It appears then, from these considerations, that that
cannot be affirmed absolutely of any whole which
may be denied absolutely of it ; and also, that things
cannot

ning of the Gospel.   In like manner John himself employs the word beginning, placed thus absolutely, in
the introduction to his First Epistle, at which beginning he states himself to have been present; and besides this, he uses the same term (λογος) Word, as if
he meant to be his own interpreter.   For there is no
reason why Jesus, whom, in his Gospel, John designates by the absolute term (λογος or) Word, should not
be here styled (ὁ λογος της ζωης) " the Word of life,"
because, as we learn from what follows, he conveyed
to us the tidings of eternal life, which, until that time,
had been buried in the counsels of the Father[9].   But

---

[9] I have stated in a preceding note what many of the ancients understood by ὁ λογος, or the Word.   Grotius comments
in nearly the same manner on this place, the Introduction to
John's Gospel, and confirms his interpretation under John
xvii. 5; and 1 John i. 1.   Socinus himself, with many others,
contends that the first verse of John's First Epistle (which
seems to correspond with the beginning of his Gospel) does
not relate to the person of the Son of God.   They who maintain that by λογος, with the article prefixed, the Son of God is
always designated, are greatly mistaken; so much so, that the
contrary, rather, may be asserted.   See only in the same Evangelist, John ii. 22; iv. 37, 41, 50; v. 24; vi. 60; vii. 36;
viii. 31, 37, 43, 51, 52, 55; xiv. 24; xv. 3, 20; xvii. 6, 14, 20;
xviii. 32; xix. 8; xxi. 23; and 1 John ii. 5, 7, &c.   In all these
instances ὁ λογος is clearly distinguished from the Son of God.

In the Old Testament, also, the Hebrew term דבר, Dabar, or
Word, is very far from denoting the Son of God, or any spiritual person.   See in reference to this subject Exodus ii. 15;
ix. 4, 5, 6; xii. 24; xxx. 17.   Numbers xv. 31; xxiii. 5, 16;
Deut. iv. 2; ix. 5; xviii. 20.   Josh. xi. 15; xxi. 45.   Judges
iii. 19, 20.   1 Sam. xvii. 29, 30.   2 Kings ii. 22.   In several of
these passages, besides, the word occurs with the article ה prefixed, הדבר.

The same may be observed of the Chaldee MIMRA Jehovah; as the author of a treatise on the Word of God (who is
said

But in what sense is it asserted that the Word was in the beginning of the Gospel?

In the following, that any one might learn that Jesus, even at the very beginning of the Gospel, was

---

said to have been William Vorstius) has demonstrated. Indeed, it is to be remarked, that the Chaldee Paraphrast expressly distinguishes Messiah from מימרא Mimra. For he thus renders Isaiah xlii. 1; " Behold my servant Messiah, I will uphold him my chosen, in whom my word (מימרא) delighteth. I will put my holy spirit upon him; he shall reveal my judgments to the people." In like manner, we find, in the introduction to the Book Sohar, that Chochamah, that is, Wisdom, (which is there used as synonymous with ὁ λογος), is never by the Cabbalists called Son: but Seir Anpin, which is found in Sephira Tiphereth, is by them constantly and properly rendered Son, or First-born. See the work above referred to, part ii. p. 80, 81, 185.

Jesus Christ, the Son of God, may, nevertheless, be correctly denominated ὁ λογος, on account of the Word of Life dwelling in him, in relation to his office. Moses is, by Philo Judæus, called νυς, that is, the purest mind, and Aaron is denominated by him ὁ λογος αὐτυ, or his word. Lib. de nom. mut. And he expresses himself in a similar manner elsewhere, Lib. quod det. pot. insid. soleat. Indeed, he calls Moses the PRINCE or CHIEF OF THE ANGELS, and THE MOST ANCIENT WORD. For he writes, that he who says, I will stand in the midst between you and the Lord (who was Moses, as evidently appears from Deut. v. 5) was, ὁ αρχαγγιλος και πρισβυτατος λογος. Lib. quis rer. div. hæres sit. With equal propriety, then, similar language might be used respecting the Messiah.

Besides what is stated above, the paraphrase of Schlichtingius on the beginning of John's Gospel, which is comprised in his Annotations on 1 Peter i. 20, deserves to be consulted; as also Brennius's notes on the same passage. It ought, moreover, to be considered, whether Luke, in the opening of his Gospel (chap. i. 2), when he says that the apostles were from the beginning eye witnesses and ministers τυ λογυ, of the word, did not mean to express the same thing as John has stated at the commencement of his Gospel, and of his First Epistle? B. WISSOWATIUS.

invested

comes ABRAHAM I am HE") is evident from those passages in this evangelist, where the same or similar forms of speech are found in the Greek. Thus chap. xiii. 19, " Now I tell you before it come, that when it is come to pass ye may believe that I am he." And xiv. 29, " And now I have told you before it come to pass, that when it is come to pass ye might believe."

What would be the sense of this reading?

It would be very excellent. For Christ admonishes the Jews, who sought to entrap him in his discourse, to believe that he was the light of the world, while yet an opportunity was afforded them, and before the divine favour, which he offered to them, was taken from them, and transferred to the Gentiles. For that the words I AM ($\varepsilon\gamma\omega$ $\varepsilon\iota\mu\iota$) are to be construed as if he had explicitly stated, " I am the light of the world," appears from the commencement of his address, verse 12,—and also from hence, that Christ twice designates himself by the same words, I AM or I AM HE ($\varepsilon\gamma\omega$ $\varepsilon\iota\mu\iota$), in verses 24 and 28. That the words " before Abraham was I am" mean what I have already intimated, may be shown from the signification of the name Abraham, which is on all hands agreed to denote THE FATHER OF MANY NATIONS. Genesis xvii. 5. But since he was not actually made the Father of many nations until after the grace of God having been manifested to the world by Christ, many nations had become, through faith, the sons of one Father, who was in token thereof called Abraham, —it is apparent that Christ might with propriety admonish the Jews to believe that he was the light of the world

world before Abraham should become the Father of many nations, and thus the divine grace be transferred from them to other nations.

It is not unusual in the sacred writings to render proper names significant of some circumstance in the condition of those to whom they are given. Thus in Ruth i. 20, " Call me not NAOMI (that is PLEASANT), call me MARA" (or BITTER). 1 Samuel xxv. 25, " As his name is, so is he ; NABAL (that is FOOL) is his name, and folly is with him." Isaiah viii. 10, " Speak the word and it shall not stand; for IMMANUEL, that is, GOD IS WITH US." Matt. xvi. 18, " Thou art PETER (that is a STONE), and on this ROCK," &c. Mark iii. 17, " He surnamed them BOANERGES;" which name, as it could not be understood in Greek, the evangelist translates, subjoining, " which is, THE SONS OF THUNDER." It may be added, that Christ might justly say that he was before Abraham, in as much as he was, by a divine appointment, before that age ; as was also HIS DAY, which, on this account, Abraham might in spirit have seen, and did see (John viii. 58), which was what Christ sought to prove [11].

What are the passages of Scripture from which it is inferred that Christ was begotten from eternity out of the essence of the Father ?

Chiefly the following :—Micah v. 2, " But thou,

[11] This last interpretation is given more at large by Schlichtingius, in his commentary on the place. Augustine and Beza confess that the words admit of this construction, and in this they are followed by Fricius Modrevius. *Syl.* i. *Tract.* i. *cap.* v. Grotius likewise is of the same opinion, and cites as parallel forms of speech, John xvii. 5 ; 1 Peter i. 20 ; Rev. xiii. 8. B. WISSOWATIUS.

Bethlehem

Bethlehem Ephratah, though thou be little among the thousands of Judah, yet out of thee shall he come forth unto me that is to be ruler in Israel; whose goings forth have been from of old, from everlasting." [*Et egressiones ejus ab initio, et a diebus seculi,* whose goings forth have been from the beginning, from the days of the age.] Psalm ii. 7, "Thou art my Son, this day have I begotten thee." Psalm cx. 3, "From the womb of the morning," &c. which the Vulgate renders—*Ex utero, ante Luciferum genui te,* "From the womb, before the morning star, have I begotten thee." Proverbs viii. 23, where Wisdom says of itself, "I was set up from everlasting, from the beginning, or ever the earth was."

What answer do you make to these testimonies?

Before I reply to these testimonies separately, it must be observed, that this generation out of the Father's essence involves a contradiction. For if Christ had been generated out of the essence of the Father, he must have taken either a part of it, or the whole. He could not have taken a part of it, because the divine essence is indivisible. Neither could he have taken the whole; for in this case the Father would have ceased to be the Father, and would have become the Son: and again, since the divine essence is numerically one, and therefore incommunicable, this could by no means have happened.

But what answer is to be given to the first of the scriptural testimonies, cited from Micah?

That this testimony states nothing whatever as to a generation from the essence of the Father; and by

no

no means proves a generation from eternity : for mention is made here of A BEGINNING and OF DAYS, which cannot apply to what is eternal: and the words which are rendered in the Vulgate " *a principio, a diebus æternitatis*"—" from the beginning, from the days of eternity,"—stand in the Hebrew " from of old, or from former time—from the days of age" [מימי עולם], but the " days of age" are the same as " days of old,"—as may be seen from the following passages : Isaiah lxiii. 9, " In his love and in his pity he redeemed them, and he bare them, and carried them all the days of old " [כל ימי עולם] ; Malachi iii. 4, " Then shall the offering of Judah and Jerusalem be pleasant unto the Lord, as in the days of old, and as in former years" [כימי עולם].   But that any thing should have been from of old, sometimes implies in the Scriptures that it had for a long period of time been noted and illustrious ; as appears from Jeremiah xxv. 5, "—dwell in the land which the Lord hath given unto you and to your fathers for ever and ever." And this holds particularly, when families are spoken of.   The meaning of the passage then is, that Christ should deduce the illustrious origin of his birth from a very remote antiquity—that is, from the time when God, after rejecting Saul, established a king and a regal family over his people—which was done in David; who was of Bethlehem, and was also the author of the stock and family of Christ : or, indeed, from Abraham himself, who was the first father and progenitor of the race of Israel [12].   What

---

[12] Calvin's observations on this passage are worthy perusal.
                                                                    But

What reply do you make to the second testimony, from Psalm ii. 7 ?

That it asserts nothing concerning the generation of Christ out of the essence of the Father, or of any eternal generation whatever : for since the words THIS DAY denote a fixed period of time, they cannot imply eternity. And that God has begotten him, does not prove that he begat him out of his own essence. This is evident from hence, that these very words, " this day have I begotten thee," were in their primary application spoken of David, who, certainly, was begotten neither from eternity, nor out of the essence of God: also because the apostle Paul quotes this passage to prove the resurrection of Christ : Acts xiii. 32, 33, " We declare unto you glad tidings, how that the promise which was made unto the fathers, God hath fulfilled the same unto us his children, in that he hath raised up Jesus again ; as it is also written in the second Psalm—Thou art my Son, this day have I begotten thee:" further, because the author of the Epistle to the Hebrews cites them in proof of the glorification of the Lord Jesus : Heb. i. 5, and v. 5, " For unto which of the angels said he at any time, Thou art my Son"&c. " Christ glorified not himself to be made an high priest, but he that said unto him, ' Thou art my Son,'" &c. and lastly, because it appears that God begets Sons otherwise than out of his own es-

But above all, the words which follow (Micah v. 4) ought to be noticed—namely, that " he shall feed in the strength of the Lord, in the majesty of the name of the Lord his God,"—which could with no propriety be spoken of the Eternal God. B. WISSOWATIUS.

sence,

sence, since the Scriptures state that believers are begotten of God. Thus, John i. 12, 13, " To them gave he power to become the Sons of God, even to them that believe on his name : which were born not of blood, nor of the will of the flesh, nor of the will of man, but of God." 1 John iii. 9, " Whosoever is born of God doth not commit sin, for his seed remaineth in him : and he cannot sin, because he is born of God." James i. 18, " Of his own will begat he us with the word of truth[13]."

What answer do you make to the third testimony, adduced from Psalm cx. 3 ?

It is to be remarked that this passage is incorrectly translated both in the Vulgate and the Greek versions : for the sense of the original Hebrew is, " from the womb of the morning thou hast the dew of thy birth," in which words David predicts of christians that they should multiply as the drops of the morning dew.

'What reply do you make to the fourth testimony, quoted from Proverbs viii. 23 ?

In order the more clearly to understand this subject, you must know that those who from this testimony would prove the generation of Christ from eter-

---

[13] That these words of the Psalmist refer to the resurrection of Christ from the dead, as they are interpreted by the apostle, (Acts xiii. 32, 33,) is admitted by Hilary, Ambrose, Calvin, and Paræus. ANDREW WISSOWATIUS.

But it ought to be remarked that the Chaldee Paraphrast instead of BEGETTING uses the word CREATING : for he thus renders the passage under consideration,(Psalm ii. 7,) " I will declare the promise which God hath spoken—My beloved, as a son is to his father, so art thou fair to me, as if this day I had created thee." B. WISSOWATIUS.

E   nity

nity, argue in the following manner :—The wisdom
of God is begotten from everlasting (Prov. viii. 23) :
Christ is the wisdom of God (1 Cor. i. 24) :—therefore
he is begotten from everlasting. But that this argument is not valid will appear from hence, that
Solomon speaks of the wisdom which existed in the
mind of God before all ages, which was afterwards
displayed in the Law, and through the Law communicated to mankind. On this account he does not add
to it the word GOD. But Paul calls Christ expressly
the Wisdom of God, and also the Power of God; because Christ crucified was a signal and illustrious effect and demonstration of the divine wisdom and
power :—and in like manner, on the contrary, Christ
crucified is styled, in respect to human wisdom and
power, the foolishness of God wiser than men, and
the weakness of God stronger than men. And thus
also, by a similar figure, the apostle a little before
(ver. 21) calls the workmanship of God in the creation
of the world, the wisdom of God. Hence it appears
that Solomon writes of a wisdom which neither is nor
could be a person : but only by a common figure (prosopopœia) introduces it as speaking; which figure is
so apparent in the words of Solomon, that no one can
fail to observe it who only reads what is declared respecting wisdom in the seventh, eighth, and ninth
chapters of this book. But Paul, by another well-
known figure (metonymy), speaks of a wisdom which
is a person. Besides, the words which are translated
"from everlasting" are in the Hebrew "from the age,"
or "from of old," [מעולם] *à seculo.* But it is one
thing

thing to have been from of old, and another to have been from eternity.   See Isaiah lxiv. 4 ; Jerem. ii. 20; Luke i. 70; and many other places[14].   Which

---

[14] That Solomon in this chapter (Prov. viii.) by no means speaks of the Son of God, but of the wisdom of God, by which he has created all things wisely (Prov. iii. 19, 20; Jer. x. 12; Psalm civ. 24), is admitted by many of the Fathers : as Athanasius, Basil, Gregory, Epiphanius, and Cyril. These things may also be understood of the wisdom which was afterwards displayed in the Law of God.—See the Apocryphal Books Ecclesiasticus xxiv. 8, 10, 25, &c.; Baruch iii. 37; iv. 1; and Wisdom of Solomon x., &c.   AN. WISSOWATIUS.

That things which are not persons, may by prosopopœia be spoken of personally, is evinced by the admirable discourse of the apostle (1 Cor. xiii.) concerning charity. Moreover, Christ is justly called, 1 Cor. i. 24, Σοφια Θευ (the Wisdom of God), on account of the treasures of wisdom and knowledge dwelling in him Col. ii. 3.   What Paul states, 1 Cor. i. 30, is also entitled to consideration, that " Christ is made unto us of God Wisdom," &c.[1]   B. WISSOWATIUS.

[1] [The following clause is added to the original in the English translation of the first edition of this Catechism.   It will serve to show the opinion of the old English Socinians respecting the Holy Spirit, which will be found more explicitly stated in the quarto Unitarian Tracts published about the close of the 17th century. They held that it was a created being, and the first in rank and dignity in the angelic hierarchy.—" Though we should admit, that by wisdome is understood a person, yet what hinders but that we may with far greater probability understand it of the Holy Spirit, who is called the Spirit of Wisdom, and hath the same things attributed to him that are ascribed to wisdome ?—See Isaiah xi. 1—5; Isaiah iv. 4; Exod. xxxi. 1—6, compared with Prov. viii. 12, 14, 15, 16, 20 ; and Gen. i. 2, compared with Prov. viii. 22, 29, 30.   Where it is observable, that Moses, describing the creation of the world, maketh mention of the Holy Spirit, but not of the Son of God ; who was as worthy to have been mentioned, and would accordingly have been expressed, had he been then present with God, as well as the Spirit.   Neither will it be amisse to cite the concurrent suffrages of holy men under the old covenant, whose writings, though put out of the Canon, as not found in the Hebrew, are

E 2   yet

Which are the passages of Scripture wherein names which properly belong to the one God, are thought to be given to Christ?

They are those wherein Jesus is supposed to be called, 1. Jehovah, Jer. xxiii. 6. 2. The Lord of Hosts, Zach. ii. 8. 3. The true God, 1 John v. 20. 4. The only Lord God, Jude 4. 5. The great God, Titus ii. 23. 6. The Lord Almighty, Rev. i. 8. 7. He who was and is and is to come, Rev. iv. 8. 8. God—who has purchased the Church with his own blood, Acts xx. 28. 9. God—who laid down his life for us, 1 John iii. 16.

What have you to urge by way of answer to these testimonies, severally; and in the first instance, to that from Jeremiah xxiii. 6, " And this is his name by which he shall be called, The Lord (JEHOVAH) our righteousness?"

I answer, first, That it cannot be hence proved that the name Jehovah is attributed to Christ: for these words ought to be applied to Israel, who is spoken of immediately before, in the very same verse, " In his days Judah shall be saved, and Israel shall dwell safely." This may easily be made to appear from what the same prophet states, chap. xxxiii. 15, 16, " In those days, and at that time, will I cause the branch of righteousness to grow up unto David; and

---

yet deservedly of great esteem among the people of God. For it is apparent from sundry passages, both of the Book of Wisdome, and that of Ecclesiasticus, that these writers, as they by Wisdome understood a creature, so did they conceive that creature to be the Spirit of God. See Wisdome vi. 24; i. 4—7; vii. 27; ix. 17, 18, 19; Ecclesiasticus xxiv. 12, 13, 14; i. 4, 5, 7, 8, 9."—p. 35, 36. TRANSL.]

he

he shall execute judgement and righteousness in the land.   And in those days shall Judah be saved, and Jerusalem shall dwell safely; and this is the name wherewith SHE shall be called—the Lord (JEHOVAH) our righteousness."   For, as commentators have observed, the pronoun (SHE) is in the Hebrew feminine, which must necessarily refer to Jerusalem, answering to Israel, in the passage before quoted (xxiii. 6). Hence it appears that in the place last mentioned the words " he shall be called" are spoken of Israel.— But though we were even to grant, that the name Jehovah might here be referred to Christ, yet it appears, from other considerations, that it could not be asserted that Christ was God : for otherwise it would follow that Jerusalem also was God.   For it must be understood that the whole clause " the Lord our righteousness" (JEHOVAH-TZIDKENU) is as it were converted into one name, and moreover given to a thing which is not God.   In the same manner, the mountain whereon Abraham was about to offer up his son is called, Gen. xxii. 14, " The Lord will see" or be seen, JEHOVAH-JIREH.   And the altar which Moses raised was called (Exod. xvii. 15) " the Lord (Jehovah) my exaltation," JEHOVAH-NISSI. And that which Gideon raised (Judges vi. 24) is called " The Lord send Peace," JEHOVAH-SHALOM. And lastly, to omit other passages, the city of Jerusalem is called by Ezekiel " a Lord to them."   Whether therefore the words in Jeremiah xxiii. 6 are to be understood of Christ, or of Israel, the meaning of them is, that the one Lord our God would then justify us : which, with

respect

respect to the Israelites, was accomplished by him, when Christ appeared.

What answer do you make to the second testimony, from Zachariah ii. 8?

The whole of the passage referred to is as follows: " Thus saith the Lord of Hosts, After the glory hath he sent me unto the nations which spoiled you; for he that toucheth you toucheth the apple of his eye." These words are applied, by a forced construction, to Jesus Christ, because it is thought to be here asserted, that the Lord of Hosts was sent by the Lord of Hosts: but they do not admit of such an interpretation, as is manifest from hence, that the words " after the glory hath he sent me" are uttered by another, that is by the angel who is conversing with the other angel and Zachariah, as plainly appears from the preceding part of the same chapter, beginning at the fourth verse, where this angel is introduced speaking. The same thing may also be perceived from hence, that the words which are here quoted, "he who touches the apple of his eye," must necessarily be those of the messenger, and not of the Lord of Hosts. For they are not here referred to the Lord of Hosts as if he had himself actually uttered them, but indirectly, as if he (the angel) had spoken in this manner: " Thus saith the Lord of Hosts—Because after the glory hath he sent me unto the nations which spoiled you, for he that toucheth you toucheth the pupil of his eye."

What answer do you make to the third testimony, from 1 John v. 20, where Christ is said to be called the TRUE GOD?

The

The whole verse runs thus :—" We know that the Son of God is come, and has given us an understanding, that we may know him that is true, and we are in him that is true, even in his Son Jesus Christ. This is the true God, and eternal life."   Now I deny that the words " this is the true God" refer to the Son of God :—Not that I deny that Christ is, in his sense of the terms, a true God, but that he is that true God who is spoken of in this passage.   Because Christ is in no instance styled absolutely God (ὁ Θεος) with the article, or the true God ; and in this very passage, as also in like manner in John xvii. 3, he is clearly distinguished from the only true God.   Neither will it at all serve our adversaries, who would have the words " this is the true God" applied to Christ, that he had been mentioned just before; for relative pronouns, such as THIS, &c. do not always refer to the nearest antecedent, but frequently to the principal subject matter under discussion, although more remote.   This appears from the following examples :—Acts vii. 18, 19, " Till another king arose, which knew not JOSEPH, THE SAME dealt subtilly with our kindred."   Acts x. 6, " He (Peter) lodgeth with one SIMON, a tanner, whose house is by the sea side, HE shall tell thee what thou oughtest to do."   2 John 7, " Many deceivers are entered into the world, who confess not that JESUS CHRIST is come in the flesh ; THIS is a deceiver and an antichrist." From these passages it appears that the relative pronoun does not refer to the persons forming the proximate, or nearest antecedent, but to those who

are

are more remote. And besides, if these words, " this is the true God," are referred to Jesus Christ, John would assert that Jesus Christ was the son of himself, for he calls him the Son of that true God. The placing of the true God in opposition to idols, in the twenty-first verse, shows that in scriptural phraseology not Christ but the Father of Christ is indicated[15].

What answer do you make to the fourth testimony from Jude, ver. 4, "denying the only Lord (δεσποτην) God, and our Lord Jesus Christ?"

It is attempted to be proved from this clause, that since in the Greek there is but one article prefixed to both the titles, they ought, conformably to a rule of Greek composition, to be considered as designating one person only, that is Jesus Christ. But it must be remarked that this rule is not always followed by Greek writers; and the circumstances of the case must determine where it does not apply. That this rule does not extend to all cases, is proved by several examples in the New Testament itself. Thus Matt. xxi. 12, " And Jesus went into the temple of God and cast out all them that sold and bought:" where in the Greek only one article is prefixed to the two words SOLD and BOUGHT. Matt. xvi. 1, " The Pharisees

---

[15] It ought to be remarked, that the Son of God is here expressly distinguished from the true God, (who, according to the same apostle, John xvii. 3, is the Father alone,) to the knowledge of whom he is said to conduct us. It is therefore necessary that the following words, which exhibit a mode of repetition usual with John, should be understood of the Father; as Erasmus and Grotius rightly observe. See also Schlichtingius on the place. B. WISSOWATIUS.

also

also with the Sadduces." Chap. xvii. 1, "Jesus taketh
Peter, James, and John." Ephes. ii. 20; iii. 5, "The
apostles and prophets." Heb. ix. 19, "The blood of
calves and goats." In all these cases, to omit many
others, one article only is prefixed, which clearly shows
that this is not a perpetual rule, because the subjects
are only coupled together in the sentence. The
reader may be referred besides, for other examples, to
Ephes. v. 5; 2 Thess. i. 12; 1 Tim. v. 21.

What answer do you make to the fifth testimony,
taken from Titus ii. 13, " Looking for that blessed
hope, and the glorious appearing of THE GREAT GOD
AND OUR SAVIOUR JESUS CHRIST ?"

It is attempted to be shown on two grounds that
the epithet " the great God" in this passage ought
to be referred to Christ. First, because the rule already referred to, respecting the construction of two
or more substantives, with only a single article prefixed, requires it to be so applied ;—and secondly, because it is the coming of the SON, and not of the FA-
THER, that we are looking for. The former of these
reasons has already been obviated, in the answer to
the preceding question. To the latter it is replied,
that Paul does not write (as in the English translation)
" looking for the glorious appearing of the great God,"
but "looking for the appearing of the glory of the great
God" ($\epsilon\pi\iota\varphi\alpha\nu\epsilon\iota\alpha\nu$ $\tau\eta\varsigma$ $\delta o\xi\eta\varsigma$ $\tau o\upsilon$ $\mu\epsilon\gamma\alpha\lambda o\upsilon$ $\Theta\epsilon o\upsilon$). Now
that it may be truly said, that the glory of God will
appear when Christ shall come to judgement, is evident from the declaration of our Lord, that " he shall
come in glory," that is, in the glory of God his Fa-
B 5   ther.

ther. There is, however, no impropriety in saying
that God the Father will come, or rather will appear,
when the Son shall come to judge the world. For
will not Christ, in judging the world, sustain and represent the person of God the Father, as the sovereign
from whom he will have derived his judicial office?

What answer do you make to the sixth testimony,
from Revelations iv. 8, " Holy, holy, holy Lord God
Almighty, which was, and is, and is to come ?"

This passage is referred to Christ, because it is assumed that no one is " to come" but he ; who is to
appear again to judge the quick and dead. But the
word ($εϱχομενος$) which is here rendered " to come,"
may with equal propriety be rendered TO BE. Thus
John xvi. 13, our Lord says of the spirit which he
promised to the apostles, that " he would show them
things TO COME, or TO BE." And Acts xviii. 21,
we read of a feast that was TO COME, or TO BE. In
both these places the Greek word is $εϱχομενος$—ven-
turus—(to BE hereafter). Besides, who does not
see that since in the former clauses the words are
" who WAS, and who IS," the third clause ought to
be rendered " and who IS TO BE ;" in order that the
whole passage may be understood of existence ; and
not the first two of existence, and the last of a future
appearance? Nor is there an individual who does
not perceive that the eternity of God is the subject
which the writer had in his mind, and which comprehends all past, present, and future time. But what
must serve still more clearly to expose this gross er-
roi is the following passage in Rev. i. 4, 5, " Grace
be

be unto you, and peace, from him which is, which was, and which is to come (or to be), and from the seven spirits which are before the throne, and from Jesus Christ who is the faithful witness." Whence it appears that Jesus Christ is a being wholly distinct from him who is, and who was, and who is to be, or, agreeably to the Greek idiom, "who is to come."

What reply do you make to the seventh testimony, deduced from Acts xx. 28, "Take heed unto yourselves, and to all the flock over the which the Holy Ghost hath made you overseers—TO FEED THE CHURCH OF GOD, which he hath purchased with his own blood?"

In reference to this passage, I answer, that the word GOD, here inserted, may and indeed ought to be understood of God the Father: both because the article is prefixed to it, even though the word is put subjectively, which is never the case when it is applied to Christ; and because in this very address Christ is throughout distinguished from God (ver. 21, 24). In the next place, the apostle calls the blood which Christ shed, God the Father's own blood, for this reason,—that whatever any one possesses through the gift of another, and is as such lawfully his own, may nevertheless still be said to be the property of him from whom it was obtained. Whatever Christ was, he was through the gift or appointment of God, and he possessed nothing which he had not received from God, and which did not, of right, still belong to him. It may therefore be said that Christ's blood was God's own blood, especially if we consider in what manner it was shed for us,—because it was shed as the blood

of

of the lamb of God, that is, of such a victim as God
provided, as it were of himself, to take away the sins
of the world.   It may be added, that the blood of
Christ may with propriety be called God's own blood,
in as much as that Christ was God's own Son, begotten
of him by the Holy, Spirit.   Nor must it be omitted,
that in the Syriac version the words OF CHRIST, and
not OF GOD, occur in this place[16].   In some Greek
manuscripts also LORD AND GOD are inserted : the
word God being added to Lord in order to intimate
that Christ was in such a sense made Lord by the
Father, that the title God might with propriety be
ascribed to him ; that by this means the dignity of his
church and the excellence of his blood might appear
so much the more conspicuously.   Agreeably to this interpretation besides, Thomas, if he addressed those
words to Christ, was not satisfied with calling him Lord,
but styled him also God, that he might acknowledge,
not his ordinary, but his divine, authority over him.

What answer do you make to the eighth testimony,

---

[16] It is thus that Jerome quotes this passage in his Commentary on Titus.   A. WISSOWATIUS.

That very ancient Greek MS. of Thecla, as Grotius observes,
reads τυ Κυριυ. of the Lord. So also the Armenian version reads
" the Church of the Lord," as a bishop of Armenia informed
Sandius, as Cingallus states in his *Scriptura S. Trin. Revela-*
trix, p. 138.[m]   B. WISSOWATIUS.

[m] [Griesbach has inserted του κυριυ, "of the Lord," in his text
as the genuine reading,—a substitution which is demanded by
the concurrent authority of the most ancient and best manuscripts which are extant of the New Testament. The common
reading is supported by no manuscript or version of great antiquity or value. See Griesbach and the Improved Version on the
place.   The MS. of Thecla referred to by Grotius is the celebrated *Codex Alexandrinus* in the British Museum. TRANSL.]

from

from 1 John iii. 16—"Hereby perceive we the love of
GOD, because he laid down his life for us ?"

In the first place, I must inform you that the word
GOD is not found in any Greek copy, except the
Complutensian; nor does it occur in the Syriac version.   But if this word were found in every copy,
would it therefore follow that the pronoun HE (εχεινος)
must be referred to God ?   Certainly not; and this
not only for the reason which I have already noticed,
in answer to the third testimony,—that words of this
class do not always refer to the proximate antecedent, or the nearest person,—but also because John,
in this very chapter, twice applies the Greek pronoun
εχεινος to Christ, although his name does not appear
for some time before, as may be seen in the fifth and
seventh verses, where he writes, " Ye know that he
(εχεινος) was manifested," &c.   And " even as HE,
εχεινος, is," &c.   The same occurs in chap. iv. 17.
And indeed this pronoun, if its proper and customary
signification be attended to, will be seen to have reference, not to the person who is named immediately
before, but to one who has been noticed more re-
motely, or even not at all.   The meaning of this passage, therefore, is, that the love of God is perceived in
this, that Christ his son laid down his life for us.

You have satisfied me so far as respects the names
of Jesus Christ :—I now wish you to explain those testimonies relating to works and operations which our
adversaries imagine to be ascribed to Christ in the
Scriptures ?

These testimonies are those in which, in their apprehension,

prehension, the Scriptures inculcate concerning Christ, 1. That he created heaven and earth with all things. 2. That all created things are preserved by him. 3. That he conducted the children of Israel out of Egypt, dwelt with them in the wilderness, leading them on their way, and acted as their benefactor. 4. That his glory was seen by Isaiah. 5. That he became incarnate.

State what those testimonies are whereby they conceive it to be proved that Christ created heaven and earth ?

They are the following :—John i. 3, " All things were made by him, and without him was not any thing made that was made." Again, ver. 10, " The world was made by him." Coloss. i. 16, " By him were all things created, that are in heaven, and that are in earth, visible and invisible, whether they be thrones, or dominions, or principalities, or powers ; all things were created by him and for him." Heb. i. 2, " By whom he made the worlds." And lastly, the words of the Psalmist, quoted Heb. i. 10, 11, 12, " Thou, Lord, in the beginning hast laid the foundation of the earth, and the heavens are the works of thine hands. They shall perish, but thou remainest ; and they all shall wax old as doth a garment, and as a vesture shalt thou fold them, and they shall be changed; but thou art the same, and thy years shall not fail."

What answer do you make to the first of these testimonies, John i. 3?

In the first place, the word here used is not CREATED, but MADE :—which I notice, lest any one should

understand

understand by creation the production of something out
of nothing.   Secondly, John writes, " All things were
made BY HIM," (*per eum*) ; a form of speech employed to
denote not the person who is the first cause of any
thing, but him who is the second cause, or medium.
Nor, indeed, can it be said that all things were made
by Christ in any other sense, than that God had made
them by him, as appears from Ephes. iii. 9, where the
apostle writes, according to the Greek, that God
" created all things by Jesus Christ" (διὰ Ιησου Χρι-
στου). From this very passage, also, it clearly appears
that the writer treats not of the first creation of all
things, but of a second creation : because in the account of the first creation there is no direct mention
of any person by whom God effected the great work,
as we find to be done in respect to the second creation.
Lastly, the words ALL THINGS are not to be here understood of all objects whatever, but are to be restricted to the subject matter of discourse, as is most
commonly done in other cases in the sacred writings,
and particularly in the New Testament.   A remarkable instance of this kind occurs 2 Cor. v. 17, where
the apostle has under his consideration the very subject of which the evangelist John is treating, and
where he states "ALL THINGS are become," or made,
" new ;" though it is apparent that there existed many
things which were not then new made.   As then the
subject matter of which John is treating is the gospel,
it follows that the terms ALL THINGS are to be understood of those objects merely which pertain to the new
creation effected under the gospel.

Why

Why does John add, "and without him was not any thing made ?"

This clause was subjoined, the better to illustrate the preceding declaration that " by him all things were made."   For these words seem to affirm generally that all things were done immediately by the Word itself, although some of them, and those too of great importance, were not effected personally by himself, but by means of the apostles, such as the calling of the Gentiles, and the abolition of legal ceremonies. For though these things originated in the discourses and proceedings of the Lord Jesus, they were not effected immediately by Jesus Christ himself, but afterwards by his apostles; not, however, without him. For the apostles did all things in his name and by his authority; as he declares John xv. 7, " Without me ye can do nothing."

Why, again, does John superadd the words, " That was made,"—for can any thing be made which is not made?

In order to show, not that all things that exist were made by God through the instrumentality of this word, which is Christ, but that all things which were made were made through him:—an evident proof that he does not speak of the old and first creation, wherein all things that are, were made by God ;—but of the new, in relation to which many things exist that were not made, since they do not pertain to it.[n]

What

---

[n] [As the distinction observed in this reply between things that EXIST, and things that ARE MADE, may not seem very intelligible to the reader, the original question and answer are subjoined.

Quo

What answer do you make to the second testimony from John i. 10, " The world was made by him ?"

First, that the evangelist does not state here, that the world was CREATED, the word creation being understood to mean production out of nothing,—but, that it was MADE. Secondly, he adopts a mode of expression which denotes an intermediate cause ;— "the world," he says, "was made BY (through) HIM." Thirdly, the term WORLD, like others which in the Scriptures are used in precisely the same sense, denotes not only heaven and earth, but, besides its other significations, designates the human race generally; as may be seen in the very verse under consideration, where the writer states, "he was in the world, and the world knew him not:" so likewise, John xii. 19, " Behold, the world is gone after him :" it is also used for the future world, to which Paul refers, Rom. iv. 13, where, speaking of Abraham, he observes, that " the promise that he should be the heir of the world, was not to him, or to his seed through the law." It is this world that Peter also has in view, 2 Pet. iii. 13, when he states that christians are " looking for new heavens and a new earth." So likewise the author of the epistle to the Hebrews in the

---

Quo vero fine addidit, quod factum est ? An enim aliquid fieri potuit quod factum non est ?

Ut doceret non omnia quæ sint per Sermonem hunc, qui Christus est, a Deo facta esse, sed omnia quæ facta sint, per eum esse facta ; evidenti documento, non agere ipsum de creatione illa vetere et prima, in qua omnia quæ sunt, a Deo facta sint, sed de nova, cujus respectu multa sunt quæ facta non sunt, quippe ad eam non pertinentia. TRANSL.]

following

following passage, (Heb. i. 6,) " And again, when he
bringeth in the first begotten into the world, he saith,
And let all the angels of God worship him." That
this writer intends here the future world, is confirmed
by what he observes in the second chapter of this epistle and the fifth verse—"For unto the angels hath
he not put into subjection the world to come, whereof we speak." But he has no where spoken of it
except in the passage just quoted, from the sixth verse
of the first chapter. There is, besides, another passage (chap. x. ver. 5), where, speaking of Christ, he
says, " Wherefore, when he cometh into the world he
saith, Sacrifice and offering thou wouldest not, but a
body hast thou prepared me." Here, since it is obvious that he speaks of the world, in which, after he
had entered upon it, Christ exercised all the func-
tions of a priest, as all the circumstances demonstrate, it is also apparent that he has reference not to
the present, but to the future world ; especially since
he says of Christ (chap. viii. 4), that " if he were on
earth, he should not be a priest."

What then do you understand by this declaration,
" And the world was made by him ?"

The words admit of two interpretations :—First,
that the human race were renovated, reformed, restored, and as it were new made, by Christ ; because
he had conveyed eternal life to them while they were
in a lost condition, and obnoxious to eternal death ;
and had imparted to them the most efficient motives to
return to God whom they had forsaken. In reference
to this John reproves the world, because that after ·

Christ

Christ had delivered it from destruction, and had il-
lumined it with the light of the gospel, it did not acknowledge him, but had spurned and rejected him.
For it is agreeable to the Hebrew language, that in
such forms of speech the words to make, and to create,
should have the same meaning as to make anew,
and recreate; because that language is destitute of
what are called compound verbs.   The second interpretation is, that the future world, which we expect,
is, as to us, made by Christ; as it is also called future
in respect to us, though now present to Christ and the
angels.

What answer do you make to the third testimony,
Coloss. i. 16, " By him were all things created, &c. ?"

Besides that the apostle speaks here of Christ as
an intermediate or secondary cause, the verb to create
is used in Scripture not only with reference to the old,
but also to the new creation.   Of this you have an
instance, Ephes. ii. 10, " For we are his workmanship, CREATED (κτισθεντες) in Christ Jesus unto good
works:" and a little further on (ver. 15) " to make"
or " create" (κτιση) in himself of twain one new man."
So likewise James i. 18, which is commonly understood to refer to the new creation, " Of his own will
begat he us with the word of truth, that we should be
a kind of first fruits of his creatures" (κτισματων).
Moreover, that the expressions, "all things in heaven
and earth," are not here used for all objects whatever, appears not only from the words of Paul further
on, (ver. 20,) where he states that " God by him
(Christ) reconciled all things unto himself, whether
                                                                they

they be things in earth or things in heaven;" but also from this very passage itself; wherein the apostle does not say that heaven and earth were created, but only all those things which are in heaven and earth.

. What then do you understand by this testimony ?

That all things in heaven and on earth are ordered by Christ, and by him transformed into a new state or condition ; and this, because God has appointed him to be the head both of angels and of men, who before acknowledged God alone as their sovereign ; whence has followed a new order of things among all beings endued with intelligence [17].

What

---

[17] That this passage of the epistle to the Colossians ought to be interpreted of the new creation, may be proved by the three following arguments :—First, A reason is here assigned, why Christ is called "the first born of every creature." Now, since the first born is of the number of those of whom he is called the first born ; and as Christ cannot, in reference to the old creation, be understood to be the first among created beings, many generations having intervened between Adam and him ; it follows, that he must be so designated in reference to the new creation, which commenced from him ;—and to this creation the reason of this designation is accommodated.

Secondly, What are here stated to be created by Christ are not heaven and earth and all the things which they contain, conformably to the language used elsewhere, when the old creation is spoken of,—but only rational natures ; as being alone susceptible of a new creation. .

Thirdly, The very enumeration of the things created by him sufficiently shows that the new creation is here spoken of. For with respect to "things in heaven," the angels are indeed said to have been created by him, but under the names of " thrones, and dominions, and principalities, and powers ;" which are not names of simple existences, but of dignities with which the Lord honours them; just as we say that a king, a prince, or a consul, has been created, not when he is born, but when he is so designated.

What answer do you make to the fourth testimony, Heb. i. 2, "By whom he made the worlds?" I ob-

---

signated. What is comprehended in the creation of "things in earth," and in what manner it is effected, may be seen from the eighteenth verse, where the church of Christ alone is mentioned, "He is the head of the body, the church:" and by this also the new creation is connected with Christ in the nineteenth and twentieth verses, since God is said to fill all things by him, and by him to have "reconciled all things to himself," he "having made peace through the blood of his cross," between those things which are in heaven and those which are on earth— things which cannot be referred to the old creation. The reader may compare with this the parallel passage, Ephes. i. 10, "That in the dispensation of the fulness of times, he might gather together in one all things in Christ, both which are in heaven, and which are on earth." It may not be foreign from the purpose to have stated the above reasons for the better understanding of the real meaning of this text. M. RUARUS.

[On the above note Schlichtingius remarks]—I concur in opinion that it may be of use to state here the reasons above given, except that in the third reason, those titles of dignities should appear to be inserted not to intimate that Christ conferred those dignities on the angels—for whence does this appear?—but to show that the highest and chief angels are not exempted from the creation made by him, since they also are obliged to acknowledge him for their head. It is in the (ανακεφαλαιωσει) "gathering together of all things in Christ," that this creation chiefly consists: Ephes. i. 10. I. SCHLICHTINGIUS.

That this creation was made by Christ as MAN is admitted by Athanasius, Cyril, Fulgentius, Salmero, Arias Montanus, &c. Piscator's observations on this passage may also be consulted. A. WISSOWATIUS.

Procopius Gazæus, in his observations on the first chapter of Genesis, thus interprets this passage of the epistle to the Colossians—" Omnia per illum condita sunt, sive quæ in terra sunt, sive quæ in cœlis: id est, RENOVATA, et in integrum RESTITUTA. "By him were all things created that are in heaven and that are in earth:—that is, RENOVATED, and RESTORED to their pristine state." Grotius likewise writes to the same purpose; and his observations should by all means be consulted.

See

I observe, that what is here explicitly stated, not that Christ made the worlds, but that God made them by him ; may be asserted in reference to mankind, or understood of the world. to come.   And in what sense both the human race and the world to come may be said to have been made through Christ, I have already explained in my observations on the second testimony, John i. 10.   That the original creation of this world is not intended here, is evident from this, that the same writer asserts that God made the worlds by him " whom he had appointed heir of all things ;" but it is evident this was no other than the MAN JESUS. Besides, the very order of the words proves that these worlds were made subsequently to his being appointed the heir of all things ; and that this was not done till after his resurrection, is declared in several passages of the holy scriptures[18].

                                        What

See also his prolegomena to the gospels, and his annotations on Ephes. i. 10; ii. 10; iii. 9; James i. 18; Rev. iii. 14; iv. 11. Grotius remarks that Chrysostom explains this passage to mean that the world was created on account of Christ.   The interpretation given of it by John Simplicius, in his Articles of Faith, § 6, may also be consulted.   This agrees with the explanation which Schlichtingius has proposed in his observations on the introduction to John's gospel, inserted in his commentary on 1 Pet. i. 20.[o]   B. WISSOWATIUS.

  [o] [Modern Unitarians concur with the authors of this Catechism, and the above annotators, in interpreting this passage of the new moral creation effected by Jesus Christ, by means of his gospel.   The reader may consult, on this subject, in addition to the authorities above referred to, an admirable essay on the creation of all things by Jesus Christ, inserted in Commentaries and Essays, vol. ii. p. 9; and also a Discourse by the Rev. Russell Scott of Portsmouth, on the same subject.   TRANSL.]

  [18] Grotius remarks that in his opinion this passage may with-
                                        out

What answer do you make to the fifth testimony, from Psalm cii. 25, &c. quoted Heb. i. 10, 11, 12, " Thou, Lord, in the beginning hast laid the foundation of the earth," &c. ?.

To this testimony I reply, that these words of the Psalmist, which were spoken of the one supreme God, are by this author applied to Christ only so far as they pertain to the scope of his argument.   For it must be observed that the discourse in this testimony refers not to one subject only, but to three distinct subjects :—First, the creation of the heavens and the earth; secondly, the destruction of all created things ; and thirdly, the endless duration of God. Now that the writer does not refer the first of these to Christ is hence evident, that he proposes to himself, in this chapter, to prove the pre-eminence of Christ,—not that pre-eminence by which he would himself be the supreme God, but that which through the divine favour he " obtained by inheritance," and whereby he was made " better than the angels,"—

---

out harshness be rendered, *propter quem mundum fecit*, " on whose account he made the world." And he shows in his commentary on this place, and on Heb. i. 10, that it was understood and believed among the Jews that the world had been created with a view to the Messiah. This interpretation would be more accordant with the bearing of the apostle's observations, and better harmonize with the preceding context :—that the son of God was for this reason appointed the heir of all things, that God had for, or with a view to, him, made the ages, or the world.   For the Greek preposition *δια* with a genitive case may be rendered FOR, or " WITH A VIEW TO," as appears from a passage of Gregory Nazianzen, which, among others, is usually quoted as an example in the Lexicons.   Δι' ἡμαν την ανθρωποτητα Θεος ὑπερη.   B. WISSOWATIUS.

which

which is to be dated from that time when he sat down at the right hand of God, as clearly appears from the third and fourth verses. For he thus expresses himself, " He sat down on the right hand of the majesty on high, being made so much better than the angels, as he hath by inheritance obtained a more excellent name than they." Since then the kind of superiority here specified, neither is, nor can be, the creation of heaven and earth, it is apparent that the words of the Psalmist were not cited by this author with the view of proving that this creation was the work of Christ.—But to explain this matter somewhat more at large.—Since it appears that these words of the Psalmist were addressed to the one supreme God, if they were applied by the author to the Hebrews, to Christ, in the sense contended for, he must have done it either that he might declare Christ to be that one supreme God, or that he might set him forth as joined with and subordinate to God. But the first cannot have been the case; because, if this fact was at the time known to those Hebrews, what occasion could there have been for their requiring these additional proofs of the pre-eminence of Christ? But if it was unknown, then this point ought the rather to have been proved and demonstrated from the scriptures. For it would have been absurd, tacitly and without evidence to assume that to be already known wherein the chief pre-eminence of Christ consisted, and which is most difficult of belief, while that which is greatly inferior in dignity, and more credible, is advanced with so much care, and

with

with so many scriptural proofs. But further :—Let it
now be supposed that Christ was the one supreme
God—what more would this scriptural testimony
prove, than that He who is the one supreme God,
created heaven and earth ? a position concerning
which, assuredly, there never was any question. Moreover, if it were assumed that Christ was the one supreme
God, there could remain no ground for the comparison
which the author institutes between him and the angels.   For to what purpose would it be to compare,
in respect to pre-eminence, the one supreme God,
the creator of all things, with the angels, his own creatures ?   Lastly, The writer would in this case himself overturn the very thing which he had undertaken
to establish.   For was there ever a time when this one
supreme God was made better or more excellent than
any created beings ?   The second case then which
I have stated must be asserted, namely—that the
words of the Psalmist are applied by this author to
Christ, because he is in the things enumerated
joined with and subordinate to God.   But this junction and subordination have no reference to the old
creation of the heavens and the earth, which is spoken
of in these words of the Psalmist: for in the old creation
God had no one joined with and subordinate to him.
To suppose this would also be assuming what ought
much rather to be proved than the very thing
for the establishment of which this testimony is adduced, and the taking of which for granted would in
like manner destroy the comparison here instituted
between Christ and the angels. For if Christ was sub-

ordinate to God in the creation of heaven and earth,
there can be no doubt but that he was also subordinate to him in the creation of the angels; and thus
the angels, no less than the heavens and the earth,
would be his creatures. Lastly, this also would destroy the very position towards the establishment of
which all the observations of the writer are directed;
namely, that Christ, after he had sat down at the right
hand of the majesty on high, was made better than the .
angels. For in this case he would have been made
more excellent than the angels, not first at this particular period, but before the creation of all things. Now
if the author take neither of these things for granted,
how could he refer to Christ the declaration of Scripture, which ascribes the creation of heaven and earth
to God, in either of the senses I have mentioned?
What could he, by the citation of this testimony, prove
to those persons who admit neither of the cases I have
stated?—It remains then, that we are to consider
these words to be referred to Christ in so far as he
is in the other particulars, that is in the destruction
of heaven and earth, subordinate t God, and united
to him in the perpetuity of his future existence:—
these, in arguing with Hebrew Christians, the author
might with propriety state as indisputable facts. For
with respect to the first, it is certain, both from the
testimony I have already cited, and from other declarations of Scripture, that Christ will reign as long as
heaven and earth and the existing age shall endure:—
on which account the destruction of heaven and earth
cannot be effected except under his reign, and accordingly

ingly by his own act. For it was no less known to the Hebrews, that those things which God was to perform during the reign of the Messiah, with a view to the salvation of his people and the punishment of the wicked (to which events the destruction of heaven and earth refers), were to be performed by the Messiah, whom for this purpose he had constituted the King and Lord of all things. And since God has put all things in subjection to Christ, who can doubt but that heaven and earth are his; and that therefore, if they are to be destroyed, they must be destroyed by Christ?—With respect to the perpetuity of his future existence, this was also not at all doubted by them; for they believed that the Messiah would abide for ever, and acknowledge that when raised from the dead, and received into heaven, he should live a celestial life with God. This then is the reason why the author deservedly, and in an appropriate sense, applies to Christ the words that were by the Psalmist addressed to God; which he does very properly and seasonably after the declaration, which has already been noticed, that the throne of Christ was to endure for ever and ever: that is to say, that he might show that, so far from the existence of Christ terminating with the end of the age during which he is to reign, it is he who is to put an end to that age, and to destroy heaven and earth,—whilst he himself will live and remain through all eternity. This certainly comprises the most conclusive proof of his superiority to angels: for, while in respect to their immortality he is in nothing their inferior, he is in regard to the power and authority implied in the de-

struction

struction of heaven and earth, far more excellent and divine[p].

But if the former part of this passage, in which the creation of heaven and earth is spoken of, have no reference to the design of the writer to the Hebrews, how happens it that he did not omit the clause ?

On this account; that the other parts, which are applicable to his argument, are connected with this by pronouns and adjectives:—As " THEY shall perish;" " ALL shall wax old;" "thou shalt fold THEM, and THEY shall be changed," &c., and he chose to repeat the whole enumeration rather than change the words of Scripture, and substitute the nouns for the adjectives and pronouns.

Have you any other similar examples of this practice ?

They are indeed sufficiently common among all writers both sacred and profane. Take for one instance Matt. xii. 18—21, " 18 Behold my servant whom I have chosen, my beloved in whom my soul is well pleased: I will put my spirit upon him, and he shall show judgment to the Gentiles. 19 He shall not strive nor cry; neither shall any man hear his voice in the streets. 20 A bruised reed shall he not break, and smoking flax shall he not quench, till he send

---

p [Few modern Unitarians, if any, would, I apprehend, subscribe to the preceding interpretation. The words of the Psalmist are understood by them to be quoted by the writer to the Hebrews with no other view than to prove the lasting or permanent duration of the spiritual sovereignty of Christ, from the immutability of God, who was the founder and is the supporter of his kingdom. TRANSL.]

forth

forth judgement unto victory.   21 And in his name
shall the Gentiles trust.".   In this quotation (from
Isaiah xlii. 1, &c.) it is sufficiently apparent, that the
nineteenth verse alone applies to the evangelist's purpose, which was to account for Christ's prohibition,
contained in the sixteenth verse, that those whom he
healed "should not make him known."   We have
another instance, Acts ii. 17—21.   17 "And it shall
come to pass in the last days, saith God, I will pour
out of my spirit upon all flesh: and your sons and your
daughters shall prophesy, and your young men shall
see visions, and your old men shall dream dreams:
18 And on my servants, and on my handmaidens,
I will pour out in those days of my spirit ; and they
shall prophesy: 19 And I will show wonders in heaven above, and signs in the earth beneath ; blood and
fire, and vapour of smoke : 20 The sun shall be turned into darkness, and the moon into blood, before the
great and notable day of the Lord come : 21 And it
shall come to pass that whosoever shall call on the name
of the Lord shall be saved."   In this quotation (from
Joel ii. 28, &c.) it is obvious that only the seventeenth and eighteenth verses are pertinent to the apostle Peter's observations, which went to show that the
Holy Spirit had fallen on the disciples of Christ.
Again, in the same chapter of the Acts, verses 25—
27.   25 "I foresaw the Lord always before my face,
for he is on my right hand, that I shall not be moved.
26 Therefore did my heart rejoice, and my tongue
was glad : moreover also my flesh shall rest in hope:
27 Because thou wilt not leave my soul in hell [HADES,

the grave] neither wilt thou suffer thine holy one to
see corruption:" in which quotation (from Psalm
xvi. 8, &c.) it is apparent that the twenty-seventh
verse alone bears upon the subject; since it was the
apostle's aim to prove that it was not possible that
Christ should be detained by death.   Lastly, in the
very chapter under our consideration (Heb. i. 9.) it is
manifest that the words, "Thou hast loved righteousness and hated iniquity," have no connection with
what the apostle undertakes to prove, which is, that
Christ was made better than the angels.

I wish to know whether there be any other instances
of words spoken of one person, being applied to another on account of some subordination or likeness?

You need not go beyond this chapter in search of
examples of this kind, as you may find some in the
context of the words which I have last quoted: for
in the sixth verse, words which in another Psalm
(xcvii. 7) are spoken of God, "Let all the angels
worship him," are applied to Christ for no other
reason than because he is subordinate to God in religious worship.   For the angels cannot worship God,
as I shall hereafter show, without first worshipping
him to whom God has subjected both themselves and
the world they inhabit: and on the other hand, in
worshipping Christ they worship God himself. Again,
in the seventh verse ("who maketh his angels
spirits, and his ministers a flame of fire") words
which in another Psalm (civ. 4,) are spoken of winds
and storms, and lightnings that dart along the heavens, are applied to angels on account of some ima-
gined

gined similitude. You may refer also to Acts xiii. 47, where the prediction of Isaiah concerning Christ, Is. xlix. 6, (" I have set thee to be a light of the Gentiles, that thou shouldest be for salvation unto the ends of the earth") is quoted by Paul and Barnabas as if it had been delivered in relation to themselves. I shall adduce some further examples hereafter, when I come to reply to the arguments grounded on expressions used respecting God in the Old Testament and applied to Christ in the New Testament.

But does it not seem harsh that when some words in passages of this kind do, on some account, pertain to Christ, the whole should not be referred to him?

It ought not to seem harsh that words of this description, spoken of another person, should be applied to Christ so far only as they correspond to his person. The writer to the Hebrews supplies us with an example of this in the fifth verse of the first chapter; where, in the following words spoken by God concerning Solomon (2 Sam. vii. 14), " I will be his Father, and he shall be my Son; if he commit iniquity, I will chasten him with the rod of men, and with the stripes of the children of men'"—he applies the former part alone to Christ; omitting the latter portion, because it might indeed be suitable to Solomon but could not be to Christ, who was free from all sin and iniquity. The same writer, in several other instances, applies expressions which are used of God, to Christ, as far as his circumstances and person required, as you shall hear in the proper place.

But

But may not the old creation of heaven and earth be referred to Christ in some appropriate sense, which would indicate his high pre-eminence above the angels?

Certainly : namely—in so far as Christ, being antecedently to all creation foreknown, especially chosen, and predestined to glory by God, was the cause of God's creating the world and all things, whereby he might carry into effect his purpose of conducting Christ to glory, and conferring through him eternal life on the human race : in which sense, indeed, the creation of heaven and earth and all things might justly be referred to Christ as its author; and this was of old known to the Hebrews, viz. that the world was created with a view to the Messiah ; furnishing, too, a clear proof of this fact, that Christ, after being advanced to his glory, was made more excellent and worthy than the angels.—If any one shall say that this was the ground on which the author attributed those words also, in which the creation of heaven and earth is attributed to God, to Christ, in the sense I have intimated, that is, a sense appropriate to him, he will find that I entirely concur with him in opinion. To this manner of speaking may be likened that wherein parents are said (Exod. xx. 12) to prolong the days of those children who honour them : which nevertheless they are not able to do, but God does it with a view to themselves or their offspring ;—and also wherein the friends of the mammon of unrighteousness are stated (Luke xvi. 9) to receive us into everlasting habitations ; which, in like manner, will not be done

by

by them, but by God on their account. To the same purpose is the saying of Salvianus in the preface of his book against avarice : *Recte ipse scripsisse dicitur, per quem factum est ut scriberetur*—" He is justly said to have written, by whom the writing was caused to be made[19]."

By

---

[19] What if to these two interpretations of this very difficult passage we add a third ?—I observe then, that the divine author applies the passage of the Psalms, which speaks of the old creation, to the new creation effected by Jesus Christ, in an accommodated sense. For if the prophets could say that God created a new heaven and a new earth when he improved the condition of the people of Israel,—with how much greater propriety may this language be used in reference to the reformation of the world by Christ! For this renovation of the Israelites induced no alteration of the heaven or the earth, or even of that small district ;—whereas the new reformation effected by Christ gave a new lord to heaven and earth, who rules them at his pleasure, and has power to destroy them; who has also made all the inhabitants of heaven and earth partakers of an entirely new state of things, introduced a new order even among the angels in heaven, with various kinds of dignities and offices—established on the earth among mankind far different principles and different manners,—and reconciling both to each other has formed them into one commonwealth. The sense of the passage would therefore be as follows :— And thou, Lord God, from the beginning of the new creation hast by Christ laid the foundation of the earth,—which a little before was convulsed by the wickedness of men, and hastening to destruction,—by new laws, and the heavens are as a new work of thine hands, in as much as they are transformed by thee through Christ into a state wholly different from that wherein they were before. But they nevertheless shall perish —being to be destroyed by Christ,—but thou, together with him whom thou hast associated with thee in the conduct of this new reformation, shalt remain : they all as a garment shall wax old, and as a vesture shalt thou fold them up by Christ ; but thou and thy Christ are the same, and thy years and his, whom thou hast made immortal, shall not fail.

In order to render this interpretation the more probable,

F 5

those

By what testimony is it attempted to be proved that Christ preserves all created things?

By that passage of the epistle to the Hebrews (chap.

---

those passages of the prophets should be consulted where some national calamity is represented by the ruin of the world, by earthquakes, by the darkening of the sun and moon and other planets, and the fall of the stars, by lightning also and by thunder: while on the other hand national prosperity is set forth by the restoration of light to the sun, moon, and other heavenly bodies. Of the former we have examples, Judges v. 4. 20; Psalm xviii. 7; lxxv. 3; lxxxii. 5; Isaiah xiii. 10. 13; xxiv. 18. 23; xxxiv. 4; li. 6; Ezek. xxxii. 7, 8; Joel ii. 10; Amos vii. 9; Mich. i. 4; Hagg. ii. 7. Of the latter, Is. xxx. 26; li. 16; lx. 20; lxv. 17; lxvi. 22. Of both, Psalm lx. 2.—Many more instances, and some of them more striking, are collected by Rabbi Moses Ben Maimon in his learned work intituled *More Nebochim*, part ii. chap. 29. M. RUARUS.

  I do not approve the third interpretation which is here added. It may be objected to it, that the author of the epistle to the Hebrews is confirming his discourse by scripture testimony; but this testimony does not at all refer to the new creation. All the testimonies of scripture which he quotes either directly prove his position, or contain something whence the superiority of Christ over angels may be inferred; which is the case in this passage, where God, as he is stated to have created the heaven and the earth, is also said to destroy them hereafter. And as it appears from the preceding testimony that this will happen in the time of Christ's kingdom, it follows that it will be accomplished through Christ. For he has on this account made him Christ and king—that he might accomplish through him all things pertaining to the salvation of his people (among which the destruction of the present heaven and earth forms a principal part)—which was admitted also by the Hebrews themselves. Hence likewise it may easily be seen how greatly Christ excels the angels. But that these words of the Psalmist were spoken or addressed to Christ, no one will be bold enough to assert, unless he take for granted that Christ is the one God. And if this be assumed, the whole force of the author's reasoning is overturned and destroyed.

Moreover, the Psalmist does not here place the creation of heaven and earth, and the destruction of them, as opposite or

dissimilar

(chap. i. 3) where Christ is said to "uphold all things by the word of his power."

What answer do you make to this?　That

---

dissimilar events, which this third interpretation requires, but as consentaneous occurrences: which objects, as they were created, it is no wonder that they should be destroyed. Neither, in fact, will those heavens in which the angels reside be destroyed. One may thus paraphrastically explain the author's meaning:—Lest any one should think that Christ is said so to reign for ever, as if an end were not to be put to this world—the scriptures elsewhere assert, addressing God, "Thou, Lord," &c. From which words it appears that under the reign of Christ, and consequently by his kingdom, an end will be put to this world, and the heavens and the earth be destroyed. Hence it is obvious to every one how superior Christ is made to the angels. In short, the author does not adduce this testimony, because that by the Hebrew title Jehovah (Lord), Christ is to be understood, or that the words are addressed to Christ,—but merely because they contain an argument in proof of the superiority of Christ over the angels. It is thus also that he cites the words spoken of God in the sixth verse, and those spoken in the seventh, of thunder and lightning. If then the angels ought to worship God, and testify their subjection to him, when he brings his first begotten into that world inhabited by the angels, it follows that the angels should worship the first begotten also, and submit themselves to him, since he is brought into that world in order that as their King and Lord he might receive it and all its inhabitants as his inheritance and possession. The author resumes this argument in the following chapter, and explains and confirms it more at large. And since the titles ANGELS and MINISTERS in the Psalms are changed, and both are used concerning STORMS and LIGHTNING—it follows that Christ is made far superior to the angels; the title of ELOHIM (God), and a "throne enduring for ever," being attributed to him. I. SCHLICHTINGIUS.

Although the new creation is not treated of in this Psalm, nevertheless the words, taken in that other sense, may be accommodated to that occurrence, as is done in other accommodations, and in this very chapter, 5—8. Cornelius Jansen, bishop of Ghent, on this Psalm, and also his disciple Estius on this place, interpret these words of the restoration of the New Jerusalem effected by Christ. But we may notice, in the first

place,

That the word translated "all things" does not
mean in this place, any more than in many others, all
things universally, without exception; but may be referred

---

place, a passage of Isaiah (li. 16), where the plantation of the
heaven and the foundation of the earth are in the primary sense
clearly attributed to the prophet. And what should hinder that
similar things should with greater propriety be asserted concerning the Messiah? Jerome, speaking of the words of Christ "My
God, why hast thou forsaken me?" says that some passages
are quoted in the New Testament from the Old, foreign from
the purpose. See also Galatinus, *lib*. viii. *cap*. 18. Bellarmine,
tom. i. *contr*. vi. *de Purgat*. *lib*. ii. *cap*. 5, writes, that the Church
is wont to quote some words, although the greater part of
them do not bear upon the purpose immediately under consideration. Bonaventura (Ps. cxviii.) says, that the Virgin Mary
from the beginning founded the world with God, because he
made the world with a view to her:—we may speak thus of
her son with much better reason. But the same words being
applied to different things do not prove that those things are
the same. As Isaiah vi. 9; Acts xxviii. 25; John xii. 39;
Matth. xiii. 14; Mark vi. 16. 27, 28. A. WISSOWATIUS.

He who desires to examine the source of the second exposition which is given above, may consult the Annotations of the
illustrious Grotius, whence these observations are taken; and
an interpretation similar to the third may be found in Enjedinus
and Brenius. And no one ought to feel surprised that many
explanations should be given of this place. After it has been
proved that the opinion which our opponents deduce from this
passage is false, and their exposition at variance with the scope
of the author—(as Augustine says in one place, *si diceretur
Christus major quam angeli, ridendum erat, incomparabiliter
enim major est creator omni creatura, (Hom. in Joh. iii.)* " it
would be ridiculous to assert that Christ is greater than the
angels, for the creator must be beyond all comparison greater
than every creature,")—if we show that many consistent interpretations can be given of the words, so much the better. To
those already produced I will therefore add one, which to me
appears plainer than any of them. Many take for granted that
the words of the tenth, eleventh, and twelfth verses relate to
the son of God: nevertheless, we do not see that any one has
hitherto

ferred to those things alone that pertain to the kingdom of Christ, which is here, in the opinion of some
very learned men, the subject of discourse,—all which.

---

hitherto stated any necessary cause for this assertion. The
apostle, both in what precedes and in what follows, is treating
of the operations as well of God the Father as of his Son.
Now the creation of heaven and earth is never attributed to
Christ absolutely, as it is here. But the supreme God (whom
we have already shown to be the Father alone) is said to
have done this, and that alone and of himself, Is. xliv. 24;
Neh. ix. 6; Job ix. 8, &c. The Hebrews also, even to the
present times, firmly believe that the creation of heaven and
earth was effected by the one person of the supreme God,
without any assistant or instrument. The divine author observes afterwards, that God had placed his Son over all the
works of his hands.

Further, the first creation, which (as reason dictates, and the
primitive Church constantly taught in opposition to heretics,)
was not made out of pre-existent matter co-eternal with God,
could not have been executed by a plurality of Lords. Besides,
Luke (whom many of the ancients regard as the author of this
epistle) clearly asserts that he had diligently inquired after and
accurately narrated all things which Jesus taught and did.
(Acts i. 1, compared with Luke i. 3.) Not a hint appears however in any part of his writings, that the Son of God had created heaven and earth. That the words under consideration
may properly be applied to God the Father, is acknowledged,
among others, by Thomas Aquinas, in his observations on the
passage. See also Pool's Synopsis on this place.

It is to be observed, moreover, that this passage is scarcely
any where employed by the ancients against those who denied
that the Son of God was the Creator. That such modes of
speaking are not unusual with the sacred writers may be seen
from Gen. xlix. 18; Rom. xi. 33, &c.; 2 Thess. ii. 8, 9; and,
as some think, Rom. ix. 5; 1 John v. 20, &c. A more ample
explanation and defence of this place is given by the ministers
of Sarmatia and Transylvania, concerning the true and false
knowledge of the one God the Father, of the Son, and of the
Holy Spirit, *lib.* ii. *c.* 13. You will find the same in the Albanian
Controversy, and other writings of the Transylvanians: for more
cannot be said here concerning this passage. B. WISSOWATIUS.

things

some of them also tempted, and were destroyed of serpents."

What answer is to be given to these testimonies?

In respect to the first, the very thing itself shows that the rock whereof the Israelites drank was not literally Christ, but figuratively; that is, because it was an image or type of him.   Hence it by no means follows that Christ was actually in the desert with the children of Israel.   Nor will it any more serve the cause of our opponents that this rock is called "spiritual," since that rock might be denominated spiritual, although it was material; for the same reason that the manna was called spiritual meat, and the water spiritual drink; because they were the figure and representation of meat and drink and of a rock, truly spiritual, or because they had a spiritual reference to him;—agreeably to what John writes (Revelation xi. 8), "the great city which spiritually is called Sodom and Egypt, where also our Lord was crucified," that is, Sodom and Egypt in a spiritual sense.   What he states of the rock following them ought to be understood of the water which, after the rock had been struck, issued out of it, and for a long way followed the people through the wilderness, which before was destitute of running water, or at least of such as was fit for drinking.   To this the Lord alludes by the prophet Isaiah (xliii. 20), " The beasts of the field shall honour me, the dragons and the owls, because I give waters in the wilderness, and rivers in the desert, to give drink to my people, my chosen."   See also Psalm lxxviii. 15, 16, and cv. 41.

With

With respect to the second testimony, " Neither let us tempt Christ, as some of them also tempted," it cannot be concluded from these words that the apostle meant to affirm that. Christ was actually tempted in the wilderness ; as may be perceived from a similar mode of speaking ;—for if some person were to say, " be not disobedient to the magistrate, as some of our ancestors were," you would not understand the same individual magistrate to be intended in both cases. Now if there are found in the scriptures forms of speech of this kind, wherein a similar declaration is made in reference to the person who is mentioned a little before, without a repetition of the name, it is only in cases wherein no other person besides him who is expressly named can be understood.   An example of this you have Deut. vi. 16, " Ye shall not tempt the Lord your God, as ye tempted [him] in Massah." But in the apostle's words under consideration, some other person besides Christ may be understood, as Moses, or Aaron (Numb. xxi. 5), since this temptation was practised against them, especially against Moses. For what Christ is now to us, they were then, in some respects, to the Israelites ; particularly Moses, who is also said (Deut. xxxiii. 5) to have been king in Israel, (which is to be Christ, or anointed of God), and indeed he is called Christ [their anointed], Habakkuk iii. 13. There is nothing then to forbid that God should be understood here, whose name the apostle might omit, because it was sufficiently known from the history who it was that had been tempted.—Thus in like manner the author of the epistle to the Hebrews

(chap.

(chap. iii. 16) states in a similar case, "Some, when they had heard, DID PROVOKE," GOD or LORD being understood [21].

Upon what testimony is it attempted to be proved that Isaiah saw the glory of Christ?

On that of John (xii. 41); "These things said Esaias when he saw his glory and spake of him."

What answer do you make to this?

First; that these words are not necessarily to be referred to Christ appears from hence—that they may be understood of God, the Father. Nor is there any thing in the words immediately following to show that Christ is here spoken of. For it must be observed that the following, or forty-second verse, does not agree with the next preceding, or forty-first verse, but with the thirty-seventh, as may easily be

---

[21] In connection with the explication of this testimony it may deserve notice, that Grotius states that in the *Codex Alexandrinus* it is not "let us not tempt CHRIST," but "GOD." But Epiphanius (*adversus hæreses, lib.* i. *tom.* iii. *edit. Petavianæ*) observes, that this passage was corrupted by Marcion, who substituted τον Χριστον (Christ), for τον κυριον (Lord). And indeed it is most probable that in the first copy the reading was τον κυριον, which the *Codex Alexandrinus* has interpreted τον Θεον (God), but which Marcion and the present common copies have converted into CHRIST. M. RUARUS.

Thomas Aquinas understands here GOD; but Haymo, MoSES, who was a type of Christ, and who might likewise be called Christ, or anointed. See Psalm cv. 15. Consult also Nic. Gorramius *Ord. Prædic.*; and Erasmus on the place. A. WISSOWATIUS.

It is besides to be observed, that the Æthiopic version expressly reads GOD; for it thus renders the passage: *Et ne tentarent* DEUM *dix't iis; et tentarunt eum, et destruxerunt eos serpentes.* It is moreover to be remarked, that in this version the word GOD is wanting in 1 Tim. iii. 16. B. WISSOWATIUS.

seen

seen by comparing them together. The intermediate passage, which speaks of God alone, is to be read as in a parenthesis. Secondly; let it be granted that the words of John do refer to Christ: it might truly be said that the glory, that is to say the future glory, of Christ, was seen in that glory of God which Isaiah beheld; since it was in some measure permitted to prophets to behold future and even long distant events, on which account they were called SEERS. For he saw the glory of God with which the earth is said to be filled. And this happened literally and perfectly when God was revealed to the whole world by Christ; in which revelation was comprised the glory of both. Nor can it be doubted that this vision was literally and perfectly, or in a spiritual sense, to be realized at a future period; that is, in the time of Christ. For John asserts that these things were then fulfilled which Isaiah had formerly foretold in this vision. Moreover, these words of John, "when he beheld his glory," properly refer to the quotation first made from the prophecy of Isaiah: and the following words, "when he spake of him," to the quotation last made. For when Isaiah spoke the words first quoted by John (verse 38), "Lord, who hath believed our report and to whom hath the arm of the Lord been revealed?" he saw, in the prophetic spirit, that "excellent glory," as Peter calls it, of Christ, which he was to attain after his sufferings; and was foretold of him (Isaiah lii. 13—15; liii. 1, &c.). But when Isaiah uses the words afterwards quoted by John (ver. 40), "he hath blinded their eyes," he

spoke

spoke of Christ in his own person (Isaiah vi. 9, 10);
otherwise it would appear useless tautology in these
words of the evangelist, if both particulars refer to
one place in Isaiah.   For to what purpose would it
be to say that Isaiah spake of Christ, when he beheld
his glory?   Could he avoid speaking of him, when he
is stating that he had seen his glory?   These words
then, " when he spake of him," refer to that passage
of Isaiah wherein he speaks of Christ in direct terms,
and without the vision of his glory ; which certainly
could not be the passage whence the first testimony
was taken : it must, therefore, necessarily have been
that adduced subsequently[22].

From what testimonies of Scripture is it attempted
to be proved that Christ became, as it is said, incarnate ?

From the following :—First, John i. 14, where, according to the common version, we read, " And the
word was made flesh."   Secondly, Philipp. ii. 6, 7, 8,
" Who (Christ) being in the form of God, thought it
not robbery to be equal with God, but made himself
of no reputation, and took upon him the form of a
servant, and was made in the likeness of men, being
found in fashion as a man."   Thirdly, 1 Tim. iii. 16,
" God was manifested in the flesh."   Fourthly, Heb.

---

[22] Some copies instead of " his glory" read " the glory of
God." This is the reading of Christopher Froschover's edition printed at Zurich A.D. 1559. The like will be found in
Robert Stephens's great Bibles. That it was the glory of God
the Father which appeared to Isaiah is maintained by Chrysostom, Theophylact, Guido Perpinian, Monotessaro, and Al-
cazar on Revelation iv. 2, 3. AND. WISSOWATIUS.

ii. 16,

ii. 16, " For verily he took not on him the nature of·
angels, but he took on him the seed of Abraham.''
Fifthly, 1 John iv. 2, " Every spirit which confesseth
that Jesus Christ is come in the flesh, is of God.''
Sixthly, Heb. x. 5, " When he cometh into the
world he saith, Sacrifice and offering thou wouldest
not, but a body hast thou prepared me.''

What answer do you make to the first of these
testimonies ?

That it is not here asserted that God became, as
they speak, incarnate, or that the divine assumed a
human nature : since it is one thing to say that " the
word was made flesh,'' and another to assert, in their
phraseology, that God became incarnate, or that the
divine, took upon it a human nature. For THE WORD
is not God himself, that is, the supreme God ; nor
does the phrase " was made flesh'' (the term flesh
being understood, as it is here, of a mortal man) signify to be made or to be born a man : but every man
is said to be made or to be born who before had no
nature. And if the Word was, strictly speaking, made
flesh (and nothing obliges us to depart from the
proper meaning of the terms), either it was actually
a person before it was made flesh, or it was not : if it
was a person, then certainly, after being made flesh,
that is, being made another substance, it must have
ceased to be that substance, and consequently that
person also, which it was before :—it was not therefore the one God ; much less could it have been the
one God, if it was not any real existing person. And
it is declared in this passage, not only that the person

of

of the Word was made in the days of the writer, but also WHAT it was made, when it was made,—namely, FLESH ; that is to say, a nature subject to sufferings and death, which is the property of all mortal men. Besides, the phrase " the Word was made flesh" may also be rendered, " the Word WAS flesh." This is asserted by a writer of the last century, who, unquestionably, was eminently skilled in the Greek language—Joachim Camerarius, in his observations on this place : and is likewise evident from other passages wherein the word εγενετο (here translated " was made") is rendered by the verb WAS. Thus in this very chapter, ver. 6, " There was a man (εγενετο ανθρωπος) sent from God :"—also Luke xxiv. 19, " Which was a prophet" (ὁς εγενετο ανηρ προφητης). See also Luke i. 5 ; Acts ix. 19 ; 2 Pet. ii. 1, &c. For the Greek verb γινομαι signifies equally TO BE and TO BE MADE. But that the language of John cannot be understood to speak of the incarnation contended for, is shown by the order of his words : because it were exceedingly harsh to say that the Word assumed a human nature, after what he had before stated respecting it, and which took place subsequently to the nativity of the man Jesus Christ ;— such as, that John the Baptist bare witness of him— that he was in the world—that his own received him not—and that to as many as received him he gave power to become the sons of God.

How then is the phrase " the Word was made flesh" to be understood ?

That the Word, although endued with as much divinity

vinity as the language of John ascribes to it, was as
to its substance a man, no less obnoxious than other
men to sufferings, afflictions, and death.   For the
Scriptures frequently employ the term flesh in this
sense, as is evident from those passages wherein God
thus speaks (Gen. vi. 3), " My spirit shall not always
strive with man, for that he also is flesh." Also
Isaiah xxxi. 3, " The Egyptians are men and not
God, and their horses flesh and not spirit."   And the
author of the epistle to the Hebrews (v. 7), " In
the days of his flesh ;" which he uses for the time
when he was mortal, or indeed for that during which
he suffered, and when the infirmity of his nature
chiefly appeared.   Nor is it to be wondered at, that
the word flesh should designate that which is weak,
since, as Peter (1st Epist. i. 24) asserts from Isaiah,
" all flesh is grass."

What reply do you make to the second testimony,
from Philipp. ii. 6, 7, 8 ?

That it does not comprise that for which our adversaries contend.   For it is one thing to assert, as
the apostle does here, that " being in the form of
God" he " took upon him the form of a servant," and
another to say that the divine assumed a human
nature.   The FORM of God cannot mean here the
NATURE of God, since the apostle states that Christ
emptied himself (ἑαυτον εκενωσε) of this form : but God
cannot in any respect empty himself of his nature.
Neither does the " form of a servant" denote human
nature, because " to be a servant" refers to the external

ternal state and condition of a man. Nor ought it to be overlooked that the word FORM is used but in one other passage in the New Testament, (Mark xvi. 12,) where it is employed in this sense, importing not a nature, but an external appearance : the words are, Jesus "appeared in ANOTHER FORM unto two of them."

But does it not appear from the words which the apostle subjoins a little further on, " being found in fashion as a man," that he had, as our adversaries express themselves, become incarnate ?

By no means : for these words have no such meaning. We read in the Scriptures (Judges xvi. 17), concerning Samson—that he should " be like any man." And Asaph (Psalm lxxii. 6, 7) threatens those persons whom he had denominated " Gods, and children of the Most High," that they should " die like men :" concerning whom it is certain it could not be said, in the language of our adversaries, that they had become incarnate.

How then do you understand this entire passage ?

To this effect :—That Christ, who, while in the world, like God, wrought wonderful works; whom, as God, all things obeyed, and who received divine worship, became, when the divine will and the salvation of men required it, like a servant and slave, and like men endued with no divine power ;—I say, LIKE, not actually, as was the case of old with Samson, but resembling a man in appearance and fashion; he being inwardly and actually full of divine energy when " he
                                        humbled

humbled himself and became obedient unto death, even the death of the cross," that is, evidently to the punishment of a slave [23].

What do you reply to the third testimony (1 Tim. iii. 16), " God was manifested in the flesh ?"

First, that it may be shown from the Latin Vulgate, the Syriac, and Arabic versions, that the word GOD was wanting in many ancient copies. Neither did Ambrosius know any thing of it. So that the entire passage may be referred to the " mystery of godliness"[24] mentioned immediately before. Nothing certain can therefore be concluded from this passage. But secondly, even though the word GOD were inserted here, there is no reason why it might not be referred to God the Father; since these things might truly be affirmed of the Father,—that he was manifested in the flesh, that is in Christ and the apostles, or by Christ and the apostles, who were flesh. And as to what is read further on, according to the common version, " received up into glory," it is in the Greek ($\alpha\nu\varepsilon\lambda\eta\phi\vartheta\eta$ $\varepsilon\nu$ $\delta o\xi\eta$) " in glory," that is, with glory, or gloriously.

What then is the meaning of this place?

That you may the better comprehend it I will re-

---

[23] See, among others, the Annotations of Erasmus, Piscator, and Grotius on this place. BEN. WISSOWATIUS.

[24] That this passage was falsified by Macedonius bishop of Constantinople, a Nestorian under the emperor Anastasius, is asserted by Liberatus archdeacon of Carthage, *Tomo Concil.* 4. Hincmarus archbishop of Rheims writes to the same effect, that the word Θεος was inserted by the Nestorians. *Inter Opusc.* lv. c. 18. Besides the manuscripts above cited; it is wanting in the Armenian version. See also Erasmus on the place, and the various readings of Curcellæus. A. WISSOWATIUS.

cite

cite the whole passage, leaving the term God, not-withstanding its being suspected, among the words of the apostle. " God was manifest in the flesh, justi-fied in the spirit, seen of angels, preached unto the Gentiles, believed on in the world, received up into glory." The meaning of this is, that very great mysteries appeared in the religion delivered by Christ ; that God revealed the hidden secrets of his will by weak men, obnoxious to various afflictions ; that by the spirit with which he filled those weak per-sons he caused men to acknowledge that he was just and true, and on this account to believe what was an-nounced by them in his name ; that the same secrets of his will were at length perceived by the angels, and were preached not to the Jews alone but also to he Gentiles ; that the world believed in God, and re-ceived him in a most distinguished manner and with the highest glory—which was done when all men glorified the word of the Lord, as we read Acts xiii. 48 ; 2 Thess. iii. 1.

What answer do you make to the fourth testi-mony, from Heb. ii. 16 ?

That it contains not even the resemblance of what is called an incarnation ; since the writer does not say that Christ TOOK, (as some translate the word, and as it is commonly understood,) but TAKETH, or rather " taketh hold of," which by no means designates a past action, such as incarnation would be, but one that is present and continued[r]. Nor does the author

---

[r] [" For verily he taketh not hold of angels, but of the seed of Abraham he taketh hold,"—Marginal rendering of the verse in the authorized English version. TRANSL.]   say

say " human nature," but " the seed of Abraham,"
which among the Hebrews implies a plurality, and in
the sacred writings denotes those who believe in
Christ, as may be seen Gal. iii. 29.

What then is the meaning of this passage?

The writer intends to assert that Christ is never
called the saviour or redeemer of angels, but of the
children of Abraham; that is, of believing human
beings: whom, as with an out-stretched arm, he emancipates from their bondage to the fear of death.

What answer do you make to the fifth testimony,
from 1 John iv. 2?

That it contains nothing whatever respecting what
is termed the incarnation: for the words which some
interpreters render " come in the flesh," are in the original " come in flesh" (εν σαρχι). Nor does John
write that " the spirit which confesseth that Jesus
Christ is come in flesh is of God;" but that " that
spirit which confesseth Jesus Christ, who came in
flesh, is of God." The meaning of these words is, that
that spirit is of God, which confesseth that Jesus,—
who lived on earth subject to the greatest weaknesses
of flesh, underwent the most ignominious death, and
was so far destitute of the human glory and power
which the Jews looked for in their Messiah,—was the
Christ, the promised king of the people of God. For
he here tacitly declares the cause why the false prophets of that time objected to acknowledge Jesus for
the Christ [25].

What

---

[25] It may in this place be considered, what kind of antichrists, or false prophets, the apostle had in view. He had

stated

What do you reply to the sixth testimony, from Heb. x. 5 ?

That there is no mention made here of what is termed an incarnation. For, first, it may be said of any person whatever, that God had fitted or prepared for him a body; and indeed these words (Psalm

---

stated before (chap. ii. 18, 19), that they had gone out from them. Now if we consult the records of antiquity it will appear that these were Cerinthians, who denied that Jesus Christ was come in flesh, or that Jesus was the Christ, or Son of God; but taught, as we may every where read in the writings of the ancients, that the Christ was immortal, and had descended from heaven into Jesus, who was only a mere man; that in the time of his passion the Christ had flown away, and that it was Jesus alone, who was mortal, that had suffered. But whether these things comport best with our opinions or with those of our adversaries, we leave to every one to judge. Moreover, the ancients testify that John, in his writings, took up his pen against these persons. It is to such persons also, who deny that the Son of God was a real man, that Ignatius the martyr, bishop of Antioch and the disciple of John, refers, when, in his Epistle to the Romans, he breaks out in the following words: —" What does it profit me if any one praises me, but blasphemes my Lord, while he does not confess that he wore flesh? He who does not confess this, wholly denies him, as one who bore about with him a dead carcase." And again in the same Epistle:—" But if these things were done by our Lord in imagination only, or in appearance, then am I also chained in imagination. And why should I deliver myself to death, to the stake, to the sword, or to wild beasts? But I, who am near the sword, am near God, and endure all things solely as a fellow-sufferer with him, being myself fortified by the consideration of his being a perfect man, whom some ignorant persons deny." These and other fragments of a similar kind Theodoret has collected together and transmitted to us in his Eranistes or Polymorphus: and we are uncertain whether, besides these, there be extant any other undoubted writings of Ignatius. In like manner also, another disciple of John, Polycarp bishop of Smyrna, uses this language against the heretics of his time; that " Jesus Christ was come in flesh." BEN. WISSOWATIUS.

(Psalm

xl. 6) are in their primary meaning to be understood of David, as the Psalmist himself shows : but
no one will affirm that he had become incarnate.
In the next place, these words, when applied to
Christ, may be interpreted of his immortal body,
which God had fitted for him [26]; especially if by his
" coming into the world," which is mentioned here,
be understood his entrance into the future world,
wherein are the palace and temple of Christ, acting
as our sovereign and priest,—concerning which I have
already spoken. There is nothing to require, nor
will the use of the phrase in the Scriptures permit,
that this coming into the world should be understood
of his nativity : for if by the term WORLD we understand the present world, that person is said, in the
Scripture meaning of the words, to have then come
into it, who has entered upon any public office among
men.

What then is the meaning of this passage ?

That God had fitted and prepared for Jesus such a
body as was suitable and proper for the performance
of his office of high priest in heaven [27].

Yoù

---

[26] Why not, rather, of a mortal body, susceptible of sufferings ? For it follows, " Lo, I come to do thy will, O God."
This profession of obedience comports better with the days of
his flesh than of his glory. Hence, by coming into the world,
may here be well understood his entrance on his public office
among men, as stated at the close of the above answer. M.
RUARUS.

What if we understand it of both ? For now also, in the
heavenly temple, he acts as a priest, or executes the will of
God towards believers. A. WISSOWATIUS.

[27] If the preceding note be approved, this answer ought to be
altered

You have hitherto explained in what manner our opponents attempt to prove concerning Christ, from the Scriptures, things which in reality they do not ascribe to him:—show me now in what manner they reason falsely from those things which the sacred writings do actually attribute to him?

The passages of Scripture from which they draw erroneous conclusions, either relate directly to Christ, or are referred to him in some accommodated sense.

Which are the texts that relate directly to Christ?

They are those wherein it is said concerning Christ, that he was God, was one with God, or equal with God; that he was the Son of the living God, was God's own or only-begotten Son; that he was the first born of every creature; that he had all things which the Father had; that he was the everlasting Father,

---

altered in this manner, or in words of similar import, [such a body] "as might be sacrificed and offered for the human race." M. RUARUS.

Some conceive that there is much force in 2 Cor. viii. 9, in favour of the doctrine of the incarnation. "Ye know the grace of our Lord Jesus Christ, that though he was rich, yet for your sakes he became poor, that ye through his poverty might be rich." But, not to notice that these words, though read as they are commonly translated, may with propriety be explained in the same manner as Philipp. ii. 7, 8, has been above, it is to be observed that the original text is ιπτωχευσι πλουσιος ων, which, as Erasmus observes, ought to be rendered, *pauper fuit*, or *mendicavit, dives existens*, "He was poor or solicited charity, though he was rich." But this is most true of Christ the Son of Man, without this incarnation, concerning which the Scripture is silent: for all riches were in his power, and all things were as tributes to which he was entitled (Matt. xi. 27; xvii. 27). These, however, on our account, he was unwilling to use, but lived in the world like a beggar. Matt. viii. 20, &c. See also Grotius on this place.   B. WISSOWATIUS.

the

the Word of God, the Image of the invisible God, the character of his substance; that being seen, the Father was seen; that he was in the Father and the Father in him; that the fulness of the Godhead dwelt in him bodily; that he had glory with the Father before the world was; that it was he whose Spirit was in the prophets; that he came down from heaven, came forth from the Father, came into the world, and was sent into the world by the Father; that he is the only Lord, the Lord of glory, the King of kings and Lord of lords; and that faith and divine honour pertain to him.

In what passages of Scripture is Christ called God?

John i. 1, "And the word was God." Thomas's exclamation, John xx. 28, "My Lord and my God." And Rom. ix. 5, where the apostle writes that Christ is over all, or over all things, "God blessed for ever."

What is to be inferred from these testimonies?

That the divine nature claimed for Christ cannot be proved from them, is manifest from hence,—not to notice what has already been advanced,—that in the first testimony the WORD of God is spoken of, which must necessarily be something else than God himself; especially as in the same place John declares that it was WITH that God. In the second testimony, Thomas (if indeed the words be not an exclamation of surprise) calls Christ God, in whose feet and hands he observes the wounds of the nails, and in whose side he sees the mark of the spear: and because he beholds him risen from the dead, he styles him his Lord and his God; as if he might style him

Lord,

Lord, who might also with propriety be called God[a]. And Paul calls him, "who was of the fathers as concerning the flesh," "God over all, blessed for ever." All which, it is evident, could by no means be affirmed of him who is the one God. For it would thence follow that that one God was two Gods, of whom one was with the other; while to have the marks of the wounds, and to be of the Fathers, are circumstances that belong altogether to a man, which to ascribe to him who is the one God were the height of

---

[a] Erasmus observes on these words, "This is one place wherein the evangelist plainly ascribes the title God to Christ." Grotius also (whose annotation on this passage is worthy perusal) states, that here for the first time the title God is attributed to Jesus by the apostles : and he subjoins this reason—namely, that "after his resurrection he had proved that it was from him life, and indeed eternal life, ought to be looked for. See John xi. 25, &c." See also Sandius[a] on the place. B. WISSOWATIUS.

[a] [Sandius's observations on this text are contained in his *Interpretationes Paradoxæ quatuor Evangeliorum*, page 257 : " The Nestorians," he writes, " denying with Paul of Samosata and Photinus that Christ was the true God, state that these words (my Lord and my God) refer to the Father, being an exclamation of Thomas astonished at the resurrection of Christ ; as appears from the ancient Synods, *cap.* 8 and 12. ' Theodorus Mopsuestænus asserts that the confession which Thomas made, when he felt the hands and side of our Lord after his resurrection, saying, My Lord and my God, was not spoken by him concerning Christ ; neither does Theodorus say, that Christ was God, but, that Thomas, astonished at the miracle of the resurrection, glorified God, who had restored the Lord to life.' To this Bellarmine replies, that it is not written in Greek with ὦ (the mark of exclamation), but with the article. But the Nestorians might again have retorted on Bellarmine, that Christ (Mark xv. 34, and Matt. xxvii. 46) says in an exclamation, ὁ Θεός μου, ὁ Θεός μου. So also Psalm xxi. 1, ὁ Θεὸς ὁ Θεός μου, and innumerable other places." TRANSL.]

absurdity.

absurdity. If any one should hold out the cloak of a
distinction of natures, I have already removed that,
and shown that this distinction can by no means be
sustained. It is moreover to be remarked, that the
word God does not occur in the last text in the Syriac; and Erasmus states that the passage stood thus
in the old manuscript of Cyprian (*Advers. Jud.* ii. 6);
that Hilary also read it so under Psalm cxxii.; and
that Chrysostom does not seem to have read it otherwise [29]. All therefore that is asserted is, that Christ
is over all blessed for ever; that is over all the Fathers and Israelites, concerning whom the apostle
is writing: and indeed it is not Paul's custom to
call Christ God, but Lord. If however he do apply
the title God to Christ in this passage, he does it in
that sense in which he calls him the one Lord, made
by God. For Christ is called God in this sense in
Psalm xlv. 6, 7, " Thy throne, O God, is for ever and
ever; the sceptre of thy kingdom is a right sceptre.
Thou lovest righteousness, and hatest wickedness;
therefore God, thy God, hath anointed thee with the

---

[29] Erasmus, although he retains the word GOD, shows that a
better reading may be given of this passage, and that the concluding words do not necessarily refer to Christ. He states
that after the words " of whom is Christ according to the
flesh," a full stop or colon ought to be placed: and that the remainder of the sentence is a doxology, or ascription of praise
addressed to God the Father—" God, who is over all, be blessed for ever." The Greek text greatly favours this rendering,
as Curcellæus rightly observes in his various readings of the
New Testament; as does also Grotius, in his annotations on
the passage. B. WISSOWATIUS.

oil

oil of gladness above thy fellows:" to which words of the Psalmist it may with reason be perceived that the apostle here alludes [30].

But Paul seems himself, in this passage, to intimate that distinction of natures, when he says that Christ was of the fathers " according to flesh ?"

By no means: for the words "according to the flesh" are in no instance put in opposition to any divine nature or substance, but only to spirit, or to some spiritual property; as appears from the third verse of this very chapter, where Paul calls the Jews his kinsmen " according to the flesh," putting them in opposition to kinsmen and brethren, not certainly according to a divine nature, but according to the spirit,—just as he elsewhere styles them, " Israel according to the flesh." For the same reason he says that Ishmael was born of Abraham according to the flesh, contrasting him with Isaac, born according to the spirit. But not to seek our examples from other quarters alone, the same apostle, in this very Epistle to the Romans, thus explains this distinction in relation to Christ himself; as he opposes his descent according to the flesh to his descent according to the spirit, when he says (chap. i. 3, 4), " Who (that is, the Son of God) was made of the seed of David ac-

---

[30] Grotius, among others, (including Erasmus,) observes that the words here quoted from Psalm xlv. 7, 8, and cited by the apostle, Heb. i. 8, 9, ought, both in the Hebrew and the Greek texts, to be construed with the nominative rather than with the vocative case.

cording

cording to the flesh, and declared to be (that is, constituted) the Son of God with power, according to the spirit of holiness, by the resurrection from the dead." Whence also it may easily be seen, that if there be any thing in the passage in the ninth chapter which should be put in opposition to the words "according to the flesh," on account of which Christ ought to be styled " God over all, blessed for ever ;" it is not the divine nature, but the " spirit of holiness" that must be opposed to them ; especially as he is God over all blessed for ever, in so far as he is the Son of God, or is constituted King and Lord of all, and over all.

But, in what sense is Christ said to be "made of the seed of David, according to the flesh," and "declared to be the Son of God according to the spirit of holiness ?"

The apostle intimates that there were in Christ two things ; the flesh, or mortal nature of man ; and the spirit of holiness, that is, agreeably to the Hebrew idiom, the Holy Spirit. In respect to the first of these, considered alone and by itself, he could not refer his fleshly origin and stock to any other persons than to David and his posterity; but in respect to the second, in as much as he imbibed from God the Spirit of holiness with which he was wholly consecrated, he was constituted the Son of God. Being restored to life by the supreme power of God, who burst asunder the gates of death, he was made the celestial Lord and king of all.

Where do the Scriptures testify that Christ is one with the Father ?

John

John x. 29, 30; where our Lord says, " My Father, which gave them (my sheep) me, is greater than all, and no man is able to pluck them out of my Father's hand. I and my Father are one."

How do you reply to this testimony?

That it does not follow from what is said of Christ's being one with the Father, that he is one with him in nature, the words of Christ (John xvii. 11), addressed to his Father concerning his disciples, demonstrate: " Holy Father, keep through thine own name those whom thou hast given me, that they may be one as we are:" and further on (ver. 22), " The glory which thou gavest me I have given them, that they may be one even as we are one." That Christ is one with the Father, ought then to be understood, according to the usual manner of speaking, of the unvarying agreement of mind between the Father and the Son. But that a divine nature in Christ cannot be proved from hence is evident' from the place itself: for Christ asserts that the Father is greater than all, and consequently than himself, as he elsewhere expressly declares; both because he had given those sheep to him, and because he had drawn an argument from the invincible power of God that it could never happen that his sheep should be taken from him, since there existed between himself and God, as Son and Father, the most intimate agreement. But would he, who was himself the supreme God, deduce from the power and protection of another person, and not from himself, the proofs of those things which he had promised? especially when that other person also would possess all

his

his power no otherwise than as he was the supreme God?

Where is Christ said to be equal with God?

John v. 18, " Therefore the Jews sought the more to kill him, because he not only had broken the sabbath, but said also that God was his Father, making himself equal withGod." Philipp. ii. 6, " Who (Christ Jesus) being in the form of God, thought it not robbery to be equal with God."

What reply do you make to these passages?

That Christ's being equal to God by no means proves him to possess the divine nature claimed for him: indeed, the contrary may be hence inferred, since no one can be the equal of himself. It is to be observed, besides, that it is not said, in the first text, that Christ made himself equal with God; but that the Jews thus pronounced concerning Christ, as well as that he had broken the sabbath. Wherefore Christ, when he replies to this accusation of the Jews, shows that there was a great disparity in the equality between himself and the Father : that he was indeed equal to God, in so far as he did the same works with the Father; but that he was unequal to him, in so far as that he could do nothing of himself, but those things only which he saw the Father do; wherein as a scholar he emulated his master and director; that is, those things the faculty and power of doing which he had received from the Father. And as to the other text (Philipp. ii. 6), a more careful inspection of it will show the same thing ; partly because in the Greek it is not that he is equal to God, but equal things (*æqualia*), that is,

conformably

conformably to the Greek idiom, that he is equally
God, is like God; and partly because he laid aside for
a time this equality with the Father,—which does not
comport with him who is God by the nature which
is claimed for Christ [31].

Where is it stated that Christ is the Son of the
living God, God's own Son, and God's only begotten
Son?

In Matthew xvi. 16, Peter says, " Thou art the
Christ, the Son of the living God." Romans viii. 32,
the apostle writes, " He (God) spared not his own
Son, but delivered him up for us all." John iii. 16,
" God so loved the world that he gave his only begotten Son :" and further on (ver. 18), " He that believeth not is condemned already, because he hath not
believed in the name of the only begotten Son of God."

What answer do you give to these passages?

That it can by no means be proved from all these
attributes of Christ that his nature was, as is contended,
divine. For as to the first, it is very obvious that Peter
confesses that the SON OF MAN, who is the subject
of discourse, is " the Christ, the Son of the living
God." But the " Son of Man" possesses no such divine nature as our opponents feign for Christ. Besides,
the Scriptures testify concerning other men that they
are the Sons of the living God. Thus the apostle

---

[31] It should be considered whether these words *υχ αρπαγμαν
ηγησατο*, may not be more correctly rendered, as they have been
by some, *noluit rapere*, (he was unwilling to seize by violence,
an equality with God). On this subject see Erasmus and Sandius on this passage, and also *M. Poli Synopsis Crit. S. Scrip.
Interpret.* B. WISSOWATIUS.

Paul

Paul (Rom. ix. 26) quotes a passage to this effect.
from Hosea i. 10, "And it shall come to pass that
in the place where it was said unto them, Ye are not
my people, there shall they be called the children
(υἱοι) of the living God." But as Peter adds the title
" Son of God" to the title " Christ" by apposition,
as it is termed, and without any conjunctive particle,
it manifestly appears that the title Son of God is
synonymous with that of Christ; which may be seen
from this confession of Peter as it is recorded by
Mark and Luke, where the words " the Son of God"
are omitted : also from other passages of Scripture,
as Matth. xxvi. 63, 64 ; Mark xiv. 61 ; compared with
Luke xxii. 67, 70 ; 1 John v. 1, 5 ; and likewise from
the thing itself. For to be the Christ of God means
that he is a king anointed by God, to whom on this
very account the title Son of God is appropriate. In
respect to the second and third testimonies, we here
read that God's own and only begotten Son was delivered up to death ; which could not be asserted of one
who was by nature God. And, indeed, it appears
from the very circumstance of Christ being the Son
of God, that he could not be God, otherwise he would
be the Son of himself. But the reason why Christ is
called God's own Son is this, that he is the Son of
the only God, begotten by the only God through the
Holy Spirit ; since a thing being one's own means no
more than that it is not another's, nor possessed in
common, but is wholly one's own. And he is styled
the only begotten, the only Son, and also, absolutely,
the Son, because among the sons of God he is the
chief

chief and the most beloved by God; which appears
from hence,—that he alone was begotten of God
through the Holy Spirit, that he alone was sanctified
by him and sent into the world, invested with the
office of Christ; that he alone has as yet been raised
from the dead by God to an immortal existence, he
alone made the heir of all things, and the partaker of
a heavenly kingdom : just as Isaac, because he was
most dear to Abraham, is called (Heb. xi. 17) his
only begotten Son, although he had a brother, Ishmael. And Solomon is called (Prov. iv. 3) "the
only begotten in the sight of his mother," although
he had more brothers by the same mother (1 Chron.
iii. 5).

Where is he denominated the first-born of every
creature ?

He is thus called in the Epistle to the Colossians,
chap. i. ver. 15.

What answer do you make to this ?

That it cannot be hence concluded that Christ had
this divine nature. For since Christ is "the first
born of every creature," it must needs be that he is
himself one in the number of creatures; the import
of the term "first born," in the Scriptures (Col.
i. 18; Rom. viii. 29; Rev. i. 5), being, that the first-
born must of necessity be of the same kind as those
of whom he is the first-born; and, as the word itself
implies, be the first of them. But that the Lord
Jesus was the first of the things made in the old creation, even our opponents cannot admit, unless they
would become Arians. They must therefore grant
that

that he is one, and indeed the first, among the productions of the new creation. Wherefore not only is this divine nature of Christ not established, but it is clearly to be inferred that he possesses no such divine nature. The reason why the apostle applies this epithet to him is, that he precedes all things else in the new creation, both in time and dignity [32].

In what passages of Scripture does he assert that he hath all things which the Father hath?

In John xvi. 15, where Christ says, "All things that the Father hath are mine." And further on, xvii. 10, "All mine are thine, and thine are mine."

What say you to these testimonies?

That it is by no means to be hence inferred that Christ has this divine nature, or the same essence with the Father: otherwise it would follow that the Son also, to whom the Father states (Luke xv. 31) "All that I have is thine," would have the same numerical essence as his Father. For it is obvious that in the term ALL THINGS in such forms of speaking, NATURE or ESSENCE is on no account to be included; but those things only which any person possesses. But nothing forbids that the same thing should be possessed at the same time by those whose natures are different, especially if one of them is on any account subordinate to or dependent upon the other, as is certainly the case in this instance. For the Son is

---

[32] Jerome thus comments on this place:—"The first-born according to the human form which he assumed, not in time but in honour: like Exodus iv. 22, "Israel is my Son, my first-born." Consult also Psalm lxxxix. 27. B. WISSOWATIUS.

subordinate to the Father, by whom he states that all
things were given to him : from which very circumstance it is apparent that the Son has not the same
nature with the Father ; for, if he had, he would possess all things of himself[33].

Where is Christ called the " Father of Eternity"
[the Everlasting Father] ?

In Isaiah, chap. ix. ver. 6.

What say you to this passage ?

That a divine nature cannot be hence proved, unless it be shown that the writer speaks here of that
Eternity which is without beginning; which can by no
means be done ; otherwise we should have two Fathers existing from all eternity. Besides, it is obvious that the author writes of a Son who was BORN
in times past and GIVEN to us, who could not have
existed from all eternity. The Greek translators [the
Septuagint], and also the Latin [the Vulgate] who
followed them, perceiving this, have rendered the
words, *Pater futuri seculi,* " the Father of a future
age." But Christ may be thus designated, although
he possessed not the divine nature which is claimed
for him ; and for this reason, because he is constituted by the Father the prince and author of the eternal life conferred upon believers. It may be added
that the prophet speaks of this child as of a king given

---

[33] Add to this, that if these things are to be understood
without limitation, and referred to essence, it would follow that
the Son had the Fathers PERSON ; that as the FATHER had a
Son, so must the SON likewise have a Son; and, *vice versa,*
that the FATHER must have a HUMAN NATURE: and other innumerable absurdities. B. WISSOWATIUS.

by

by God; and good kings, such as it is predicted he would be, are wont to be called the FATHERS of the people. But lest any one should think that this signal blessing would be of no longer continuance than in the case of other kings, even the most excellent, on account of the frailty of their lives, the prophet asserts that this king would be the Father of Eternity, that is, according to the Hebrew idiom, ETERNAL, which, through the great kindness of God, is actually accomplished in Christ.

In what passages of Scripture is Jesus styled the " Word of God," " the Image of the invisible God," " the express image of his person" or substance? And where is it asserted that " he who has seen Jesus has seen the Father," that " the Father is in him and he in the Father," and that in Jesus " dwells all the fulness of the Godhead bodily ?"

In John i. 1, " In the beginning was the word," compared with Rev. xix. 13, " and his name is called the Word of God:" Col. i. 15; " Who is the image of the invisible God:" Heb. i. 3, "Who being the brightness of his glory, and the express image of his person, &c.:" John xiv. 3, " He that hath seen me hath seen the Father :" ver. 10, " I am in the Father, and the Father in me:" Col. ii. 9, " In him dwelleth all the fulness of the Godhead bodily."

What say you to these testimonies ?

That it cannot be proved from Christ's being the Word of God that he possesses a divine nature : indeed the contrary is the rather to be inferred ; for since he is the WORD of the one God, it is evident that

that he is not that one God.   And the same may be
replied to those testimonies wherein Christ is called
" the image of the invisible God," and " the express
image of his person."   But Jesus is called the Word
or Speech of God because he is the immediate interpreter, and at the same time the executor, of the
divine will: for this properly belongs to the Word
of God.   In the Greek, the article is prefixed to
the term WORD (ὁ λογος) in order to designate this
illustrious, or most excellent and divine interpreter
and executor of the divine will; by whom, as we
learn from what follows, God effected the new creation of the world and of all things.   John himself, explaining this title of WORD a little further on, writes
(John i. 18), " No man hath seen God at any time ;
the only begotten Son, who is in the bosom of the
Father, he hath declared him."   Hence also the author of the Epistle to the Hebrews states (chap. i. 2)
that " in these last days God hath spoken unto us by
his Son."   The same may also be observed of Christ
when he is called " the image of the invisible God;"
that he has caused God, whom no one hath seen at any
time, to be seen and known by us in all those things
relating to our salvation, which it was of consequence
should be seen and known.   He was the " express
image of the person," or substance of God, and likewise " the brightness of his glory," in so far as the
power, wisdom, and goodness of God shone in him
during his abode on earth, (the period concerning
which the author speaks, as the succeeding context
evinces,) and God's invisible substance itself was displayed

played and placed before the eyes of men in the divinest attributes and works. If, however, any one should contend that all these titles, " the image of God," " the express image of God's person," " the brightness of the glory of God," are applied to Christ because God has made him the most like himself by the communication of a divine nature and glory, and that he requires to be worshipped and adored by all in him, he will by no means find me an opposer of his opinion. As to the declaration of Jesus, " He that hath seen me hath seen the Father," it cannot be certainly proved from it that any one has a divine nature; since this vision cannot refer to the essence of God, which is absolutely invisible, but ought to be understood of the view, that is, the knowledge of those things which Christ said and did, as he himself asserts in the verse immediately following. He who sees and knows these things sees and knows God himself, as far as he can be seen and known by men, and as he ought to be, if they would obtain salvation. Neither can this divine nature be inferred from the words, " I am in the Father, and the Father in me," since Christ says to his disciples (John xv. 4, 5), "Abide in me, and I in you. As the branch cannot bear fruit of itself, except it abide in the vine; no more can ye except ye abide in me. I am the vine and ye are the branches. He that abideth in me and I in him, the same bringeth forth much fruit; for without me ye can do nothing." Which comparison of the vine and the branch indicates, not an unity of essence, but the junction of the branch with the vine. And again,

further

further on (John xvii. 21, 23), speaking to the Father of his disciples, and on their behalf, he says, " that they also may be one, as thou Father art in me, and I in thee, that they also may be one in us. I in them, and thou in me." To the same effect he speaks John xiv. 10, 11, 20. But shall we on this account say that the disciples ought also to have a divine nature? Christ, then, by this manner of speaking, declares the intimate connexion of the Father with him, and, on the other hand, of himself with the Father; whence it comes to pass that the Father never forsakes him, and that he in no case acts in opposition to the Father. The demonstrative proofs of this are the divine works of Christ, from which he desired that the truth and certainty of his words should be inferred (John x. 38), "Though ye believe not me, believe the works; that ye may know and believe, that the Father is in me and I in him." But these works were no evidence that Christ had the divine nature which the Father possessed; for, if he had, it could never have been evinced by those works that he had been sent by the Father, he having himself, without any mission, the power of doing them. Nor, in the last place, can the divine nature of Christ be proved from these words, " In him dwelleth all the fulness of the Godhead bodily." For, first, since the apostle puts Christ in opposition to philosophy and the law, it is evident that he speaks of that deity or divinity of Christ which is derived to us through his doctrine and spirit: but this is true and celestial wisdom, the solid knowledge of the divine will. The same is also to be inferred from the

phrase

phrase "all the fulness, &c." for these words indi‑
cate that that kind of divinity is here spoken of which
may exist somewhere without being complete, or full
in all its parts, which cannot happen in respect to the
divine essence. Add to this, that the word BODILY
is here opposed to legal shadows, as may be per‑
ceived from the seventeenth verse, compared with these
and the preceding words. Whence it may be seen that
BODILY signifies TRULY and SUBSTANTIALLY; and also
that the writer is here treating of that which had
existed as it were in shadow elsewhere, namely in the
law:—which, again, evinces that the divine essence is
not here spoken of, but rather the true and solid
knowledge of the divine will, and the fulness of that
kind of divinity whereof the Colossians themselves
were, in their measure, made partakers by Christ.
For the apostle immediately adds (ver. 10) "and ye
are complete in him," alluding, in the expression
COMPLETE, to the FULNESS of divinity which he had
stated to dwell in Christ; as is shown not only by the
similarity of the Greek words, but also by the con‑
nexion of the things: as if he had said, "And of his
fulness ye are filled;" or, as John expresses himself in
a similar case (chap. i. v. 16), "And of his fulness
have we all received:" which passage, taken from the
close of the fourteenth verse, where the Word is said
to have been full of grace and truth, to the end of the
eighteenth verse, excellently illustrates the text under
consideration. In like manner also the apostle ex‑
presses to the Ephesians (chap. iii. ver. 19) his wish
that they "might be filled with all the fulness of God."

But

But the " fulness of God," and " the fulness of the Godhead," are the same ; and this, although it dwells first, and far more abundantly in Christ, as the head, is derived through him to the members, according to the measure and capacity of each.

Where do the Scriptures assert concerning Christ, that he had glory with the Father before the world was ?

In John xvii. 5, our Lord himself, in his prayer to God, says, "And now, O Father, glorify thou me with thine own self, with the glory which I had with thee before the world was."

What reply do you make to this ?

That the divine nature of Christ cannot be hence proved : for that a person may have had something, and consequently may have had glory, with the Father before the world was, without its being to be therefore concluded that he then actually existed, or that he possessed the same nature as the Father, is evident from 2 Tim. i. 9, where the apostle says of believers, that grace was given to them before the world began. Besides, it is here stated that Christ prayed for this glory ; which is wholly incompatible with a divine nature. But the meaning of the passage is, that Christ beseeches God to give him in actual possession, with himself, the glory which he had with him, in his purposes and decrees, before the world was.   For it is often said that a person has something with any one, when it is promised, or is destined for him : on this account believers are frequently said by this evangelist to have eternal life.   Hence it happens that

Christ

Christ does not say absolutely that he had had that glory, but that he had had it WITH THE FATHER; as if he had said, that he now prayed to have actually conferred upon him that glory which had been laid up for him with the Father of old, and before the creation of the world[34].

[34] That this is the true sense of the passage is directly shown by Augustine and Beda. Musculus explains it in the same manner, as does also the great Grotius, who is himself a host. B. WISSOWATIUS.

The Arabic version renders this passage as follows :— " Now therefore, O my Father, glorify thou me with the glory which was for me with thee before the world was." *Nunc igitur glorifica me tu, Pater mi, gloriâ quæ erat mihi apud te ante existentiam mundi.* But the Æthiopic, as follows :—" And now glorify me, O Father, with my glory which is with thee, which was before the world was created." *Et nunc glorifica me, Pater, cum gloriâ mea, quæ apud te* EST, *quæ* FUIT *prius quam crearetur mundus.*

It ought also to be observed here, that it has been the unanimous opinion of the Jews down to the present day, that the Messiah had no existence before the creation of the world, except in the divine decrees. In the Babylon Talmud, where the origin and ancient lineage of the Messiah are treated of, no higher excellence is attributed to him, than that his name was created before the world was produced. The passage (In Tract. PESACHIM *cap.* iv.) is to the following effect : " Seven things were created before the world was produced; namely, the Law, Repentance, Gen Heden (or Paradise), Gehenna (or Hell), the Throne of Glory, the Place of Sanctuary, and the Messiah's name. The LAW, because it is written (Prov. viii. 22), " The Lord possessed me in the beginning of his way, before his works of old." REPENTANCE, according to the words of the Psalmist (xc. 2, 3), "Before the mountains were brought forth," &c. " Thou turnest man to destruction, and sayest, Return, ye children of men." GEN HEDEN, because it is said (Gen. ii. 8), " The Lord planted a garden eastward in Eden." GEHENNA, as it is written (Isaiah xxx. 31), " Tophet is ordained of old." The THRONE OF GLORY, and the PLACE OF SANCTUARY, according to the prophet's words (Jer. xvii. 12), " A glorious high throne from the beginning, the place of our sanctuary."

H

Where do the Scriptures assert that the Spirit of Christ was in the Prophets?

In the first epistle of Peter, (chap. i. 10, 11), " Of which salvation the prophets have inquired and searched diligently, who prophesied of the grace that should come unto you, searching what, or what manner of time, the Spirit of Christ which was in them did signify."

What answer do you make to this testimony?

That the existence of a divine nature in Christ cannot be proved from it.   For this Spirit which was in the prophets may be called the Spirit of Christ, not because it was given by Christ, but either be-

tuary."   The NAME OF THE MESSIAH, as it is said (Psalm lxxxi. 17), " His name was first, before the sun," *Ante solem primum nomen ejus*; [rendered in the common English translation "His name shall be continued as long as the sun."] See also the Talmud *de Votis*. The Chaldee Paraphrase thus reads the last passage : "A name was prepared for the Messiah before the sun:" *Ante solem præparatum est nomen Messiæ.* It is evident from these quotations that the Messiah's name cannot be said to have been created before the world, in any other sense than that wherein the creation of the other six things is to be understood.   The Hebrew interpreters themselves give this explanation of the matter : that God, before he produced the world, made a decree for the creation of these things, and for sending the Messiah: and adduce in support of this meaning the following axiom, That the INTENTION is first, afterwards the EXECUTION. The most ancient Jewish interpreters do not ascend higher in treating of the descent of the Messiah ; and those of more modern times agree with them in opinion.   Among others may be consulted Rabbi Solomon Iarchi, on the cited passages ; R. Moses Ben Maimon, *Tract. Melochim in Misnajoth, cap. ult.* ; D. Isaac Abarbanel on Isaiah, chap. xi. ; and others whose names may be seen in a work already referred to—*Disceptatio de Verbo, vel Sermone Dei*, which also may be consulted on these points.   B. WISSOWATIUS,

cause

cause it announced those things which pertained to
him, or because it, as it were, wholly breathed and
contemplated him, or because it was the same as the
Spirit which was to dwell in Christ, in as much as it
predicted those very things which Christ was to announce. This Peter himself intimates in the passage,
when he adds concerning the Spirit, that "it testified
beforehand the sufferings of Christ, and the glory
that should follow."   Christ foretold the very same
things through his own Spirit ; only the Spirit being
more abundant in him, his prediction was far more
explicit and perfect than the predictions of the prophets.   John adopts the same manner of speaking,
in a contrary case, when he says (1 John iv. 3) of that
" Spirit which confesseth not that Jesus Christ is
come in the flesh," that it is the Spirit of Antichrist ;
and he adds, " whereof ye have heard that it should
come, and even now already is it in the world," that
is to say, was in those Antichrists which were then the
forerunners of the great Antichrist ; since that great
Antichrist, of which he speaks, did not at that time
exist.   He thus expresses himself also because that
spirit was wholly antichristian, and breathed and in
culcated doctrines accordant with those which have
been introduced into the world by Antichrist. For he
who asserts that Jesus is the most high God himself,
denies that he is the Christ of God, that is, a celestial king of God's appointment, which is the spirit
of Antichrist (1 John ii. 22).   Not unlike this is the
mode of speaking employed by the same writer (chap.
iv. 6), " Hereby know we the spirit of truth and

the

the spirit of error;" where it is called the spirit of truth, and the spirit of error, not because truth and error, as if they were persons, bestowed this spirit; but because the spirit of truth speaks what is of the truth, the spirit of error, what is erroneous. It may be added, that it would not at all follow that Christ had a divine nature, even though it should be proved that he communicated his spirit to the prophets; since any one might impart to others the spirit which he received from God, as indeed Peter openly testifies concerning Christ, subsequently to his exaltation, Acts ii. 33.

Where do the Scriptures assert concerning Christ that he came down from heaven, came forth from the Father, and came into the world?

John iii. 13: " No man hath ascended up to heaven, but he that came down from heaven, even the Son of Man which is or WAS in heaven:" and further on (chap. x. 36), " Whom the Father hath sanctified and sent into the world." Also chap. xvi. 28, " I came forth from the Father and am come into the world; again I leave the world and go to the Father." And chap. xvii. 18, " As thou hast sent me into the world, even so have I sent them into the world."

What answer do you make to these passages?

That the divine nature of Christ cannot be proved from them is evident from hence; that the expressions in the first testimony, " came down from heaven," may be understood figuratively; as in James i. 17, " Every good and perfect gift is from above, and cometh down from the Father of lights," &c. And Revelation

velation xxi. 2, " I John saw the holy city New Jerusalem coming down from God out of heaven," &c.
But if they ought to be understood literally, which I
most freely admit, it is apparent that they were spoken
of no other than the SON OF MAN, who, since he had
necessarily a human nature, could not be God, nor,
indeed, have existed antecedently to his birth. Add to
this, that it is expressly stated, that he had ascended
into heaven, that is, before he declared these things;
which could be asserted of Christ not on account of
his divine, but only of his human nature[35]. Moreover,
as to what the Scriptures testify concerning Christ,
that " the Father sent him into the world," we read
the very same thing concerning the Apostles, in the
passage quoted from John xvii. 18; " As thou hast
sent me into the world, even so have I sent them into
the world." Hence it is that Paul expressly states,
that " God sent his son, made or born of a woman,
made under the law :" which implies, not that Christ
was sent in order that he might subsequently be born of
a woman, but was sent, now that he had been born of
a woman. It cannot therefore be hence inferred that

---

[35] That Christ was in heaven antecedently to his nativity, it
were absurd to suppose ; for he would in that case, especially,
if he was the creator of heaven, have descended thence with
perfect knowledge and wisdom. But that he was MADE perfect in these respects is testified not only by the Baptist, but
also by himself, (John iii. 32 ; viii. 26, 28, 38; xii. 49, 50). On
which point see more in the following section. Luke also
(chap. ii. 52) expressly states, that, after his birth, he increased
in wisdom, and in favour with God:—these therefore he had not
before, or if he had he had lost them, which were no less absurd. B. WISSOWATIUS.

he

he had existed before he was born of the Virgin, or that he was endowed with a divine nature. The declaration that Christ " came forth from the Father," imports the same thing as the phrase that he had " come down from heaven;" from which I have just shown, that it cannot be proved that Christ possesses the divine nature which is claimed for him. I assert the same concerning his " coming into the world." For he did not come into the world before he was sent by the Father, but rather was sent in order that he might come into the world. But it has just been proved that he was not sent by the Father in order to be born of the Virgin, but after he had been born of her. . Whence also the Scriptures place his coming into the world subsequent to his nativity. Thus our Lord states (John xviii. 37), " For this end was I born, and for this cause came I into the world, that I might bear witness unto the truth." Add to this, that John (1 Epist. iv. 1) states, in similar phraseology, that " many false prophets are gone out into the world," who certainly neither existed before they were born, nor had a divine nature. This last mode of speaking imports no more than this, that Christ had begun to preach publicly among mankind ; and the preceding, that he had for this purpose been commissioned by God from heaven [36].

Where

---

[36] In proof of the existence of Christ before his nativity are adduced John i. 15 and 30, John bare witness of him, and cried, saying, This was he of whom I spake, He that cometh after me is preferred before me: for he was before me." " This is he of whom I said, After me cometh a man which is preferred before

Where do the Scriptures style Christ the " one Lord," " the Lord of glory," " the King of kings and Lord of lords ?"

In 1 Cor. viii. 6, " To us there is—one Lord, Jesus Christ, by whom are all things, and we by him." 1 Cor. ii. 8, " Had they known it, they would not have crucified the Lord of glory." Revel. xvii. 14, " Then shall they make war with the lamb, and the lamb shall overcome them, for he is Lord of lords and King of kings." And chap. xix. 16, " And he hath

fore me : for he was before me." But that the word πρωτος (BEFORE) denotes in these passages a priority in DIGNITY and not in TIME, has been sufficiently proved by Erasmus, Grotius, and Beza (who reads here, *antepositus est mihi*, " he is placed before me.") Cingallus, in the work above referred to, gives a catalogue, p. 127, of other writers, both ancient and modern, who held the same opinion. The same thing is illustrated by parallel places in Matt. iii. 11 ; " He that cometh after me is mightier than I, whose shoes I am not worthy to bear." Mark i. 7 ; " There cometh one mightier than I after me, the latchet of whose shoes I am not worthy to stoop down and unloose." Luke iii. 16; " One mightier than I cometh, the latchet of whose shoes I am. not worthy to unloose." Genesis xlviii. 20 may also be considered; " And he blessed them that day, saying, In thee shall Israel bless, saying, God make thee as Ephraim and as Manasseh : and he set Ephraim BEFORE Manasseh." t B. WISSOWATIUS.

t [The Polish Socinians, believing that Christ after his baptism, and before he entered on the duties of his office, was taken up into heaven, in order to be taught the great truths he was to communicate to the world, interpret the first two clauses of John iii. 13, " No man hath ascended up to heaven, but he that came down from heaven," of his literal ascent and descent on this occasion. In the last clause they put the verb in the past tense, and read the passage, " the Son of Man who WAS in heaven." In what sense modern Unitarians understand the whole verse has been shown above, page 67, note k, to which the reader is referred. TRANSL.]

on

on his vesture, and on his thigh, a name written, King
of kings and Lord of lords."   .

What do you allege against these testimonies ?   .

As to the first, the divine nature of Christ cannot
be inferred from the apostle's styling him the " one
Lord;" for he clearly distinguishes him from the one
God, whom he calls the Father ; and whom alone I
have already stated to be that one God. Again, the
apostle shows by the expressions he uses respecting
him, " by whom are all things," that he is not the
one God ; since it appears, as I have before proved,
that this preposition BY (*per*) designates not the
primary but the secondary cause, which can by no
means be affirmed of him who is the one God. And
although the Scriptures sometimes say of the Father,
that " all things are by him," yet this is to be understood of the Father in a sense different from that in
which it is understood of Christ : since no one can,
as his superior, do any thing by or through the Father.   For this is asserted of the Father, not because
any person does any thing by or through him, but because all things are first ordained by his counsel and
also accomplished by his power, although he may
sometimes employ other intermediate or secondary
causes.   But this is affirmed of Christ because some
one else, namely, God, performs all things by him, as
I have already shown, and as appears from this very
passage ; since the declaration " BY WHOM are all
things" (*per quem omnia*) is opposed to "OF
WHOM are all things" (*ex quo omnia*), which designates the primary efficient cause. I will not re-
                                        peat,

peat, what has already been stated more than once, that the expression ALL THINGS refers to the subject. matter of discourse, as the prefixing of the article in the Greek text evinces. Now the apostle is treating of all those things which pertain to christians, as— not to notice the term FATHER, and the phrase the ONE LORD JESUS CHRIST—is demonstrated by the words TO US, so often repeated, and which can designate no other persons but christians. Wherefore the divine nature of Christ cannot be proved from this testimony [37]. With respect to the second testimony, as this speaks of the person who was crucified, it is evident that the divine nature contended for cannot be proved from it, since this could not be asserted of one who, in consequence of that nature, was God, but only of a man; who is styled the "Lord of Glory," that is, the GLORIOUS LORD, because he was by God crowned with glory and honour. For Christ is described by these terms, not so much because he was actually such at the time of his crucifixion, as because he was so when the apostle thus designates him: though at the time of his crucifixion also he was the "Lord of Glory" in so far as he was destined for celestial glory. In relation to the third testimony, as it treats of one who was a lamb and had a robe, and whom the same writer distinctly states to have been slain, and

---

[37] That the expression ALL THINGS (ταυτα) is hardly ever used in the Scriptures in an unlimited sense, may be seen in the *Bibliotheca Ravanellis*. So also, in this passage, the word must necessarily admit of limitation; otherwise God, the Father, would be BY CHRIST.—B. WISSOWATIUS.

to

to have redeemed us by his blood, things which do not
comport with a being who is by nature GOD,—it is
evident that the divine nature of Christ cannot be
established by it.   But all the titles which are attributed to Christ in these testimonies denote the supreme authority which God has given to him over all
things.

What testimonies of Scripture may be adduced for
Faith in Christ, and ascribing divine honour to him?

Christ himself says (John xiv. 1), " Ye believe in
God, believe also in me." And John v. 22, 23, " The
Father judgeth no man, but hath committed all
judgement unto the Son, that all men should honour
the Son, even as they honour the Father." Also Philippians ii. 9, 10, 11, " Wherefore God hath highly
exalted him, and given him a name which is above
every name, that in the name of Jesus every knee·
should bow of things in heaven, and things in earth,
and things under the earth, and that every tongue
should confess that Jesus Christ is Lord to the glory
of God the Father."—To these, other passages might
be added.

What answer do you make to these testimonies?

In respect to the first, so far is it from proving
Christ to be by nature God, that it is evident it es-
tablishes quite the contrary : for Christ makes here
a distinction between himself and the one God. As
to what our adversaries affirm, that faith is not to be
placed in any one besides God; this is in another place
(John xii. 44) explained by Christ, when he says,
                                        " He

" He that believeth on me, believeth not on me, but on him that sent me." Whence it is evident that Christ did not claim for himself faith in the sense in which it is due to God. For that faith is due to God alone, which terminates in him, and has respect to him as the original author of all things : but it is evident from the cited verse that such a faith is not to be attributed to Christ. For we therefore believe in Christ, because he has promised to us supreme felicity, having been sent by God for this purpose ; and because he received from God the power of making us happy, and was charged with this office. So that our faith in Christ is in this manner directed to God himself as its ultimate object. To this purpose is the testimony of Peter (1 Epist. i. 21), " Who by him do believe in God, that raised him up from the dead, and gave him glory, that your faith and hope might be in God."

But our opponents allege from Jeremiah (xvii. 5) " Cursed be the man who trusteth in man ?"

To this I reply, that it is not said absolutely, " Cursed be the man who trusteth in man," but who so trusts that he " maketh flesh his arm ;" that is, who rests his hope on the strength of a mortal man, and not on the divine spirit or energy which is discernible in that man. Wherefore MAN is to be understood here, as he is wont to be, according to the mortal nature of men only, without any portion of divine energy and power ; for whoever has had these communicated to him by God is placed so far beyond and above man. For this is all that is to be understood

stood by the term FLESH,—the following words
being added, " and whose heart departeth from the
Lord." But we who place our hope in Christ, do
not "make flesh our arm;" since Christ, although
mortal, was endowed with the divine spirit, and is
now made a living spirit. Neither does our heart
" depart from the Lord;" for by trusting in Christ
we trust in God, and thus our heart approaches towards God instead of departing from him.

What answer do you make to the other testimonies
which speak of the divine honour of Christ?

As all the testimonies which speak of the divine
honour of Christ do also most distinctly speak of a
divine honour given and granted to him, at a particular period, and for a certain reason, it is evident,
that it cannot be proved from them that he has a
divine nature. Our adversaries indeed oppose to this
that passage of Isaiah (chap. xlii. 8) " My glory will
I not give to another." But I answer, that what
was intended by the term ANOTHER is sufficiently
evident; for it is immediately added, " neither my
praise to graven images." God therefore speaks in
this place of those who have no communion with him,
and to whom if any glory or honour were ascribed,
it would not redound to him. Whence also it appears
that the words " I will not give" signify nothing
more than " I will not permit;" and not absolutely,
" I will not of my own accord communicate to any one
of my supreme glory." For who does not know that
God will communicate of his glory to a person who
depends upon him, and is subordinate to him? For by
this

this means his glory suffers no diminution, since the whole reverts back to him. Such a person is the Lord Jesus: as he is from God, and is altogether subordinate to him,—whatever honour is shown to him redounds wholly to God himself.

I have now heard you concerning those passages of Scripture which seem directly to relate to the Son of God;—I wish next to be informed concerning those which are applied to him in some accommodated sense, and seem to prove him to have a divine nature?

These are comprehended in those testimonies, which were in the Old Testament spoken of the one God of Israel, and which in the New Testament are either actually applied to Christ, or believed to be applied to him. The first of these is Isaiah xxxv. 4, 5, 6, " God will come, and save you. Then the eyes of the blind shall be opened, and the ears of the deaf shall be unstopped: then shall the lame man leap as an hart, and the tongue of the dumb sing:" which things seem to be repeated concerning Christ in Matthew. xi. 5, " The blind receive their sight," &c. To this may be added a passage of a similar kind from Malachi iii. 1, " Behold, I will send my messenger, and he shall prepare the way before me:" which is applied to Christ in the tenth verse of the same chapter of Matthew, and Mark i. 2. In Isaiah xli. 4 ; xliv. 6 ; xlviii. 12, we read, " I am the first, and I am the last :" and the same thing is said concerning Christ, Revelation i. 17 ; ii. 8. In Psalm lxviii. 18, we read, " Thou hast ascended on high, thou hast led captivity

captivity captive, thou hast received gifts for men :"
things which are repeated concerning Christ, Ephesians iv. 8.   In several places in the Scriptures
(Psalm vii. 9; Jer. xi. 20; xvii. 10) we find it written
that " God searches or tries the heart and the reins:"
and the same is affirmed of Christ, Revel. ii, 23.
It is said, Psalm xcvii. 7, "Worship him, all ye gods"
[angels] : which is referred to Christ, Heb. i. 6.   To
the same purpose is Isaiah xlv. 23, " I have sworn
by myself, that unto me every knee shall bow:"
which is spoken of Christ (Rom. xiv. 11).   In Isaiah
viii. 14, it is said that God should be for " a stone
of stumbling and a rock of offence to both the houses
of Israel :" which is applied to Christ, Luke ii. 34;
Rom. ix. 32; 1 Peter ii. 7.   Zechariah (xi. 10)
writes, " They shall look upon me whom they have
pierced :" which John applies to Christ in his gospel
xix. 37, and Revelation i. 7.   Lastly, Psalm cii. 26,
" They shall perish, but thou shalt endure," and
what follows, concerning the destruction of the heavens, are applied to Christ, Heb. i. 10.   From these
testimonies our adversaries reason as follows :—Since
those things which, under the Law, were spoken of
God, are under the Gospel affirmed concerning Christ,
it is apparent that Christ is the God of Israel.

What reply do you make to these things?

First, that all those passages of the Old Testament are not actually quoted in reference to Christ.
For Matthew xi. 5, does not at all show that Isaiah
xxxv. 4, 5, 6, was spoken of Christ; neither is the
sense of the two passages the same.   Nor, again, in
those

those places where Christ is said to be "the first and the last," and to "search the heart and the reins," are the passages of the Old Testament cited as quotations: that being merely affirmed concerning Christ which had before been asserted of God :—though possibly there may be some allusion to those passages; as it is customary for all writers to apply to their own subject, in an accommodated sense, the words of both sacred and profane authors, though originally used in reference to other things; especially when by this means they are not so much endeavouring to prove any thing, as to explain and exemplify. But although all those testimonies of the Old Testament, spoken of God, were applied to Christ, (which indeed I admit in respect to some of them,) it would not hence follow that he possessed a divine nature. For this might be done for some other reason; namely, on account of the intimate union subsisting between God and Christ, and the similitude which is essential to that union. Their union is discernible in this, that God, from the very beginning of the new covenant, has, through the instrumentality of Christ, performed, and hereafter will finally accomplish, all things that in any way relate to the salvation of mankind, and also, consequently, to the destruction of the wicked. Whence it is necessary that he should be like God as to authority and dominion, power and wisdom, and, to omit other particulars, as to honour and worship, and therefore united to him as to the author of all these things : so that if any thing were committed to Christ, the same would,

in

in consequence of this, be also necessarily committed
to God himself. Now if the Scriptures declare concerning Moses that he brought the children of Israel
out of Egypt (Exodus xxxii. 7), and that he was the
Redeemer of that people (Acts vii. 35), and affirm
of other persons, the very same thing which is most
explicitly predicated of God himself, when neither
Moses nor those other persons were joined with God
by such an union as subsists between him and Christ,
—with much more justice may those things which in
their first application were spoken of God, be referred
in an accommodated sense to Christ, on account of
that peculiar and most intimate union which subsists
between them.

Apply your observations to the several passages separately?

In respect then to the first and second of the cited
testimonies;—since God brought salvation to us
through Christ, and came to mankind by him, as his
distinguished ambassador, who, evidently in an un-
precedented manner, sustained and represented his
person, and performed all things in his name, and by
his authority and power; those things which are
written of the coming of God to mankind, of the salvation given by him, of the angel (or messenger)
sent before his face, and the preparing of the way,
may justly be applied to Christ in an accommodated
sense, although he were not that God concerning
whom those things were first predicated. This is
sufficiently shown by the words of Malachi, quoted by
Matthew and Mark (see Mal. iii. 1; Matt. xi. 10;

Mark

Mark i. 2). For in this passage, what God says, according to the prophet, " before ME," or " before MY face," is written by those evangelists, " before THY face," or " before THEE ;" by whom is meant God, who speaks Malach. iii. 2. And if you look to the prophet's words, you will see that God says that he would come, not in his own person, but in the person of Christ, and that John would prepare the way before the face of God, so far as he would prepare it before the face of Christ, whom God had designed to be the messenger of the covenant. Moreover, as God so prosecutes the scheme of salvation by Christ, as that he, having been first delegated by him for this purpose, has begun it, and will ultimately complete it, he is said, like God, to be, in relation to our salvation, "the first and the last [38]." Because, again, God,

---

[38] That the SON of God is absolutely the FIRST, none will venture to assert, who maintain that the Father is the first person of the Trinity. Erasmus well observes in his Annotations on John viii. 25: *Quod in Apocalypsi dicitur principium et finis, constat intelligendum, Christum esse initium et consummationem Ecclesiæ, quam priore adventu constituit, posteriore perficiet.* " As to what are called in the Revelation ' the beginning and the end,' it is evident that we must understand by them that Christ is the beginning and the consummation of the Church, which was founded by his first, and will be completed by his second, appearance." We read nearly to the same effect in Hermas *Simil.* 9; where, speaking of the Church, he calls the Son of God, " the old rock and the new gate ;" and for these reasons, because the Church is founded upon him, and is older than every creature, and because he will in the last days appear for its completion, that those who are about to be saved may enter through him into the kingdom of God: which accords with the words of Paul, whose disciple he was (Col.

God, like a conqueror, in him, ascended on high,
(Col. ii. 15; Ephes. iv. 8) led captive enemies, displayed the conquered and the spoiled, and by him gave
gifts to men; and because Christ descended into hell
that he might vanquish and destroy hell and death,
and the devil, who held the empire of death ;—that
passage of the Psalms (lxviii. 18) which was spoken
of God, is applied to Christ.   Because God, in order
to be able to judge the secrets of men by him, has
given him so much wisdom, that he can search the
heart and the reins, Christ applies to himself what
is, in reference to this subject, asserted of God.   Because Christ is seated at the right hand of God in
heaven, and has had a name given him which is
above every name, he is also to be worshipped by
the angels, (Heb. i. 6, compared with the third and
fourth verses of the same chapter).   Because every
knee ought now to bow, and hereafter actually will
bow to him (Phil. ii. 9, 10) when he shall appear on
the judgement-seat, in the glory of his Father, and
shall thus represent his person and majesty (Matt.
xvi. 27), which adoration and genuflexion will be referred to God himself; the words of the Psalmist
(Psalm xcvii. 7, 13) and of Isaiah (chap. xlv. 23) are
quoted in reference to Christ. (Romans xiv. 11, compared with Philipp. ii. 9, 10, and John v. 22, 23, 24.)
Because, in consequence of this, he who is offended in

(Col. i. 15, 18), and also with Revelation i. 17, and xxii. 13,
as Grotius also has remarked. To the same effect are likewise Heb. ii. 10; xii. 2; Acts iii. 15, 31; Eph ii. 20, &c. B.
WISSOWATIUS.

Christ

Christ is offended in God, who has placed him a stone
in Zion; and because he who touches and hurts him,
touches the apple of God's eye and hurts God himself
—therefore the words of Isaiah (viii. 14) and Zechariah (xii. 10) are accommodated to him.   And because, finally, God will hereafter by him destroy the
heavens, and burn this world for the punishment of
the wicked; the words of the Psalmist (cii. 26) spoken
directly concerning God, are applied to Christ.   (2
Thess. i. 8; 2 Peter iii. 7 ; Heb. i. 10.)

Are there any passages of scripture besides these,
wherein words used in the Old Testament in reference to some one thing or person, are applied in
an accommodated sense to another in the New Testament ?

There are :—for, not to notice the passages wherein
those things formerly spoken of the TYPE, are in the
New Testament applied to the ANTITYPE, of which
the number is considerable ;—we perceive that what
was predicted concerning Christ in Isaiah xlix. 6,
" I will give thee for a light to the Gentiles, that
thou mayest be my salvation to the end of the earth,"
is applied (Acts xiii. 47) to Paul and Barnabas.
That which is said of the Law (Deut. xxx. 12, 14)
is applied (Rom. x. 6, 7, 8) to the righteousness of
faith.   What is stated of the heavens (Psalm xix. 4)
is quoted in an accommodated sense (Rom. x. 18).
What is said of treading oxen (Deut. xxv. 9) is applied (1 Cor. ix. 9) to the teachers of the Gospel generally.   What is affirmed (Psalm civ. 4) concerning
winds and lightnings, you have already been informed,

ed, is applied (Heb. i. 7) to angels. The first of these accommodations is made on account of subordination, the others on account of some similitude.

I perceive that Christ has not the divine nature which is claimed for him; but that he is a real man :—inform me now in what way the knowledge of this eminently conduces to salvation?

This you may perceive from hence : first, because the contrary opinion greatly tarnishes the glory of God; secondly, because it materially weakens and nearly destroys the certainty of our hope; and thirdly, because it makes one thing of Christ, and another of the Son of God; so that divine honour being transferred to the latter, the divine honour of him who is actually the Christ and the Son of God, is either taken away, or essentially impaired.

How does the opinion of our adversaries tarnish the glory of God?

Not only because the glory of the one God, which pertains to the Father alone, is transferred to another, concerning which I have already treated; but also because God is deprived of that glory which he seeks in the exaltation of Jesus Christ. For if Christ were the most high God, he could not be exalted; or if he could, his exaltation could refer to nothing but the reception of his divine nature entire. Paul, however, says (Ephes. i. 17—21) that " the God of our Lord Jesus Christ, the Father of Glory,—wrought his mighty power in Christ, when he raised him from the dead, and set him at his own right hand in the heavenly places, far above all principality," also (Philipp. ii. 9, 10), that "God had highly exalted Christ, and given him a name which is above every name, that in the name of Jesus every knee should bow, and every tongue should confess that Jesus Christ is Lord to the glory of God the Father :" " To THE GLORY," the apostle writes, " OF GOD THE FATHER," who GAVE him such a name, and such glory.

How, secondly, does the opinion of our adversaries destroy or weaken our hope?

Because the greatest force which pertains to the resurrection of Christ, as a proof of our resurrection, is taken away by attributing this divine nature to him. For it would hence follow that Christ rose from the dead by virtue of his divine nature, as indeed is commonly maintained, and that, on this account, he could by no means be detained by death. But we have nothing in us by nature, which, after we are dead, can recall us to life, or which can in any way prevent our remaining dead perpetually. How then can the certainty of our resurrection be demonstrated from the example of Christ's resurrection, as the apostle Paul has done (1 Cor. xv.), when there exists such a disparity between Christ and us? And, indeed, if this opinion be admitted, Christ, in reality, could not die, and rise from the dead; since it would follow from it, that Christ was not a person, or, as they say, *suppositum humanum*[u], that is, a man subsisting of himself. But to die and to rise from the dead can comport with no other than a subject, [*sup-*

---

[u] [Vide *Martinii Lexicon*, v. *Suppositum.* TRANSt.]

positum]

positum] or thing subsisting of itself. A divine person could not die. If therefore Christ was destitute
of a human person, capable of dying and rising
from the dead, how could he die, or rise from the
dead? The same reason shows that Christ was not
truly a man, since every one who is a real man is a human person. But that opinion which acknowledges
Christ as subsisting of himself, and therefore truly
a man, who was obedient to his Father unto death;
and asserts and clearly determines that he died, was
raised from the dead by God, and endowed with immortality; does in a wonderful manner sustain our
hope of eternal salvation; placing before us the very
image of the thing, and assuring us that we also,
though we be mortal and die, shall nevertheless, if
we follow his footsteps, be in due time raised from the
dead, and be brought to a participation of the immortality which he now enjoys.

How, thirdly, does the opinion of our adversaries
make one thing of Christ, and another of the Son of
God?

Because it makes of Christ, the one God himself,
and calls him the Son of God, who actually existed
before the conception of the man Jesus by the Holy
Spirit, and his birth of the Virgin, and indeed before all
ages, and directs to the worship of him, our honour and
faith:—while in the mean time, either he who is truly
Christ and the Son of God, is to them an idol, if they
worship him; or else it does not appear how he is
at once the one God, and a man, and can be worshipped

shipped both as God, and as a man whom God has exalted [39].

SEC-

---

[39] If some difficulties should still occur to any one in respect to other passages of Scripture besides those which have been examined, he will find them explained in the *Bibliotheca Fratrum Polonorum*, in Enjedinus, or Volkelius; also in Felbinger's Demonstrations of Christianity, and in the Annotations of Grotius and Brenius. It ought not to seem to any one a matter of surprise, that more should be said on this subject than on the others; for extreme is the hatred which these churches endure from all, on account of this confession concerning the Son of Man.

It remains that we subjoin a few things concerning ANTIQUITY, about which many make so much noise. That the first Christian teachers, who are called Fathers, believed, until the year 300 and afterwards, that the Father alone was the supreme God, will appear from an examination of their writings: and for this purpose their collected opinions are given by Petavius in his work on the Trinity, by Zwicker in his *Irenicum Irenicorum*, by Sandius in his Nucleus of Eccles. Hist., and in others of his publications. I do not however deny that most of them ascribed two natures to the Son of God; asserted his existence before the creation of the world; and taught nearly the same things concerning him as were afterwards maintained by the Arians. Nevertheless, in the most ancient of them, those who lived nearest the time of the Apostles, nothing of this kind appears; indeed the contrary may plainly be collected from them. To omit at present other proofs, Eusebius (*Hist. Eccles. lib.* v. *cap.* 28), speaking of the Artemonites, who flourished about the year 200, and acknowledged no other for the Son of God besides or before him who was conceived of the holy Spirit, and born of the Virgin, (constantly asserting that the primitive Christians, and indeed the Apostles themselves taught the same doctrine, as Theodoret testifies, as well as Eusebius) mentions an ancient writer refuting them by the authority of Justin, Miltiades, Tatian, Clemens, Irenæus, and Melito, who, he says, taught opinions contrary to those of the Artemonites. Justin, the first of these authorities, flourished about the year 160. Undoubtedly then the disciples of the Apostles, who were anterior to him, taught the same as the Nazarenes, the first Christians:

indeed

SECTION V.

OF THE PROPHETIC OFFICE OF CHRIST.

I UNDERSTAND what relates to the Person of Christ, proceed now to those things which pertain to his offices.

By

---

indeed nothing to the contrary is to be gathered from their genuine writings. Now that the first Christians in Judæa, who confessed that Jesus was the Christ, were called Nazarenes, is evident from Acts xxiv. 5, 14; and from the existing records of antiquity; which also among others, Grotius in his *Proleg. in Matth.* and Curcellæus, *Diatr. de Esu Sangu. cap.* vi. have clearly demonstrated: and that the Nazarenes taught the same doctrines as were afterwards maintained by the Artemonites is declared by Theodoret, Epiphanius, Jerome, and Augustine. Indeed that this was the unanimous opinion of the primitive Church appears besides from that creed alone which is called the Apostles', and to which we assent. [x] B. WISSOWATIUS.

[x] [The English reader, who may wish for further information on this subject, may consult Dr. Priestley's elaborate and masterly work, " The History of Early Opinions concerning Jesus Christ," in four volumes octavo. He should also peruse the Tracts which were published by both the learned combatants in the controversy between Dr. Horsley and Dr. Priestley. These have lately been reprinted, the one by the bishop's son, the Rev. Heneage Horsley, and the other by the London Unitarian Society, under the editorial direction of the Rev. Thomas Belsham, who has added to this edition a Review of the Controversy by Doctor Priestley, in four letters never before published. Mr. Belsham has also personally distinguished himself in the discussions on this subject: first, by a "Review of the Controversy between Dr. Priestley and Dr. Horsley," inserted in his " Calm Inquiry into the Scripture Doctrine concerning the Person of Christ:" afterwards in his " Claims of Dr. Priestley in the Controversy

with

By all means : you must know then that the offices of Christ consist in his being a PROPHET, or the Mediator of the New Covenant; our HIGH PRIEST; and our KING.

Where in the Scriptures is he called a PROPHET, and the Mediator of the New Covenant ?

There is a singular testimony to this effect which Peter quotes from Moses, who had spoken it to the Fathers, (Acts iii. 22) "A Prophet shall the Lord your God raise up unto you of your brethren, like unto me; him shall ye hear in all things whatsoever he shall say unto you." The author of the Epistle to the Hebrews, also, writes (chap. xii. 24), "Ye are come—to Jesus the Mediator of the New Covenant:" and uses the same language, chap. viii. 6. For Moses, also, in so far as he was the Mediator of the Old Covenant (Gal. iii. 19), was at the same time a prophet.

Wherein consists his prophetic office ?

In perfectly manifesting to us, confirming, and establishing, the hidden Will of God.

Whence do you prove that Christ has perfectly manifested to us the Will of God ?

From hence;—that Christ himself told his disciples (John xv. 15), " All things that I have heard of my Father, I have made known unto you :"—and there was nothing pertaining to his Will which he had not heard. And also because John testifies concerning

___

with Bishop Horsley, restated, and vindicated, in reply to the Animadversions of the Rev. Heneage Horsley, &c." and lastly, in his " Letters to the Unitarians of South Wales," a work written in reply to the present Bishop of St. David's, who had entered the lists as the champion of Dr. Horsley, and the antagonist of Dr. Priestley and Mr. Belsham. TRANSL.]

I   him

him (John i. 14 and 16), that he "dwelt among his disciples full of grace and truth:" and that himself, as well as others, had " received of his fulness, and grace for grace:" in illustration of which he adds (ver. 17, 18), " For the Law was given by Moses, but grace and truth came by Jesus Christ. No man hath seen God at any time; the only begotten Son, which is in the bosom of the Father, he hath declared him." To the same purpose are the words of Paul (Col. ii. 9), that ", in him dwelleth all the fulness of the God-head bodily;" or, as he had stated before (ver. 3), that " in Christ," (or rather, " in the mystery of God and of Christ,") " were hid all the treasures of wisdom and knowledge." Hence he is styled the " Word of God" and the " Image of the invisible God;" the import of which titles I have already explained.

But by what means did the Lord Jesus himself acquire his knowledge of the divine Will ?

By ascending into heaven, where he beheld his Father, and that life and happiness which he was to announce to us; where also he heard from the Father all those things which it would behoove him to teach. Being afterwards sent by him from heaven to the earth, he was most largely endowed with the Holy Spirit, through whose inspiration he proclaimed what he had learnt from the Father.

By what testimonies of Scripture do you prove these things ?

That Christ ascended into heaven, he himself tes-tifies, John iii. 13, where he thus speaks : " No man hath ascended up to heaven, but he that came down from heaven, even the Son of Man which is in heaven."

heaven." And that he saw his Father he testifies in the same Gospel, chap. vi. 46, where he states, " Not that any man hath seen the Father, save he which is of God, he hath seen the Father." That he beheld the life and happiness which he announced to us, is evident both from what he himself declares (John iii. 11), that he testified what he had seen; and also from what John the Baptist asserts concerning him in the same chapter (ver. 31, 32), where he observes, " He that cometh from above is above all," " What he hath seen and heard, that he testifieth." That he heard and learnt from the Father what he was to teach to others, appears partly from the passage just cited, and partly from what Christ declares, John viii. 26, " I speak to the world those things which I have heard of him:" and (ver. 28), " As my Father hath taught me, I speak these things." With which agrees ver. 38, " I speak that which I have seen with my Father:" and also, what he states chap. xii. 49, 50, " I have not spoken of myself; but the Father which sent me, he gave me commandment, what I should say, and what I should speak." " Whatsoever I speak, therefore, even as the Father said unto me, so I speak." Whence likewise it is, that he says, his doctrine and word are not his, but the Father's who sent him. That he had descended from heaven, or come forth from the Father, is intimated in some of those very passages which I have just quoted; namely, John iii. 13 and 31 : to which may be added John vi. 38, " I came down from heaven not to do mine own will, but the

will

will of him that sent me:" and chap. xvi. 28, " I
came forth from the Father, and am come into the
world." That he was largely endowed with the
Holy Spirit, is sufficiently evident from the history of
his baptism, not to adduce other testimonies—such as
that of Isaiah lxi. 1, quoted (Luke iv. 18) by Christ
concerning himself, "The spirit of the Lord is upon
me, because he hath anointed me to preach the gospel to the poor," &c.; and that of the apostle Peter
(Acts x. 38), that " God anointed Jesus of Nazareth
with the Holy Ghost and with power." And lastly,
that he spoke the words of God by virtue of his spirit,
John the Baptist testifies, John iii. 34, where, dis-
coursing of Christ, he says, " He whom God hath
sent speaketh the words of God; for God giveth not
the spirit by measure unto him." To which may be
added Acts i. 2, where it is said that Christ had
given commandments unto the apostles " through
the Holy Ghost," that is, by the direction and impulse of the Holy Spirit [y].

---

[y] [The doctrine maintained in the former part of this answer respecting the literal ascent of Jesus into heaven, his
vision of God and of celestial happiness, and his instruction in
the divine truths he was afterwards to promulgate to the
world, constitutes one of the chief points of difference between
the opinions of the old Socinians and those of the Unitarians
of the present day. In what sense the latter interpret the passages upon which the former grounded their hypothesis, has
already been shown above, page 67, note (k), in respect to one
of the principal texts. The reader is again referred to that
note; and he may consult the authorities there cited for the modern Unitarian exposition of the other texts adduced by the
authors of this Catechism in support of their system. TRANSL.]

What

What is that Will of God which has been declared to us by Jesus Christ?

It is that contained in the New Covenant which God has made with the human race through this Mediator (Heb. viii. 6; 1 Tim. ii. 5).

What does this New Covenant comprise?

It comprises both the perfect Precepts, and the perfect Promises of God, together with the mode whereby, and the ground upon which, we ought to conform to these precepts and promises; which ground is itself a command of God, and has respect to his promises.

CHAPTER I.

OF THE PRECEPTS OF CHRIST, WHICH HE ADDED TO THE LAW.

What are the perfect Precepts of God comprised in the New Covenant?

They are in part included in the commands delivered by Moses, together with those which were added to them by Christ and his apostles: and in part contained in those which were delivered exclusively by Christ and his Apostles.

What are those of the former class?

They comprehend all the moral precepts; that is, all those laws which relate to the duties of virtue and probity.

Are there then other precepts delivered by God through Moses?

There are: Of these some pertain to external rites,

rites, commonly denominated Ceremonial; and other
to judicial proceedings. But Christ has abrogated,
either expressly or tacitly, those of the ritual kind.
He has by the Apostles, and especially by the apostle
Paul, openly abrogated and annulled a great part of
the precepts relating to external rites or ceremonies:
and the other external rites or ceremonies, that are
not openly abrogated, ought to be considered as annulled by the property of the New Covenant, for the
very reason on account of which those that we find
to have been openly abrogated were done away.
The judicial precepts belonged to the constitution
of this commonwealth.

But what is the property of the New Covenant?

It is altogether spiritual; being placed not in external things which from their nature conduce nothing to virtue, but in things internal, possessing
some natural moral value. But external rites, commonly denominated ceremonial, are not spiritual;
nor do they of themselves, and from their nature, at
all conduce to virtue and piety. Unless, then, there
exist in the New Testament some express command
concerning things of this kind, it is by no means to
be believed that they are to be observed under the
New Covenant. It must therefore be understood,
that what is commanded in the Old Covenant in respect to what are usually called ceremonies, in no
way pertains to the New.

On what account were certain ceremonies belonging to the Old Covenant openly abrogated?

Because those ceremonies were shadows of things
future;

future; which are now present, and have appeared in the New Covenant. Wherefore, the body being come, the shadows retire.

Do the Scriptures contain any express testimony in proof of this?

There is one in Paul's Epistle to the Colossians (chap. ii. ver. 16, 17), "Let no man therefore judge you in meat or in drink, or in respect of an holyday, or of the new moon, or of the sabbath days: which are a shadow of things to come; but the body is of Christ." Hence it happens that all the other ceremonies, although not openly abrogated, are to be considered as tacitly done away, since it is evident that they were all shadows of those things which have appeared in the New Covenant. Add to this, that some of the ceremonies of the Old Covenant were of such a kind that they were abolished because they related only to the Israelites.

State, what were the ceremonies of this class?

You have examples of them in the Paschal Lamb, and the Feast of Tabernacles. These, and some others of a similar kind, pertained to the Israelites alone; because they were instituted in commemoration of benefits conferred upon them exclusively, or which they alone had obtained. But they in no way relate to the Gentiles, converted to God by Christ, who at this day compose the largest part of God's people.

But what say you respecting the judicial precepts —are not Christian governments bound by these?

By no means: since many of them contain laws which

which were proper and peculiar to that people and government.

What is the reason of this?

First, Because under the Old Covenant severity and rigour obtained; but under the New, favour and mercy, whereby the rigour which these laws exacted is mitigated, as far as can be done without public detriment: for, to adopt here also the words of the apostle, " we are not under the Law but under Grace." Secondly, Because under the Old Covenant God's people had a form of government prescribed and instituted by God himself; which government terminating, the laws and judicial regulations especially adapted to it, also vanished. Hence it happens that that class of laws which in their first application referred to earthly happiness, and the preservation of peace, are sometimes applied in an accommodated sense to a covenant which holds out to us scarcely any other than spiritual and celestial benefits, promising earthly advantages but very sparingly:—whereas, on the contrary, in the Old Covenant, nothing but the blessings of this life was expressly and openly promised to the Israelites, as I will show you hereafter. If then any of the judicial laws of Moses are admitted into Christian governments also, it is not because they were published by him, but because without them civil society could not be preserved and maintained.

Have not then the government and administration of magistracy and of earthly commonwealths been done away?

By

By no means; since all power is from God (Rom.
xiii. 1). Mankind could not exist without society, nor
society be maintained without a magistrate and governor: and indeed the church of Christ itself supports
civil government, since it could not assemble except
where civil government existed.　Hence the apostle
exhorts (1 Tim. ii. 1, 2) " that first of all supplications, prayers, intercessions, and giving of thanks be
made for all men, for kings, and for all that are in
authority, that we may lead a quiet and peaceable
life in all godliness and honesty."　And any person
may engage in the magistracy, provided that in undertaking and discharging its duties he so conduct
himself as not to offend against the laws and institutions of Christ[40].

.　　　　　　　　Explain

---

[40] There is not room in this place to say much upon this
difficult question concerning magistracy.　It is justly shown
above that we are no longer bound either by the ceremonial
or the judicial laws of the Old Covenant; for both the political
and sacerdotal order of the Jewish Church, as the shadows of
future things, have ceased; and new rites, and new laws, by
which Christians ought to be judged, have been instituted by
Christ, our supreme legislator, priest, and king; and also new
penalties, of a corresponding nature, against those who disobey
these laws. This king has also established a new government in
the commonwealth of the New Covenant, and that, as already
stated, a spiritual one, conformable to the property of this
kingdom and covenant. Ephes. iv. 11; 1 Cor. xii. 28.　But
we no where read that he instituted, besides this government, any other magistracy; or ordained any kings or princes
besides himself, who might exercise coercive authority, and
the power of life and death, over his subjects and brethren.
Indeed, it appears from Matthew xx. 25, &c.; Mark x. 42,
&c.; Luke xxii. 25, &c.; that he forbade his disciples in such
a way as this to exercise dominion over one another in his
church and kingdom (which is not of this world, John xviii. 36),

　　　　　　　　and

· Explain, at length, what are the moral precepts of the Law, and what Christ has added to them?

· They are of two kinds : some general, and others particular,

---

and enforced his precept by his own example. Hence it may be concluded, that it best becomes Christians, who have here no continuing city (Heb. xiii. 14), but whose πολιτευμα is in heaven (Philipp. iii. 20), to remain in that state wherein their Lord founded the first church, and in which it flourished about three centuries, that is, under afflictions, and under persecution ; to relinquish civil magistracy to the men of this world ; and to refrain from usurping for themselves the right of exercising authority over others, and much more of shedding human blood, without the express command, or at least the permission, of the supreme Lord. For the persons above referred to, whom Paul directs to be obeyed, or for whom he exhorts that prayers should be offered up, were heathen magistrates. Should difficulties occur to any one, respecting these passages of Scripture, or others of a similar kind, he will find explanations of them by J. L. Wolzogenius in his Treatise *de Natura et Qualitate Regni Christi*, and also in his writings against Schlichtingius. For the latter, with many of his contemporaries, members of these churches, was of a contrary opinion. But, it must be observed, that the first persons in Poland, of the confession which is set forth in this Catechism, called first Pinczovians, afterwards Racovians,—of whom the leaders were Gregory Paul, Peter Gonesius, George Schoman, Martin Czechovicius,—maintained that it was not lawful for a Christian to bear the office of a magistrate. It seems that the Fathers of the Church for nearly the first three centuries were also of this opinion, as will appear from an examination of their works^z. B. Wissowatius.

^z [The question considered in the preceding note, and in the answer in the text that led to it,—Whether it were lawful for a Christian to exercise magistracy and bear arms,—was one upon which the Unitarians on the continent were greatly divided in opinion, and holds a prominent place in their controversial writings. Among the earliest persons who maintained the negative of this question were Gregory Paul, Peter Gonesius or Conyza, George Schoman, and Martin Czechovicius, mentioned above by Wissowatius. To these names might be added Joachim

particular, whereby the general are explained; and
are comprised in the Decalogue.

What are the general precepts?   Those

Joachim Stegman, jun., Daniel Brenius, and above all J. L.
Wolzogenius, who has entered at great length into the subject
in the three following tracts above referred to, inserted among
his works in the *Bibliotheca Fratrum Polonorum,* viz. *De Natura et Qualitate Regni Christi:—Annotationes ad Questiones
J. Schlichtingii de Magistratu, Bello, et privata Defensione:—
Responsio ad J. Schlichtingii Annotationes in Annotationes de
Bello, Magistratu, et privata Defensione.* On the other side, the
controversy was carried on by Stanislaus Budzinius, who addressed a letter on these points to the Synod of Racow, and
another to Gregory Paul; by Jacob Paleologus in Transylvania; by Simon Budnæus, Samuel Przipcovius, Jonas Schlichtingius, Daniel Zwicker, and Faustus Socinus. The reader
has seen above a specimen of the reasoning of those who
contended for the negative of the question;—the following extract comprises a summary of Socinus's sentiments in support
of the affirmative. It is a part of a letter to Elias Arcisse-
vius (*Socin. Op. fol. p.* 603), and is here inserted in Dr. Toulmin's translation (Life of Socinus, p. 235, &c.): " I think it
lawful for a Christian to bear the office even of a chief magistrate, if, in the execution of his office, he do not any thing
contrary to Christian charity. I can scarcely think that
Christian charity by any means allows the putting of the guilty
to death, or mutilating their limbs. Nor will any Christian
magistrate, if he regard my advice, venture to do this. The
question relative to war, whether it can be vindicated or not,
is much more difficult. Whether, for instance, a Christian who fills the post of the supreme magistrate, can, without the violation of Christian charity, use the assistance of
those who are disposed to hire themselves to him:—notwithstanding I am of opinion that it is not allowable for a private
Christian, even in order to keep off a war, to kill any one, or
to mutilate him in any limb, though the supreme magistrate
command him to do it: otherwise, it appears to me lawful for
a Christian to be armed, and to march with others to suppress,
without the murder of any one, the attack of assailing enemies:—when he has first tried every measure that he may not
be compelled to march forth, but may be allowed to purchase
                                                        with

Those wherein Christ states that the Law and the Prophets are comprised; namely, the Love of God and of our neighbour: both of which are in the Decalogue explained by particular precepts.

What is the general precept concerning the love of God?

This is expressed in the following words of Moses (Deut. vi. 5, 6), "The Lord our God is one Lord; and thou shalt love the Lord thy God with all thy heart, and with all thy soul, and with all thy might:" which command is thus quoted by Mark (xii. 30) and Luke (x. 27), "And thou shalt love the Lord thy God with all thy heart, and with all thy soul, and with all thy mind, and with all thy strength."

What is the meaning of this precept?

That we devote to the worship and service of God, since he is ONE ONLY, whatever we possess of affection, whatever of capacity, either in respect to our will, our understanding, or our bodies, or to those powers and faculties which have been granted to us. For this precept, even as it is expressed by Moses, appears so comprehensive as to embrace the whole of the commandments of God delivered in the Law. But as

---

with money a leave of absence from personal services of this kind: which if he cannot obtain, it is better, in my judgement, to run some danger of giving offence to the weak in the faith, than to draw most certain ruin on himself and his connections. I will not allege that offence is not less given, nay much more offered, to a great number, when any one refuses to obey the supreme magistrate; who, all agree, in things not plainly repugnant to the precepts of Christ, is to be entirely obeyed." TRANSL.]

Christ

Christ has distinguished it from that precept which directs us to love our neighbour, it is applied particularly to the worship and honour of God, and implies chiefly, that we are to attach ourselves to no other God besides him, and abstain from all spiritual adultery.

Has Christ added any thing to this precept?

He has added a requisition that we should love himself also, and thus love God in him; and, therefore, that we love him with the same kind of love as we do God himself. To this duty relates, in the first place, that declaration of the apostle (1 Cor. xvi. 22), " If any man love not the Lord Jesus Christ, let him be Anathema Maranatha:" and also Ephesians vi. 24, " Grace be with all them that love our Lord Jesus Christ with incorruption," or incorruptly; that is, sincerely and constantly. John xiv. 15, 21, 23, 24, may also be consulted, where the nature of this love is explained.

But has Christ added nothing to this precept relating to this perfection of love?

If you look at the words alone, Christ will not seem to have added any thing to them; but if you attend to the sense of them, you will perceive that this love is much more perfect under the New, than it was under the Old, Covenant. For these words, since they are general, may with propriety be understood as applicable to the particular precepts. Wherefore, if the particular precepts are of a more perfect and sublime kind, those general terms, also, will themselves acquire a more perfect sense, and demand a more intense measure of love towards God:

God : but if the particular precepts be of a less perfect kind, the general terms will demand a less measure of love. For in both cases that measure of love is required which is necessary to the observance of the particular precepts. Now, that the particular precepts of the New Covenant are more perfect and sublime than those of the Old, will appear from an examination of each. This, likewise, the supreme excellence of the promises of the New Covenant requires, as well, as its unbounded grace, declared by Jesus Christ. For it is agreeable to reason, that the greater things God has promised to us, and the greater love he has manifested towards us, so much the greater ought our love towards him to be. Hence it is that we are commanded to be "fervent in spirit" (Rom. xii. 11); that is, to engage with great vigour and earnestness in promoting the glory of God, and in those other concerns, such especially as the salvation of mankind, which are well-pleasing in his sight.

Before you proceed to another general precept of God, I wish you to explain to me those particular precepts whereby you have stated that the first general precept is explained ?

There are four commandments of the Decalogue, which are denominated the first table of the Law; whereof the last, as you shall hear in its proper place, is peculiar to the Old Covenant.

Which is the first commandment of the Decalogue ?

The first in order is, " Thou shalt have no strange gods," or " no other gods before me."

What

What is implied in this commandment?

These two things: first, That we acknowledge God, for our God; that we place our trust in him, and pay him suitable honour and worship. This, the very words of the commandment, considered alone, require; much more will they appear to do so, if we compare them with those which precede and lead to them (Ex. xx. 2, &c.; Deut. v. 6, &c.), " I am the Lord thy God, which have brought thee out of the land of Egypt, out of the house of bondage." Secondly, That we receive not the god of any other nation, or strange gods, to place them as rivals in the presence of our God, who is the true God; and consequently, That we worship no other God besides him, since he only and alone is the God of Israel: all others being, in respect to Israel, foreign, strange, and new.

As I now understand who is to be acknowledged for God, and for what reason he is to be so acknowledged, I wish in the next place to learn in what manner trust is to be placed in him?

By cherishing a firm conviction that he is able to do all things; and that if you seek his favour he will serve you, and accomplish all his promises.

What kind of worship is suitable to God?

Such as excels every worship and honour that is commonly wont to be paid to any human beings or angels; and wherein we are so to conduct ourselves as if we every where beheld him, though to us invisible.

Wherein do the worship and honour of God consist?

Briefly

Briefly speaking, in adoration and invocation.

How is adoration to be paid to God?

The adoration we owe to God is of two kinds, internal and external.

What is the nature of internal adoration?

It is such as comprehends in it the greatest reverence of our minds towards God, and the self-abasement thence arising; so that from our very heart and soul we acknowledge his infinite wisdom, power, and benevolence in respect to us.

What is external adoration?

It is a kind of sign or index of the internal, which, while we bend our bodies reverently before the invisible God, and fall down on our knees or faces, leads us, either with our tongue and speech to celebrate his name, or to say or do something else that has a direct view to his honour. Hence prayers, as far as we honour God in them, are to be referred to this: for the invocation of the invisible God is necessarily included in adoration, although adoration be not necessarily comprised in invocation. The acknowledgement of the divine name, and of the doctrines derived from God, may also be referred to external adoration.

But is the external adoration under the New, the same as it was under the Old, Covenant?

There is a wide difference between them; as the Lord Jesus himself intimates when he says (John iv. 21), "The hour cometh when ye shall neither in this mountain, nor yet at Jerusalem, worship the Father." And ver. 23, "The hour cometh, and now is, when
the

the true worshippers shall worship the Father in spirit
and in truth." He makes here a twofold distinction: first, that formerly it was required that sacrifices and oblations should be offered at Jerusalem
alone; but that now it was not only lawful, but had
become men's duty, to do this in every place. Secondly, that the former worship, of oblations and sacrifices, consisted for the greater part in ceremonies
and things, which, so to speak, were carnal and ty-
pical; whereas the present worship is placed in oblations, sacrifices, and things, spiritual, real, and solid,
conducive, from their nature, to the glory of God.

What has the Lord Jesus added to this command?

He has, in the first place, commanded us in a general way, to pray;—and has also prescribed what
things we ought to supplicate.

Did not the worshippers under the Old Covenant
pray to God?

Prayers were certainly offered to him not only
under the Old Covenant, but also antecedently; the
worshippers being in some instances excited by the
divine wisdom, power, and goodness, which were
known to them; and, in others, urged by their need
and desire of those things for which they supplicated.
But in no part of the law of Moses, wherein all the
terms of the Old Covenant are declared, do we read
a single express command binding the Israelites universally to pray at all, although afterwards we observe exhortations to this duty in some of the Prophets. But under the New Covenant the precepts
for it are clear and frequent.

What

What is meant by praying to God?

To pray to God, as you may sufficiently understand from the word itself, is to ask something of him.

What are the things for which it is necessary we should pray?

These the Lord Jesus has comprised in that form of prayer which he delivered to his disciples, and is inserted in Matthew vi. 9, &c. and Luke xi. 9, &c. "Our Father, which art in heaven," &c.

What does this prayer contain?

Petitions of two kinds;—whereof the one relate to the glory of God, and the other principally to our necessities.

Which are those that relate to the glory of God?

The three placed first in order.

What is the first petition?

" Hallowed be thy name."

Explain this petition?

We pray that God would cause his name to be acknowledged and celebrated by all men, as the holy name of the true God.

What is the second petition?

" Thy kingdom come."

Explain the meaning of this?

We pray that God would cause all men to acknowledge his jurisdiction and sovereignty over them, as their creator, and to submit themselves to his rule and authority.

What is the third petition?

" Thy will be done on earth, as it is in heaven."

Explain

Explain the meaning of this petition ?

We pray God to cause all men to do his will on earth in their concerns and actions, as it is performed in all things by the angels in heaven. In all these petitions the gift of the Holy Spirit ought certainly to be considered as included; since, in order to the performance of these things by men, there is the utmost need of the assistance of the Holy Spirit.

What are the petitions which relate principally to our necessities ?

The remaining three, which follow the others in order.

What is the first of these ?

"Give us this day our daily bread."

Explain this petition ?

We pray God to supply us, for the time to come, with those things which we every day need for the sustenance and preservation of life.

What is the second of these petitions ?

"Forgive us our debts as we forgive our debtors."

Explain this also ?

We acknowledge and confess that we are sinners in the sight of God; and pray that through his grace and mercy our sins may be forgiven; and likewise that he would confer upon us eternal life, which is the proper consequence of the remission of sins; the condition of true penitence and regeneration being implied; whereof one part, relating especially and by a kind of just propriety to the obtaining of this grace and mercy from God, is that which Christ adds,

that

that we also —miserable beings—do the same to other men, by whom we have been injured; being ourselves to experience hereafter what we shall have done to others, either in forgiving or not forgiving them.

. What is the third of these petitions ?

" Lead us not into temptation, but deliver us from evil."

. State the meaning of this petition ?

Conscious of the infirmities of our flesh, we pray God that he would not permit us to be tempted, but would deliver us from the evil into which we might possibly fall,—and principally from the devil, the author and the active promoter of temptations *. For, if while we thus constantly pray, and acknowledge and confess our infirmities before God, it should nevertheless be his pleasure to permit us to fall into any temptations, the most effectual assistance of God will not be withheld from us ; whereby, being delivered from every evil work, we may overcome with the highest glory to God, and be preserved for the heavenly kingdom of Christ our Lord.

Is it not lawful to pray in any other manner ?

Certainly it is : for our Lord does not forbid this, either here or elsewhere,—since we may pray to God for the same things, in other words, or for other things which are not expressed or necessarily comprehended in this form of prayer,—provided only that

---

* [On the subject of dæmoniacal temptations, &c., the reader is referred to note (ª) page 7, and the authorities there enumerated. TRANSL.]

we

we ask not for such things as are opposed to what is clearly prescribed to us by the divine will. But if we pray for any thing concerning which the divine will has not been declared to us, our petition is in such case to be wholly submitted to the will of God.

For what purpose then has the Lord Jesus delivered this form of prayer?

Partly that it might appear to us what the things are which ought necessarily to be asked of God; and partly that he might keep us from vain repetitions, or such frequent repetitions of the same thing as are not occasioned by the desire of possessing it, or by the fervour of the Spirit,—and which, so far, is nothing but senseless babbling.

What else has the Lord Jesus added to the first commandment?

That we are required to acknowledge the Lord Jesus himself as one who has divine authority over us, and in that sense as God; that we are bound, moreover, to put our 'trust in him, and to pay him divine honour.

In what way ought we to put our trust in Christ?

In the same way as we put our trust in God: namely, by firmly believing that he is able to perform all things; that if you seek his favour he will do you good, and accomplish all his promises.—As to the distinction which, in this respect, exists beyond this, between God and Christ, you have already been informed.

But wherein consists the divine honour due to Christ?

In adoration likewise and invocation. For we ought

at

at all times to adore Christ, and may in our necessities address our prayers to him as often as we please: and there are many reasons to induce us to do this freely.

Does not the rite of breaking bread pertain to the honour of Christ?

It does: but this is a ritual, and not wholly a moral, observance, to which my observations now relate.

Whence do you prove that divine worship is due to Christ?

Authorities for this are furnished by many passages of Scripture. For instance, Christ says (John v. 22, 23), " The Father hath committed all judgement" (all rule and government) " to the Son; that all men may honour the Son as they honour the Father." And (Philipp. ii. 9, 11) the apostle writes, "Wherefore God hath highly exalted him, and given him a name which is above every name; that in the name of Jesus every knee should bow, of things in heaven, and things in earth, and things under the earth; and that every tongue should confess that Jesus Christ is Lord to the glory of God the Father." It would appear also from these testimonies,—although there existed not, in so many words, an express command for adoring Christ,—that that sublime sovereignty wherewith he has been invested by God requires from us the divine worship of him. For in every government honour is due from the subjects;—in the divine government, divine honour; in human governments, human honour. And for this reason also, when

Christ

Christ was about to be introduced into the future world, it was said, " Let all the angels of God worship him" (Heb. i. 6); which honour certainly is no other than divine. But if the angels, as they adore God, ought to adore Christ also, as a Lord given to them by God—how much more ought men to do this, to whom he is with peculiar propriety given as a Lord, and to whom alone he is given for a Saviour!

But how do you show that we may in our necessities address our prayers to the Lord Jesus?

First, from this consideration,—that he is both able and willing to afford us assistance; and understands our prayers. Secondly, because we have exhortations to this duty given us by our Lord himself and by his Apostles. And lastly, because examples of this practice may be seen in holy men.

Whence do you prove that Christ is able and willing to afford us assistance, and that he understands our prayers?

That he is able to assist us in all cases appears from hence,—that " all power is given to him in heaven and in earth" (Matthew xxviii. 18); that his power and strength are such that " he is able to subdue all things to himself" (Phil. iii. 21); to release us from death (John vi. 40, 54); and confer immortality (2 Cor. iv. 14, &c.), than which no power can be greater. That he is willing, appears from hence : first, because he has promised this ; secondly, because he is by affection so disposed towards us, who are united to him by the bond of nature, that he has at one time laid down his life for us, and now

does

does not disdain to call us his brethren, and having
tasted of our sufferings knows how to afford us prompt
assistance : and thirdly, because he is for this very
reason constituted by God, our saviour, priest, king,
and head, that he might have the care of our salvation, and yield us succour.   That he understands our
prayers appears from hence; that he knows all things
(John xvi. 30); that he searches the heart and the
reins (Revel. ii. 23), and perceives the hidden things
of darkness (1 Cor. iv. 5); and also because he has
himself said, he would do whatsoever we should ask
in his name (John xiv. 13) ; whence it is necessary that
he should also know what we pray for.

  But where has Christ, and where have his apostles,
proposed to us these inducements ?

  First, John xiv. 13, 14, where our Lord himself
says, " Whatsoever ye shall ask in my name that will
I do, that the Father may be glorified in the Son.   If
ye shall ask any thing in my name I will do it."
Whence it is to be understood,—since Christ himself
states and inculcates, that he would do what we asked
in his name,—that he incites us in this to venture in
all our necessities to fly to him, and in his person to
pray for the assistance of God.   And secondly, Heb.
iv. 14, 15, 16, where the author writes as follows :
" Seeing then that we have a great high-priest that
is passed into the heavens, Jesus the Son of God,—let
us hold fast our profession.   For we have not a high-
priest which cannot be touched with a feeling of our
infirmities, but was in all points tempted just as we
are, yet without sin.   Let us therefore come boldly to
                                                    the

the throne of grace, that we may obtain mercy, and grace to help us in time of need." Also Rom. x. 13, " Whosoever shall call on the name of the Lord shall be saved." In which words the calling on the name of the Lord is declared to be the means of obtaining salvation: for verses nine to fifteen show that by Lord, Christ was understood by the apostle.

Where are the examples of this practice to be found?

The apostles say, Luke xvii. 5, "Lord, increase our faith." Matthew viii. 25, " Lord, save us, or we perish." Acts vii. 59, Stephen, invoking, says, "Lord Jesus, receive my spirit." And again (ver. 60), "Lord, lay not this sin to their charge." Again, 2 Cor. xii. 7, 8, "And lest I should be exalted beyond measure through the abundance of the revelations, there was given to me a thorn in the flesh, the messenger of Satan to buffet me, lest I should be exalted above measure. For this thing I besought the Lord thrice that it might depart from me." Again, 1 Thess. iii. 11, " Now God himself, and our Father, and our Lord Jesus Christ direct our way unto you." The same thing is to be seen in all the apostolic salutations, wherein grace, mercy, and peace, are supplicated for believers, as from the Father so also from his son Jesus Christ, as our Lord. Lastly : Christians are in several places in the sacred scriptures described as calling upon the name of our Lord Jesus Christ (Acts ix. 14, 21; 1 Cor. i. 2; 2 Tim. ii. 22) ; which words so far comprise the general worship paid to Christ by believers, as that they express it by one, and

that

that the chief part of it, that is, by the imploring of his assistance; since it is necessary that he whose name you invoke. should be worshipped as, in an adequate sense, a God.

I perceive that we may address our prayers to the Lord Jesus:—state now what the reasons are which impel us to do this freely?

These you may have understood from the preceding declarations : for all that has hitherto been said concerning the invocation of Christ incites us to pray to him ; but chiefly his most tender and benevolent affection towards us, and that union of nature which leads us to venture with a somewhat greater confidence to approach him whose condition of life was at one time the same as our own : while, on the contrary, the sublimity of the nature of the supreme God, which is at all times most distantly removed from ours, may in a manner overawe our humility. And this was the very reason why God committed to the man Christ the charge of our salvation—that he might thus succour our weakness, and excite and maintain our confidence.

Is not the first commandment of the decalogue altogether changed by this addition ;—that we are bound to acknowledge Christ as God, in the stated sense, and to approach him with divine worship?

That commandment is in no respect changed; for it only requires that we have no other Gods before God. But Christ is not another God, since God has communicated to him of his divine and celestial majesty, and has so far made him one and the same
with

with himself. Nor has God by this commandment deprived himself of the power of conducting his Christ to celestial authority, and by this means extending his own glory; but only bound us down, by his law, that we presume not, of our own accord, to join any one with himself in divine worship and honour. The command, therefore, to have and worship but one God only, remains in force; the mode, alone, of worshipping him is changed, in so far as that the only God was formerly worshipped without Christ, but is now worshipped through Christ.

Why then do the Scriptures say (Jer. x. 11), "The Gods that have not made the heavens and the earth, even they shall perish from the earth, and from under the heavens ?"

Because they speak of the idols and statues, and the false gods of the Gentiles. Since these had received no divinity from God, neither had created heaven and earth, and so had no divinity of themselves, and yet were erroneously worshipped by men for gods; the prophet justly wishes that they and their names (for they were nothing else besides empty names) might perish from the earth, and from under the heavens. By which very thing he shows that he speaks of gods who have no place in heaven, but whose statues and images alone are found only on the earth and under the heavens. Wherefore this passage does not relate to those who dwell with God in heaven, sometimes designated in the Scriptures by the title gods, such as the angels; nor indeed to those

who,

who, being invested among men on earth with the supreme direction of human affairs, are entitled to be addressed by God himself,—" Ye are gods, and sons of the most high :" so that the words cannot, without impiety, be referred to Christ seated at the right hand of God in the heavens.

Is there any difference between the honour of God and the honour of Christ?

There is this difference, that we adore and worship God as the first cause of our salvation, but Christ as the second. We direct this honour to God, moreover, as to the ultimate object; but to Christ as an intermediate object : or, to speak with Paul (1 Cor. viii. 6), we worship God as him " from whom are all things, and we in him ;" that is, are in him while we direct all our religious service to him ;—but Christ, as him by whom are all things and we by him : that is, are by him, while we direct our religious service and worship to God by him.

What think you of those persons who believe that Christ is not to be invoked or adored ?

Since they alone are Christians who acknowledge Jesus to be the Christ, or the heavenly king of the people of God, and who, moreover, worship him on a religious ground, and do not hesitate to invoke his name; on which account, we have already seen that Christians are designated as those who called on the name of the Lord Jesus Christ,—it is easily perceived that they who are disinclined to do this, are so far not Christians ; although in other respects they con-

fess

fess the name of Christ, and declare that they adhere
to his doctrine[b].   You

---

[b] [The editors of this Catechism have given above the doctrine held by most of the Polish Socinians concerning the worship of Christ.   As this formed a remarkable feature of their
creed, and is the principal article respecting which modern
Unitarians in this country differ from them in opinion, it may
not be amiss to subjoin here the sentiments of Socinus himself concerning it, in the compressed form in which he has
embodied them in his replies to the propositions of Francis
David.   The reader will find the propositions and the answers translated in Dr. Toulmin's Life of Socinus, p. 453, &c.

"Jesus is truly the Christ, or the king of God's people :
moreover, the kingdom of Christ promised by God, was to be
not an earthly, but a future and heavenly one, as Jesus himself and his disciples have shown by their explanation of the
divine oracles."

"Having obtained the kingdom promised to him, he governs the whole church ; and at the same time, by means of
the divine power communicated to him, and the overruling
agency of God in subduing his enemies, he enjoyeth rest ; till
he hath subjected all things to him except one, i. e. death."

"He may, therefore, with the utmost propriety be called
God ; since he filleth an office of the greatest dignity, and is
invested with the highest divine power in heaven and earth."

"On this account, though absent, religious adoration is to
be paid to him ; since, even before he received his kingdom,
while he dwelt on earth, he was deservedly worshipped with
more than civil homage : they who neglect it offend shamefully against God."

"Therefore, we are altogether obliged, besides observing
his commands, to serve and worship him, as appointed by
the Supreme Being to be our Lord and God, now in the fullest
degree reigning over us."

"And we ought to place our hope and trust in him, as in
that person who, with the approbation of God, hath himself
promised and can bestow upon us the greatest felicity."

"And to invoke him, i. e. to implore his aid and assistance
in our necessities, is the same as if any one pray unto God himself ; since it is certain that, by power from God, he can both
hear our prayers and grant what things we want."

"We

You have asserted that next to God, Christ ought to be worshipped—say whether there be any one besides to be worshipped ?

Certainly

" We may even ask him to pray to God on our behalf, and to obtain of God favours for us ; yet so that by these modes of expression we acknowledge before God, that all the power of assisting us possessed by Christ he derived not from himself but God ; for, in this sense, the Scripture saith he intercedeth for us. For he is a mediator between God and us in a more eminent degree in heaven, than he was on earth. On earth he announced the goodness of God to us, and prayed to him for us : in heaven he carries into effect the same goodness ; and all the blessings which are derived from God to the church, are given through him." *Socin. Op. Tom.* ii. *p.* 801.

The old English Socinians entertained the same views on this subject as their Polish brethren ; maintaining that Christ was to be worshipped, but only so as that the divine honour thus paid to him might redound to God. " All the express worship," they observe, " to be exhibited to Christ has this ground and foundation ; namely, that the Father, even God, has given him that power, authority and dominion, which make him a fit object of that worship ; and the glory thereof is not terminated in him as in its utmost scope, but passes by and through him to the Father."—See a treatise " Of Worshipping the Holy Ghost," &c. page 7, inserted in the " Second Collection of Tracts, proving the God and Father of our Lord Jesus Christ, the only true God," &c. quarto, 1692.

The Unitarians of the present day, in this country, universally concur in rejecting this system of subordinate worship altogether. Their unanimous opinion on this head may be said to be comprised in the following sentence of the venerable Theophilus Lindsey :—" Love, honour, reverence, duty, confidence, gratitude, and obedience are, and will be certainly for ever, due from us of mankind to the Lord Jesus for his immense love to us, and on account of his perfect holiness, excellency, power, dignity and dominion : but religious worship is the incommunicable honour and prerogative of God alone." *Apology*, &c. p. 137.

The interpretations given by modern Unitarians of those passages of scripture which have been thought to require divine

Certainly not.   For there is no divine testimony whence it would appear that God has given this honour to any one, except Christ.   The worship which is at this day paid in the Roman Church to the Virgin Mary and the Saints is grounded altogether on their own opinion.

---

vine worship for Jesus Christ, may be seen in various parts of the writings of this excellent person. Also in Belsham's Calm Inquiry, pages 249, &c. 1st edition. Dr. Carpenter's Unitarianism the Doctrine of the Gospel, page 216, &c.

The reader will observe with regret the uncandid reflection cast in the above answer by the Polish Socinians upon those who differed from them on this point of doctrine. In the first edition their feelings are somewhat more strongly expressed:—the question and answer as there given are thus rendered in the old translation.

"What think you of those men which doe not invocate Christ, nor think that he must be adored?

"That they are no Christians, since indeed they have not Christ; for though in words they dare not deny him, yet in reality they do." p. 86.

Acting upon this view of their opinion and character, some of them did not scruple to persecute their opponents when they had the power; and in Transylvania the excellent and venerable Francis David sacrificed his life, in circumstances the most honourable to himself, through the bigotry of Socinus and Blandrata on this question. At a later period, however, they entertained more just and enlightened sentiments respecting religious liberty, and the right of private judgement in those concerns which lie between man and his Maker. "The genuine disciples of Christ," says Schlichtingius, "who profess the plain and solid truth, which is on all sides supported by its own strength, and fears no heresies, are not accustomed to pursue others for the sake of religion: so that it may be justly laid down as a fixed point, that persecution on account of the faith, hath never been endured by any but by the good from the hands of the bad, or at least by men of inferior virtue from those of worse dispositions." See more of this excellent paper in Toulmin's Life of Socinus, page 115, &c. TRANSL.]

May

May they not justly be excused, since they do this with the view of worshipping God?

By no means:—for in paying divine worship to any one, it is not enough to rest on opinion, however specious it may be, and to do it with a good intention: but it is necessary, for this object, to have also the very truth itself; indeed, the clear declaration of the divine will. For all religious worship is due to the one God alone; nor can it be lawfully given to any other except by the divine will: but of any will of God, in this respect, nothing can be known to us, unless revealed by himself. The divine or religious worship, therefore, which is given to any other, when there exists no revelation of the divine will on the subject, ought to be regarded as idolatry.

But they assert that they do not pay to the saints *latria*, or the highest kind of divine worship, but only *dulia*, a worship of an inferior kind?

They deceive themselves by this distinction of terms, since both these words signify SERVICE; and in every case wherein service is used for religious worship, it means *latria*, or such worship as is due to God alone. In Hebrew, certainly, when the *latria* (worship) of idols and false gods is prohibited, the word SERVICE is employed, the whole import of which is expressed by the term *dulia*. It ought not therefore to be conceded that that service alone is *latria* which is paid to any person or thing instead of the supreme God; for otherwise the human nature of Christ would not receive this kind of worship; nor would the inferior gods among the heathens, or their images, have been
honoured

honoured with this worship; and yet the worship of these is, both in common speech and in the sacred scriptures, styled IDOLATRY. It is hence apparent that it is not lawful to worship any one, either with the highest, or even with an inferior, degree of honour, at least of a religious kind, besides God, and him whom God himself has testified to be worthy of this distinction.

I perceive that no one is to be worshipped besides God and Christ:—but may we not invoke the Virgin Mary and the Saints; not that they may themselves bestow any thing upon us, but may procure it for us by their prayers to God and Christ?

This is by no means permitted: for, as I just now observed, in paying to any one religious worship, such as is the invocation of dead saints, it ought to be clearly apparent that it is done in conformity with the will of God. But no testimony can be adduced from the sacred scriptures to show that the Virgin Mary and other saints have any charge of things which are done by us; that they either know or any ways understand them, or that they hear our prayers;—circumstances of which he ought, however, to be fully convinced who would address his supplications to them. It is, besides, sufficiently evident, both from reason and the sacred scriptures, that the dead, while they remain dead, cannot actually live; and therefore can neither know any thing, nor hold any charge, nor supplicate any thing of God. Whence Christ proves that it is necessary God should raise Abraham, Isaac and Jacob; because he would otherwise be the God of the dead, and not of the living. And hence also Paul shows, 1 Cor. xv. 19, 20, 30, 32, that if there be no resurrection of the dead, we are of all men the most miserable, and evidently lost; and that there would be no reason why we should expose ourselves to so many perils on account of Christ :—which could not be asserted, if dead saints exist in heaven previously to the resurrection. That also would be false which David asserts, Psalm vi. 5; xxx. 9, 10; cxv. 17, 18; and Isaiah, chap. xxxviii. 18, 19,—that in death there is no remembrance of God.

I conceive that I understand what force the first commandment has in the Christian religion; proceed therefore to the second?

The second commandment is this : " Thou shalt not make unto thee any graven image, or any likeness of any thing that is in heaven above, or that is in the earth beneath, or that is in the water under the earth. Thou shalt not bow down thyself to them, nor serve them."

But why do you make this the second commandment, when the majority of Christians consider that it is comprised in the first?

In this they greatly err, since it contains a prohibition wholly distinct from the first : otherwise there would either be only nine commandments in the decalogue, or the last would be divided, as is absurdly done by them, into two :—that is, the words " Thou shalt not covet thy neighbour's house" would be formed into a separate commandment, though in fact

it

it is comprised in the concluding words of the last commandment, wherein it is forbidden us to covet ANY THING that is our neighbour's. Add to this, that in Deuteronomy (chap. v. ver. 21), WIFE, and not HOUSE, is first mentioned:—thus, "Neither shalt thou desire thy neighbour's wife, neither shalt thou covet thy neighbour's house, his field," &c. On which account the ninth commandment would be, " Thou shalt not covet thy neighbour's wife:" and thus what in Exodus is the ninth, would in Deuteronomy form a part of the tenth, commandment;—and, on the other hand, what in Deuteronomy is the ninth, would in Exodus form a part of the tenth, commandment. Besides, the " other Gods" mentioned in the first commandment are, properly, those only which are falsely deemed gods. Those images also are referred to here, which were not taken for the gods themselves; such were in general all the images of the heathens. For the heathens did not consider these as being properly the gods themselves, but as the figures or representations of their gods. Such also formerly were, such at this day are, and such may be, the images formed of the true God, and the making of which, with a view to the worshipping of him, he expressly prohibits: as may be seen, among other places, Deut. iv. 12, 15, 16, " The Lord spake unto you out of the midst of the fire; ye heard the voice of the words, but saw no similitude, only ye heard a voice. Take ye therefore good heed unto yourselves; for ye saw no manner of
similitude,

similitude, on the day that the Lord spake unto you in Horeb out of the midst of the fire, lest ye corrupt yourselves, and make you a graven image, the similitude of any figure, the likeness of male or female." But images formed of God himself cannot properly be called " other Gods ;" nor will you readily find them so designated in the sacred scriptures [41].

What does this commandment forbid ?

Four things are here forbidden : First, that we do at our own pleasure, and without the express command of God, make any image which can furnish occasion to men to adore and worship it ; and principally that there be formed from any religious opinion or fancy a cause of worship and religious service. Secondly, that any image, without in like manner the clear consent of God, be worshipped : that is, that either the mind or the body be devoutly inclined before it ; that there be paid before it the religious worship of him, with a view to the representing of whom it was made ; or that any honour of this kind be shown to any image. Thirdly, that any image, formed at our pleasure, be served, that is, be honoured by any religious act. Fourthly, that adoration and religious service be in like manner, at our choice, any where paid to any one thing, although otherwise good, and made by God. So that, the wor-

---

[41] And yet the calves set up by Jeroboam in Dan and Bethel are called " other Gods," 1 Kings xiv. 9 ; which, nevertheless, were designed to represent the God who brought Israel up out of the land of Egypt. Id. xii. 28. M. RUARUS.

ship

ship and service of all these things being done away, the worship and religious service of the images placed in their stead, will also cease.

What are those images which may furnish occasion to men to worship them?

All those which represent persons or things, in which there is or has been any thing of divinity, or some other quality that seemed to entitle them to religious respect; or, at least, wherein any thing of this kind is believed to exist or to have existed:— Such are the images of God, of Christ, of the Holy Spirit, of the Apostles, of the Virgin Mary the mother of Christ, and of other holy persons, of the cross of Christ also, and of other things of a similar nature. These images furnish so much the greater occasion for this kind of worship, from being deposited in holy places, and likewise from being consecrated.

But did not God himself command some images to be placed in his sanctuary, and afterwards permit others to be placed in the temple by Solomon?

It by no means follows from this conduct of God, that it is lawful for us to do the same thing without his command and permission: for God established the law not for himself, but for us. And that he might indulge that carnal people, who were governed more by their senses than by their minds and understanding, with something whereby he might the more effectually draw them from forming for themselves images or statues, he commanded those representations of cherubim, and the ark which contained the covenant, to be placed in the sanctuary:

in

in order also that that covenant might be esteemed
the more sacred, and that the people might know
him to be a present God, he placed his visible glory
round the ark and the cherubim; published from
thence his answers; and from thence administered
assistance : and he appointed those figures of cherubim as emblems of the guardian angels,—to which
the wings, extending from one to the other, and
overshadowing the ark of the covenant, were added,
that they might in this manner represent the throne
of God, seated on the wings of cherubim, and pro-
tecting his people. Add to this, that God ordained
that those images which he had commanded to be
placed in the sanctuary, namely, the cherubim,
should not be ordinarily visible, not to the people
only, but not even to the priests. For it was allowed to the high-priest to enter there but once in
the year ; and if the ark was to be removed, it could
not be delivered to the Levites to be carried, until it
had first been covered over by some priests (Numbers v. 5, 6, 15). Hence happened what we read of,
1 Samuel vi. 19, that the men of Bethshamesh, to the
number of fifty thousand three score and ten, were
slain, because they had looked into the ark of the
Lord. Those images, therefore, could not furnish
occasion for idolatry. For though the ark and its
cover, with the cherubim, were worshipped, yet neither
was the ark itself, nor were those representations of
cherubim, any image of God. Nor were those cherubim worshipped in themselves : but all the worship
was directed to God ; because not only his holy covenant,

nant, but also he himself, as in an especial manner
on his throne, was there present.   But if, to add this
by the way, the worship of the ark and the mercy-
seat, did not weaken the divine commandment concerning the worship of the one God, or was not in
opposition to it, as might have been the case had
God so determined,—how much less can this be supposed in relation to the worship of Christ, the son of
God; who is the true and mystical ark of God,
wherein are hidden all the treasures of wisdom and
knowledge; that true PROPITIATORY or mercy-seat
held out by God to all men,—the living, not carved,
image of God himself, and not of cherubim ; the character of the substance of God, the brightness and
splendour of his glory.   The oxen placed by Solomon under the brazen laver, on account of their situation and mean use, never drew any to the worship
of them ; and the same might be observed of some
other images placed-in the temple.

But as God has exhibited his image, why may it
not be painted, or in some other way pourtrayed ?

Since God exhibited himself to the view of some
of the prophets under a certain kind of image or appearance, it does indeed follow that he may in some
way be delineated by men under some figure; not
as he actually is in himself, but as he sometimes
displayed himself ;—but not, nevertheless, so as to
allow of his being worshipped by the adoration of
that figure [43].   For God has not by such appear-
ances

---

[43] It seems indeed exceedingly dangerous to attempt to de-
lineate

ances abrogated the commandment delivered, and so strongly enforced, in the covenant. Add to this, that the kind of figure under which God has appeared, is far different from the inanimate representations formed by men from earthly and frail materials. For besides that that figure must necessarily have been far more venerable, and more suitable to the living God, than these can be, it cannot by any means interfere with the worship of the one God, since the person who worships that, worships God himself; whereas the contrary is the case in respect to the images made by men for this purpose, that is to say, those which God prohibits.

I sufficiently understand the first two things which are comprised in this commandment: I wish you now to explain the third?

Images are honoured by some act, or a service is paid to them, when, for example, tapers are lighted up before them, incense is burnt to them, vows are made to them, and pilgrimages are undertaken to them; when they are carried about in solemn procession, and ornamented with apparel and other decorations.

But our adversaries say that these services are not paid to the images themselves; and that not the images, but those whom they represent, are worshipped?

This evasion avails them nothing; even when, by

---

lineate God by any image under which he exhibited himself to be seen, for this would easily furnish an occasion for idolatry. A. WISSOWATIUS.

those images, they worship, in the way I have explained, the persons whom they represent. This indeed is the very thing forbidden in the prohibition,— that either God or any thing else be worshipped by images. This is evident in the first place from hence, that it was in a manner prohibited in the first commandment, that we worship any thing by itself besides God, for that which is worshipped by itself is taken for God. Secondly, because even the heathens, to whose idolatry all agree that this commandment was opposed, worshipped not in reality the images themselves, but by them worshipped the gods whom the images represented. Thirdly, the same thing is shown in the case of the calf which the Israelites cast in the wilderness, and of those calves which Jeroboam afterwards proposed to them to be worshipped. For it is certain that the worship which was paid to those calves was not in their opinion paid to the calves themselves, but to the God of Israel; since they conceived that the God of Israel was represented by them. That this worship was, however, contrary to the command of God, is sufficiently known from the history.

But how do you prove that the Israelites worshipped God in the calf which they cast in the wilderness?

This may be learnt from the conduct of Aaron himself, and of the people:—from the conduct of Aaron, because he thus speaks concerning the calf, when he was about to dedicate it (Exodus xxxii. 5), " To-morrow is a feast unto the Lord:"—from the

conduct

conduct of the people, because they said of the calf, that he was the God which had brought them out of the land of Egypt. But it was well known to them that it was not the calf, which they had just seen cast by themselves, long after they had been brought out of Egypt, but the Lord, that had effected their deliverance out of that country;—since the whole of this proceeding, of leading them out of Egypt, was conducted by Moses, expressly in the name of the Lord himself.

How do you prove the same thing in respect to the calves made by Jeroboam?

First, from this circumstance, that those calves were proposed to the people, by Jeroboam, to be worshipped, in these words :—" Behold thy gods, O Israel, which brought thee up out of the land of Egypt" (1 Kings xii. 28). It is, in the next place, sufficiently evident from the history itself, and is, indeed, stated in it, that those calves were made by Jeroboam, in order that the people might not go to Jerusalem for the purpose of worshipping God. For they never would have desisted from going to Jerusalem, nor have acquiesced in the worship of the calves, had they not been persuaded that in those calves the God of Israel was worshipped by them.

What is required of us towards fulfilling this commandment?

That we not only do not worship idols, but also take heed that we do not join in those acts which in any way relate to idolatry; and likewise that we carefully shun those places where idols are worshipped.

shipped. Whence it is that Paul so earnestly warns
the Corinthians against being partakers of the tables
of dæmons, that is, not to associate with idolatrous
company; and if they were told that any thing had
been offered in sacrifice to idols, not to eat of it, to
the offence of others (1 Cor. x. 21, 28, 32, compared with Revelation ii. 14, 20). To this subject
pertain also those words (1 Cor. x. 14), " My dearly
beloved, flee from idolatry;" as appears from what follows. The words of John (1 Epist. v. 21), " Little
children, keep yourselves from idols," may also be
applied to this case.

But why is it that we are required to shun these
things?

Because it does not in itself comport with the holiness of a Christian to be a partaker of those things
or actions which relate to dæmons; because such
conduct may easily offend our weaker brethren, and
confirm those who are without in their errors; and
lastly, because it may by degrees teach us to view
idolatry with less abhorrence, and insensibly inspire
us with a partiality for it.

But why is it that God forbids that he should be
represented by an image, in order to be worshipped
under it?

Because an image cannot but be mere vanity and
a lie,—a thing whereby the nature and majesty of
God are materially obscured and diminished, when
he is likened to corruptible man,—and much more
when he is delineated, as he formerly was, under the
forms of beasts : concerning which much may be seen
in

in the Prophets (Isaiah xliv. 19, &c.; Jer. x. 14, 15; li. 17, 18; Heb. ii. 18), as also in the Wisdom of Solomon, chapters xii. xiii. xiv. xv.; in the declaration of Paul in Acts xvii., and in the first chapter of his Epistle to the Romans. It would hence happen that God would by degrees be thought, especially by the ignorant, to be such a thing as the image is; and as they would perceive in this nothing excellent and above the lot of men, they would divest themselves of that kind of reverence which is due to God. Secondly, because an idea of divinity would by degrees be attached to the images themselves; and while, with your eyes directed to them, you were worshipping and invoking God, whom you believe to be represented by them, the very form of the eyes and ears which you saw in the images, would so bear away your mind that you would fancy that they beheld you, that they heard your prayers, and even that sometimes they inclined their heads towards you—as experience testifies.

What is the third commandment?

" Thou shalt not take the name of the Lord thy God in vain; for the Lord will not hold him guiltless that taketh his name in vain."

What is it to take the name of the Lord in vain?

It is to call God to witness, or to swear by his name, in false matters. Hence the Lord Jesus, quoting this commandment, says (Matthew v. 34), "Thou shalt not forswear thyself." That IN VAIN, is put for FALSELY, is evident from the ninth commandment, in Deuteronomy v. 20, " Thou shalt not

bear

bear false witness,"—where the same term is employed.

But is that alone swearing, when the name of God is expressly mentioned, and God is called to witness?

No: but every religious asseveration, that is, an asseveration with which any thing divine, or in any way sacred, or of divine appointment, is connected: so that he who makes it does, at least tacitly, call upon God as the witness and supporter of his word.

What is added to this commandment under the New Covenant?

First, That we may call not only God, but also the Lord Jesus Christ as our witness, since the Lord Jesus " searcheth the reins and the hearts" (Rev. ii. 23); and is appointed by God to be the judge and rewarder of all. Secondly, that it is not only not lawful for us to forswear ourselves, but also, not to swear even what is true, unless in the most weighty affairs, those particularly wherein the glory of God is concerned, and in which we are constrained by some necessity: and even then we are not to do it rashly, but with great fear of God, and the utmost caution.

Where is there any thing written on this subject ?

Matthew v. 33—37, " Ye have heard that it hath been said by them of old time, Thou shalt not forswear thyself, but shalt perform unto the Lord thine oaths: but I say unto you, Swear not at all; neither by heaven, for it is God's throne; nor by the earth, for it is his footstool; neither by Jerusalem, for it is the city of the great king: Neither shalt thou swear by thy head, because thou canst not make one hair white

white or black. But let your communications be yea, yea; nay, nay : for whatsoever is more than these cometh of evil." To the same purpose is James v. 12.

But as our Lord forbids to swear at all—whence do you prove that we may swear in very weighty matters ?

The expression AT ALL is not to be understood as if it were not lawful, in any case, to swear : for it is employed for the sole purpose of excluding all the oaths of which Christ is speaking, and others of the same kind. But he is speaking of those oaths which are uttered without any necessity or just reason ; such as those which are introduced into our daily conversation, and proceed spontaneously from a depraved habit. This appears from what is opposed to them—" Let your communications be yea, yea; nay, nay." Oaths of this kind, if they were true, the Law of Moses did not forbid, as appears from the vows that the Law permitted to be made with an oath, and of which the Lord Jesus makes mention here ; where he plainly intimates what kind of oaths he had in view, and wished to prohibit [43]. For in respect to

oaths

---

[43] It must be observed that Christ opposes this prohibition not to swear, to promissory oaths, that have a view to future occurrences ; concerning which men are uncertain, and may therefore easily forswear themselves. It ought to be remarked that we scarcely ever read in the Old Testament of any other kind of swearing besides such as respects the future. Cicero, also, defining an oath (*Lib. iii. de Officiis*), says, *Jusjurandum est affirmatio religiosa; quod autem affirmatè, quasi Deo teste, promiseris, tenendum est.* "An oath is a religious

oaths extorted by some necessity or weighty cause, and especially those which relate to the divine glory, not only is there no reason that he should wish to prohibit them, but every reason that he should not. And hence we read that the apostles swore, as may be seen, Rom. i. 9; 2 Cor. i. 23; xi. 31; Phil. i. 8; 1 Thess. ii. 10:—And to swear by the name of God is placed among the parts and kinds of divine honour in the sacred writings; Deut. vi. 13; x. 20; Isaiah xix. 18; xlv. 23; Jer. xii. 5, 16, &c.

But wherefore does the Lord Jesus forbid us to swear even in things that are true?

That the name of the most high God, and of our Lord Jesus Christ, should be held by us in the highest veneration, and that we should not degrade it, in this manner, by daring to call either as a witness like some familiar acquaintance, at our pleasure, and

ligious affirmation, and what you solemnly promise, as if God were your witness, should be performed." From such oaths, therefore, though we find no examples of them in the New Testament, Christians ought generally to abstain. On the other hand, the religious asseverations of which the New Testament furnishes examples are not to be resorted to, except (as above stated) in the weightiest matters, relating to the glory of God; and even then with the greatest circumspection. In other matters, we must be careful that our words be believed as if they were oaths—as intelligent heathens also have inculcated;—whose opinions, as well as those of the first christians, concerning swearing, which they also deemed unlawful, Grotius has collected in his work *de Jure Belli et Pacis, lib.* ii. *cap.* 13; but chiefly in his annotations on Matt. v. 33, &c. where he confirms the interpretation of Christ's words which I have here proposed. You will find the same in Faustus Socinus's Commentary on the same passage; and also in Andrew Wissowatius's annotations on James v. 12.

B. WISSOWATIUS.

even

even in trifling matters. And also, lest by levity of swearing we should acquire a habit of perjuring ourselves, and thus incur the penalties to which in swearing we often bind ourselves. Upon this point the son of Sirach elegantly expresses himself (Ecclus. xxiii. 9), "Accustom not thy mouth to swearing; neither use thyself to the naming of the Holy One."

Is it not lawful to swear by others besides God and Christ?

By no means; for God hath not privileged any one besides Christ to be the searcher of hearts.

What is the fourth commandment?

"Remember the sabbath day to keep it holy."

What do you think of this commandment?

I conceive that what was ritual and carnal in it has been done away, with the other legal rites :—in the stead of which, Christ, the master of a more perfect devotion, has introduced the true holydays of a perpetual sabbath, which consist in the constant celebration of the divine name, and a perpetual abstinence from sin.

But why was it inserted in the Decalogue?

Principally for this reason, that the sabbath was in a peculiar manner the sign of the covenant between God and the Israelites, by which he gave them rest from their toils in Egypt; as appears from some passages of Scripture (Deut. v. 15; Exod. xx. 12). On which account the observation of the sabbath was somewhat more holy than the other ceremonies. God seems besides to have designed that there should exist some memorial that the most excellent part of

the

the Mosaic Law was not perfect, and that a Law more perfect than that of Moses should succeed, namely, the Law of Christ [44].

Has

---

[44] As in almost every instance in which the rest of the sabbath is commanded, it is stated as the reason, that God, on that day, rested from the work of creation, and afterwards sanctified it, why is this reason suppressed here? We see that it is done, lest, as this reason is common to all mankind, the observation of the sabbath should seem to be obligatory upon us also in the present times. This therefore ought to be explained. M. Ruarus.

With respect to the question concerning the sabbath, I think this answer might be given;—that the sanctifying of it was decreed by God even from the beginning of the world, on account of the previous completion of the creation; that nevertheless no law was then given for keeping it holy which should bind the whole human race; but that a law was first given to the Israelites, accompanied with additional reasons peculiar to themselves, and which therefore could not be obligatory on other nations, unless they dwelt interspersed among them. The Jews themselves, if I remember correctly, do not include the religious observation of the sabbath in the precepts delivered to Adam and Noah. The first mention of it, therefore, we have in Exodus, chap. xvi., where the observation of it was imposed on the Israelites by the visible evidence of the cessation of the manna.

If it be further inquired whether we, who give our names to Christ, are also under the yoke of the sabbath, I would answer with the apostle (Col. ii. 16), that no man has authority to "judge us (ιν μερει) in respect of a holyday, or of the new moon, or of the sabbath days," which were the shadows of things to come,—for as much as we hold the body, which is of Christ. For the same apostle elsewhere (Rom. xiv. 5) commands both him who esteemeth every day alike, and him who esteemeth one day above another, to be fully persuaded in their own minds; that is, to act conscientiously in what they do, since "whatsoever is not of faith is sin." Besides this, we do not read in Acts xv., that at the Council of Jerusalem, when some ritual laws were instituted for the Gentile converts to christianity with the view of establishing peace between them and the Jewish converts, any thing was decreed

L   by

Has not Christ appointed that the day called the Lord's Day should be observed instead of the sabbath?

By

---

by them concerning the religious observation of the sabbath. It is indeed stated there (ver. 21), that " Moses of old time had in every city them that preached him, being read in the synagogues every sabbath day;" but no law was passed enjoining this practice to be perpetuated in the churches of Christ. But although I do not think that we are directly bound by the command of the Decalogue respecting the sabbath, yet I apprehend it may justly be concluded, that if the Israelites were commanded to consecrate a seventh part of their lives to divine worship, it is fit that we, to whom, not, as in their case, a terrestrial but a heavenly happiness is promised, should do the same. And again, that if God willed that the Israelites should indulge themselves, their families, and cattle, with rest every seventh day, it is certainly proper that we should not burthen them with more work, and fatigue our family and cattle by labour. In like manner, also, I conceive that other ritual laws may be adopted for the use of Christians. For instance :—the Israelites were commanded to consecrate to God the first fruits of their corn, their first born, and a tythe of the produce of their land ;—so much, or even more, ought Christians likewise by right to set apart from their possessions, to expend either in advancing the divine glory, or in relieving the poor, should they need their assistance. M. RUARUS, *Epist. ad Steph. Curcellæum, Cent. secunda.*

The digression of Curcellæus on this question respecting the sabbath, forming the sixth chapter of his dissertation *de Esu Sanguinis,* is worthy of being read in this connection. It is besides certain, as he has there demonstrated, that the early Christians observed both the sabbath and the Lord's day. The Jews do not however enumerate the observation of the sabbath among the seven precepts delivered by God to Adam, and Noah, and their posterity. These they state to be, 1. Not to worship idols ; 2. Not to blaspheme God or his holy name ; 3. To abstain from theft and rapine ; 4. Not to shed human blood ; 5. Not to enter into incestuous marriages after the multiplication of the human race ; 6. To appoint judges who should decree justice according to these precepts. These

they

By no means ; since the Christian religion, as it takes away other ceremonies, as they are called, does also wholly abolish the distinction of days, as the

apostle.

---

they say were delivered to Adam, and repeated to Noah with the addition, 7. Not to eat the member of a living animal, or, as it is in the text (Gen. ix. 4), not to eat " the flesh with the life thereof, which is the blood thereof."

It might be considered here, as the occasion leads to the subject, whether this prohibition against eating blood, as enjoined by God on Noah and his posterity, and therefore on the human race (Gen. ix. 4), and afterwards renewed by the Holy Spirit through the apostles of Christ (Acts xv. 20, 29; xvi. 4; xxi. 25), be not also obligatory upon us? That this command is perpetual, is professedly demonstrated by S. Curcellæus in the dissertation already referred to on eating blood. Grotius was of the same opinion, as may be seen in his Annotations on Acts xv. 20. Indeed, it ought to be observed that this was the unanimous sentiment of the primitive church, as both these authors have abundantly shown. Among the Polish brethren, likewise, some were of the same opinion, and in the number M. Czechovicius. See also the commentary of A. Wissowatius on Acts xv. 20, inserted in the *Bibliotheca Fratrum Polonorum*[c]. B. WISSOWATIUS.

[c] [The length of the preceding note precludes the introduction in this place of much additional remark on the two important topics which it brings to our notice. They have, both of them, been largely and ably discussed since the publication of this Catechism by several writers, who have espoused different sides of the questions,—but the controversy has had no necessary connection with Unitarianism.

In respect to the perpetuity of the command concerning the sabbath, and the sabbatical observance of the Lord's day, the reader will do well to peruse the "Digression," above referred to, of Curcellæus, inserted in his *Diatriba de Esu Sanguinis.* This is a very masterly little treatise, exhibiting a luminous and comprehensive view of the subject. Among more modern publications, he may be directed to the Theological Repository, conducted by Dr. Priestley, the fifth and sixth volumes of which contain several able and interesting papers upon this question. To these may be added, on one side, Mr. Belsham's

L 2

Sermon

apostle plainly intimates, Coloss. ii. 16; Rom. xiv. 5, 6; Gal. iv. 10, 11. But as we perceive that the Lord's Day was in early times observed by Christians, we assume the same liberty ourselves, and freely allow it to other Christians.

I seem sufficiently to understand those commandments of the decalogue wherein the general precept concerning the love of God is explained; state to me now the other general precept?

This

Sermon on " Popular Errors;" and on the other, a discourse by Dr. Estlin, intituled " An Apology for the Sabbath."

With regard to the other question, concerning abstinence from blood, it may be observed that few topics have been more amply or more ably discussed. But after all that has been advanced on either side by the illustrious host of writers who have entered the lists as champions in the controversy, and who seem to have exhausted the arguments which could be brought forward in support of their respective hypotheses, few persons, who will be at the pains of examining and carefully weighing the subject for themselves, will rise from the investigation with the conviction that it has been satisfactorily and finally set at rest. The reader will have learnt from the preceding note, that on this interesting topic the Polish Socinians were divided in opinion. Faustus Socinus's sentiments may be seen in his Life, by Dr. Toulmin, p. 244, &c. He maintained that the precept forbidding to eat blood was " repugnant to christian liberty, and to the spirit of the Christian religion, which is averse from ceremonies of this kind, and to the express rule laid down by the apostle Paul, and often repeated by him, which is, that no kinds of meat are to be avoided by a Christian." The contrary side was advocated by Andrew Wissowatius, in his commentary on the fifteenth chapter of the Acts, which is inserted in the *Bibliotheca Fratrum Polonorum,* among the works of Wolzogenius. The treatise of Curcellæus, already mentioned, inserted in his collected works by Limborch, and printed separately, in duodecimo, in 1659, is a powerful vindication (hitherto, certainly, unrefuted,) of the perpetuity of the prohibition against the use of blood delivered

to

This is expressed by Moses in these words (Levit. xix. 18), "Thou shalt love thy neighbour as thyself."

What is to be understood by the term NEIGHBOUR?

By the term neighbour, as used by Moses, is to be understood, a person of the same nation, or any Israelite. For in the same context (Levit. xix. 15—18) he uses the titles, "thy neighbour," "thy brother," and the "child of thy people," "as synony-

---

to Noah, and subsequently renewed and confirmed by the decree of the Council of Jerusalem. An able advocate on the same side arose in the early part of the last century, in a work intituled "Revelation examined with Candour," &c. Against this appeared, in 1732, an anonymous pamphlet intituled "The Question about Eating of Blood stated and examined," &c.; and another by a Prebendary of York, in 1733, under the title of "An Enquiry about the Lawfulness of Eating Blood:" which was followed in 1734 by a second tract by the same writer in defence of the first. To the first two of these tracts the author of "Revelation examined with Candour" published in 1734 a spirited reply, under the title of "The Doctrine of Abstinence from Blood defended." In the same year appeared another learned tract on the same side, intituled "The Apostolical Decree at Jerusalem proved to be still in force, both from Scripture and Tradition." The chief aim of this writer was to state more at length the argument in support of the perpetuity of the prohibition grounded on the opinion and practice of the primitive church. These are all the tracts published on the subject at this period that have fallen into my hands. The reader may be referred, besides, to Dr. Ward's Dissertations, and Dr. Lardner's remarks upon them, inserted in Dr. Kippis's edition of his works, vol. xi. p. 305, &c. also to Grotius's annotations on Acts xv. 20; Dr. Doddridge's Lectures, prop. cxlvii. schol. 1, and the authorities subjoined. The controversy was partially revived in the Theological Repository: two papers upon it are inserted in vol. iii. p. 212, and vol. iv. p. 421. TRANSL.]

mous,

mous, although nearly the same reason applied to strangers dwelling among the Israelites, concerning whom there is a specific law in the same chapter (Levit. xix. 33).

What is meant by loving our neighbour as ourselves?

It is to wish well to him, and to act well towards him, for the like reason that you wish well to yourself and provide for your own accommodation; and especially, that you do to others what you may justly require others to do to you. Wherefore justice, and kindness, and, what depends on both these, the desire of peace, are comprehended in this love. But how far this is extended in the Law of Moses, may be learnt from the special precepts of that Law, relating to our neighbour, and from the rule and analogy of the whole of the Mosaic religion.

What has the Lord Jesus added to this commandment?

He has given to the term NEIGHBOUR a more enlarged signification, and made the love of our neighbour more comprehensive; and has also required that it should be more perfect.

In what way has he enlarged the signification of the term neighbour, and made the love of him more comprehensive?

By requiring us to regard as our neighbour not only him who is of the same nation as ourselves, or of the same religion, but also every man whatever, as united to us by nature, of whose assistance we may have any need, and whom we may be able to serve or

to

to injure :—such was the Samaritan formerly to the Jew, and, on the other hand, the Jew to the Samaritan, as Christ intimates in the parable. He, however, is in a higher sense, and may with better reason be styled, our neighbour, who is jointly with ourselves a member of the same body of Christ; as appears from Ephes. iv. 25, "We are members one of another." Hence it is that we are commanded to do good to all men, but especially to the household of faith; and also to cultivate and pursue peace with all men, but chiefly with those who are joint partakers with ourselves of the Christian religion, with whom we ought to be one.

How has he required that we should more perfectly love our neighbour?

This you will understand if I explain to you how perfectly Christ desires that all our neighbours universally should be loved by us; and, in the next place, how he commands that we should love our brethren and enemies in particular.

How perfectly does he desire that all our neighbours universally should be loved?

After this manner: First, we are to offer up prayers and thanksgivings to God for all men: in the next place, we are to seek and promote their eternal salvation by every other means in our power; to guard against giving them cause of offence; and abstain even from things in themselves lawful, if our use of them should in any way be detrimental to their salvation: lastly, when we have received injuries, we are not to retaliate, or return evil for evil, but rather, in

giving

giving and lending, even without hope of repayment, are to expose ourselves to injuries, and overcome evil with good.

But was not revenge prohibited even by the law of Moses?

That which is inflicted by the magistrate, was prohibited only in part; that is, the revenging of those injuries which the very length of time ought then to cancel. To this relates the precept (Levit. xix. 18), " Thou shalt not avenge nor bear any grudge against the children of thy people." In other respects, the words of the Law are very explicit, and several times repeated, as quoted by Christ, Matth. v. "An eye for an eye, and a tooth for a tooth;" which allowed the magistrate to avenge recent injuries [45].

But where has the Lord Jesus forbidden revenge?

In Matthew v. 38, &c., where, putting his own precepts in opposition to those of the Law, he says, " Ye have heard that it hath been said, (Ex. xxi. 24; Levit. xxiv. 20; Deut. xix. 21;) an eye for an eye, and a tooth for a tooth; but I say unto you that ye resist not evil." In which words Christ not only forbids revenge, considered simply in itself, or the

---

[45] This limitation of revenge seems to promise that something would be said concerning the revenge which any person might inflict on his own behalf;—nothing nevertheless is observed respecting this, which indeed should chiefly be treated of, in as much as the principal difference lies in it between the Old and the New Covenant. It ought to be remarked, that under the Old Covenant it was lawful for a neighbour to avenge the death of his kinsman, if he found the murderer without the border of the city of refuge. Numb. xxxv. 27. M. RUARUS.

retaliating

retaliating of evil for evil, and pain for pain, even though inflicted by the magistrate, and authorized by the law,—but also commands us to give place to injuries,' lest the provocation to exact an eye or a tooth, prohibited in that other law, and countenanced by the law of retaliation, and other inconveniences, should be aggravated; and to do this with so much patience and meekness that we are even to permit our cheek to be stricken a second time, to give our cloak to him who has taken away our coat, and to go two miles with him who has compelled us to go one mile, rather than oppose force to force, or sue any man at the law on account of our coat :—neither of which things was prohibited to any by the Law.

Are then those words of Christ, " turn to him the other (cheek) also," to be understood absolutely according to their plain literal import?

No :—for we read concerning our Lord himself, that when a blow was given him on the cheek, he not only did not expose himself to a repetition of the insult, but resisted his persecutors in those words, (John xviii. 23,) " If I have spoken evil, bear witness of the evil; but if well, why smitest thou me?" We read the same thing of the apostle Paul, Acts xxiii. 3.

May we not then institute proceedings through the civil magistrate to retaliate injuries?

Certainly,—only without revenge: for it is this alone that our Saviour forbids :—and this revenge is the returning pain or evil for evil, which the Law allowed for the solace of the injured party.

But

But how perfectly does Christ command that we should love our brother in particular?

Many things are prescribed on this subject in different parts of the Scriptures of the New Testament; but a compendium of the principal of them is exhibited, 1 Peter iii. 8, 9, when the apostle directs that all should be " of one mind, having compassion one of another:" "Rejoicing," as Paul says (Rom. xii. 15), "with them that do rejoice, and weeping with them that weep:" endued with brotherly love, or imitating in our love towards other Christians that natural affection which is wont to exist between brothers: disposed to pity, and to beneficence towards the poor and distressed, which includes hospitality also; and lastly, to be courteous and humane. He who observes these things will easily accomplish all that the apostle writes concerning charity, 1 Corinth. xiii. But the highest perfection of this love consists in this, that we firmly and patiently sustain all the inconveniences that may befall us from our brethren or on their account, and lay down our lives for them.

What is meant by laying down our lives for our brother?

That in order to serve our brother we are not only not to withhold any thing else, but are also not to refuse hazarding our lives :—of this we perceive an example held out by Paul (Rom. xvi. 3, 4) in Priscilla and Aquila, and in Epaphroditus (Phil. ii. 30).

In what way are we required by Christ to love our enemies?

As

As an enemy may be of various kinds, our love towards him must also be various. For we are required to bless those who curse us; to do good to those who hate us; to pray for those who despitefully use and persecute us. When they ask, we are to give to them; when they hunger, we are to give them food; when they thirst, we are to give them drink; and when they supplicate any thing of us, they are not to be refused.

I comprehend those things which the Lord Jesus added to the general precept of Moses, concerning the love of our neighbour: state to me what are the particular commandments of the Decalogue in which he inculcates it?

They are the remaining six, which compose the second table of the Decalogue.

Which is the fifth commandment of the Decalogue?

" Honour thy father and thy mother; that thy days may be long upon the land which the Lord thy God giveth thee."

What is it to honour our parents?

To esteem them highly in our mind, and show them every respect in our words and actions; to obey them in all things which are not repugnant to the commands of God (for the maxim holds universally, that God is to be obeyed rather than men), to evince our gratitude to them, and do them every kind office, for our education and for other benefits received from them. Ephes. vi. 1, 2, 3; 1 Tim. v. 4.

What

What has the Lord Jesus added to this commandment?

Nothing seems added to this. Nevertheless we may enumerate in this place the duties of parents and sons, on account of their bearing some resemblance or analogy, those which are delivered in the Scriptures of the New Testament concerning subjects and magistrates, wives and husbands, and servants and masters.

What is the duty of parents ?

That they "provoke not their children to wrath, but bring them up in the nurture and admonition of the Lord." Ephes. vi. 4.

What is meant by provoking their children?

To treat them with undue severity; which is done when they either chastise them without cause; or in chastising them exceed the proper bounds; or always exact their right, and remit nothing; or lastly, when they do not concede to them those things which the kindness and affection of parents towards their children demand to be conceded with tempered prudence. For by these means children are alienated from their parents, and depressed in mind: but the apostle (Col. iii. 21) commands "fathers not to provoke their children to anger, lest they be discouraged."

What is meant by bringing them up in the nurture and admonition of the Lord?

It is to introduce them from their earliest years into the ways of the Lord, to obey God's commandments,

ments, by pious instructions, by exhortation, by moderate and prudent chastisement, by example and conversation. There is, indeed, a remarkable command of God respecting pious instructions (Deut. xi. 19), where he requires that parents should speak with their children concerning his Law, not only at home when they " lie down and when they rise up," but also " when they walk by the way." And Solomon has given many precepts concerning chastisement.

What is the duty of subjects towards the magistrate?

To submit to his government, whatever may be its nature, whether it relate to religion or to morals, in those things which do not trespass on the authority of God as the supreme Lord of all; to pay him tribute and custom, to honour and respect him, not from fear only, but for conscience sake, knowing that the magistrate is of God's appointment, and acts as his vice-gerent on earth.

What is the duty of the magistrate towards his subjects?

To acknowledge that his authority over others is derived from God, and to employ it for the protection of the good, and the intimidation of the wicked,—as is inculcated at large, Rom. xiii. 1—5 [46].

What

---

[46] We no where read in the New Testament the duties prescribed to the magistrate, and according to which he ought to conduct himself, as we do in respect to those of the other classes of persons in the Church of Christ. In the passage referred to (Rom. xiii.), the duties not of the magistrate, but of

What is the duty of husbands towards their wives?

To love them "as Christ has loved the church," and "as their own bodies;" to "dwell with them according to knowledge," that is, to conduct themselves discreetly towards them, adapt their commands to their temper, and carefully avoid those things which might irritate their minds and alienate their affections from them. To give them honour, as to the weaker vessel;—that is, to make up to them, by every mark of kindness, what, as the inferior sex, is wanting to them of dignity and excellence, that they may hold them in affectionate esteem, and not despise them: moreover, not to be bitter or angry towards them, or inhuman, severe and cruel. See Ephes. v. 25, 28; 1 Peter iii. 7; Coloss. iii. 19.

What is the duty of wives towards their husbands?

To be subject to their husbands in every thing, as the church is subject to Christ; to reverence them; also, not to usurp authority over the man, but to be in silence: that is, not to presume to rule the men, or to teach them with a kind of magisterial authority, or reprove them with harsh expressions. With these duties must be classed the following: that they do not take from their husbands and transfer to themselves the authority and rule over their families; that they do not revile, and quarrel with them; but that, on the contrary, they rather attend respectfully to the words and commands of their husbands, and

of subjects towards the magistrate, are enumerated:—and at that time, which ought to be noticed, Christians obeyed heathen magistrates, especially at Rome. B. WISSOWATIUS.

display,

display, incorruptly, a meek and quiet spirit. Eph. v. 24, 33; Col. iii. 18; 1 Tim. ii. 12; 1 Peter iii. 1, &c.

What is the duty of servants towards their masters?

To be obedient to them "with fear and trembling, in singleness of heart, as unto Christ; not with eye service, as men pleasers, but as the servants of Christ, doing the will of God from the heart; with good will doing service, as to the Lord, and not to men: knowing that whatsoever good thing any man doeth, the same shall he receive of the Lord, whether he be bond or free:" Ephes. vi. 5—8. To be "subject to their masters with all fear; not only to the good and gentle, but also to the froward:" 1 Peter ii. 18. To please their masters, "not answering again, not purloining, but showing all good fidelity:" Titus ii. 9, 10. "As many servants as are under the yoke" are to "count their own masters worthy of all honour, that the name of God and his doctrine be not blasphemed. And they that have believing masters," are not to "despise them because they are brethren; but rather do them service, because they are faithful and beloved, partakers of the benefit:" 1 Tim. vi. 1, 2.

What is the duty of masters towards their servants?

To "give to their servants that which is just and equal;" to forbear threatenings or severity; knowing that both have a master in heaven, and that there is with him no respect of persons. Ephes. vi. 9; Col. iv. 1.

What

What is the sixth commandment?

" Thou shalt not kill."

What has Christ added to this?

He has commanded us not to be angry with our brother; and not to offend him by severe epithets, proceeding from anger, which our Lord describes by the terms Racha, and fool. (Matth. v. 22.) To this duty belong those words of the apostle (Ephes. iv. 31), " Let all bitterness, and wrath, and anger, and clamour, and evil speaking, be put away from you, with all malice."

But what is meant by calling any one Racha, or fool?

It is the same as to say that he is worthless, and destitute of reason.

But if it so happen that we offend our brother, what ought to be done?

He is most carefully to be reconciled : for, unless we be reconciled to our brother, our religion is vain ; and unless this be done quickly, there is danger of our falling beneath the judgement of God.

Is it, then, not allowable to be in any way angry?

It is not lawful to be angry in the way forbidden by our Lord,—that is, to seek a wicked revenge with the full approbation of our minds. Nevertheless, it is not forbidden that any one should be angry when he is moved by the sinfulness of an action, provided he do not meditate any wicked revenge [47], be not ex-

cited

---

[47] For " wicked revenge," (*ultio vitiosa*) here twice repeated,.

cited in an undue measure, and do not persist in his anger, but rather feel reluctant to indulge it.

But wherein does this prohibition of Christ against anger and railing differ from that against revenge?

In this,—that the prohibition against revenge applies to cases wherein we have sustained real injury; whereas that against anger and railing refers to cases wherein, in reality, we have not been injured by our brother, or at least not in such a way as will justify anger and railing, although it may to us seem otherwise. Whence it is that in the Greek the word (εικη) causelessly, or RASHLY, is added. Matth. v. 22.

What is the seventh commandment?

" Thou shalt not commit adultery."

What has the Lord Jesus added to this ?

First, that we are not only not actually to commit adultery, but also not to " look on a woman to lust after her," Matth. v. 28 : affirming that he who does

---

peated, I would rather substitute, MALEVOLENT (*malevola*) or MALICIOUS (*maligna*) or HURTFUL (*inimica*.) M. RUARUS.

It is truly surprising that a distinction should be made by Christians between a revenge which is wicked, and one that is not wicked, when the sacred scriptures (Rom. xii. 19) expressly forbid revenge, without any distinction whatever. Might it not, with equal reason, be excepted, that when fornication, adultery, and idolatry are prohibited by God, WICKED fornication, adultery and idolatry are intended? Some of the papists scruple not to make a distinction similar to this, in respect to that passage, 1 Peter iv. 3, concerning " abominable idolatries ;" as if it might be inferred from the words that there is some idolatry not abominable. They seem in this, however, to act with greater propriety, than those who make a distinction, in the present case, respecting revenge, concerning which there is no passage of this kind in the sacred Scriptures. F. C.

this

this "hath committed adultery with her already in his heart." But the person who thinks and purposes with himself to possess a woman, is not the only one who is to be deemed to have committed adultery with her in his heart; but he also who so sets his mind upon her that he cherishes the impure thought in his heart, and would if possible commit the act itself. Christ added besides, that " whosoever shall put away his wife, saving for the cause of adultery," and marries another, commits adultery; and that whosoever marries her that is divorced also commits adultery. From this commandment it likewise appears that the Lord Jesus forbade polygamy. For if he who marries another wife after he has divorced his former, commits adultery, certainly he does no less so, who while he retains one wife marries a second. Hence Paul directs (1 Cor. vii. 2) that every man have his own wife, and every woman her own husband. Lastly, he forbids all fornication and impurity, all indecent and obscene conversation, all " foolish talking and jesting." Heb. xiii. 4 ; 1 Thess. iv. 1, 4 ; Ephes. v. 3, 4, 5.

Is there any thing else that pertains to this commandment?

Yes :—that a believer do not marry an unbelieving wife, and that a believing wife do not marry an unbelieving husband (1 Cor. vii. 39; 2 Cor. vi. 14), lest by such an union the hearts of believers be seduced: —on which account we see that such marriages were expressly prohibited by God under the Law. Exod. iii. 4 ; Deut. vii. 3, 4.

Should

Should it happen that one of the unbelieving married parties become a believer, must the unbelieving one be deserted by the believing?

By no means, if the unbelieving party be pleased to dwell with the believing: but if the unbelieving party be unwilling to dwell with the believing, there is in such case no bondage (1 Cor. vii. 10, 12, 13). And hence the believing party is not to be held to bear all the inconveniences and injuries, in order to dwell with the unbelieving who is separated from him.

What is the eighth commandment?

"Thou shalt not steal."

What is forbidden in this commandment?

The taking away of what belongs to another without the knowledge and consent of the owner; with which, indeed, may be classed every method of embezzling the property of our neighbour: but this is, in the intention of the Law, included in the tenth commandment.

What is the ninth commandment?

"'Thou shalt not bear false witness against thy brother."

What is prohibited in this commandment?

All lying whatever; not only that which proceeds from a mind desirous of deceiving, but also that which arises from levity. Likewise, every kind of calumny, condemning and malignity, which is perceived in taking from the praise of others, and in tarnishing their good actions by a sinister construction.

What is the tenth commandment?

"Thou

" Thou shalt not covet thy neighbour's house, thou shalt not covet thy neighbour's wife, nor his man servant, nor his maid servant, nor his ox, nor his ass, nor any thing that is thy neighbour's."

What is meant by coveting that which is our neighbour's?

According to the intention of the Law, to covet our neighbour's property, is to set our minds upon it, so as to endeavour, even by fraudulent means, to draw it to ourselves, and thus, as far as may be in our power, to deprive our neighbour of it. Wherefore the commandment is thus expressed in Mark x. 19, " Defraud not," or deprive not, " another of his property;" and that, because it is said immediately before, " Do not steal." And this very thing is demanded by the spirit of the Law of Moses, for as much as the Decalogue forbids no taking away of another's property besides that which is done by theft: but it can on no account be thought that this is not prohibited in the Decalogue, since such a prohibition is in the highest degree necessary to the security of civil society, and to the exercise of that charity towards our neighbour which the Law requires. Hence Paul also shows that, because charity doeth no evil to our neighbour, all the commandments of the second table are comprised in love towards our neighbour; intimating that the tenth commandment, no less than the others, prohibits this alone, that no one do his neighbour an injury. The word covet is in other places also wont to be employed in a sense which includes its external effect. Exod. xxxiv. 24; Deut.

Deut. vii. 25; Prov. i. 10; Isaiah i. 29; and elsewhere.

In what way may our neighbour be deprived of his
property?

By force, or by fraud.   In what manner he may be
deprived of it by force is obvious to every one:—but
there are many kinds of fraudulent artifices: for it
is easy to discover them in buying, selling, or ex-
changing, in hiring or letting, in borrowing or lending, and in other transactions.   Respecting selling,
we have an old divine prohibition, Levit. xix. 35, and
Deut. xxv. 14, 15: "Thou shalt not have in thine
house divers measures, a great and a small; but thou
shalt have a perfect and just weight, a perfect and a
just measure shalt thou have."

May not usury be referred to this commandment?
Certainly.

What is usury?

The usury of which I here speak, that is unlawful
usury, is the extortion of interest on money loans, to
the oppression or injury of another.   Such is properly the import of the Hebrew term rendered usury
in several places in the Old Testament, which signifies
BITING.   But reason itself teaches, that to receive
interest for money lent, without biting or injuring
another, indeed, even with advantage to him, is neither a sin, nor unlawful usury;—especially if the
lender himself stand in need of the profit of such
money, and do not extort it from the poor, from
whom the Mosaic Law expressly forbade the receiving of usury.   Whence it happens that the Law
openly

openly permits the receiving of usury from strangers. It is apparent, therefore, that to receive interest for money lent, is not absolutely and in its own nature unjust : on which account it is that usury is never expressly forbidden in the Gospel, notwithstanding those things which are repugnant to the spirit and doctrine of Christ are in the sacred Scriptures minutely described, and in some way or other enumerated. But unlawful usury is to be considered as forbidden among other things, when injustice is prohibited : for charity and beneficence are required of us ; and we are commanded to do to others, what we would wish them to do to us.

What is added to this commandment in the New Covenant ?

If you look not to the words but to the intention of the commandment, this is added to it ; that we are not only not to endeavour to obtain, by unjust means, the property of our neighbour, but also not even to wish, or to purpose in our thoughts, to do this. For that which it is not lawful for a Christian to do, it is not permitted him to wish or design.

But is not the prohibition not to covet our neighbour's wife added to the seventh commandment ?

It certainly is, but in another sense. For here it is only forbidden us to desire another man's wife that she may be our own, as is evident from the other things which are in this place joined with WIFE. But in the other case it is prohibited to us to desire to enjoy her while she remains the wife of another.

CHAP-

CHAPTER II.

OF THE PRECEPTS OF CHRIST, DELIVERED BY HIM SEPARATELY.

You have stated the precepts of Christ contained in the laws of God delivered by Moses, and those which he added to the Mosaic commandments;—it remains that you explain to me those also which Christ has delivered separately?

These are of two kinds ;—for some relate to morals, and some to external religious acts, commonly denominated ceremonies.

What are those which relate to morals?

These are of three kinds : some relate to the religion and devotion of the mind ; some to contempt of the world ; and some to fortitude and patience.

What are the precepts of the first kind?

These three, which Paul comprises in the following passage to the Thessalonians (1 Epist. v. 16, 17, 18), " Rejoice evermore. Pray without ceasing. In every thing (and at all times also) give thanks : for this is the will of God in Christ Jesus respecting you."

What is prescribed in the first of these?

That we constantly delight ourselves in the hope of immortal life which we derive from the religion of Jesus Christ, and in the enjoyment of it deem ourselves truly happy. Hence the same apostle commands elsewhere (Rom. xii. 12) to " rejoice in hope," or Philipp. iv. 4, and 1 Tim. i. 1, " to rejoice in the

Lord

Lord alway," as in him " who is our hope ;" that is, the author and cause of our hope. To this rejoicing is opposed that solicitude which is wont to be excited in the mind either by the fear of impending evils, or by the feeling of those which are present; against which the apostle exhorts in the cited passage of the epistle to the Philippians (chap. iv. 6).

What are the precepts of the second kind ?

That we cease not to pray to God at any proper season ; but that, as far as we can, we offer up our prayers constantly and assiduously; and watch with them. He is assiduous in prayer, who prays as frequently as possible, intermingles deep sighs with the actions of life, interrupts his proceedings to create opportunities for devotional exercises, and on account of them takes away something from his sleep. This precept is repeated in several passages of the Holy Scriptures, and principally in those places where the writers speak of avoiding the evils of the last judgement, and other impending dangers. Luke xviii. 1, &c.; Rom. xii. 12; Ephes. vi. 18; Philipp. iv. 6; Coloss. iv. 2.

What qualifications ought those who pray to possess ?

First, That they confide in God ; nor doubt that he is able to give what they ask, and also willing to confer it, if they possess, besides, the other qualifications which I shall presently mention. Secondly, That they pray in conformity with the will of God ;— that is, ask for those things which are not at all repugnant to the divine will as declared in the doctrine

of

of Christ; those things which are either promised in it, or are at least on some account agreeable to the things promised. Thirdly, that they do the will of God; and that, especially, if they bear any enmity to any individual, they forgive him, and thus " lift up holy hands without wrath and doubting." (1 Tim. ii. 8.) Lastly, that they pray with great humility, and with all possible devotion. Devotion requires that, having withdrawn our thoughts as much as possible from other things, we fix them on God; and excite and invigorate in ourselves our desire of the thing for which we pray;—whence fervour is wont to arise. This is what James meant (chap. v. ver. 16), when he said, the prayer of a righteous man, made effectually, or fervently, availeth much.

What are the precepts of the third kind?

That as frequently and assiduously as possible we testify our gratitude to God for all his other blessings, but especially for the eternal life and the remission of sins offered to us: and that we devoutly celebrate these his distinguished gifts :—upon which subject, there are remarkable precepts Ephes. v. 18, 19, 20; Coloss. iii. 16, 17; Heb. xiii. 15. And again, that we return our thanks for all things that happen to us, though they may seem adverse and afflicting, knowing that all these things shall work together for our good.

What are the precepts which relate to contempt of the world?

These John has briefly comprised in the following

M   passage,

passage, (1 John ii. 15, 16,) " Love not the world,
neither the things that are in the world," &c. " For
all that is in the world, the lust of the flesh, and the
lust of the eyes, and the pride of life, is not of the
Father, but is of the world."

What is prohibited in these words ?

That we set our minds on the present world, and
the things which are found in it ;—that is, so as to
pursue them beyond what necessity may require, and
thoroughly to enjoy them ; and consequently, that we
love the men of this world, that is, so far as such
are the enemies of God, and their morals, which are
in opposition to the divine will ; but hold them in
thorough aversion. Their morals comprise the " lust
of the flesh;" that is, those vices wherein the flesh
is indulged, to which is opposed continence or temperance :—" the lust of the eyes ;" that is, the pursuit of unlawful pleasures which are drawn from objects of sight, especially avarice, which for the gratification of the eyes heaps up gold and riches : to this
is opposed αυταρχεια, or a mind contented with its
lot: lastly, " the pride of life;" to this belong
haughtiness, ostentation, ambition, and supercilious-
ness;—vices to which are opposed modesty and humility.

Ought not these vices to be considered as prohibited in the Old Covenant?

Only in so far as they are joined with injuries and
affronts offered to others, or with the neglect of some
other divine precept. But in the New Covenant they
are

are forbidden on their own account; and this under pain of the loss of salvation, as may be sufficiently perceived from this passage of John.

Wherein does the " lust of the flesh" consist?

Partly in gluttony, drunkenness and revellings; and partly in impurity.

What is gluttony?

The immoderate use of food.

What is drunkenness?

The immoderate use of drink, which may be of a greater or less degree.   Peter (1 Epist. iv. 3) denominates the former " excess of wine," and the latter more generally, " banquetings."

What are revellings?

Revellings are repetitions of banquets or luxurious feasts, with company, noise, songs and dancing: with which ought to be classed all kinds of feasts provided for the gratification of the appetite.   For the appetite is gratified not only by the immoderate use of meat and drink, but also by other pleasures, to which men are wont to be more agreeably enticed, when allured by meat and drink.   Of this kind are dances, lascivious conversation, light sports, and many other things abhorrent to the gravity and holiness of a Christian.

Wherein consists continence, or temperance?

In sobriety and chastity : sobriety imposes moderation in eating and drinking, and sometimes even demands fasting; and chastity requires abstinence from all impure pleasures ; that is, from those pleasures

M 2   which

which lie beyond the limits of lawful and honourable marriage.

What is meant by moderation in eating and drinking?

That we eat and drink just as much as suffices for the preservation of our health and strength; and carefully guard against oppressing our hearts, and rendering them unfit for serious and pious thoughts and actions.

What is fasting?

Abstinence from all meat and drink throughout the day, and sometimes longer, for the mortification of the body.

Is it not fasting, when men abstain from certain kinds of meats?

You may perceive, from the definition of fasting, that to abstain from a particular kind of meat is by no means to fast. This is rather the choice of a certain meat, made with detriment to christian liberty, and without any necessity, and joined besides with no small danger of error; since we see that the common people, who are in other respects inclined to superstition, and captivated principally by external things, follow this practice, and pursue it more attentively than they do those things which are commanded by God himself; and, on account of it, form a higher opinion of their holiness, believe their sins to be expiated, and condemn others who do not the same, just as if the essential condition of salvation were placed in this. It is not to be disguised, however, that

that it behooves us, in the season of fasting, to abstain from meat and drink of the more delicate and costly kind;—which practice, having been formerly observed by those who fasted, the perverted discipline of the church has converted into fasting; and fasting itself has been lost in the name.

Ought those who fast to be restricted to certain days?

Certainly not: for this also is contrary to the nature and freedom of the Christian religion, which ought not to be bound down to stated times.

Is it required of Christians, universally, to fast?

It is not: but we are nevertheless incited to do so of our own accord by the example of pious men, and by the effect which we may observe to arise from it: for it is of use towards controlling the desires of the flesh, and testifying our humility before God; and has power, besides, to move his compassion, if it be accompanied by prayers and almsgivings. Add to this, that it is of service for this end also, to enable us to attend the more to meditations, to prayers, and other pious acts. To conclude: it behooves the Christian, in other respects likewise, to withdraw himself, as much as his necessary avocations may permit, from those pleasures which are common to him with brutes.

What is avarice?

It is the anxious desire of possessing more than is necessary for comfortably and honestly maintaining yourself and family. 1 Tim. vi. 8, 9.

How is this sin committed?

In

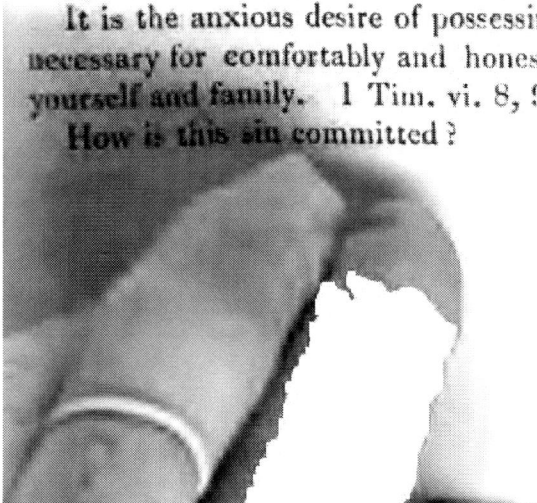

. In two ways: first, when men anxiously seek more than they want; and secondly, when they carefully hoard up and keep what they obtain. Matth. chap. vi.; Luke, chap. xii.

. To what uses then ought Christians to apply what they possess beyond what a just necessity may require for themselves?

When there is occasion, they ought to devote it to the advancement of the divine glory, to the support of the poor, especially of the household of Faith, and to other acts of beneficence,—with this reserve, however, that they be not actuated by any view to their personal glory. This is what Christ inculcates in these words (Matth. vi. 3); " Let not thy left hand know what thy right hand doeth."

Wherein may be discerned a mind contented with its lot?

. In this,—that, so far from anxiously seeking any thing beyond what is of just necessity, although it may stand in need of something of just necessity, it yet bears its condition patiently. We have an example of this in the apostle Paul, who thus speaks of himself to the Philippians (Chap. iv. ver. 11, 12); " I have learned, in whatsoever state I am therewith to be content. I know both how to be abased, and I know how to abound : every where and in all things I am instructed both to be full and to be hungry, both to abound and to suffer need." To this subject refer also those words, 1 Tim. vi. 8, " Having food and raiment, let us be therewith content :" and Heb. xiii. 5, " Be content with such things as ye have."

I have

I have heard you concerning the "lust of the flesh" and "the lust of the eyes;" I wish now to know what is meant by "the pride of life?"

It is the pursuit of vain-glory; and that glory is vain which is not merited, or does not relate to the glory of God, or is otherwise destitute of real utility. To this are to be referred all arrogance, all self-conceit as to ourselves, and contempt of others, and all ostentation; every kind of excess also relating to a splendid exterior, either as to the decoration of the body, as to attendants, or edifices, or other circumstances of this kind.

What is humility?

It is the submission of our minds though we be the superior persons—it is aversion to vain-glory; and a readiness to perform even the meanest offices for others, however low may be their condition (Philipp. ii. 3, 4), which Christ evinced in himself when he washed the feet of his own servants, the apostles, John xiii. 4, 5.

Explain now the precepts relating to self-denial?

The substance of them is comprised in those words of Christ, (Matth. xvi. 24,) "If any man will come after me, let him deny himself, and take up his cross and follow me."

What is meant by denying oneself?

It is to have no concern for ourselves in respect to the flesh, that we may constantly attach ourselves to Christ: or to be prepared to give up life, and much more those things which are equally or less dear to us than existence, in order to follow even to the last

extremity

extremity Christ and the doctrine and devotion that he has prescribed to us:—which duty Christ has explained in these words, recorded by Luke (chap. xiv. ver. 26 and 33), " If any man come to me, and hate not" (that is, and place not after me) " his father and mother, and wife and children, yea, and his own life also, he cannot be my disciple." " So likewise, whosoever he be of you that forsaketh not all that he hath, he cannot be my disciple."

What is meant by bearing one's cross ?

It is to prepare the mind to undergo and endure, on account of Christian truth and piety, not only troubles and afflictions of other kinds, but even death, —and that not of any particular description, but the most cruel and ignominious,—whenever it shall so please God:—just as if we were bearing our cross on our way to a place of cruel and of infamous punishment.

What is meant by following Christ ?

To follow Christ is to be his disciple, and to imitate his example in patience, and in submitting even to the most cruel death. To this refer, among others, the words of Peter (1 Epist. chap. ii. ver. 21), " Christ also suffered for us, leaving us an example that we should follow his steps." See also Heb. xii. 1, 2, 3.

Ought we not to follow Christ in other things also ?

We ought, indeed, to imitate him in all the actions of his life ; in those at least which were not peculiar to his office, or which had the appearance of virtue.

Hence

Hence John observes (1 Epist. chap. ii. ver. 6), " He that saith he abideth in him ought himself also so to walk even as he walked."   But we are in particular and expressly commanded to imitate him, as we have seen, in patience, in love towards others, in gentleness and humility—which virtues shone in the whole of his life, and above all in his death.   In respect to love, you may consult John xv. 12, 13 ; Ephes. v. 2 ; 1 John iii. 16 ; concerning gentleness and humility together, Matth. xi. 29 ; concerning humility separately, Matth. xx. 27, 28 ; Philipp. ii. 5, 6, to which add Rom. xv. 1, 2, 3.

CHAPTER III.

OF THE BAPTISM OF WATER.

EXPLAIN now those things which relate to external religious acts, or sacred rites.

The external religious acts, or sacred rites, always observed in the church of Christ, are baptism, and the breaking of the sacred bread[d].

What

[d] [In the first edition of this Catechism the account of the Lord's Supper preceded that of Baptism, and is thus introduced in the old English translation, p. 104:—Q. " What are Christ's ceremonial precepts, as they call them ?—A. There is but ONE, namely the Lord's Supper." From this it would appear that when the Catechism was first published, baptism was not considered by the Polish churches as a Christian institution of perpetual obligation. This, however, was not exactly the case, as we learn from the controversies to which the subject gave rise. The chief advocate of this opinion was Faustus Socinus, by whom, no doubt, as the Catechism was compiled under his sanction and with his assistance, baptism was here excluded from the number of Christian rites. Socinus's senti-

ments

What is your opinion respecting the Baptism of Water?

. That it is a rite of initiation, whereby men, after admitting

---

ments are collected by Dr. Toulmin in the Memoirs of his Life (p. 251, &c.); and, as they are of some importance towards elucidating the History of the Reformation in Poland, seem entitled to insertion in this place.

" ' As to the baptism of water, I apprehend it is not a perpetual ordinance of the church, and was not prescribed for them who in any other way have publicly given their names to Christ, or from their earliest years have been educated and instructed in the Christian discipline. Yet I should think, if it is to be retained in these days, it is to be retained principally on their account who have been converted from other religions to the Christian: and I do not see why such may not be baptized by those who have preached Christ to them: or if they have no spiritual father in Christ amongst men, why he may not perform this service, who has been fixed upon for this office by the congregation to which they are willing to join themselves: since the baptism of water, administered in the name of Jesus Christ, is only shadowing forth the forgiveness of sins in the name of Christ, in open profession of his name, and a kind of initiation into his religion: nothing is really communicated by it, but it is a recognizance of what hath been granted, and will most certainly be bestowed.' *Socini Opera,* tom. i. *p.* 350, 351.

" Amongst the other sentiments and practices of the Calvinists, or Evangelical, which Socinus regarded as erroneous, he reckons their opinion concerning baptism. One mistake, as he thought, which they espoused on this article, was an apprehension, that baptism was a seal from heaven of the remission of sins, and a confirmation of the faith of the adult. On this he remarks, ' That the nature of a seal consists in its being a proof or evidence of a transaction; but this is not true of baptism, though an holy rite: for, by the washing of the body, it is only a shadow and emblematical representation of the remission of sins, the doctrine of which had been previously explained by words. As to its being a confirmation of the faith of the adult who receive it, nothing more need be said, than that there is no trace of this in the sacred writings;
but

admitting his doctrine, and embracing faith in him,
are gained to Christ, and planted among his disciples,
or in his Church; renouncing the world, with its

manners

---

but a cordial faith was required, as a pre-requisite of baptism.
Neither is this ceremony endowed with any such power or
efficacy; but whatever confirmation faith might receive
through this rite, must be derived from the Holy Spirit, which
was bestowed after baptism, to afford a public evidence of the
truth of Christianity, and the effects of which were visible and
conspicuous.'

"He reckoned also the practice of infant baptism, as a
great and hurtful error; particularly because the stress laid
upon it by the Calvinists as well as the Papists, disposed
them to hold in detestation those who did not approve of it or
practise it, whom they could scarcely regard as Christians. 'It
is surprising (says Socinus) how much they depart, in this instance, from Christian charity, and so deviate from the true
way of salvation. For what can be more plain, and evident
from reason and Scripture, than that to the right administration of baptism, it is previously necessary that the baptized
person should be a believer? For Christian baptism was administered in the name of Jesus Christ, in whom the baptized
person professed to believe, and was by this mode declared to
be the disciple of Christ (Acts ii. 38, 41; viii. 16, 37; x. 48;
xix. 5), as all the examples and circumstances of the baptism
administered by the apostles after the resurrection evidently
show; nor doth one example of infant baptism occur in the
Scriptures. For as to what some allege as a proof of this,
that the baptism of an household or family is several times
mentioned, (Acts xxv. 15, 33; 1 Corinth. i. 15;) they do not
reflect that this must be understood of those members of a
family who were capable of baptism; as is expressly pointed
out in the second of these passages. To this let it be added,
that to justify such a conclusion, it must be clear from other
evidences and circumstances that there were infants in those
families; but nothing of this appears.' *Opera, tom.* i. *p.* 702.

"Whilst Socinus thus discarded the general and prevailing
sentiments held by the reformer on the subject of baptism, he
likewise disapproved of the opinions of the Unitarian churches
in Poland on this head; as appears from a particular tract on

this

manners and errors, and professing that they have for their sole leader and master in religion, and in the whole of their lives and conversations, the Father, the Son, and the Holy Spirit, who spoke by the apostles;—declaring, and as it were representing by their very ablution, immersion, and emersion, that they design to rid themselves of the pollution of their sins, to bury themselves with Christ, and therefore to die with him, and rise again to newness of life: binding themselves down, in order that they may do this in reality; and, at the same time, after making this profession, and laying themselves under this obligation, receiving the symbol and the sign of the remission of their sins, and so far receiving the remission itself. Acts ii. 38.

Do infants at all belong to this rite ?

If you look to the custom of the ancient apostolic Church, and to the end for which this rite was instituted by the apostles, it does not pertain to infants; since we have in the Scriptures no command for, nor any example of, infant baptism, nor are they as yet capable, as the thing itself shows, of the Faith in Christ, which ought to precede this rite, and which men profess by this rite.

What then is to be thought of those who baptize infants ?

---

this point, and from a letter to Simon Ronemberg, an elder of the church of Racow; in which he endeavours to prove that the Unitarian churches were in a grievous error, and imposed a burden on the brethren, as they would receive none under this character, nor admit them to their communion, who did not in mature life submit to immersion, as an avowal of their faith in Christ." *Socini Opera, tom. i. p. 429.*—TRANSL.]

You

You cannot correctly say that they baptize infants.. For they do not BAPTIZE them,—since this
cannot be done without the immersion and ablution of the whole body in water :, whereas they only
lightly sprinkle their heads—this rite being not only
erroneously applied to infants, but also, through this
mistake, evidently changed.   Nevertheless, Christian
charity incites us, until the truth shall more and more
appear, to tolerate this error, now so inveterate and
common, especially as it concerns a ritual observance,
in persons who in other respects live piously, and
do not persecute those who renounce this error [48].

What

---

[48] It is to be lamented that this sacred rite, which was appointed by God from heaven (John i. 6, 33; Matth. xxi. 25, 32;
Mark i. 2, &c.; Luke iii. 2, 3; vii. 29, 30), sanctioned by the
example (Matth. iii. 15, 16) and by the command (Matth.
xxviii. 19; Mark xvi. 16) of our Lord, confirmed by the practice
of his apostles and of the primitive church (John iii. 22; iv.
1, 2; Acts ii. 38, 41; viii. 12, 13, 16, 38; ix. 18; x. 47, 48;
xvi. 15, 33; xviii. 8; xix. 5; xxii. 16), and held in high estimation by their successors in every age; should be by some
wholly done away, and by others (as is here justly intimated)
shamefully changed by human comments.   That infant baptism was not in use in the primitive churches, and that none
but Catechumens (that is, persons who had been instructed)
were baptized, will clearly appear from an examination of the
writings of the ancients.   The words of Tertullian, in his
book on Baptism, are well known; wherein, adverting to
Matthew (chap. xix. ver. 14), he would have little children
come to Christ in order to be TAUGHT—but not to be BAP-
TIZED, until after they had understood the design of baptism.   Similar language may be found in his book De Corona
Militis.   See also the epistle of Victor bishop of Rome to
Theophilus bishop of Alexandria; and likewise Walfredus Stra-
bo, De Rebus Eccles. cap. 26. To the same purpose writes Erasmus, Paraphr. in Matth. xxviii. et Act. ii.   But the point for
which

What is to be thought of those who conceive that men are regenerated by this rite ?

That

---

which we contend is most clearly proved by the sixth canon of the celebrated Council of Neocæsarea, held A.D. 315 ; where the question was discussed, whether the foetus were baptized at the same time as the pregnant mother? It was thus decreed—" A pregnant woman may be baptized whenever she wishes : for there is in this nothing common to the parent with the foetus ; because the personal intention of each must be shown by their profession." The same thing is also evinced by examples :—thus Gregory Nazianzen—whose father was a bishop, and who was for a long while educated under his direction—was not baptized until he had attained the age of manhood. So likewise Chrysostom—born of Christian parents on both sides, and instructed by Meletius, a bishop—was baptized at the age of twenty-one. Thus also Basil the Great, Jerome, Ambrose, Augustine, the emperor Theodosius—all born of Christian parents, and educated in the Christian religion—were not baptized till they were of adult age. The first canon respecting the necessity of infant baptism was made at the Council of Carthage, commonly called *Milevitanus*, held A.D. 418. Even among more modern authorities, many persons, in other respects our adversaries, admit that infant baptism is not grounded on the Holy Scriptures, and was not practised by the ancients. Such as L. Vives in Augustine *De Civit. Dei, l. v. c.* 27 ; Polydore Vergil *de Invent. Rer. l. iv. c.* 4 ; Bellarmine, *tom.* i. *lib.* 4, *c.* 3 *et* 4 ; Zwinglius, *lib. de Sedit. Author. et Artic.* 18, *de Confirm.* Brentius *Prol. in Catechesin.* Peter Martyr *Comm. in* 1 *Cor.* i. 5 ; Bullinger *Dec.* 2, *Ser.* 1. The Remonstrants in their "Apology," p. 358, &c. G. Cassander, in his book on the Baptism of Infants, confesses that it was introduced in the third century. But above all are deserving to be read in proof of this, Grotius on Matth. xix. 14, and Episcopius *Institut. sect.* i. *c.* 14 : also M. Czechovicius's book on this subject ; and the thirty-six arguments of the Transylvanians against infant baptism, subjoined to the Albanian Controversy.

After the practice of infant baptism was admitted into the churches, the mode of administering this ordinance was also clearly changed. For it is very evident that this sacred rite ought to be administered in no other way than by immersion, and

that

That they greatly err:—for regeneration is the
changing of our reason, will, and affections, and
the

---

that it was so administered from the earliest antiquity. The
celebrated Grotius comprises the reasons for this in the following brief observations in his Commentary on Matth. iii. 6.
*Mersatione, non perfusione, agi solitum hunc ritum, indicant et
vocis (nimirum βαπτιζιιν) proprietas, et loca ad eum ritum de-
lecta. Joh. iii. 23 ; Act. viii. 31, et allusiones multæ apostolorum,
quæ ad aspersionem referri non possunt. Rom. vi. 3, 4; Coloss.
ii. 12. Serius aliquanto invaluisse videtur mos perfundendi, sive
aspergendi, in eorum gratiam, qui in gravi morbo cubantes, nomen dare Christo expetebant, quos cæteri κλινικυς vocabant, vide
Epist. Cypriani ad Magnum. Quod autem* TINGERE *pro* BAP-
TIZARE *usurpant Latini veteres, mirum videri non debet, cum La-
tinè* TINGENDI *vox et propriè et plerumque idem valeat quod*
MERSARE. "That this rite used to be performed by immersion and not by sprinkling, is indicated by the signification of
the word (βαπτιζιιν), by the place chosen for the ceremony, and
by many allusions of the apostles, which cannot be referred to
sprinkling. Somewhat later the custom of pouring or sprinkling seems to have obtained in accommodation to those who,
while labouring under severe disorders, wished to give their
names to Christ, whom others denominate κλινικυς, Clinics. See
Cyprian's Epistle to Magnus—That the ancient Latins should
use *tingere*, to sprinkle,—instead of *baptizare*, ought not to excite our surprise, as in the Latin language the verb *tingere* properly and most frequently signifies the same as *mersare*—to
dip or immerse." Thus far Grotius:—to which may be added,
that the mode of baptizing in use among the Jews was by the
immersion of the whole body. On which point may be consulted Grotius on Matt. iii. 16, and on Mark vii. 4. And to
the same purpose are Erasmus in his Paraphrase, and Beza
in his Annotations on this place ; also Hammond on Matth. iii.
1, and Lightfoot *Horæ* 46. Buxtorf likewise, among others,
treats largely of this subject in his work *de Synagog. Jud.* It
ought, above all, to be considered, that for such a baptism as
now commonly obtains, there could be no necessity for going
to a river, or for descending into, and coming out of, the water, as was the case in respect to Christ and others, It was
this

the conforming of them to the doctrine of Christ our Saviour,—as the term regeneration itself, when ap-plied

---

this practice that gave occasion to the well known verses of Lactantius,

Candidus egreditur nitidis exercitus undis,
Atque vetus vitium purgat in amne novo.

Moreover, all lexicographers affirm that βαπτιζειν properly signifies *immergere*, to immerse or dip ; but principally, Henry Stephens, who is himself a host, demonstrates this at large, and adds the following remarkable words—*Qui lavare seu abluere, pro baptizare, itidemque ablutionem seu lotionem, pro baptismo, seu baptismate, dicere ausi sunt, explosi jure optimo fuerunt. Thes. Linguæ Græcæ.* They who presume to write *lavare*, or *abluere*, TO WASH, for TO BAPTIZE, and *ablutionem* or *lotionem*, WASHING, for BAPTISM, are with the greatest justice rejected.

That the ancients administered baptism in this manner, their own writings everywhere declare. In proof of this may be consulted Coccius, who in his *Thes. Cath. tom.* ii. *lib.* v. *art.* 16, demonstrates, that the mode of baptizing for which we contend was in use in every age among Christians.

The observations we have produced from Grotius, and which we have thus far advanced, are substantiated by many learned men, although not otherwise agreeing with us in opinion: as Luther, *tom.* vi. *Sermo de sacr. bapt.* John Pomeranus on the xxixth Psalm. Bellarmine, *tom.* iii. *lib.* 1, *de Baptism. cap.* 1 ; Calvin, *Institut. lib.* iv. *cap.* 15, § 19, and on Acts viii. 38, and John iii. 23 : also Osiander and Piscator on this place. Flaccius Illyricus in his *Clavis Sacræ Scripturæ*; *Centuriatores Magd. cent.* 1, *lib.* 2, *cap.* 6; Pamelius; *in Tertullianum de Bapt.* and in 76 *Ep. Cypriani.* Valesius, *in Euseb. lib.* vi. *cap.* 43. Camero, Camerarius, and Casaubon on Matth. iii. 6. Lightfoot on John iii. 23. Beza on Gal. iii. 27, and Coloss. iii. 9, and in his second epistle. Estius, Aretius, and Menochius on Rom. vi. 4 ; Coloss. ii. 12. Also Davenant on these places. Marloratus on John iii. 23. Ravanellus *in Bibl. Sac. tit. Baptismus—num.* iii. *dist.* 2. Danhawerus *in Mysterio Sophia.* Dietericus *Inst. Catech. Art. de Cœna Dom.* § 1. Salmasius *in Appar. de Prim. et de Cæs. et Coma.* Vossius *in Etym. Ling. Lat. et in Disp. de Bapt.* Altingius *in Dissert. Acad.* Bren-ius

plied to the mind, imports.   But a change of this
kind cannot take place in infants, who are ignorant
of

---

ius on Matth. iii. 6. Curcellæus *Inst. lib.* v. *c.* 2, *et Diat. de
Esu Sang. c.* 13. But I should want time and room, were I to
attempt to insert here all the testimonies which favour our
opinion[1].   B. WISSOWATIUS.

[1] [On the subject of baptism, the Unitarians in this country
are divided into four parties.   A considerable number of them
concur with the editors of this Catechism and the learned
author of the preceding note, in regarding adult baptism by
immersion as alone the ordinance of divine institution, sanctioned by the precepts and the practice of Christ and his
apostles.   These comprise at present a large proportion of
that very respectable body denominated GENERAL Baptists, in
contradistinction to the PARTICULAR, or Calvinistic, Baptists.
Others adopt the practice of infant baptism by sprinkling,
as of apostolical, and therefore of divine, authority and obligation.   Under this class may be ranked the major part of
those who, from among the members of the established
church, and the Pædo-baptist dissenters, have embraced Unitarianism.   A third party look upon baptism as a rite intended only for proselytes, and to be applied, under the Christian
dispensation, as it was under the Jewish, to such persons
alone as are converts from other religions.   They consider it,
therefore, as having no reference to the descendants of Christian parents, either infants or adults.   A fourth class have
adopted the opinion of Faustus Socinus and some of the earlier Socinians,—rejecting baptism altogether, as an ordinance
never intended to be perpetual, and of no further obligation
upon Christians.   The writings of Unitarians on this subject
have not of late years been very numerous.   Early in the last
century Mr. Emlyn published his " Previous Question," in
which he contended against the application of baptism to the
posterity of baptized Christians.   The late Mr. Gilbert Wake-
field also, in his " Short and plain Account of the Nature of
Baptism according to the New Testament," espoused the
same hypothesis.   The late Dr. Toulmin, who was a zealous
antipædo-baptist, published two tracts on the perpetuity of
the ordinance : and Mr. Belsham has this year stood forward
as the champion of Pædo-baptism, in a work of great learning
and

of right and wrong, and much more that a thing of such importance concerns them. And that adult persons, who are capable of such a change of mind and will, can be regenerated by water, or by an external rite which reaches the body only, is so far from the truth, that it seems somewhat like idolatry; since that effect is ascribed to water and the external rite, or connected with them without the declared permission of God, which ought to be ascribed to God himself, and to his holy word made intelligible to the minds of those who are regenerated. For it is God "who of his own will begat us with the word of truth," James i. 18; and that seed, "not corruptible, but incorruptible," whereby we ought to be regenerated, formerly spoken of by the apostle (1 Peter i. 23), is "the word of God, which liveth and abideth for ever."

Why then does Christ say (John iii. 5) that we must be born again of water and of the spirit?

Christ does not thus speak because he intended by water, the water of baptism :—but he meant spiritual water, or water which is spirit; just as elsewhere (Matth. iii. 11; Luke iii. 16), to baptize with the spirit and with fire, is to baptize with spiritual fire, or with the spirit, which is a kind of divine fire. This is evident from hence, that Christ, in the continuation of this discourse with Nicodemus, makes no further mention of water, but speaks of spirit alone.

and ability, intituled "A Plea for Infant Baptism," wherein he may be said to have exhausted his subject, and set it forth to the utmost advantage. Transl.]

But

But he asserts that we must be born again of water,
with the view of intimating that our regeneration
consists in a certain ablution and cleansing of the filth
of our minds : and he adds the term spirit, in order
to point out that not a terrestrial but a spiritual and
celestial water is requisite for this purpose, since the
filth of the mind can be washed away by the latter
only, and not by the former. Nor is it a new thing
to designate the Holy Spirit by the term water. You
have examples of this further on in the same evangelist (John iv. 10, 14, and vii. 38), on which account it
is frequently said to be poured out. Paul also explains
to us these words of Christ, when he says (Titus iii.
5, 6) that God had saved us " by the washing of
regeneration, and renewing of the Holy Spirit, which
he shed on us abundantly, through Jesus Christ our
Saviour." For he asserts that this washing of regeneration, and renewing of the Holy Spirit, was effected
as it were by water from heaven poured upon us by
Christ.

But the apostle, in this very passage, seems to attribute regeneration to the baptism of water, since he
speaks of washing ?

He does indeed mention washing : but does not
assert that that washing of regeneration is the baptism of water itself, as they also who mostly urge this
passage against us are themselves forced to confess ;
because they contend that infants alone are regenerated by baptism, and that in adults, regeneration,
having been made by faith before baptism, is only in-

dicated

dicated by baptism. But in this passage, and in others of a similar kind, adults are intended: since, therefore, the apostle speaks here of the washing of regeneration of adult persons, it is evident that he does not treat of the baptism of water, but of a certain spiritual ablution. Nor is it unusual in the Scriptures to call that purgation of our minds, that is, that act of God and Christ whereby our minds are cleansed from the filth of our vices, which is effected by the word or doctrine of the Gospel, figuratively by the name of washing. For Paul writes to the Ephesians (ch. v. ver. 26) that Christ cleansed the Church " by the washing of water by the Word," that is through the Word, namely, of the Gospel;—wherein he alludes to the custom of washing new-married women; to which God also refers, in part, in Ezekiel (ch. xvi. ver. 9), where, speaking to the people of Jerusalem, he says, " then washed I thee with water;" which, the passage itself most clearly shows, is to be understood figuratively. The writer to the Hebrews also (ch. x. ver. 22, 23) exhorts those who had long before given their name to Christ, and no further stood in need of the baptism of water, to have their " hearts sprinkled from an evil conscience, and their bodies washed with pure water;"—alluding to the legal ablutions, which persons who had become accidentally unclean were obliged to use before they could approach sacred things or places. Lastly, the apostle himself, in the very passage under our consideration, explains what he means by the washing of regeneration, subjoining

these

these words in illustration of the preceding—" and the renewing of the Holy Spirit ;" wherein he shows that he meant a washing which is a regeneration and renovation, by the genitive of difference or of species; which spiritual washing of regeneration he asserts to have been made by the shedding of celestial water, that is of the Holy Spirit, upon men, as appears obviously from what follows: but the shedding of the Holy Spirit upon men was in no way connected with the baptism of water, since we see that it never was done in the baptism itself, but most frequently followed it; and indeed after the laying on of the hands of the apostles, but in no instance before. Acts x. 44.

But what is to be understood by those words addressed to Paul by Ananias (Acts xxii. 16) ;—" Arise and be baptized, and wash away thy sins."

It is by no means to be understood by them that the mere ceremony of baptism, or as Peter observes (1 Epist. chap. iii. ver. 21) " the putting away of the filth of the flesh," has of itself the power to wash away sin; but that this power belongs to those things in this ordinance, or resulting from it, which pertain to the mind and spirit, among which is to be ranked, as Ananias subjoins, the " calling on the name of the Lord." From these things follow the remission of sins, and, as Peter also states, " the answer of a good conscience towards God." For it is to be held, and this consideration may throw light on many other passages of Scripture, that where, in the writings of the New Testament, that wherein our salvation generally is comprised, or that whence our salvation

vation results, is ascribed to a rite or ceremony, this is by no means done as if by such ceremony, of itself, this were effected; but because by that external act a certain adumbration only is made of this matter, and an obligation to it established :—since we see clearly that the ground of our eternal salvation is placed in things of a far different description; and that, on the other hand, nothing would be more easy than to gain possession, by such ceremonies, of the kingdom of heaven. On the same principle rest the declaration (Gal. iii. 27), " As many as have been baptized into Christ have put on Christ ;" and others of a similar kind.[49]

CHAP-

---

[49] It is rightly stated that this external rite alone cannot effect our salvation. The water itself avails us nothing,—but the benefit results from the observance of our Lord's command. That maxim of the Theologians is well known, *Non privatio baptismi, sed contemptus damnat.* It is not being without baptism, but a contempt of the ordinance, that exposes to condemnation. That which is internal is not therefore to be separated from that which is external. A true faith superadded to the baptism of water, and the profession of this faith, may deservedly be said to regenerate and save us, and " to wash away our sins." These are therefore joined together Mark xvi. 16, &c. 1 Pet. iii. 21. On which place Grotius thus comments : *Plerumque apostoli, cum baptisma nuncupant, simul comprehendunt doctrinam baptismi,* &c. " The apostles frequently, when they speak of the ordinance of baptism, include at the same time the doctrine of baptism." See on this point Heb. vi. 2 ; also Rom. vi. 3, 4; Ephes. iv. 5; Gal. iii. 27 ; Col. ii. 12. The same writer on the passage quoted above (Titus iii. 5) explains the washing of regeneration to mean baptism joined with the doctrine of baptism, and with the thing signified ; and presently adds, " one part of the new birth is the extirpation of our vices, which is promised in baptism :" " After baptism is given the Holy Spirit, which operates the

greatest

CHAPTER IV.

OF THE BREAKING OF THE HOLY BREAD.

What is the rite of breaking bread?

It is an institution of the Lord Christ, that believ-ers in him should break and eat bread, and drink of a cup together, with the view of commemorating him, or of showing forth his death;—which institution. ought to continue until his coming.

Do you then consider the commemoration of Christ to be the same as showing forth his death?

They are the same; as the apostle Paul clearly explains that commemoration in this sense (1 Cor. xi. 26), " For as often as ye eat this bread, and drink this cup, ye do show the Lord's death till he come." For as to those persons who by commemoration, in the words of Christ, wherein he instituted this rite,. understand recollection, or use the latter term for the, former,—conceiving that this sacred rite was instituted in order that it might recall the death of Christ to our memory,—they do in this manifestly err. For he who would rightly comply with this ordinance, and in this way show the death of the Lord, ought to. have the death of Christ familiarly and at all times in his mind.

What is meant, then, by showing the Lord's death?

It is, in the observance of this rite, to celebrate

greatest things. This is the other part of the New Birth." On this subject are deserving of being read the observations of Schlichtingius in his *Confessio Fidei Christiani, edita nomine Ecclesiarum Polonicarum*; and in his Vindication of that work.— B. WISSOWATIUS.

the

the great kindness of Christ, in that, from his un-
speakable love towards us, he suffered his body to be
tormented and lacerated, and thus in a manner broken, and his blood to be shed: or solemnly to testify
by this act how great that kindness is, and how beneficial and salutary to us, to the glory of his name,
and the perpetual commemoration of so distinguished
a blessing.

But why does our Lord wish the remembrance of
this to be above all other things celebrated in his
Church ?

Because of all the actions of Christ, which he un-
dertook with a view to our salvation, this was the
most difficult, exhibited the strongest proof of his
love towards us, and was the most proper to him.
For the resurrection of Christ from the dead, and his
exaltation, were the work of God the Father, and not
of Christ himself.

Is there no other stronger reason, on account of
which the Lord Jesus instituted this ordinance ?

There is no stronger reason,—although some assert that he instituted it, in order that from the observance of it the remission of sins and the confirmation of our Faith might follow; and others, that it is
a sacrifice for the living and the dead.

What is to be thought of these opinions ?

That they cannot be maintained. For as to the
first, since this rite is to be observed for the purpose
of commemorating or showing forth the kindness
manifested by Christ towards us, and no other end
besides this is intimated by Christ, it is evident that
it

it was not instituted with the view that we might receive any benefit from Christ at the celebration of it, except in so far as it is worthily observed it forms a part of Christian piety [50]. And as to the confirmation of our faith, so far is our faith from being confirmed by the mere use of the bread and wine, that he who would worthily partake of them ought to be already assured of the remission of his sins on the part of God ; and the more certain he is of this, the more worthily will he be able to comply with this ordinance.

What is to be thought of the opinion that the Lord's Supper is a sacrifice for the living and the dead ?

That it is altogether a great and pernicious error: for the Scripture testifies (Heb. viii. 2, 3, 4; ix. 24) that the offering of the body of Christ, which followed his death, was made in heaven, and could not have been made on earth ; and that the body of Christ now dwells not on earth, but in heaven. Besides, as Christ is himself both the priest and the victim, it follows that no one can offer Christ but himself. Let

---

[50] If it be a part of Christian piety, surely it conduces to our justification, and so to the remission of our sins, which however in the beginning of this question is absolutely denied. M. RUARUS.

This rite may be justly styled a part of Christian piety, for it is a command of Christ, having a view to his own glory and consequently to the glory of GOD also. Although therefore this external act was not ordained in order that we might by it obtain the remission of sins, yet nevertheless, (as we have observed above concerning baptism,) it may be said to assist us in obtaining justification and salvation ; for obedience to the commands of Christ is required as a condition of salvation.— B. WISSOWATIUS.

it be added, that it were absurd to suppose that he who has offered himself to God could be offered by another. Lastly; since the Scripture asserts (Heb. vii. 27; x. 14) that the sacrifice of Christ is but one, and that it was so perfect that " by this one offering he perfected for ever them that are sanctified," it neither ought to be, nor can be, repeated; otherwise it would be neither a perfect, nor yet a single, offering.

What is the meaning of these words, " This is my body ?"

They are not understood by all persons in the same sense : for some think that the bread is actually changed into the body, and the wine into the blood of Christ, which change they denominate transubstantiation. Others imagine that the body of Christ is in the bread, or under it, or with it. And there are some who suppose that in the Lord's Supper they are partakers, but nevertheless spiritually, of the body and the blood of the Lord : all which opinions are erroneous and false.

How do you prove this in respect to the first of these opinions ?

As follows—Because it might otherwise be in like manner maintained that the cup is changed into the testament, or that the testament was in, under, and with the cup, or was drunk spiritually : since it is written by Luke and Paul, " This cup is the new testament in my blood," as absolutely as it is before said, "this is my body,"—the words from which these persons deduce their opinion. Moreover, in respect to this transubstantiation, as it is called, since the Scrip-

tures

tures designate the bread we take by the name of
bread in the very use of it, (as is clear from the words
of Paul, 1 Cor. x. 16; xi. 26, 27, 28,) it is evident
that the bread remains there, without any trans-
mutation whatever into the body of the Lord.   The
Scripture, besides, testifies (Acts iii. 21) that the
body of Christ is in heaven, and must abide there
"until the time of the restitution of all things." He cannot therefore be any more existing on earth. Whence
it is that the Holy Scriptures assert that the Lord
Jesus will descend and come to us from heaven: but
if he be now here under the form of bread and wine,
he can no more come ; for no one can come to the
place where he already is.   The body of Christ,
moreover, is only one; whereas the bread, or the
hosts, as they call them, are many, and indeed infinite in number.   It would follow, therefore, that the
body of Christ is at the same time both numerically
one, and many and infinite in number.   It would also
follow, that this one body of Christ was at one and the
same time seen and not seen by the same person, was
eaten by him and not eaten, was within him and not
within him; that it is at the same time superior and
inferior to itself, is greater and less than itself; that it
retains its stature and does not retain it ;—all which
things overturn one another, and are clearly self-
contradictory.   It is above all most absurd, as common sense itself shows, that the immortal body of
Christ should be capable of being chewed and mas-
ticated by our teeth, as the host is chewed and mas-
ticated ; and also that it should be capable of being

burnt,

burnt, and in many other ways destroyed. It is evident in the next place, that Christ speaks of that body of his wherein he was crucified, which was a terrestrial and animal body;—but that which he now has is neither terrestrial nor animal, but celestial and spiritual, as clearly appears from Paul (1 Cor. xv. 44—49). And besides, in instituting this rite, he considers his body, and proposes it for our commemoration, as, on account of suffering, without life and blood; and therefore appoints a peculiar commemoration, by the use of the cup, of his blood drawn from his body. But the body of Christ is now living, and no longer obnoxious to any pains or to death. Let it be added, that that which now exists, cannot be made out of any thing else;—but the body of Christ now exists, therefore it cannot be made out of bread.

How do you prove the second opinion to be erroneous and false?

That this opinion cannot stand, appears from most of the reasons already stated, and principally from hence, that the body of Christ dwells in heaven, and that this opinion takes away altogether from the body of Christ the properties of a body, and thus becomes self-contradictory.

How do you prove the same in respect to the third opinion?

This opinion also cannot stand; since it can by no means happen that the very substance of the body of Christ, abiding in heaven, can be actually taken by us, who dwell on earth; and this too in an infinite number

ber of places at the same instant. For this real partaking requires that the one should be actually brought
into contact with the other. But if they should assert
that this is done by faith, which looks to the substance
of Christ, existing in heaven, as its object, and through
this, as a medium, derives a certain efficacy or advantage flowing from Christ to mankind ;—it may be
replied, first, that this is not a real participation of
the body of Christ; since, according to this, the
substance itself is not partaken, but the fruits of it :
and they themselves affirm, that the real participation of the body of Christ is such that it cannot be
comprehended by the mind, nor expressed by the
tongue; whereas that participation which has just
been noticed, may be both understood by the mind
and expressed in words [51]. In the next place, this
may be done without this eucharistic rite, as well
as by it. Besides, if this was the intention of Christ
in the words " this is my body," they could not
have been spoken either of the bread or of this act
absolutely ; but only with this condition, that those
who came to the Lord's table were possessed of this
faith. As, however, those persons observe the ordinance who are without this faith,—and sometimes all
may be of this description who eat this sacred bread
together,—neither the bread nor the act can have any
such conjunction with the body of Christ as they desire : not to repeat at this time other things tending
to the refutation of this opinion.

[51] *Vide Calvini Instit. lib. iv. cap. xvii. 57.* M. RUARUS.

What

. .What then is to be understood concerning the eating of the body and the drinking of the blood of Christ in the sixth chapter of John's gospel?

Christ is not speaking there of this ordinance; for in that chapter he ascribes eternal life unconditionally to him who eats his flesh and drinks his blood, and withholds eternal life absolutely from him who does not eat his flesh and drink his blood; which that he did not assert in reference to this rite is hence evident, because a person might partake of this ordinance and nevertheless perish, and because, on the other hand, a person who had not partaken of it, never perhaps having had an opportunity, might be saved. Hence it follows that the power of conferring eternal life upon men can on no account be attributed to this rite, unless it be certain that the very flesh and the very blood of Christ be actually taken in it. But I have just demonstrated that this cannot be done. And, indeed, Christ himself sufficiently shows that his words are to be understood not in a literal but in a spiritual sense, when he tells those who were offended by the harshness of them (ver. 63), " It is the spirit that quickeneth; the flesh profiteth nothing: the words that I speak unto you, they are spirit, and they are life;" that is, they ought to be, understood of a spiritual thing suited to the obtaining of eternal life. Christ does not therefore, in this passage of John's gospel, speak of the eucharistic ordinance; but he calls his body, deprived on our account of life and blood, MEAT, and his blood, drawn forth from his body, DRINK, because his death has the

power

power of imparting eternal life to men, (inasmuch as Christ died for the life of the world,) just as material meat and drink have the power of sustaining corporeal and temporary existence. But as it is necessary to take meat and drink, or to eat and drink, if we would support this temporary existence, so also ought we to eat the flesh and drink the blood of Christ, (the comparison being pursued by him,) if we would obtain eternal life through his death.   Since then the flesh and blood of Christ are by him called meat and drink, by way of similitude, it follows that to eat this flesh and drink this blood, was also spoken by him no otherwise than by way of similitude, and so ought to be understood by all.   And what else can this be but to believe and be thoroughly convinced, that Christ died for us and for our sins?   For from this belief, if it be productive of piety, follow eternal life, the wonderful refreshing of our minds, and the firmest assurance of the forgiveness of all our sins and of the obtaining of eternal life.

But how are those words of Paul to be understood (1 Cor. x. 16), "The cup of blessing which we bless, is it not the communion of the blood of Christ; the bread which we break, is it not the communion of the body of Christ?"

In this manner:—that all who bless this cup, that is, sanctify it by thanksgiving and the celebration of the name of the Lord; and, in like manner, they who break this bread together; provided they practise this rite worthily, have the communion of the body and blood of Christ; that is, of all the benefits which

Christ

Christ procured for us by his death; and attest this also in this ordinance. For that they have communion among themselves is apparent from hence, that they are one bread and one body; that is, they are companions [*companes, sive companiones, et concorpores*], because all partake of one bread. In like manner, immediately after, (ver. 18,) explaining by another example the matter concerning which he is there treating, he says that Israel after the flesh, who eat of the victims slaughtered at the altars, are partakers of the altar, and therefore of the worship and the sacrifices, and that this was testified by this very act. Hence he comes to the conclusion he had had in view, that they were to abstain from things sacrificed to idols. Not that an idol is any thing, or that that which is sacrificed to idols is any thing; but that those things which the Gentiles, who were ignorant of God, sacrificed, they sacrificed to dæmons,—wherefore they who ate of those things had communion with dæmons, or made fellowship with dæmons, and testified so much by this act.

Explain to me, then, the true and genuine sense of these words, " This is my body ?"

This you will easily understand, if you only bear in mind that, in the sacred writings, and indeed in common practice, figures, images, and commemorating signs, are called by the names of those things of which they are the figures, images, and memorials. Wherefore, when Christ designed that in this rite his bloody death should be declared by us, under a kind of shadow or representation, he said that this bread
which

which is broken is his body, delivered for us : that is
to say, is a commemorating sign, a kind of emblem
of his body to be shortly, on our account, broken, that
is, lacerated, pierced, wounded, and tortured : and
also, in like manner, that the cup, or the wine contained in it, was for the same reason his blood, to be
shortly shed for us.   For the wine is no otherwise in
the cup than as it is poured out of his vessel, or at
least drawn from his grapes.   It is by way of figure
or emblem only that it is said in Ezekiel (chap. v.
ver. 1—5) concerning the hair, whereof a part was to
be cut, a part burnt, a part scattered, and a part
preserved, to be afterwards consumed: "THIS IS JE-
RUSALEM :" that is, this is an emblem of Jerusalem,
or a shadow of what she is to become.   As to what
is stated in the account of Luke and Paul,—that this
cup is the new testament in the blood of Christ,—
this must be understood as if they had said, This is a
certain memorial, or commemorating sign, of the New
Covenant confirmed by the blood of Christ.   In like
manner circumcision also was formerly called a Covenant (Gen. xvii. 13), namely, between God and
Abraham; that is, was a kind of commemorating token
of the Covenant, as the Scriptures themselves explain
it (Gen. xvii. 11).   So likewise the sabbath is called
(Exod. xxxi. 16) a Covenant between God and the
Israelites; that is, a sign of that Covenant, as the
Scriptures in like manner explain, Exod. xxxi. 13
and 17.   For a similar reason it is said concerning that
remarkable rite of eating the paschal lamb (Exod.
xii. 11), that " it is the Lord's passover," by which

name, PASCHA, or rather PESACH, the passover, namely, of the Lord, the lamb itself also is called, because
it was the memorial of his passover. In like manner both the rite itself of breaking bread, and the
bread and the cup, may be denominated the body and
the blood of Christ.

But if such be the case, why does Paul say (1 Cor.
xi. 9) that "whosoever shall eat this bread and drink
this cup unworthily, shall be guilty of the body and
blood of the Lord;" and (ver. 29) that " he does not
discern the Lord's body?"

Paul does not thus speak because such a person
takes the very body or blood of Christ, which, as far
as it can be taken by us, can be taken only worthily:
—but because that while he eats this bread and drinks
of the cup of the Lord, unworthily, he offends against
the very body and blood of Christ, and is guilty
of his sufferings, whereof this rite is the memorial
or emblem, and for the proclaiming and commemorating of which it was instituted. This Paul himself intimates, when from this circumstance—that as
often as we eat this bread, and drink this cup, we do
show forth the Lord's death—he draws this conclusion,
that whosoever eats and drinks unworthily, is guilty of
the body and blood of the Lord. Nor do the words
" not discerning the Lord's body" imply any thing
else than that he does not value and esteem, as
highly as he ought, the singular dignity of the body of
Christ, delivered to death on our account; nor distinguish those sacred symbols, the representations of
Christ's body, or the act appointed for the celebration

tion of it, from ordinary and profane food, and the eating of such food; nor treat the one with any more religious respect than the other[52].

What is meant, then, by eating this bread and drinking this cup unworthily?·

It is not to observe this ordinance with due reverence and piety, or in such a way as we ought, and the reason of its appointment demands. Whence may easily be understood what is meant by observing it worthily.

I wish you to explain this to me a little more at large?

In order to the worthy observation of this ordinance, it is requisite, first, that you carefully consider what is to be done in it, for what purpose it was instituted, and is to be observed by you; that you devoutly reflect how severely Christ suffered; what great blessings he has procured for you by his agonies and death, and how resplendently the love both of Christ and of God shines forth here; that, in this manner, you excite your mind to venerate and worship God and Christ, and to offer them thanksgivings; that you do this continually in this rite; and that you cautiously avoid doing any thing, which is

---

[52] An example of this may be taken from the use of the paschal lamb, which it was not lawful for any one to eat unless he had been previously purified, as appears from Numb. ix. 7, and 2 Chron. xxx. 3. In consequence of some neglecting this requisition it appears that they were visited with certain plagues, from which they were delivered by the prayers of Hezekiah: ver. 20.—M. Ruarus.

not

not accompanied by the highest reverence of God and Christ. And because we testify in this ordinance that we have the body of Christ, crucified on our account, for the spiritual food of our souls, and his blood shed, for our saving drink; also that we have communion with him, and thus belong to the New Covenant, and together with other Christians are members of one body (all which demand a faith working by love), we ought at the same time, and above all things, to study to be what in this ordinance we profess ourselves to be, that we may not lie to God and Christ: and if, as yet, we are not such, we should at all events resolve to become such as soon as possible; and not suffer this determination of our mind to be afterwards of none effect. In order that we may accomplish all this, Paul commands us to examine and judge ourselves, and so observe the ordinance.

What is meant by examining and judging ourselves?

Carefully to scrutinize ourselves and our actions: not those actions alone which are passed, as if we would punish what was criminal in them, amend them, and pray God to forgive them; but those also which are present; carefully to deliberate upon whatever we undertake, that we may not in any thing offend God, but conduct ourselves in all our proceedings as we ought, and the divine commands require[33].

CHAP-

---

[33] The ordinance of breaking bread is denominated the Lord's

CHAPTER V.

OF THE PROMISE OF ETERNAL LIFE.

You have explained to me the perfect precepts of Christ, I wish you to explain his promises also ?

The

Lord's Supper in the sacred scriptures (1 Cor. xi. 20), and every where among Christians to this day : for this ceremony was observed by our Lord in the evening, or at night. And it is plainly to be gathered from the writings of the ancients that it used to be celebrated at this season in the primitive churches : and we have an instance of this, Acts xx. 7, &c.

There is a difference of opinion among Christians as to the kind of bread which ought to be used in the holy communion. That Christ himself - used unleavened bread appears from Matth. xxvi. 17, compared with Ex. xii. 18; and the apostle seems to allude to this, 1 Cor. v. 7, 8. Christians therefore would act most safely if in these things also they were to follow the example of their Lord.

But it is of more consequence to consider whether that holy act of humility, the washing of feet, which our Lord instituted at the time of this his last supper, and sanctioned by his example and command,—adding that happy were they who should do these things (John xiii. 17),—ought not still to be practised in the Christian Church ? That it should, seems evident from the cited passage : and it is dangerous to depart from the literal import of the words, or assert that the command does not extend to all countries and times. That this holy custom was held in esteem and observed by the ancients appears from the writings of some of them. See Tertullian, *lib.* ii. *ad Uxorem*; Cyprian *de Lotione pedum.* Ambrose (*lib.* iii. *de Sacram.*) affirms that this holy custom was retained in the church of Milan down to his time : which Grotius likewise notices under John xiii. 15. So also Bernard, like those writers already named, regarded the washing of feet as a sacrament; *Sermo de Cœna.* Moreover, the 17th Council of Toledo, held in the year 694, commands (c. iii.) that "bishops and priests should wash the feet of the faithful at the celebration of the Lord's Supper, after the example of Christ,"—adding, " in order that this neglected custom may be again introduced." See also on this

subject

The greatest of all is eternal life, wherein is comprehended at the same time the remission of sins. But

---

subject Danhawerus, *Arist. rediv. dial.* ii.   Thus likewise Zacharias bishop of Rome, in reply to the inquiry of Boniface, bishop of Mentz,—whether it were allowable for holy women, as was the custom among the men, to wash one another's feet at the Lord's Supper and at other times,—states, "This is a command of our Lord," &c.   See Baronius, *an.* 751, § 11. See also to the same purpose Augustine, *Epist.* 119; and Rupertus, *lib.* v. *de Div. Offic. cap.* 20 *et* 21, and also Polydore Vergil *de Inv. Rer. lib.* 4, *cap.* 13; and Bellarmine *de Sacr. lib.* ii. *cap.* 24, &c.   In the Unitarian churches of Poland also, the great Schlichtingius particularly asserts that this command is obligatory upon us—*Comm. in Johan.* xiii. And Wolzogenius on this passage writes, that it would be a praiseworthy act to ordain the washing of feet in Christian churches—by this means the practice of humility might be perpetual among Christians.

It ought to be inquired here, besides, whether, and at what time, the command given by the apostle James (chap. v. ver. 14), to anoint the sick with oil in the name of the Lord, have ceased to be obligatory upon Christians?   Most Protestants think, that it ceased with the gift of healing which existed in the primitive church; for if this were now practised, it would have no effect.   But it ought to be observed that these miraculous healings were chiefly applied to unbelievers; for had they possessed this gift, no Christian would have died in consequence of natural disorders: the contrary of which appears from 1 Cor. xi. 30.   (See also Phil. ii. 27, and 2 Tim. iv. 20.)   That the power of healing had not then ceased appears from what follows, chap. xii. 28, 30.   It is also plain from the same place, that all presbyters were not endued with this gift of healing the sick: but James speaks here without limitation.   It is dangerous to argue from the event: for in like manner it might be proved that even baptism and faith had ceased, because the signs which were to follow these (Mark xvi. 17, 18) are not now to be seen.   Nor indeed would prayers be now to be offered up for the sick, because these also do not always succeed.   It is therefore to be ascertained in such cases (and also in all other practices), whether it be the will of the

But there is another, besides, exceedingly conducive to the obtaining of the first, namely the gift of the Holy Spirit.

What

---

the Lord; which rule is discussed by many theologians, and in reference to this place. But, in the meantime, it is sufficient if by this medium the disorders of the mind can be removed, and the remission of sins be obtained: for that the relief of the mind is spoken of here may be plainly inferred from ver. 13, 16, 19, 20. which also D. Brenius observes.

It ought above all to be considered, whether the words *σωσει*, which literally signifies to serve (commonly to save), and *ηγειρει*, which properly signifies to awaken, refer not to the future rather than the present? Some conceive that oil was at that time the natural remedy for curing diseases. But in this case the physicians rather than the elders of the church would be commanded to be sent for. Besides, this could not be the case in all disorders and in all the countries through which believers were dispersed (James i. 1; 1 Peter i. 1). But the apostle speaks in general terms. Nor would this have been then noticed as any thing extraordinary (Mark vi. 13). Some imagine that by oil the Holy Spirit is here intended. But there is no necessity to oblige us to depart from the literal import of the words. Besides, it were absurd to ascribe to presbyters the power of anointing with the Holy Spirit. But the most copious explanation of this opinion is given (among other writers) by G. Estius in his observations on this place, as also by Maldonatus on Mark vi. 13, &c. Estius asserts that this rite was observed among the primitive Christians after the time of the apostles; and, although, as we have seen in respect to other things, somewhat changed, prevails even yet in many churches. In ancient authors, but above all in Tertullian, we find this unction joined with other sacred rites. It is regarded as a command of our Lord by Innocent, 1 *Epist. ad Decentium Episcopum*; Cyril, *Catech. Myst.* 5; *et lib. de ador. in Spir.* Augustin *in Psalm.* 44; *et de Temp. scr.* 215; Chrysostom, *lib.* iii. *de Sacerd.*; Beda and Theophylact on Mark vi. 13, &c., all of whom testify that this rite was in their time observed in the Church. Polydore Vergil (*de Inv. Rer. lib.* 5, *cap.* 3) also intimates that it prevailed under Felix IV. bishop of Rome. Further information respecting this sacrament may be found in the proceedings of the general council of Florence.

What is the remission of sins?

The free deliverance from the guilt and penalties of sins. As the penalties are of two kinds, some temporal and some eternal, an exemption from both is promised through Christ, but principally from those which are eternal.

Is the remission of all sins promised to us through Christ?

Yes, of all; including those which were committed by us before we had believed in Christ, whatever were their kind or measure; those which through any ignorance or human infirmity are committed by us, while we believe in him, and are walking in newness of life; and those heavier trespasses committed after faith,—provided they be followed by true and sincere penitence, and amendment of life.

---

rence. It is well known that in the Church of Rome, and the churches subject to that see, this rite is to this day held in esteem. That it has been observed to this time in the Greek and Russian Churches appears from the censure of Cyril of Berrhœa, patriarch of Constantinople, passed at a synod in that city in 1638, and sanctioned by the patriarchs of Alexandria and Jerusalem, and by most of the Eastern bishops; and also from another decree of a synod of Constantinople, held in 1642 under the patriarch Parthenius, sanctioned by the metropolitan of Kiow, and other Russian bishops. It is said that the same custom obtains in the rest of the East. Grotius likewise observes the same thing on James v. 14; whose annotations on this passage, as also on Mar. vi. 13, may be added. Consult likewise Baronius, *tom.* 1, *an.* 63, § 13, 14, 15, 16. Nor is it foreign to the purpose to observe that this external rite is suited to those who derive their name from CHRIST—i.e. the ANOINTED: and especially in respect to those who are infirm either in body or in mind; for oil is the symbol of gladness. But more cannot be said here on this subject.—B. WISSOWATIUS.

But

But the Lord Jesus asserts (Matth. xii. 32), that blasphemy against the Holy Spirit shall not be forgiven, either in this world or the next?

He does indeed so assert; but for this reason, which he tacitly assumes, that God will close against a person of this kind, who knowingly and purposely dares to rail against the Holy Spirit with contumelious language, the avenue to faith and penitence, without which he cannot obtain the remission of sins [54].

Was not the same promise of the remission of sins comprised in the Old Covenant?

You shall hear concerning this when I come to treat of the expiation made for sins by Christ.

I have heard you concerning the remission of sins; I wish you now to explain to me the promise of eternal life?

By the eternal life promised to us by Christ, according to the meaning of holy writ, I understand not that only which the words of themselves signify, namely, a life never to terminate, or immortality, but also an existence the most replete with joy and pleasure wholly divine, passed in heaven with God and Christ, and the holy angels.

Was not eternal life promised also in the Law of Moses?

If by the word promise you understand, as you

[54] It was proper to take this occasion to explain in what sense it is to be understood that sins are remitted in this world, and in that which is to come; since the notion of purgatory furnishes but an awkward exposition of the subject. On this point may be consulted Socinus on 1 John v. *Op. tom.* i. *p.* 231. —M. RUARUS. [And Brenius on Matth. xii. 32. F. C.]

ought

ought to do, some explicit declaration of the divine will, on account of which a person may upon sure grounds hope for some good which is destined for him,—there is in the Law of Moses no promise of this kind of eternal life, which is now first revealed to us by Christ,"who hath abolished death, and hath brought life and immortality to light through the gospel:" 2 Tim. i. 10. Hence also the Gospel is said (Heb. vii. 19) to be " the bringing in of a better hope," and (Heb. viii. 6) " a better covenant, established upon better promises," than the old.

But it appears, surely, that some hope of eternal life existed among the people of God before Christ?

Nothing prevents your hoping for something, although you have not God's promise for it, provided the thing be greatly to be desired, and such as it is credible God would give to those who serve him. Now eternal life is above all things to be desired; and it is exceedingly credible that God will bestow it upon those who serve him, as a reward eminently suited to his majesty, without which, other blessings, though proceeding from God, are scarcely entitled to the name of a divine recompense [55].

Shall

[55] It might be added, that the hope of eternal life was not a little cherished by pious men under the Old Covenant, on this account, that they perceived that the most constant worshippers under the Law were sometimes oppressed by the heaviest misfortunes. Whence they might infer, either that those persons were wholly disappointed of the reward of piety promised in the Law, or that God had wherewith to recompense them even after death. For this reason this hope of a future world seems

Shall they have eternal life who have hoped for it, notwithstanding it was not promised to them?

Certainly; provided only that from their hearts they worshipped God, and were obedient to his commands: for nothing hinders but that God may perform more than he has promised. And Christ clearly teaches this (Luke xx. 27, 28), when from the words of God himself he truly and acutely infers, that Abraham, Isaac, and Jacob, shall rise from the dead and live: and the author to the Hebrews, in imitation of him, (chap. xi. ver. 16) says, that " God is not ashamed' to be called their God, for he hath prepared for them a city," namely, a heavenly one.

If God will give eternal life to those men, why did he not promise it?

God deferred a promise so excellent until the advent of the promised saviour Christ (Acts xxvi. 22, 23), that it might the more evidently appear to all that so precious a blessing flowed from his own good pleasure and free bounty alone [56].

Are there not in the New Covenant, besides the promise of eternal life, promises relating to this life also?

The Scripture indeed testifies (1 Tim. iv. 8) that godliness even under the New Covenant has the promise

---

seems to have been excited in the breasts of the worshippers of God, particularly in the time of the Maccabees.—M. RUARUS.

[56] This may be a general reason for all times ; but the reason of its being deferred until the coming of Christ seems chiefly to have been this,—that we might be the more bound to Christ, to whom we are indebted for such glad tidings.—M. RUARUS.

not

not of the future life alone, but also of the present : and likewise, as we read in Mark (chap. x. 29, 30), that if any one for the sake of Christ and his gospel shall give up all things, " he shall receive a hundred-fold now in this time, with persecutions, and in the world to come eternal life."

Is then the New Covenant equal to the Old, as respects the promises of the present life ?

Since it appears from other passages of Scripture that Christians ought to rest contented with those things which are necessary for the support of existence, it is evident that the promises relating to this life, made under the New Covenant, ought to be understood as inculcating, that Christians shall not want any thing that may be necessarily requisite for the support of this life; unless indeed God design to try their faith by want, distresses, and death. But under the Old Covenant, wealth, affluence, and pleasure, honours and dignities, were also to be looked for by those who obeyed the Law. Whence it is the more clearly seen that eternal life was not expressly promised in the Old Covenant, otherwise the New Covenant would not have " better promises" than the Old, but the latter would not a little excell the former in this respect, contrary to what I have before maintained.

CHAPTER VI.

OF THE PROMISE OF THE HOLY SPIRIT.

EXPLAIN to me the other promise, and state what the Holy Spirit is ?

The

The Holy Spirit is a virtue or energy flowing from God to men, and communicated to them : whereby he separates them from others, and consecrates them to his own service.

Is the Holy Spirit promised to all believers in perpetuity ?

Yes : It ought however to be observed that this gift, as respects its effects, is two-fold, the one continuing for a time only, the other perpetual ; whereof the former may be called visible, the latter invisible.

What is the temporary and visible gift ?

It is such a divine power as operates, either in those to whom it is given, or by them, effects that are astonishing, and clearly out of the course of nature. This gift was in the beginning conferred upon believers in Christ.

Why is it that this gift has not always continued ?

Because it was bestowed for the confirmation of the gospel of Christ. When it appeared to God that this was sufficiently confirmed, this gift, by his will and pleasure, was discontinued.

What do you mean by the gospel of Christ being sufficiently confirmed ?

I mean that they who were disposed to believe the gospel had sufficient evidence, in what was done for its confirmation, to believe it ever afterwards.

Who are those persons ?

They who are endued with integrity and simplicity of mind, or who are not averse from true piety. For God does not intend that they who are not of this class should have no cause for rejecting the doctrine

of

of Christ; and many of them at least would have had none, if this confirmation had been perpetual. Because he must have been eminently and singularly wicked who would not have acknowledged the doctrine of Christ to be true, and embraced it, not so much from the love of virtue and piety, as through the evidence of such unceasing miracles. Hence it would have happened, that in the Christian religion, which by the will of God is to distinguish the honest from the dishonest, there would have appeared no difference between them.

Tell me then what the gift of the Holy Spirit is which is perpetual among Christians?

Before I explain this, I must show that under the New Covenant there is a certain gift of the Holy Spirit which is perpetual, that is, existing at all times in the church of Christ.

I beg you would do this.

You must observe then, that, independently of other testimonies, this is made evident by the words of Christ, (Luke xi. 13,) where he shows that God would give the Holy Spirit to his children who asked it of him; which, indeed, he infers from a reason that is adapted to all ages. In the same sense ought properly those words also of Christ, (John xiv. 21, 23) to be interpreted, wherein he promises those who love him, and keep his sayings, that he and his Father will come to them, and make their abode with them, and manifest themselves to them; which indeed God and Christ accomplish by the Holy Spirit.

What then is this gift of the Holy Spirit?

It

It is a divine inspiration of that kind whereby our minds are filled with a more enlarged knowledge of divine things, or with a more certain hope of eternal life; also with joy in, and a certain foretaste of, future happiness, or with an extraordinary measure of divine glory and piety.

But do we not acquire the hope of eternal life through the preaching of the gospel?

We certainly do; for from the preaching of the gospel, that hope may be acquired of eternal life which is promised in it,—otherwise, wherefore is it promised?   But in order to fix in our minds a more firm and certain hope, by the power of which we may in every trial remain invincible, it seems requisite that that promise, outwardly made to us by the gospel, should be inwardly sealed in our hearts by God through the Holy Spirit.

Does this inward sealing extend to all to whom the gospel is announced?

By no means,—but to those persons alone who believe the gospel after it has been preached to them, who properly appreciate the outward means employed by God in confirmation of the promise of eternal life, and rightly use the gospel.   For if that gift of the Holy Spirit, which continued only for a time, was given to none but those who believed the gospel, much more, surely, are we to think that that gift of the Holy Spirit which is perpetual, is to be given to them alone who have sincerely believed, and from their hearts embraced the gospel; and who besides supplicate this gift from God with fervent prayers.

Is

Is there not need of this internal gift of the Holy Spirit in order to believe the gospel?

No: for we do not read in the Holy Scriptures that it was conferred upon any one besides those who had believed the gospel. Acts ii. 38; viii. 16, 17; x. 17; xv. 7, 8, 9; xix. 2; Ephes. i. 13.

But is there not, besides this special gift of the Holy Spirit promised to believers in Christ, another spirit common to them all?

There certainly is, which arises in the minds of all believers from the acknowledgement, and the reception through faith, of the gospel of Christ, wherein that paternal and unbounded grace of God towards the human race is proclaimed: by which spirit all ought to be governed, and the deeds of the body be mortified; and which spirit if any man have not, he is not of Christ. To this is opposed that spirit of bondage, which the discipline of the law inspired. For this reason the law is called the LETTER, and the gospel SPIRIT, and the law is said to kill, but the spirit to give life—because the law was nothing but letters and writing, proposing laws, and denouncing death against transgressors: but the gospel fills men with a filial spirit, and sets at liberty those who are incited to yield a filial obedience to God, and armed with the powers of eternal life: when there is added to this spirit that promised gift, poured forth from heaven, which the apostle, in reference to those times, rightly joins with the former, (Rom. viii. and elsewhere), nothing is wanting towards the perfecting of the Christian in this world.

After

After you have explained to me what the gift of the Holy Spirit is, I wish you to inform me also, whether the Holy Spirit be a person of the Godhead?

That the Holy Spirit is not a person in the Godhead you may learn from hence:—First, because many things which in the Scriptures are attributed to the Holy Spirit, are not applicable to a divine person; and not a few of them, not even to any person whatever: such are, that it is given by God, and this either according to measure or without measure; that God pours it out, and that it is shed forth from him; that men drink into it, and are baptized by or into it; that it is given in double portions, and distributed into parts; that there are first-fruits of it; that it is itself taken away, and that a portion of it is taken away; that at some time it was not; that it is quenched;—and similar things which are met with in the Scriptures (Acts v. 32; 1 John iv. 13; Eph. iv. 7; Acts ii. 17, 33; 1 Cor. xii. 13; Heb. ii. 4; Rom. viii. 23; Psalm li. 12; Num. xi. 17 and 25; 2 Kings ii. 9; John vii. 39; 1 Thess. v. 19). Secondly, because it is evident that the Holy Spirit is said to be given by God to men, and that this is asserted concerning it even in those places wherein it is commonly believed to mean a divine person. But a divine person cannot be given or bestowed by any one; for he who is given or bestowed must be under the authority of another, which can on no account be said of a divine person, which is the supreme God himself. Thirdly, because Christ declares concerning it (John xvi. 13), that it would not speak of itself, but whatsoever it should hear, that it

o   would

would speak : but a divine person could not but speak of itself. Fourthly, because Christ says (Matth. xi. 27) that "no one knoweth the Son but the Father, neither knoweth any one the Father save the Son, and he to whomsoever the Son shall reveal him." But if the Holy Spirit were a divine person, the Father would not alone know the Son, and the Son alone know the Father; but the Holy Spirit also, without a revelation from any one, would know both. Fifthly, because in several places (as John v. 17 ; viii. 16; xiv. 21; xvii. 3 ; 1 John i. 3, ii. 23 ; 2 John 3 and 9 ; Luke ix. 26 ; Mark xiii. 32 ; 1 Tim. v. 21 ; Revel. iii. 5, 12, v. 13), where mention is made of the Father and the Son, sometimes of angels, and occasionally of men also, and other things—no notice is taken of the Holy Spirit, although if he were a divine person he ought to be named equally with God and Christ, and much more than angels, or men, or other things. Sixthly, because the Holy Spirit is in many places called the Spirit of God : but that which is OF God cannot be God, and therefore not a divine person ; for to be OF God, and to be God, are opposed to each other. To this reason may be added, that the Holy Spirit is denominated the power or the finger of God, which cannot be asserted of a person of the Deity, that is, of the supreme God himself (Luke i. 35; xxiv. 49; Matth. xii. 28, compared with Luke xi. 20). Seventhly, because the Holy Spirit is OF God (1 Cor. ii. 12), and proceedeth from God (John xv. 26); for unless it were of God, Paul could not compare the Spirit of God with the spirit of a man which is in man,

man, as he does when he says (1 Cor. ii. 11), "for what man knoweth the things of a man, save the spirit of man which is in him? Even so the things of God knoweth no man but the Spirit of God." But since the Holy Spirit is OF God, and it cannot be said reciprocally that God is OF the Holy Spirit, it is apparent that the Holy Spirit is not a person of the Godhead. Besides, as I have already proved that there is only one person in the Godhead, and that this is no other than the Father, it is evident that the Holy Spirit, which certainly is not the Father, is not a divine person. Eighthly, if the Holy Spirit were a person, it would be God himself; for those things are attributed to it which are peculiar to the divine essence. But I have already shown that since God is numerically one, he has not a plurality of persons, and that the one numerical essence of God is not common to many persons; it is therefore clear that the Holy Spirit is not a person of the Godhead. It may be added, that if the Holy Spirit be a person, since Christ was conceived of the Holy Spirit, it would necessarily follow that Christ was the son of the Holy Spirit[57].

How

---

[57] To these observations may be added, that if the Holy Spirit be a person proceeding from the essence of God, he also must be the Son of God. Moreover, that the Holy Spirit is not itself God is also proved from hence, that it is never called God in the Holy Scriptures: neither indeed do we find it so denominated by ancient Christian writers. Hence Erasmus rightly observes: *Nemo priscorum audebat claré pronunciare, Spiritum Sanctum esse Patri Filioque homousion, na tum quidem quum*

quæstio

How then are those passages of Scripture to be understood wherein actions which properly pertain to persons,

---

quæstio de Filio tanta contentione per universum orbem agitaretur. And he adds further on: *Nunc audemus profiteri Spiritum Sanctum homousion Patri et Filio, et Deum verum de Patre Deo vero, et de Filio Deo vero.* " No one of the ancients ventured plainly to assert that the Holy Spirit was of the same substance with the Father and the Son;—not even when the question concerning the Son was every where discussed with so much warmth: but now we scruple not to declare that the Holy Spirit is of one substance with the Father and the Son, very God, of the Father very God, and of the Son very God." *Annot. in* 1 Cor. vii. 39. Similar observations occur in his preface to Hilary. The same thing is acknowledged by Petavius, *Dogm. Theol. tom.* iii. See also Curcellæus, *Instit. lib.* i. *cap.* x., *et lib.* ii. *cap.* 19, *et* 21. Hilary, in the twelve books which he wrote concerning the Trinity, never styles the Holy Spirit God—but only the gift of God (*donum Dei*), and clearly distinguishes it from God himself. Among other things, he thus writes towards the beginning of his second book: *Baptizare jussit in nomine Patris, et Filii, et Spiritus Sancti: id est, in confessione et auctoris, et unigeniti, et doni,* &c. " He commands us to baptize in the name of the Father, of the Son, and of the Holy Spirit: that is, into a confession of the author, of the only-begotten, and of the gift," &c. The doxology also of the ancients was addressed to God the Father, by or through Christ, in the Holy Spirit; as may be seen in the Apostolic Decrees, *Can.* 35, and every where among the early writers. See also Grotius on Matth. xxviii. 19. Neither again did the ancients address prayers to the Holy Spirit; and they assigned this as their reason—That a gift was not to be asked of a gift, but of the giver of the gift. See on this point Cardinal Hugo's Explanation of the Mass; and also the Cracovian Missal, in the Order of the Holy Office. Thus also writes Hilary in concluding his work: *Conserva rogo hanc fidei meæ religionem,* &c.; *ut, quod in regenerationis meæ symbolo baptizatus, in Patre, et Filio, et Spiritu Sancto, professus sum, semper obtineam: Patrem scilicet te nostrum, Filium tuum una tecum adorem, et Sanctum Spiritum tuum, qui ex te per unigenitum tuum est, promerear, &c.* " Preserve, I pray, this form of my faith, &c. that I may always maintain what in the symbol of my

persons, and refer to God himself, are attributed to the Holy Spirit?

We are to understand them in this manner, viz. That, in the Scriptures, that is frequently attributed to things which pertains to persons, without nevertheless those things being on this account thought to be persons : as for instance (Rom. vii. 11), it is asserted of Sin that it DECEIVED and KILLED ; Rom. iii. 19, of the Law that it SAID; and Gal. iii. 8, of the Scripture that it FORESAW and SPOKE. Of Charity

my regeneration I professed, when baptized into the Father and the Son and the Holy Spirit;—namely, that I may worship thee our Father, and with thee thy Son; and may obtain thy Holy Spirit, which is of thee by thy only-begotten."

It was first decreed in the council of Constantinople, A.D. 381, that the Holy Spirit was Lord. But if any among the ancients thought the Holy Spirit to be a person, they never regarded him as the supreme God, but only as the chief of those spirits which are called angels. Of which opinion there have been many in our own times. But it appears from what has been said that this notion cannot be maintained. Others, perceiving these difficulties, have suggested, whether by the Holy Spirit may not be understood the race of holy spirits, that is of angels? as may be seen in C.C.S. [C. C. Sandius] Paradoxical Proposition concerning the Holy Spirit, lately published. But neither has this opinion, though more probable than the other, a solid foundation in the Holy Scriptures. Nor can it evade all the difficulties which are here enumerated. Besides, the Holy Spirit is said to be only one, and is manifestly distinguished from the angels (1 Pet. i. 12, and Ephes. chap. iii. ver. 5, compared with ver. 10, as also Matth. iii. 16, iv. 1; Luke iv. 1; John i. 32, 33, compared with Matth. iv. 11, John i. 5). Add to this, that the Jews even to this day have never acknowledged the Holy Spirit to be a person. It is most safe therefore, adhering to the proper import of the word, to believe the Holy Spirit to be the power and energy of God, and consequently his gift ; as is clearly revealed to us in the Holy Scriptures both of the Old and the New Testament.—B. WISSOWATIUS.

it

it is stated (1 Cor. xiii.), that it " suffereth long and
is kind; that it envieth not, vaunteth not itself, is not
puffed up; doth not behave itself unseemly; seeketh
not her own, is not easily provoked, thinketh no evil,
rejoiceth not in iniquity, but rejoiceth in the truth;
beareth all things, believeth all things, hopeth all
things, endureth all things." And lastly, it is said of
the Spirit, that is, of the wind (John iii. 8), that "it
bloweth where it listeth, and thou hearest the sound
thereof, but canst not tell whence it cometh, and
whither it goeth." Since then the Holy Spirit is the
power of God, those things which pertain to God are
attributed to it; and by the title Holy Spirit, God
himself is often to be understood, since he manifests
himself by his spirit.

But how say you that the Holy Spirit is the power
of God, when the Holy Spirit and the power of the
Highest are separately named in the words of the angel to the Virgin Mary, Luke i. 35 ?

Frequently, in written compositions, the same
thing is expressed by two different words, for the
better elucidation of the subject. Many examples of
this practice occur in the Holy Scriptures, one of
which I have already adduced in reference to the very
term Holy Spirit, from Matth. iii. 11, and Luke iii.
16 :—It is there written concerning Christ, that he
should baptize with the Holy Spirit and with fire;
whereas in Mark it is merely stated that he should
baptize with the Holy Spirit. Thus also it is said
of John, that he should go before the Lord in the spirit and power of Elias : and God is stated to have
anointed

anointed Christ with the Holy Spirit and with power, where any one may perceive that this power is identical with the Holy Spirit ; for no one can be anointed with a person. This is still more evident in respect to what I have said of the words of the angel : because in Matthew (chap. i. ver. 20), the angel, speaking of the same thing, mentions the Holy Spirit alone : nor indeed was there need of any other power besides the Holy Spirit in order to the conception of Christ.

But Paul (2 Cor. vi. 6, 7) distinguishes between the Holy Spirit and the power of God, and mentions them as two distinct things ?

Paul does this, because he understood by the Holy Spirit, a power communicated to him by God, and displaying itself in him ;—such a power of God as I have stated is to be understood by the Holy Spirit. But by the Power of God he meant in this place the miracles which God, by his own power, without the instrumentality of Paul, performed in confirmation of his discourses and preaching. For the Holy Spirit of which I speak does not comprise all the power of God.

CHAPTER VII.

OF THE CONFIRMATION OF THE DIVINE WILL.

It has been shown in what manner Jesus declared to us the divine will ; I wish you now to state how he has confirmed it ?

In respect to what Christ himself did towards confirming the divine will which he had declared, these three things present themselves—The perfect innocence of his life, his great and innumerable miracles,

and

and his death; as may be perceived, not to mention
others, from that testimony of John (1 Epist. v. 8),
where he states that " there are three that bear witness in earth, the Spirit, and the water, and the
blood." For undoubtedly by SPIRIT, he means the
Spirit of God, by the power of which it is manifest
those miracles were wrought by Christ; and indeed
the greatest miracle of the Holy Spirit was the being
itself given in the name of Christ to his disciples : the
water denotes the purity of his life; as the blood does
his sanguinary death.

What was the innocence of the Lord Jesus's life,
and how was the will of God confirmed by it ?

The innocence of his life was such, that not only
he did no sin, neither was guile found in his mouth,
nor could he be convicted of any offence,—but also
that he lived so holy a life, that neither before nor
since has any one equalled him in holiness; so that
in this he approached the nearest to God himself,
and was in respect of it, exceedingly like him. Hence
it follows that the doctrine delivered by him was most
true; since such holiness could have pertained only
to a man truly divine, and imposture and a design to
deceive others in religious matters could not have existed in such holiness.

Of what kind were his miracles, and how did they
confirm the divine will ?

His miracles were such as no one before him had
performed (John xv. 24); and so numerous that John
does not scruple to assert (John xxi. 25) that he supposes " if they should be written every one, even the
world

world itself could not contain the books that should be written." And the will of God declared by Christ is on this account confirmed by them—that God would never have communicated such a power of working miracles, which must needs be altogether divine, to any one, unless he had been sent by him.

CHAPTER VIII.

OF THE DEATH OF CHRIST.

Of what kind was the death of Christ?

It was such a death as was preceded by various afflictions, and was in itself most dreadful and ignominious; so that the Scriptures testify (Heb. ii. 17) that he was on account of it " made in all things like unto his brethren."

But why was it necessary that Christ should suffer so many afflictions, and undergo so cruel a death?

First, because Christ, by the divine will and purpose, suffered for our sins, and underwent a bloody death as an expiatory sacrifice. Secondly, because they who are to be saved by him, are for the most part obnoxious to the same afflictions and death.

What was the ground of the divine will and purpose that Christ should suffer for our sins?

First, that a most certain right to, and consequently a sure hope of, the remission of their sins, and of eternal life, might by this means be created for all sinners. " For if God spared not his own Son, but delivered him up for us all, how shall he not with him also freely give us all things?" (Rom. viii. 32.) "And if

while

while we were yet sinners Christ died for us, much more then, being now justified by his blood, we shall be saved from wrath through him. For if when we were enemies, we were reconciled to God by the death of his son, much more being reconciled shall we be saved by his life" (Rom. v. 8, 9, 10). Secondly, that all sinners might be incited and drawn to Christ, seeking salvation in and by him alone who died for them. Thirdly, that God might in this manner testify his boundless love to the human race, and might wholly reconcile them to himself. All which things are comprised in that divine declaration of Christ (John iii. 16), "God so loved the world that he gave his only-begotten son, that whosoever believeth in him should not perish, but have everlasting life."

But what reason was there that Christ should suffer the same afflictions, and the same kind of death, as those to which believers are exposed?

There are two reasons for this, as there are two methods whereby Christ saves us : for, first, he inspires us with a certain hope of salvation, and also incites us both to enter upon the way of salvation and to persevere in it. In the next place, he is with us in every struggle of temptation, suffering, or danger, affords us assistance, and at length delivers us from eternal death. It was exceedingly conducive to both these methods of saving us, that Christ our captain should not enter upon his eternal life and glory, otherwise than through sufferings, and through a death of this kind. For as to the former, since we perceive in

his

his case that the termination of that way which seemed to lead to destruction is so happy,—following our
leader with the utmost firmness, we enter this way
and persevere in it, with the certain hope that the
same end remains for us also : and as to the latter,
since having himself experienced how heavy, and of
themselves intolerable to human nature, such trials
are, and being not ignorant of sufferings, he might
learn to succour the distressed.   The former cause
of the sufferings and death of Christ is intimated in
the words of Peter (1 Epist. ii. 21), " Christ also suffered for us, leaving us an example that we should
follow his steps." And also in Hebr. ii. 10, where the
sacred author asserts that " it became God, in bringing many sons unto glory ;" that is, as is to be understood from what follows, by afflictions and death,
" to make the captain of their salvation perfect,"
or to conduct him to eternal glory, " through sufferings :" that thus, the happy termination of their afflictions, and of a death so dreadful, being perceived,
those persons might shake off the fear of death, who
through this fear had been all their lifetime subject
to bondage.   The latter cause is proved by what we
read in the same chapter (Heb. ii. 17, 18), that " in
all things it behoved Christ to be made like unto his
brethren, that he might be a merciful and faithful
high-priest in things pertaining to God, to make reconciliation for the sins of the people.   For in that
he himself hath suffered, being tempted, he is able to
succour them that are tempted."   And also further
on in the same epistle (chap. iv. 15), " For we
                                                    have

have not an high-priest which cannot be touched with the feeling of our infirmities; but was in all points tempted like as we are, yet without sin." And (chap. v. 8), "Though he were a son, yet learned he obedience by the things which he suffered:" that is, how hard and difficult soever it was, he was obedient to God in every adversity, in suffering, and a dreadful and ignominious death.

Could not God have caused that believers should not be exposed to afflictions and a violent death?

He could indeed, had he thought proper to change the nature of things. But God has not done this, except sometimes, and that very rarely, in some remarkable cases and for a time; not always nor commonly, as would in this instance be absolutely necessary, if he purposed that believers in Christ should be exempted from afflictions and a violent death: and God has done this the less, where he would as far as possible exercise and prove their faith and their devotion to him.

But why was it absolutely necessary to change the nature of things, if believers in Christ were to be exempted from afflictions and a violent death?

Because believers in Christ are endued with singular piety and innocence of life, and also with patience. Of these, the former naturally cause them to be exposed to the hatred of all wicked men, of whom both the number and the power are the greatest; so that they are vexed by them, and also, if occasion or opportunity offer, put to death: and the latter is even a greater incitement to the wicked, and furnishes them

them with the power of carrying all these things into
execution.

But how has the blood or the death of Christ confirmed to us the will of God?

In two ways.   First, because he did not suffer
himself to be deterred from inculcating his doctrine
even by the most painful death; but particularly,
because he ratified the New Covenant by his blood,
and confirmed the New Testament by his death (Heb.
xiii. 20).   Hence the blood of Christ is called
" the blood of the New Testament, which speaketh
better things than that of Abel" (Matth. xxvi. 28;
Heb. xii. 24). And Christ is himself called " the true
and faithful witness" (Rev. i. 5, iii. 14).   Secondly,
because through his death he was led to his resurrection, from which principally arises the confirmation of the divine will, and the most certain persuasion of our resurrection and the obtaining of eternal
life.

Explain more at large—in what manner we are assured by the resurrection of Christ, and consequently
by his death; of our own resurrection and eternal
life?

First, we are assured by the death and resurrection
of Christ, of our own resurrection, because we behold
placed before our view, in the example of Christ, what
is promised in his doctrine—that they who serve God
shall be delivered from every kind of death, however
violent.   Secondly, since Christ was thus raised in
order that he might obtain supreme authority over all
                                                things,

things, every cause of doubt concerning our salvation has been taken away.

But in what manner?

In two ways. First, because we perceive a certain beginning of the fulfilment of God's promises, particularly as God has made an especial promise that Christ himself should deliver us from death, and confer upon us eternal life. Secondly, because we see that the power of fulfilling the divine promises made to us is placed in the hands of him who is not ashamed to call us brethren, and who so greatly loved us,—though until then wicked, and enemies to him,—that, with a view to our everlasting salvation, he submitted to a death as cruel as it was infamous; who endured in himself all those afflictions to which we must be exposed if we would obey him; and can therefore commiserate us, and be touched with a feeling of our infirmities, as I have before shown. Having then our salvation in his hands, how should he not bestow it upon us, especially as the conferring of it is connected with the highest glory both of himself and of his Father?

I observe then from hence, that in the business of our salvation more depends upon the resurrection than upon the death of Christ?

Certainly, in as much as the death of Christ would have been useless and inefficacious, unless it had been followed by his resurrection (which indeed, in respect to the divine decrees, could not but have happened), which also, in a wonderful manner,

gave

gave force to his death, and rendered it effectual in the business of our salvation.   Hence Paul writes (1 Cor. xv. 17), " If Christ be not raised, your faith is vain, you are yet in your sins."   That is to say, as the same apostle intimates Romans iv. 25, connecting together the effects of his death and of his resurrection, Christ " was delivered for our offences, and was raised for our justification."   And again (Rom. viii. 33, 34), " Who shall lay any thing to the charge of God's elect ? It is God that justifieth, who is he that condemneth ?   It is Christ that died, yea rather that is risen again, who is even at the right hand of God, who also maketh intercession for us."

But why do the Scriptures so often ascribe all these things to the death of Christ ?

Because the death of Christ the Son of God, made effective, as I have stated, by his resurrection (which principally declared him to be the Son of God), had of itself, as I have shown, great and extraordinary power in effecting our salvation.   And, in the next place, because it was the way to the resurrection and exaltation of Christ : for, from the nature of the thing, his death was necessary to the former, and, through the divine will and purpose, was essential to the latter. Lastly, because of all the things done by God and Christ with a view to our salvation, the death of Christ was the most difficult work, and the most evident proof of the love of God and of Christ towards us.

But did not Christ die also, in order, properly speaking, to purchase our salvation, and literally to pay the debt of our sins ?

Although

Although Christians at this time commonly so believe, yet this notion is false, erroneous, and exceedingly pernicious; since they conceive that Christ suffered an equivalent punishment for our sins, and by the price of his obedience exactly compensated our disobedience. There is no doubt, however, but that Christ so satisfied God by his obedience, as that he completely fulfilled the whole of his will, and by his obedience obtained, through the grace of God, for all of us who believe in him, the remission of our sins, and eternal salvation.

How do you make it appear that the common notion is false and erroneous?

Not only because the Scriptures are silent concerning it, but also because it is repugnant to the Scriptures and to right reason.

Prove this, in order.

That nothing concerning it is to be found in the Scriptures appears from hence; that they who maintain this opinion never adduce explicit texts of Scripture in proof of it, but string together certain inferences by which they endeavour to maintain their assertions. But, besides that a matter of this kind, whereon they themselves conceive the whole business of salvation to turn, ought certainly to be demonstrated not by inferences alone but by clear testimonies of Scripture; it might easily be shown that these inferences have no force whatever: otherwise, inferences which necessarily spring from the Scriptures, I readily admit.

How is this opinion repugnant to the Scriptures?

Because the Scriptures every where testify that
God

God forgives men their sins freely, and especially under the New Covenant (2 Cor. v. 19; Rom. iii. 24, 25; Matth. xviii. 23, &c.) But to a free forgiveness nothing is more opposite than such a satisfaction as they contend for, and the payment of an equivalent price. For where a creditor is satisfied, either by the debtor himself, or by another person on the debtor's behalf, it cannot with truth be said of him that he freely forgives the debt.

How is this repugnant to reason?

This is evident from hence; that it would follow that Christ, if he has satisfied God for our sins, has submitted to eternal death; since it appears that the penalty which men had incurred by their offences was eternal death; not to say that one death, though it were eternal in duration,—much less one so short,—could not of itself be equal to innumerable eternal deaths. For if you say that the death of Christ, because he was a God infinite in nature, was equal to the infinite deaths of the infinite race of men,—besides that I have already refuted this opinion concerning the nature of Christ,—it would follow that God's infinite nature itself suffered death. But as death cannot any way belong to the infinity of the divine nature, so neither, literally speaking (as must necessarily be done here where we are treating of a real compensation and payment), can the infinity of the divine nature any way belong to death. In the next place, it would follow that there was no necessity that Christ should endure such sufferings, and so dreadful a

death;

death; and that God—be it spoken without offence,—
was unjust, who, when he might well have been contented with one drop (as they say) of the blood of
Christ, would have him so severely tormented. Lastly, it would follow that we were more obliged to
Christ than to God, and owed him more, indeed owed
him every thing; since he, by this satisfaction, showed
us much kindness; whereas God, by exacting his debt,
showed us no kindness at all.

State in what manner this opinion is pernicious?

Because it opens a door to licentiousness, or, at
least, invites men to indolence in the practice of piety,
in what way soever they urge the piety of their pa-
tron. For if full payment have been made to God by
Christ for all our sins, even those which are future,
we are absolutely freed from all liability to punishment, and therefore no further condition can by right
be exacted from us to deliver us from the penalties of
sin. What necessity then would there be for living reli-
giously? But the Scripture testifies (Tit. ii. 14; Gal.
i. 4; 1 Pet. i. 18; Heb. ix. 14; 2 Cor. v. 15; Eph.
v. 26) that Christ died for this end, among others,
that he might " redeem us from all iniquity, and pu-
rify us unto himself a peculiar people zealous of good
works;" " that he might deliver us from the present
evil world;" " might redeem us from our vain conversation, received by tradition from our fathers," in order that being " dead to sin" we might " live unto
righteousness," that our consciences might be " purged
from dead works to serve the living God."

But

But how do they maintain their opinion?

They endeavour to do this first by a certain reason, and then by the authority of Scripture.

What is this reason?

They say that there are in God, by nature, justice and mercy: that as it is the property of mercy to forgive sins, so is it, they state, the property of justice to punish every sin whatever. But since God willed that both his mercy and justice should be satisfied together, he devised this plan, that Christ should suffer death in our stead, and thus satisfy God's justice in the human nature, by which he had been offended; and that his mercy should at the same time be displayed in forgiving sin.

What reply do you make to this reason?

This reason bears the appearance of plausibility, but in reality has in it nothing of truth or solidity; and indeed involves a self-contradiction. For although we confess, and hence exceedingly rejoice, that our God is wonderfully merciful and just, nevertheless we deny that there are in him the mercy and justice which our adversaries imagine, since the one would wholly annihilate the other. For, according to them, the one requires that God should punish no sin; the other, that he should leave no sin unpunished. If then it were naturally a property of God to punish no sin, he could not act against his nature in order that he might punish sin: in like manner also, if it were naturally a property of God to leave no sin unpunished, he could not, any more, contrary to his nature, refrain from punishing every sin. For

God

God can never do any thing repugnant to those properties which pertain to him by nature. For instance,
since wisdom belongs naturally to God, he can never
do any thing contrary to it, but whatever he does he
does wisely. But as it is evident that God forgives and punishes sins whenever he deems fit, it appears that the mercy which commands to spare, and
the justice which commands to destroy, do so exist in
him as that both are tempered by his will, and by the
wisdom, the benignity, and holiness of his nature.
Besides, the Scriptures are not wont to designate the
justice, which is opposed to mercy, and is discernible
in punishments inflicted in wrath, by this term, but
style it the SEVERITY, the ANGER, and WRATH of God:
—indeed, it is attributed to the justice of God in the
Scriptures that he forgives sins : 1 John iv. 9 ;. Rom.
iii. 25, 26 ; and frequently in the Psalms.

What then is your opinion concerning this matter ?

It is this ;—that since I have shown that the mercy
and justice which our adversaries conceive to pertain
to God by nature, certainly do not belong to him,
there was no need of that plan whereby he might satisfy such mercy and justice, and by which they might,
as it were by a certain tempering, be reconciled to
each other : which tempering nevertheless is such that
it satisfies neither, and indeed destroys both ;—For
what is that justice, and what too that mercy, which
punishes the innocent, and absolves the guilty ? I do
not, indeed, deny that there is a natural justice in
God, which is called rectitude, and is opposed to
wickedness : this shines in all his works, and hence
they

they all appear just and right and perfect ; and that, no less when he forgives than when he punishes our transgressions.

What are the passages of Scripture whereby they endeavour to support their opinion ?

Those which testify that Christ died for us, or for our sins; that he took away our sins ; that he hath redeemed us ; that he has given himself, or given his soul, a ransom for many : also that he is our mediator ; that he has reconciled us to God; that he is the propitiation for our sins : and lastly, they infer it from the death of Christ being compared with the sacrifices of the law, as with figures whereby it was shadowed.

What do you reply to these passages ?

As to those testimonies wherein it is affirmed that Christ died for us—that no satisfaction can be inferred from the phraseology itself, much more that it could not be such satisfaction as they contend for, is manifest from hence, that the Scriptures declare (1 John iii. 16), that "we also ought to lay down our lives for the brethren :" and Paul wrote concerning himself (Col. i. 24), "I now rejoice in my sufferings for you, and fill up that which is behind of the afflictions of Christ in my flesh for his body's sake which is the Church." But it is certain both that the believers did not give satisfaction for the brethren, and that Paul did not give satisfaction for the Church.

What then is the meaning of the phrase " Christ died for us" ?

The

The words have two significations, which however resolve themselves into one. First, that Christ was as a victim substituted for us. For we, on account of our sins, were doomed to eternal death; but Christ, that he might deliver us from our sins, and procure for us the pardon of them, endured the death of the cross,—being himself, as became such a victim, guiltless of every sin. " Christ," says the apostle (Gal. iii. 13), " hath redeemed us from the curse of the law, being made a curse for us ; for it is written, Cursed is every one that hangeth on a tree." The second signification is, that Christ died for the highest benefit of us all. When Christ is said to have " died for us," the words may bear both these significations; which are therefore used interchangeably, the one for the other. Thus, what the apostle Paul in his epistle to the Romans (chap. xiv. 15) writes, "for whom" (pro quo, ὑπερ οὑ) that is " thy brother," " Christ died ;"—he writes (1 Cor. viii. 11), in expressing the same things, " for (or on account of) whom [propter quem, δι' ὁν] Christ died." For the example of those very victims which were sacrificed for men who had sinned, shows that no substitution of things equivalent to each other can be inferred from these words ; and therefore that they were not offered as an actual compensation for an offence, but for the forgiveness of it. Nor indeed can any substitution be inferred from the words taken by themselves. For, not to proceed further, when the Scripture says (1 Cor. xv. 3) that Christ died for our sins, it does not

certainly

certainly declare that he died in the place or stead of sinners, but that he died ON ACCOUNT OF (*propter*, δια) our offences, as is stated Rom. iv. 25.

In what sense then is Christ said to have died for, or on account of, our offences ?

In the same sense as (though in a far more extensive and perfect one than) that wherein victims are said to have been sacrificed for, or on account of, the sins which were expiable by those victims. That is to say, the sins of men were the cause of the sacrificing of those victims, and the victims were sacrificed that the sins of men might be pardoned. Thus, also, our sins were the cause of the death of Christ, himself guiltless of every sin, which he endured that he might free us from the guilt of them all; and the power of his death is such, that it at once takes them away and destroys them. For Christ delivered himself to death for our sins, in order that he might claim and emancipate us for himself; and by his stripes we have been healed. For by this his great love he turns back to himself those who had gone astray (1 Peter ii. 24, 25).

What answer do you give to those passages (Isaiah liii. 4; 1 Peter ii. 24) wherein it is said that Christ bare our sins ?

That the satisfaction contended for cannot be proved even from hence. For, besides that Christ is justly said to have borne our sins in himself, in as much as he suffered on account of them, and thus in a manner received the punishment upon himself,—which Peter seems to refer to when he says that " Christ his own self bare our sins in his own body on the tree;"—it is

also

also written concerning God (Exod. xxxiv. 7; Numb. xiv. 18), according to the Hebrew text, that "he keepeth mercy for thousands, and BEARETH iniquity and sins," [in the English translation, "forgiving iniquity and transgression."] And Matthew expressly states (chap. viii. ver. 17), that when Christ healed many diseases, that "was fulfilled which was spoken by Esaias, saying (Is. liii. 4), Himself took our infirmities, and bare our sicknesses." God, however, gave no one satisfaction for sins—neither did Christ receive upon himself and bear the diseases of men, but bore them away from them. In the same sense also Christ has borne away from us all our sins, and the penalties of them, just as if he had conveyed them to a far distant region: as the Scripture likewise declares (John i. 29), he was "the Lamb of God who took away the sin of the world:" and (Heb. ix. 28) that he "was once offered to bear [or take away] the sins of many [58]."

What

---

[58] Grotius excellently remarks on this passage (1 Peter ii. 24): *Est hic μεταληψις, non enim proprie Christus, cum crucifigeretur,* VITIA NOSTRA ABSTULIT, *sed causas dedit per quas auferrentur. Nam crux Christi fundamentum est predicationis; predicatio vero pœnitentiæ, pœnitentia vero aufert vitia.*— "There is here a metalepsis; for literally speaking Christ did not, when he was crucified, take away our sins—but furnished the means whereby they might be removed. For the cross of Christ is the foundation of preaching—preaching of penitence, and penitence takes away sin." Other similar observations of this writer may be found in his Annotations on Matth. xx. 28; John i. 29; Acts xx. 28; Rom. iv. 25; Ephes. i. 7; Rev. i. 5: and also in others of his works which he wrote after Crellius had published his admirable reply to Grotius's book against Socinus on Satisfaction. Compare also with what
is

What answer do you make to those testimonies (such as Rom. iii. 24) which declare that we are redeemed by Christ?

That the doctrine of satisfaction cannot be inferred from the word redemption, is evident from hence, that it is affirmed of God himself, both in the Old and in the New Testament, that he redeemed his people out of Egypt; that he sent redemption to his people; that he redeemed Abraham and David: and likewise of Moses, that he was a redeemer (deliverer): and it is stated moreover that we are redeemed from our iniquities, or from our vain conversation. (Isaiah xxix. 22; Psalm xxxi. 5; cxi. 9; Acts vii. 35; Titus ii. 14; 1 Peter i. 18; Gal. iii. 13.) But it is certain that neither God nor Moses gave satisfaction to any one: nor can our iniquities or vain conversation be said to be satisfied. Let it be added, that God himself has redeemed us, and given his most beloved son for us, without however paying any one any thing for us; and that Christ has bought us to God in order that we might thenceforth be his servants.

But what do you conceive to be the meaning of

---

is here advanced concerning the death of Christ, what is said on this subject in the Confession of Faith of the Polish Churches. Consult also Curcellæus, *Instit. lib.* v. *cap.* 8 & 19; and his dissertation against Maresius, *Diss.* i. *de voc. Trin.* &c. § 30, 31. Besides, the death of Christ may justly be said to have procured our salvation—in this respect alone,—that by this event, and his obedience to God the Father, he was invested with supreme power over all things, and thus obtained a full right to forgive our sins and bless us with eternal life. He may therefore justly be said to have redeemed and purchased us with his blood.—B. WISSOWATIUS.

P   the

the declaration,—that Christ has redeemed us and given himself a ransom for us ?

The term REDEMPTION, in most passages of Scripture, means simply LIBERATION ; but by a more extended figure, it is put for that liberation for effecting which a certain price is paid. And it is said of the death of Christ that he has liberated us by it, because by means of it we have obtained our freedom both from our sins themselves, that we no longer serve them ; and also from the punishment of them, that being snatched from the jaws of eternal death we may live for ever.

But why is this deliverance expressed by the term redemption ?

Because there is a very great similarity between our deliverance and a redemption properly so called. For as in a proper redemption there must be a captive, the person who detains the captive, the redeemer, and lastly, the ransom, or price of the redemption; so also in our deliverance, if we speak of our sins themselves, man is the captive—they who detain him are sin, the world, the devil, and death : the redeemer of the captive are God and Christ; and the ransom, or price of the redemption, is Christ, or his soul paid by God and by Christ himself. The only difference lies here, that in this deliverance of us from our sins themselves, no one receives any thing under the name of ransom, which must always happen in a redemption properly so called. But if we speak of our deliverance from the punishment of our sins, we owe this to God, Christ having delivered us from it
when,

when, in compliance with the will of God, he gave
himself up to death for us, and through his own blood
entered into the heavenly place : which obedience of
his son unto death, and the death of the cross, God
accepted as an offering of all the most agreeable to
him.   But this is not to be understood nevertheless
as importing that God, literally speaking, had received the full payment of our debts ; since Christ was
a victim of his own, provided by himself, as was also
the case in the yearly sacrifice (the type of the sacrifice of Christ) ; and owed every thing to God through
himself, and in his own name; and although his obedience was the highest and most perfect of any, yet
he received an incomparably greater reward for it.
Wherefore this ought to be ascribed to the unbounded
grace and bounty of God ; because he not only did
not receive any part of what we owed to him, and
because he not only forgave us all our debts ; but also
because he gave a victim of his own, and that his
only-begotten and best-beloved son, that lamb without blemish, for us and our sins, not that he might
pay himself any thing for us (for this would be a
fictitious not a real payment), but might create for us
so much greater and more certain a right to pardon
and eternal life, and might bind himself by such a
pledge to confer this upon us ; and might also con-
vert us to himself, and bless us with the other signal
benefits of which we stood in need.

Why does the Holy Spirit use a metaphorical rather than a literal term ?

Because this metaphorical term expresses more ele-

gantly

gantly the expense which God and Christ bestowed on our deliverance, and therefore the love of both towards us : for a deliverance may possibly be accomplished without love, and particularly without great love ; but the deliverance which is procured at the expense not of money but "much more of his own blood," could not be effected without the highest love.

What say you to these things, that Christ is the mediator between God and men, and the mediator of the New Covenant ? (Heb. xii. 24 ; viii. 6 ; ix. 15 ; 1 Tim. ii. 5.)

Since we read that Moses was a Mediator (that is, between God and the people of Israel, and of the former Covenant), and as it is certain that he made no satisfaction to God for the sins of the people,— it cannot be inferred from the circumstance of Christ's being a mediator between God and men, that he made the alleged satisfaction for the sins of all men.

Why then does the Scripture give to Christ the title of Mediator ?

When Christ is called a Mediator, with the word Covenant subjoined, it is to be understood, that in establishing the New Covenant he was the medium between God and men, in proclaiming to them the perfect will of God, in confirming it, and at length sealing it with his blood. But when Paul, while about proving that " God will have all men to be saved, and to come unto the knowledge of the truth," says, "For there is one God," that is the Creator and Lord of all men, " and one Mediator between God and men, the man Christ Jesus," who, because he is

a man,

a man, has an union of nature with other men, and
therefore no man ought to be rejected by him; nothing
hinders but that the apostle may be supposed to refer
in the title Mediator not only to the office of Christ
which he formerly sustained in the establishment of
the Covenant, but also to that which he now holds;
with which he connects it so much more strongly—
teaching that all men have access to God not only by
the covenant made by Christ, but also by Christ himself, now living, acting, and reigning in heaven; that
is to say, as he hears their vows and prayers, and does
every thing for them with God.   For Moses also, acting as the shadow and type of Christ, was in such respects a Mediator as not only to declare the will of
God by the law delivered by him to the Israelites, but
also to approach the presence of God in the name of
the children of Israel, who through him applied to
God for, and obtained, what they wished.

What say you to this, that he reconciled us to God?

First, That the Scripture never asserts that God
was reconciled to us by Christ, but that we were
reconciled to him; which indicates no wrath on his
part, but our aversion to him, and our enmity against
him.   Wherefore the satisfaction, which they fancy,
can by no means be inferred from any of those passages.   Secondly, it is expressly asserted in the Scriptures (2 Cor. v. 18; Col. i. 20, 22), that God has
reconciled us to himself. Whence it would follow that
God himself had made satisfaction to himself.

What think you concerning this reconciliation?

That Christ Jesus showed to us, who, on account

of

of our sins, were enemies of God, and alienated from him,—the way whereby we might be turned to God, and thus be reconciled to him; and strongly impelled us to this by his death also, wherein appeared the great love of God towards us.

What say you to this, that the Lord Jesus is called a Propitiation (1 John ii. 2) ?

That what they assert is not to be inferred from hence, because the Scripture declares (Rom. iii. 25.), as the apostle expressly speaks, that God himself hath set forth Christ for a propitiation; and John writes (1 Epist. iv. 10), " Herein is love, not that we loved God, but that he loved us, and sent his son to be a propitiation for our sins." And in the next place, because even the cover of the ark, to which Paul alludes (Heb. ix. 5; Exod. xxv. 22), is called a propitiatory (or mercy-seat), when nevertheless it is evident that this in no way gave satisfaction for sins, except in so far as an offering was appointed by God to be presented there for obtaining the forgiveness of them. Lastly, it is one thing to give satisfaction to any one in the way contended for, and another to render him propitious : since he who is rendered propitious, or is appeased, may remit much of his just right ; but he who is in this way satisfied remits nothing.

What is your opinion concerning this matter ?

When Paul says (Rom. iii. 25) that God hath set forth Christ to be a propitiation through faith in his blood, his meaning is, that Christ has, by the will of God, shed his blood for the sins of all men. Wherefore, whoever would experience God propitious,

and

and obtain the forgiveness of his sins, must come to Christ through faith in him. This is the only refuge of all sinners. But when John calls him the propitiation for our sins, he means that our sins are expiated by him. For the Greek term (ἱλασμος) which in Latin is rendered *propitiatio*, frequently denotes in the Holy Scriptures expiation, or a deliverance from the guilt of sin. Hence our sins are said, Heb. ii. 17, [according to the original] to be PROPITIATED, that is EXPIATED.

What answer do you make to those testimonies wherein it is declared that the death of Christ was figured and shadowed forth by the sacrifices of the Old Covenant?

In the first place, it must be considered that in the sacrifices the death of Christ merely and by itself, was shadowed by the death alone of the victim, and principally of that which was sacrificed annually, and with the blood of which the high priest entered into the holy of holies. But as this slaughtering of the victim was not the whole of the sacrifice, but only a certain commencement of it (for the sacrifice itself was certainly then made and completed, when the high priest entered with the blood into the holy of holies, as the author of the epistle to the Hebrews testifies, chap. ix. ver. 7), so also the death of Christ was not the whole of his expiatory sacrifice, in the sense in which that author also understands the sacrifice of Christ, but a certain commencement of it : for the sacrifice was then offered when Christ entered into heaven—concerning which you shall hear presently. Besides, it would

would not follow from the type of the sacrifices, that God was, by the death of Christ, satisfied for our sins in the sense contended for, since the Scripture never inculcates that those sacrifices had the effect of satisfying God for sin, and reason evidently teaches quite the contrary. If, however, it ought to be inferred from the sacrifices of the law, as from a type, that Christ made satisfaction for our sins, it is necessary that those sacrifices should have had some power of satisfying God. For there must necessarily exist a likeness between the figure and the thing figured. Wherefore from the type of the sacrifices, the contrary ought to be inferred: that is to say; as those sacrifices were not made properly speaking for the payment of sins, but for the remission of them, so also the death and sacrifice of Christ were designed, as the Scripture every where testifies, for the remission of sins, and not literally speaking for the payment of them.

What then do you think of those sacrifices?

Principally this, that by those sacrifices the sins of God's people, which were expiable by them, were expiated in the manner which the law permitted: that is to say; those sacrifices being offered, their sins, in respect of some temporal penalties, were by the favour and appointment of God remitted.

CHAPTER IX.

OF FAITH.

HAVING thus far treated of the precepts and promises of God, I wish you now to explain to me the way and manner whereby we are to conform to both. This

This way and manner is comprised in faith in our Lord Jesus Christ, whereby we keep our attention fixed upon his promises, and willingly submit ourselves to obey his precepts : which faith renders our obedience more estimable and more acceptable in the sight of God ; and, provided it be real and sincere, supplies the deficiency of our obedience, and causes us to be justified by God.

What then is this faith in our Lord Jesus Christ ?

In order to understand this, you must observe, that faith in Christ is of two kinds. Sometimes it means that faith which, unless something else be added to it, is not attended with salvation ; and sometimes that which is of itself followed by salvation.

What is that faith which taken by itself is not attended with salvation ?

It is a bare assent alone of the mind, whereby we acknowledge the doctrine of Jesus Christ to be true ; which assent is not attended with salvation, unless something else be added to it. This appears, first, among many other things, from the apostle James, who asserts that faith cannot save him who has not works,—that without works it is dead ; and that this is only such a faith as even the dæmons entertain : secondly, from those rulers concerning whom John writes (John xii. 42), that " many of them believed, but because of the Pharisees they did not confess him lest they should be put out of the synagogue."

What is the faith which is by itself followed by salvation ?

It is such an assent to the doctrine of Christ, that

P 5　　　　　　　　　　　　we

we apply it to its proper object : that is, that we trust in God through Christ, and give ourselves up wholly to obey his will, whereby we obtain his promises ; for without this, our trust were vain, and without trust our assent would also be vain.

What is meant by trusting in God through Christ?

It is so to trust in God as at the same time to trust in Christ, whom he has sent, and in whose hands he has placed all things ; and also both to expect the fulfilment of the promises which were given by him, and to observe the precepts which he delivered : that is, to obey God not only in those things commanded in the law delivered by Moses, that are not annulled by Christ, but also in all those which Christ has delivered beyond and in addition to the law.

You include then in that faith to which alone and in reality salvation is ascribed, not only trust, but obedience also ?

I do so : partly because the thing itself shows that he who has conceived a firm and confident hope of eternal life, which Christ has promised to those alone who obey him, must be impelled to yield him obedience, in as much as immortality is such a blessing that no one can knowingly and willingly despise it: but if any one should despise it, or not so esteem it as to give himself to obey Christ with the view of attaining it, what can this excellent faith avail him? And partly because faith, unless obedience follow, when life is continued after faith has been embraced, has no power to effect our salvation, as James expressly testifies (chap. ii. 26), as we have already seen:

who

who also says (ver. 21, &c.) that Abraham likewise was justified by works, and that by these " his faith was made perfect, and the Scripture was fulfilled, which saith, ' Abraham believed God, and it was imputed unto him for righteousness.' " Now if piety and obedience, when life is continued after the acknowledgement of Christ, be required as indispensable to salvation, it is necessary that the faith to which alone and in reality salvation is ascribed, or which alone is necessarily followed by salvation, should comprehend obedience [59].

How happens it, then, that the apostle says (Rom. x. 9), that he who "shall confess with his mouth the Lord Jesus, and believe in his heart that God hath raised him from the dead, shall be saved?"

He does not so assert, as if this alone and of itself were sufficient for salvation in those who live subsequently to this faith, or the occasion of embracing it; but because from this faith follow, by a certain natural tie and connexion, the other things which are necessary to the attainment of salvation: for he who believes that Jesus is raised from the dead, must believe also that he is made by God both Lord and Christ: he who believes this will place faith in him, and invoke his name: he who does this will wholly devote himself to obey him; and thus will have a lively faith working by love, which is followed by salvation.

---

[59] The papists object to Luther, that these words of Paul are corrupted by the addition of the word ALONE—which indeed is never found in Paul, and therefore it ought not to be so often repeated here.—M. Ruarus.

Why

Why then does the apostle Paul oppose faith to works?

In those places where the apostle opposes faith to works,—as Rom. iii. 28; iv. 5; Gal. ii. 16; Ephes. ii. 8, 9.—he speaks of such works as absolutely exclude every transgression of the law; such works as must be performed by every one who seeks to be justified by the law, especially to the obtaining of eternal life: but not of such works, or of such obedience, as God requires, and with which he is satisfied, in those whom he justifies by his grace, and to whom he imputes faith for righteousness.

What then is this obedience?

Under the Gospel it is this,—that after being adopted by God for his sons, and endued with a filial spirit, we conduct ourselves as becomes obedient children, doing with our whole heart and with all our strength those things which we know that our heavenly Father requires us to perform, and giving all heed not to offend him in any thing. That is, that we put off the old man with his works, and desist from all our former sins; that we walk not after the flesh, but by the spirit mortify the deeds of the body. In short, that we continue in the habitual practice of no sin, but be endued with every christian virtue; so that, if a fault occur in our pious course, it may proceed not from any evil disposition or design, from any habit or custom, but from some weakness of human nature or from ignorance: all which indeed the Scripture is wont to comprise under the name of penitence: and as such an obedience is not servile, but filial and vo-

luntary,

luntary, so also our religious duties under the gospel require much more perfect things from us as free-men than the law formerly exacted or could exact from slaves, whom it was permitted to treat with severity.

CHAPTER X.

OF FREE WILL.

Is it in our power to obey God in the way you have stated?

It is, when strengthened by the divine aid, and by that filial spirit of which I have spoken. For it is certain that the first man was so created by God as to be endowed with free will; and there was no reason why God should deprive him of it after his fall. And the equity and justice or rectitude of God will not allow that he should deprive man of the will and power of acting rightly; especially since, subsequently to that period, he requires, under a threat of punishment, that he should will and act rightly (Deut. xxx. 19). Nor is there any mention of a punishment of this kind among the penalties with which God punished the sin of Adam.

Is not this free will depraved by original sin?

It is not yet agreed among its advocates themselves, what original sin is. This is certain, that by the fall of Adam the nature of man is by no means so depraved as that he is deprived of the liberty and power of obeying or not obeying God in those things which he requires of him under the threat of punishment or the promise of reward. Nor can it otherwise be shown,

from

from any testimony of Scripture, that it has this effect; while the declarations are innumerable which demonstrate the contrary clearer than the sun. And the fall of Adam, as it was but one act, could not have power to deprave his own nature, much less that of his posterity. That this was not inflicted upon him by God as punishment I have just shown. I do not deny, however, that, by the habit of sinning, the nature of man is infected with a certain stain, and a very strong disposition to wickedness; but I do deny both that this of itself is a sin, and that it is of such a nature that a man, after he has imbibed the divine spirit, cannot create for himself the power of obeying God as far as He, in his infinite goodness and equity, requires.

But yet, that there is original sin, seems to be taught by these testimonies: Gen. vi. 5, " Every imagination of the thoughts of man's heart is only evil continually." And Gen. viii. 21, " The imagination of man's heart is evil from his youth."

These testimonies speak of voluntary sin, as even the very term imagination itself evinces, which denotes an internal act. Such an original sin as our adversaries contend for cannot, therefore, be proved from them. For as to the first, Moses shows that it was that kind of sin on account of which it had repented God that he had made man, and clearly intimates that he had decreed to punish him for it by a deluge; which certainly can by no means be asserted of sin that is in man by nature, such as original sin is thought to be. In the other testimony, God does not

positively

positively affirm that the imagination of man's heart is evil from his youth; but only says that THOUGH it were, which would in fact be a voluntary thing, it should not any more have the effect of inducing him, on account of it, to punish the world with a flood, as he had done before: which also does not comport with such an original sin as our adversaries imagine.

What think you of what David says (Psalm li. 7), " I was shapen in iniquity, and in sin did my mother conceive me ?"

It must be observed that David does not speak here of all men generally, but of himself alone. In the next place, though he should seem to speak of some innate propensity to sin, yet he does not refer the origin of it to Adam, but only to his mother; as, indeed, we see that a propensity to certain vices is derived from parents, although the remoter ancestors of those parents were not inclined to them. Nor does he state this propensity to be such, that he was not able to abstain from the sins he is deploring, and on account of which he thus adverts to it, and from others also of a similar kind, had he chosen to create for himself the power. Not to notice that David uses a certain hyperbolical exaggeration—of which we have an example in his own writings (Psalm lviii. 3), " The wicked are estranged from the womb: they go astray as soon as they are born, speaking lies." Similar instances are found in Isaiah xlviii. 8, " I knew that thou wouldst deal very treacherously, and wast called a transgressor from the womb." John ix. 84, " Thou wast altogether born in sins." And also,

also, in an opposite case; Job xxxi. 18, " From my youth he was brought up with me, as with a father, and I have guided her from my mother's womb." And Psalm lxxi. 5, 6, " Thou art my trust from my youth, by thee have I been holden up from the womb." Original sin cannot therefore be proved from this testimony.

But does not original sin appear to be established by those very passages which you have cited from the Psalms, Isaiah, and John?

By no means: for otherwise there would exist no reason why it should be attributed to the wicked rather than to others, and they in particular be by name reproached with it;—especially by persons who could not be ignorant that it pertained to themselves in common with the wicked. Moreover, the wicked would by this means be exonerated; because it would indicate the depravity which was innate in them, and not their own acquired criminality, while nevertheless the latter is said to contribute so much more to their condemnation. Let it be added, that the words used by David and Isaiah denote the act or habit of sinning; and that in John mention is expressly made not of one sin, as original sin would be, but of SINS.

But Paul states (Rom. v. 12) that all have sinned in Adam?

It is not there said that IN ADAM all have sinned; since neither the order of the words,—Adam's name being mentioned long before, and not implied in the proximate antecedent,—nor yet the Greek particle (επι) which Paul uses, will bear this interpretation. Those

words.

words therefore which some interpreters render " in
whom" ought to be rendered, as by some they are,
" for that," " since," or " because," as may be seen
from similar passages ; as Rom. viii. 3; 2 Cor. v. 4;
Heb. ii. 18. So that Paul asserts, that " death passed
upon all men, SINCE, or FOR THAT, all have sinned[60]."

[60] So the Syriac and Arabic versions render this passage.
And it is interpreted in the same manner by Theodoret, Pho-
tius, Erasmus, Castellio, Calvin, the Zurich and Geneva an-
notators, by Osiander, Bucer, Martyr, Piscator, Junius, &c.
To the references given above, add Philipp. iii. 12; iv. 10.—
A. WISSOWATIUS.

Erasmus's observations on this passage are above all worthy
of perusal. But though the other reading were retained, a
consistent interpretation of these words might be given, and
this has been supplied to us by Grotius, whose words are as
follow :—Εφ' ᾧ hic est PER QUEM : quo modo ιτι cum dativo su-
mitur Luc. v. 5; Act. iii. 16; 1 Cor. viii. 11; Heb. ix. 17.
Frequens est μετωνυμια Hebræis dicere PECCATUM pro PŒNA, et
PECCARE pro.PŒNAM SUBIRE : unde et, procedente longius figu-
ra, per μεταληψιν ΝΩΠ, sive PECCARE dicuntur qui malum aliquod
etiam sine culpa ferunt, ut Gen. xxxi. 36, et Job vi. 24, ubi ΝΩΠ
vertitur per δυσπραγιν. Chrysostomus hoc loco, Εκεινου πεσοντος,
&c. i.e. Ipso cadente, etiam qui non comederunt de ligno, ex ipso nati sunt omnes mortales. "Εφ' ᾧ means here BY WHOM : so
ιτι with a dative is taken Luke v. 5; Acts iii. 16; 1 Cor. viii. 11;
Heb. ix. 17. It is a common metonymy in Hebrew writers,
to say SIN for PUNISHMENT, and SINNING for UNDERGOING
PUNISHMENT. Whence also, extending the figure, by a metalepsis, they are said ΝΩΠ, ' to sin,' who do any wrong even
without guilt—as Gen. xxxi. 36; Job vi. 24, where ΝΩΠ is rendered by δυσπραγιν. Chrysostom, on this passage, writes,'He
having fallen, they also who have not eaten of the tree, are all
born of him mortal.'" So far Grotius. See also on this subject Curcellæus, Diss. 2, contra Maresium de peccat. origin.—
and his Institutiones, lib. iii. cap. 16. Moreover, among other
writers, the author of Apostasia Christianorum, who is said to
have been.the most noble Lancelote of Brederode, has refuted
this inveterate error concerning original sin in twelve arguments; which C. C. Sandius has inserted in Latin, in his book
de Origine Animæ, p. 72.—B. WISSOWATIUS.

But he speaks throughout of actual sin, as the words following indicate, when he says (ver. 13), " For until the law sin was in the world : but sin is not imputed when there is no law." For these words show that we are to understand the sin prohibited by the law, which was not original, but actual sin.

Having now shown that free will could not be depraved by original sin, state to me, in the next place, how far the power of free will extends ?

Commonly there exists in men by nature but little ability to do those things which God requires of them: but all are naturally capable of inclining their will to the performance of them ; and if divine assistance be obtained, the ability to execute them will not be wanting. For it is not to be thought that God exacts from any one what is beyond his power, since he is most wise and just and good ; or that he denies his assistance to any one of those persons to whom he has declared his will ; otherwise he could not, as he now does, justly punish the disobedient; nor indeed would the disobedient be deserving of any punishment, nor the obedient be entitled to any praise.

What is this divine assistance ?

It is of two kinds—internal and external.

What is that which is external?

It comprises the excellent promises and the threatenings of the New Covenant ;—of which, however, the promises have by far the greater power. Wherefore, because the promises and the grace of the New Covenant are far more excellent than those of the Old, it is easier to do the will of God under the

New

New than it was under the Old Covenant, although
his will is much more perfect under the New Covenant,
for we are now treated not as slaves but as freemen.

What is the internal divine assistance?

It is this—when God, by his spirit, imprints and
seals what he has promised more and more upon the
hearts of believers, and causes them to be incited by a
certain peculiar fondness for the divine promises. And
also, when by the same spirit he points out more
clearly to their understanding the duties of religion,
furnishes their minds with discretion, especially in
more difficult circumstances, directly inspires their
will with a certain zeal for the vigorous practice of
piety, represses the violence of opposing passions, ex-
pels sloth, and excites the mind to virtuous actions by
certain sacred incentives. The first of these aids is
chiefly manifested in afflictions.

If, as you state, there be free will, how comes it to
pass that so many deny it?

They do this because they think they have certain
testimonies of Scripture, wherefrom they imagine they
can make it appear that there is no free will in those
things of which I have spoken.

What are those testimonies?

They are of two kinds;—the one, from which they
persuade themselves that they can infer this; the
other, by which they conceive that free will is expressly taken away.

Which are those testimonies whence they endeavour to infer this?

All those which treat of the predestination of God.
                                          What

What is their opinion concerning predestination?

That God, by an absolutely irrevocable and unchangeable decree, did from all eternity elect and appoint unto salvation certain individuals in particular, from the whole human race who were ever to be born; and doom all the rest, by the same immutable decree, to eternal damnation;—not because he foresaw the obedience of the one or the disobedience of the other, but because such was his pleasure.

What is your opinion of this matter?

That this notion of predestination is altogether false,—and principally for two reasons; whereof one is, that it would necessarily destroy all religion; and the other, that it would ascribe to God many things incompatible with his nature.

Show me how the admission of this opinion would altogether destroy religion?

This is evident from hence, that all things relating to piety and religion would be in us from necessity: and if this were the case, there would be no need of our efforts and labour in order to be pious. For all exertion and application is wholly superfluous where all things are done through necessity, as reason itself shows. But if exertion and application be taken away from piety and religion, piety and religion must perish.

Show me what things incompatible with his nature would be attributed to God if this opinion were admitted?

They are four in number. First, injustice: for it would

would be extremely unjust to punish any one for not doing what he could by no means perform. And when God punishes the wicked, and those who disobey him, what does he but punish those who do not that which they have not ability to execute? For, if the opinion of our adversaries be true, it is clear, they cannot, on account of the absolutely immutable decree of God, become by any means pious and obedient to him. Secondly, hypocrisy, joined with deceit: for God, after having by his decree excluded from salvation a great, indeed the greatest, part of those to whom the gospel is proclaimed, does nevertheless, by the preaching of the gospel, offer salvation to all; and thus acts in one way while he pretends to act in another, which conduct properly belongs to hypocrites and deceivers: and, what is worse, he does this in a case wherein it would be evident that they were very greatly injured; since they would be eternally punished because they rejected the gospel. Thirdly, the greatest imprudence: for God would be prosecuting, or at least seem to be prosecuting, what he certainly knew could never be accomplished. And what is more foolish, what more trifling, than to prosecute, or pretend to prosecute, what we certainly know can by no means be executed, and thus expose ourselves to scorn? Fourthly, wickedness: because it would make God the author of sin: for since it is altogether necessary that sin should precede damnation, certainly he who absolutely decrees that any one shall necessarily be damned, does also ordain that he should necessarily sin.

How

How do they maintain this opinion of theirs concerning predestination?

They endeavour to support it by some testimonies of Scripture, among which the principal are those contained in the eighth and ninth chapters of the epistle to the Romans. The first is Rom. viii. 28, 29, 30, " We know that all things work together for good to them that love God, to them who are the called according to his purpose. For whom he did foreknow, he also did predestinate, to be conformed to the image of his son, that he might be the first born among many brethren. Moreover whom he did predestinate, them he also called; and whom he called, them he also justified : and whom he justified, them he also glorified." The other is Rom. ix. 11, 12, 13, where the apostle writes concerning Jacob and Esau; " For the children being not yet born, neither having done any good or evil, that the purpose of God according to election might stand, not of works, but of him that calleth, it was said unto her (Rebecca), The elder shall serve the younger. And it is written, Jacob have I loved, but Esau have I hated." And a little further on (ver. 21); " Hath not the potter power over the clay of the same lump, to make one vessel unto honour, and another unto dishonour?"

What answer is to be given to the first testimony?

In order that you may understand this testimony and others of a similar kind, I must first inform you what is meant in the Scriptures by predestination, election, and calling.

This I wish you to explain.

The

The predestination of God means nothing more in the Scriptures than a decree of his made before the foundation of the world, concerning mankind, to give eternal life to those who should believe in him, and yield him obedience, and to punish with eternal damnation those who should refuse to believe in and obey him. For Christ, the perfect interpreter of the divine will, has thus explained to us the purpose and decree of God : He that believeth shall certainly be saved, but he that believeth not shall certainly be damned.

What say you concerning election ?

Election, when our salvation is spoken of, has in the sacred writings two significations ; for sometimes all who give their assent to the gospel when preached to them are said to be elected of God : and sometimes they who not only assent to the gospel, but also regulate their lives by its precepts, are called the elect. You have an instance of the first signification, 1 Cor. i. 26, 27, "You see your calling, brethren, how that not many wise men after the flesh, not many mighty, not many noble are called ; but God hath chosen the foolish things of the world to confound the wise, God hath chosen the weak things of the world to confound the things which are mighty," &c. Also in those words of Peter (2 Epist. chap. 1, ver. 11), " Give diligence to make your calling and your election sure," that is by good works, as some copies subjoin.   Of the second signification you have an example, Matth. xxii. 14, where Christ says, " Many are called, but few are chosen."

What say you of calling ?

Calling

Calling signifies the invitation of men by God to faith and salvation; but so however as that the CALLED mean in the Scriptures the same as the ELECT in the first sense. For according to Scripture usage they are not denominated the CALLED, or κλητοι, with whom the vocation of God was through their own fault ineffectual and vain.

How then do you reply to that testimony, Rom. viii. 28, &c. ?

I answer, that this testimony makes nothing at all for the predestination of our adversaries: for they hold a predestination without any regard whatever to good works; whereas Paul here speaks of a predestination of God which respects such men as love God —and I have already shown that this is in the power of men who are called to it by God.

I wish you then to explain this passage to me.

It was the purpose of God, before all ages, to call men to faith in Christ, and to give eternal life to those who believed with an efficacious faith, and loved God. They therefore who have this faith are called according to that purpose of God: they were also foreknown of God, that is, from eternity approved and loved by him. Such persons were in like manner, from eternity, appointed and predestinated to be conformed to Christ in life and glory, in order that he might not be himself alone partaker of these, but might have many brethren joint participators of the same life and glory; of whom, however, he should be the first born, that is, the first and principal heir of that glory. Hence it is with certainty concluded that all things, even

those

those which are most afflicting, work together for
good to them, no less than they did to Christ himself.
After the apostle has demonstrated this, he describes
certain degrees whereby men attain to immortality;
showing that God, by the preaching of the gospel,
invites those to enter into his heavenly kingdom,
whom he had predestinated to be conformed to the
image of his Son in immortality; then that he frees
them from all the guilt of their sins, and, lastly, con-
ducts them to immortality and eternal life.

What answer do you make to the second testimony, Rom. ix. 11, &c. ?

If you look to the history, you will perceive that
nothing is said there concerning predestination to
eternal salvation or damnation; but only concerning
the dominion of Jacob and of his descendants over
Esau and his posterity, and on the contrary concerning the servitude of the latter. And if you bear in
mind the point to which the apostle accommodates
this history, you will observe that by Esau and Jacob
he does not designate two particular individuals, but
two classes of men; as also in the history itself two
actual nations are to be understood—by Esau, his descendants, or the Edomites—and by Jacob, the Israelites; as may be seen both from the two passages
cited by the apostle and from the thing itself. For
Esau himself never served Jacob, but only the posterity of the former served the posterity of the latter.
Now by the posterity of Jacob, or the people of Israel,
is signified the whole race of believers; as by the
posterity of Esau, or the people of Edom, are intended

Q

the

the whole race of unbelievers. The apostle therefore designed to state, that God had purposed to justify and eternally to save all believers, and to damn all unbelievers, though perhaps they might in other respects excel:—and this, not because either had merited their portion by their previous conduct, but because it seemed fit to God to propose to men, to every man according to his own choice, the mode of attaining justification and salvation ; to love and make happy those who should receive it, but punish and destroy those who should refuse to embrace it. It by no means follows from hence that God has decreed absolutely and necessarily concerning each individual man before his birth, and therefore without any regard to the good or evil of his conduct, that one should perish everlastingly, and another by saved : but rather, that having made a general decree for the salvation of believers and the damnation of unbelievers, he has left to every one at his own will to join the body of believers or of unbelievers : for otherwise he could not, with justice, punish any one because he had not believed.

What reply do you make to the third testimony, Rom. ix. 21 ?

That it does not follow from this passage either that God, out of the collective race of mankind, which corresponds to the lump of clay, has destined some in particular, unconditionally and before their birth, to everlasting honour, and others to everlasting dishonour ; or that after they have been born, he has, without any regard to their obedience or disobedience, their

faith

faith or unbelief, placed the one in a state of salvation and the other in a state of perdition : but only that, at his own pleasure, God has purposed to confer upon believers of the human race everlasting glory, and to consign unbelievers to everlasting contempt,—as is stated a little before. Certainly, those passages in the Prophets, whence Paul has in a manner borrowed this comparison, clearly show that God is so far like a potter as that he determines to punish the wicked ; and that on the contrary, if they repent, he again, at his pleasure, revokes his penal decree, and pardons them ; which will be evident to any one on inspecting the passage in Jeremiah (chap. xviii. 4). From which it likewise appears that this decree for punishing men is not unconditional, and will be changed in respect to them on their reformation : but that their reformation is left to their own option : which is also taught by Paul in a similar passage (2 Tim. ii. 20, 21), where, after saying that in a great house some vessels are to honour and some to dishonour, he adds, " If a man therefore purge himself from these,"(that is, separate himself from the vessels of dishonour by purging himself from all pernicious errors and vices,) " he shall be a vessel unto honour, sanctified and meet for the master's use, and prepared unto every good work." But if God had placed men in such a condition that those who are the vessels of dishonour cannot but be such, how could Paul a little further on, in that passage to the Romans (Rom. ix. 22), assert that God " endured with much long-suffering the vessels of wrath,"—for what long-suffering would it be

to

to endure what he had himself so fixed that it could not be otherwise ? And to what did that long-suffering and forbearance tend but to their repentance? (Rom. ii. 4.) But what repentance could be expected from those who were so created, and from eternity appointed to this, that they could not repent ?

What are those testimonies whereby our adversaries conceive that free will is expressly taken away ?

These relate either to all men in general, or to certain persons in particular.

Which are those that relate to all men ?

Among others, the following. First, Rom. ix. 16, " It is not of him that willeth, nor of him that runneth, but of God who showeth mercy." Secondly, John vi. 44, where the Lord Jesus says, " No man can come to me except the Father which hath sent me draw him." And thirdly, Acts xiii. 48, where Luke states, that " as many as were ordained to eternal life believed."

What do you reply to the first ?

The apostle does not in this passage speak of a will and endeavour to obey the commands of God, or to run according to his will as revealed to us; since this would be repugnant to the whole of the Scriptures, which inculcate scarcely any thing more frequently than an endeavour to live according to God's commandment:—but he speaks of such a will and endeavour, whereby we move God to confer his favours upon us, although he has not himself appointed the manner in which we will and endeavour to obtain them. That such is the case, appears from the very

position

position of the apostle; which is to this effect:—
that not all who are born of Abraham after the flesh,
are truly his sons, and those to whom pertain the promises wherein eternal happiness is proposed to the
posterity of Abraham; but those persons alone on whom
God is pleased to bestow this favour, without any regard to their descent according to the flesh: and these
are they who have believed in God through Christ,
from whatever parents descended, or whatever their
previous moral conduct may have been, and who are
in this manner made the spiritual children of Abraham: that therefore not the Israelites born of Abraham
after the flesh, although perhaps superior to believers
in respect to their antecedent works, are the true
children of Abraham, and the heirs of spiritual blessings, but believers in Christ: and that unless he
enter this way of attaining justification, every one will
both will and run in vain, since the compassion of
God will neither direct his will nor attend his course.
Such is the true meaning of this passage. Wherefore, while I freely admit that no man by his willing
and running, when not ordered according to the will
of God, could or can succeed in moving God to confer
any benefit upon him;—so, on the other hand, that,
after God has offered his grace, a man is not able to
accept and embrace the proffered boon; and to regulate his life by the direction of the divine will, I hold
to be a pernicious error : particularly as Paul is so far
from denying that a man is able to will and run so as
to please God, that he on the contrary rather intimates
with sufficient plainness that he can do this; only he

asserts

asserts that all this will be in vain unless the compassion of God accompany it, and this running be pursued in conformity with the will of God. And that such a running will not be in vain, but be conducive to salvation, is sufficiently evident from hence,—that the apostle exhorts the Corinthians to run, and so to run as to obtain the prize held out to the runners; and states that he had not himself run in vain: 1 Cor. ix. 24, 26; 2 Tim. iv 7, 8. See also Heb. xii. 1.

What reply do you make to the second testimony?

That this mode of drawing does not take away free will: for it is not done in such a way that constraint is put upon men by God; but he draws men to his Son by displaying the excellence and certainty of his promises. That this mode of drawing is not effected by force appears, in the first place, from what Christ himself subjoins (John vi. ver. 45), where he explains the manner of this drawing: "And they shall be all taught of God. Every man therefore that hath heard, and hath learned, of the Father, cometh unto me." Whence it is obvious, that to be drawn by the Father means nothing more than to hear and to be taught of the Father. And that this is done through Christ is manifest from his words inserted a little further on (ver. 46); "Not that any man hath seen the Father, save he which is of God; he hath seen the Father:" as if he had said, He, having been first taught by the Father face to face, teaches others. It is again evident from hence, that this manner of drawing relates to all whom the gospel reaches, as may be easily inferred from those words of Jesus

(John

(John xii. 32), "And I, if I be lifted up from the earth, will draw all men unto me." Christ's meaning is, that no one can be his disciple unless the Father himself draw him, the preaching of the gospel co-ope-. rating with his divine power[61]. He would therefore draw all; but all are not in effect drawn, from their obstinacy and guilt.

What do you say to the third testimony?

That this testimony does not take away free will may be perceived from hence,—that no mention is made here of God, who had ordained these persons to eternal life; but it is merely written that " as many as were ordained to eternal life, believed;" which may be understood of some ordination made by the men themselves: as if he had said, As many as had ordained themselves, or as many as were fit, from the probity of their minds, to embrace the doctrine of Christ, and so to lay hold on eternal life,—as is written a little before in the same chapter (Acts xiii. 46) in a contrary case, that others judged themselves unworthy of everlasting life; and as Christ says further on (Acts xviii. 10), that he had much people in Corinth, for no other reason than because there were many who were fit to become his people. Let it be added, that although this ordination were referred to God, it might still be understood of the fitness of men to embrace the gospel and attain eter-

---

[61] This power does not then belong to preaching, as was stated above, when this drawing was ascribed to the excellence and certainty of the promises; but is added to it. What then is it? Perhaps the Holy Spirit? But this is given to none but those who are already believers. M. RUARUS.

nal

nal life ; since whatever is done according to the will of God may and rightly is wont to be ascribed to him as its author. But if we will have it that some decree of God concerning the salvation of those persons is intended in these words, it by no means follows either that this decree preceded the probity of their minds, much less their birth and that very age; or that it was unchangeable—so that their guilt could be made of no consequence ; or that to others it should close the way to repentance.

What are the testimonies that relate to particular persons ?

They are, among others, those wherein it is said that " God hardened the heart of Pharaoh," Exod. iv. 21 ; vii. 3 ; x. 1, 20 ; xi. 10 ; xiv. 4, 8 ; and that Judas, who was an apostle of the Lord, was destined to betray him, Acts i. 16.

What answer do you make to these testimonies?

I grant that God does sometimes so reject from his grace certain wicked men,—not before their birth, but after they had merited this by their crimes,—that they can scarcely, and not even at all, repent and be amended. But these acts and proceedings of God do not take away free will, absolutely;—first, because these examples are singular[62]; and secondly, because,

as

---

[62] I allow that free will is not taken away from other men in consequence of particular instances : but it may be objected, that, at least, it is taken away in these. In the next place, as it follows that those persons had merited this fate by their prior voluntary wickedness, it seems to be tacitly granted that after they had deserved it free will was taken away from them —which is confirmed by what is subjoined, that their will was

free

as I have stated, these persons had merited this by their antecedent voluntary offences. Whence it appears that, before God punished them in this manner, they were possessed of free will; nevertheless they refused to obey God when it was in their power, and therefore were for a long time worthy that God should execute his judgements upon them, which at length, when he saw fit, he did execute. Of this kind was Pharaoh, who, long before, had for a considerable period afflicted the people of God; and also Judas, who was a miser and a thief. God therefore, that he might

---

free before God had in this manner punished them. . Whence it may be inferred that they then had it no longer,—which is contrary to what the author designed to prove by these two reasons. I conceive that the hardening and blinding, and other divine judgements, are thus brought on these wretched men. First, because some powerful, but nevertheless not all, means of repentance are withheld from them: Secondly, because occasions of error and sin are presented to them, which are not indeed wholly inevitable, though nevertheless with difficulty to be avoided by such profligate persons. Free will is not by this means wholly taken from them—and the justice of God remains, so that the guilt of the offences they may commit after their hearts are hardened cannot be imputed to him. Concerning the hardening of Pharaoh's heart in particular, it ought to be observed, that it is attributed not only to God, but also to Pharaoh himself, as a certain act of wickedness. (Ex. vii. 13, 22; viii. 15, 19, 32; ix. 7, 34), which could not have been the case if God had effected this by some irresistible power, and Pharaoh himself had not submitted to it of his own accord. Besides, it may also be plainly inferred from several of the cited passages, by what means God hardened the heart of Pharaoh:—namely, partly by permitting his magicians to work the same miracles as Moses, and partly by removing, at the prayers of Moses and Aaron, the plagues which he had inflicted on account of Pharaoh's disobedience.—M. RUARUS.

punish them, and at the same time employ them for the execution of his purposes, hardened them, or gave them up to the power of Satan. But let me add, the Scriptures never testify that Judas had been from of old specially destined to betray Christ; but only in a general way that some one of Christ's companions should rise up against him. That Judas was the person, arose, as I have observed, from his antecedent wickedness[63].

CHAPTER XI.

OF JUSTIFICATION.

SINCE I understand what faith in Christ is, and how far it is in our power, I wish you to explain to me what justification is which we obtain by that faith?

Justification is, when God regards us as just, or so deals with us as if we were altogether just and innocent. This he does in the New Covenant in forgiving our sins and conferring upon us eternal life.

Is no one justified then without faith in Christ?

No one whatever. But this must be understood of the time after Christ had appeared—in reference to which also those words of Peter (Acts iv. 12) are to be interpreted, that " there is none other name (besides that of Jesus) under heaven given among men whereby we must be saved." For this cannot be af-

---

[63] It may be added, that in order to bring about this matter, and that the prophecies might thus be fulfilled, our Lord furnished him with the occasion when he committed the purse to the miser, and provoked his avarice by the loss of the three hundred denarii, when he accepted such valuable ointment.— M. RUARUS.

firmed

firmed in respect to the time which preceded the appearance of Christ.   For though all who at any time
believed in God were justified through faith, as may
clearly be gathered from the eleventh chapter of Hebrews, yet they were not justified by faith in Christ,
but simply by faith in God.   For though all are justified by faith in Christ, they are also justified by faith
in God, provided they believe in God through Christ,
but not else.   Let it be added, that even that mode
of justification by faith in God, once in use under the
law, was not comprehended in the Covenant given by
Moses, but depended merely on the grace of God;
but that now the mode of justification by faith is comprised in the Covenant itself.   Whence the apostle
states (Gal. iii. 22 &c.) that faith came by the gospel.

But this opinion seems to be opposed by that passage in the Acts (chap. xv. ver. 11), where the apostle says that " through the grace of the Lord Jesus
Christ we shall be saved even as they," the Fathers ?

In this passage the term FATHERS does not occur,
the words are only " even as THEY."   And the pronoun THEY does not refer to the words immediately
preceding, where the Fathers are mentioned, for the
discourse did not relate to the Fathers, but to those
more remote where the Gentiles are spoken of, who
properly are here the subjects of discourse, and are
before several times opposed to the believing Jews, as
the Jews are also to believing Gentiles.   For thus we
read (ver. 8, &c.)—" And God, which knoweth the
hearts, bare them (the Gentiles) witness, giving them
the Holy Ghost, even as he did unto us (Jews); and

put

put no difference between us and them, purifying their (the Gentiles') hearts by faith. Now therefore why tempt ye God to put a yoke (the ceremonial law) upon the neck of the disciples (the Gentiles) which neither our fathers nor we were able to bear? But we believe that through the grace of the Lord Jesus Christ we shall be saved even as they;" namely, they of whom I have said that they were saved by the grace of Christ. Nor does it constitute any objection to this interpretation, that the word Fathers is nearer than the word Gentiles, as I have shown from the passages (Acts vii. 19; x. 6; 2 John 7), which I quoted formerly in a similar case. Nor even is it of any consequence that the pronoun THEY is here masculine, and the word GENTILES, in Greek, of the neuter gender, and that it should therefore seem that the pronoun THEY cannot refer to the Gentiles: for the term Gentiles is elsewhere also in the Scriptures (Rom. ii. 14; Matth. xviii. 19) joined to the masculine gender, or else relates to it. But if any one should object to refer the pronoun THEY to the word GENTILES, it may with propriety be referred to the word DISCIPLES, immediately preceding it, which is of the masculine gender as well as the pronoun. But it is certain that by ' disciples' believing Gentiles are here to be understood.

SECTION

SECTION VI.

OF THE PRIESTLY OFFICE OF CHRIST.

———

I SEEM to have sufficiently understood those things which are comprised in the prophetic office of Christ; proceed to his other offices, the priestly and kingly—and I desire to know from yourself concerning which of these I ought first to inquire?

The order of things demands that I should treat of the priestly office of Christ before his kingly office: for although while he abode on earth, and before his death, he executed both offices together, as far as was practicable in the condition of a mortal nature,—yet in his death he first became properly a victim, and having ascended into heaven he continually presents himself an offering for us, and appears in the presence of God as a priest: which offering and appearance were so pleasing and acceptable to God, and also so efficacious, that he thereupon invested Christ with all the power of saving us, constituted him our king and the head over all things, and consequently by him conferred salvation upon us. And he is styled a priest, and the priestly office is ascribed to him, that it might appear that he is a king through the grace of God, and that the grace of God is the sole fountain of whatever blessings flow to us from his kingly office. For God also is a king: the one God cannot however be at the same time king and priest: but it was ne-

cessary

cessary that a man should be raised by him to both these dignities for the good of men.

Wherein then consists the priestly office of Christ?

The priestly office of Christ consists in this—that he not only offered up prayers and supplications to God for himself and for us while he dwelt on earth, but also sanctified himself and gave himself as an offering for us, shedding his own blood for our sins; and thus, after being restored to life by God and made immortal, he has by his own blood entered the holy celestial place, and offered himself to God, appearing for ever in his presence, and interceding for us : by which one offering of his he has obtained for all who believe in him eternal redemption, and deliverance from their sins.

Are all these things asserted of Christ in strict propriety of speech ?

These things are spoken of Christ by way of comparison and likeness with the legal priesthood :—because, as under the Old Covenant the high priest, having entered the holy of holies, performed those things which pertained to the expiation of the sins of the people (Heb. ii. 17 ; iv. 14 ; v. 1 ; ix. 24); so Christ has now entered into heaven, that he may there appear before God for us, and perform all things relating to the expiation of our sins.   But though the offering of Christ is so denominated by way of similitude, it has nevertheless a real and a far more perfect sense than sacrifices and offerings properly so called.

What

What is that expiation which Christ makes for our sins?

It is a deliverance from the guilt of our sins, and from the penalties, both temporal and eternal, which follow them; and also from the sins themselves, that we no longer serve them.

How does Jesus make expiation for our sins in heaven?

First, He does this while he delivers us from the guilt and punishment of our sins by the efficacy of his death, which, by the will of God, he endured for our sins. For so costly an offering, and such obedience as that of Christ, have continual power in the presence of God to keep us who believe in Christ, and are partakers of his death, from the guilt and the punishment of our sins, that we may not live in wickedness. Secondly, he makes expiation for our sins, while by the full and absolute authority which he has obtained of the Father he continually protects us, and by his intercession averts from us the wrath of God, that is wont to be poured out on the wicked, which the Scripture calls "making intercession for us." Thirdly, he delivers us from the servitude of our sins, partly while he emancipates us for himself by the death he endured for us, and binds us to obedience to his doctrine; partly while he sets before us in his own person an example of the highest faith in God, and of the most ardent charity towards other men, of gentleness also, and exemplary patience; and at the same time shows what he will obtain who submits himself entirely to the will of God, and thus incites us to imitate

tate him by the happiness of his glorious state;—and partly, while as the supreme overseer of holy things he directs the worship of God on earth, appoints various ministers for the performance of it, and by the assistance of his spirit renders efficacious their labours in propagating religion and extirpating sin.

What is the difference between the expiation of sins under the Old, and that under the New Covenant?

The expiation of sins under the New Covenant is most widely different from that under the Old, and is far more excellent;—and this principally for three reasons. First, because under the Old Covenant expiation was appointed by the legal sacrifices for those sins alone which were committed through ignorance or infirmity; whence also those sins are called infirmities and ignorances, Numbers xv. 24, 25, &c. But for heavier sins, which were committed by any one with an outstretched arm, and a contempt of the commandments of God, no sacrifices were appointed, but the penalty of death was denounced against them. And if God forgave any one such sins, he did it not in virtue of the Covenant, but through his especial mercy, which he displayed beyond the Covenant when and to whomsoever he saw fit. But under the New Covenant, not only are those sins expiated which are committed through ignorance and infirmity, but also the heaviest sins,—provided only that he who has committed them do not persevere in them, but repent with sincere contrition, change his life for the better, and do not any more relapse into such sins. Secondly, because under the Old Cove-

nant

nant the expiation of sin was effected in such a manner that temporal penalties alone were taken away
from those whose sins were expiated : for by carnal
sacrifices, only carnal punishment was removed. But
under the New Covenant, the expiation is such that
it removes not only temporal but also eternal penalties ; and instead of punishment, offers eternal life,
promised in the Covenant, to those whose sins have
been expiated. Thirdly, because those sacrifices did
not reach the mind, and had not power to withdraw
sinners from their sins ; and it was necessary to repeat
them often in consequence of men's relapsing into the
same offences : but the sacrifice and offering of Christ
penetrates the mind, and has the power of sanctifying
men for ever to God.—Concerning this matter the author of the epistle to the Hebrews speaks in more than
one place, and particularly chap. x. 1—4, 11, and 14.

How do you prove the first two reasons ?

That the sins which could not be expiated under
the Old Covenant may all of them be expiated under
the New, the apostle Paul testifies, Acts xiii. 38,
39, where he says, " Be it known unto you therefore,
men and brethren, that through this man is preached
unto you the forgiveness of sins, and by him all that
believe are justified from all things from which ye
could not be justified by the law of Moses." The
same thing may be seen, Rom. iii. 25. And that
sins are expiated under the New Covenant in such
a manner as that eternal punishment is taken
away, and eternal life bestowed, appears from Heb.
ix. 12, where the author says that Christ " by his
own

own blood entered in once into the holy place, having obtained eternal redemption for us." And it is said (ver. 15), that "for this cause he is the Mediator of the New Testament, that by means of death for the redemption of the transgressions that were under the first Testament, they which are called might receive the promise of eternal inheritance."

Why is this sacrifice of Christ offered in heaven?

Because it required a tabernacle suitable both to the priest and the offering. Now as the priest himself was immortal, and as that also which he offered, namely, his body, was rendered incorruptible, it was necessary that he should enter into an eternal tabernacle. And since heaven, in which God himself dwells, is such a tabernacle, it was necessary that he should enter into heaven, in order there to execute his priestly office,—as the author of the epistle to the Hebrews expressly testifies, (Heb. vii. 26,) when he says, " Such an high priest became us, who is holy, harmless, undefiled, separate from sinners, and made higher than the heavens." And he adds below (chap viii. 4), "for if he were on earth he should not be a priest."

What—was he not a priest before he ascended into heaven, and particularly while he hung on the cross?

Christ was indeed a priest, even while he lived on earth, and when he hung upon the cross. For, as I have lately said, he presented prayers and supplications to God for himself and for us, sanctified himself as an offering to God, and had the right of entering the holy place in heaven: and if he makes us kings and priests unto God, even while we are in this mortal life, how much more might he himself be said to have been a king and priest? As however the priestly office of Christ consisted chiefly in the offering of his body, and his appearance in the presence of God, it was necessary that both these should be done in heaven as a suitable sanctuary;—and on this account his body was endued with immortality, that living for ever he might make intercession for us. Hence the writer to the Hebrews (chap. viii. ver. 4) does not hesitate to declare, that if he were on earth he should not be a priest, because there are on earth others who offer gifts according to the law. Besides, as the same author testifies (chap. ii. ver. 17), " that in all things it behoved him to be made like unto his brethren, that he might be a merciful and faithful high priest in things pertaining to God, to make reconciliation for the sins of the people,"—it is evident that as long as he was not like unto his brethren in all things, that is, in afflictions and death, it was necessary that he should be perfected by means of these. And, on this account, the sufferings and death of Christ were not themselves that full and perfect expiatory sacrifice of which I speak, but a certain way and preparation for the offering of it, or a certain commencement of it. For the sacrifice could not be completed until the priest had himself been made perfect. Wherefore the writer to the Hebrews says (chap. v. ver. 9, 10), that after " being made perfect," " he was called of God an high priest after the order of Melchisedec." " For the law," he states (chap. vii. ver. 28),

" maketh

" maketh men high priests which have infirmity; but the word of the oath, which was since the law, maketh the Son, who is consecrated for evermore ;"—that is, is perfected a priest. Hence he says (chap. v. ver. 5) that " Christ glorified not himself to be made an high priest," intimating that Christ was made a priest by his glorification: and he quotes these words from Psalm ii. 7, " Thou art my son, to-day have I begotten thee:" in which he states that he was made a priest by God :—but God, as the apostle Paul testifies (Acts xiii. 33), addressed Christ in these words after he had raised him from the dead.

Why then does the apostle say (Ephes. v. 2) that " Christ hath given himself for us an offering and a sacrifice to God for a sweet-smelling savour ?"

First, You must observe that I do not separate the death from the offering of Christ ; but constantly assert that Christ no otherwise offered himself than by the intervening of his death: what I maintain is, that his expiatory sacrifice, in which he is compared with the high priest under the law, was not actually completed and perfected, until, after being raised from the dead, he had entered into heaven. For in that annual legal sacrifice, which principally shadowed forth the sacrifice of Christ, in order to the completion of the offering it was absolutely necessary that the blood of the slaughtered animal should be carried into the holy of holies, as the author of the epistle to the Hebrews testifies, chap. ix. ver. 7. In the next place, though I were to admit that the death of Christ was, in the apostle's meaning, an offering and sacrifice to God for

a sweeta sweet-smelling savour, it would not thence follow that it was that perfect expiatory sacrifice whereof the author of the epistle to the Hebrews speaks: since the apostle may, in these words, refer to those offerings which were called peace-offerings, as the expression "for a sweet-smelling savour" indicates, which are very frequently used in reference to peace-offerings, but scarcely ever in relation to expiatory sacrifices. Nor ought the word GIVEN to be joined with OFFER-ING, but should be read by itself, and understood to mean that Christ GAVE, or delivered, himself to death. For the word GIVE is used in this sense in other places in the Scriptures (Ephes. v. 25; Gal. ii. 20; Rom. viii. 32). Moreover, the words follow-ing, "an offering and a sacrifice to God for a sweet-smelling savour," connect with the pronoun HIM-SELF, to which they are joined by apposition; and are an illustration or commendation of this work of Christ—that he gave himself for us,—by which the apostle exhorts believers to imitate this act of Christ's in loving their neighbour. Other good works are else-where commended by a similar mode of speaking, as Phil. iv. 18. Wherefore also doing good and commu-nicating are called sacrifices with which God is well pleased (Heb. xiii. 16); as are likewise all good works performed by believers in Christ;—which good works of Christians were shadowed forth in the legal sacri-fices (Heb. xiii. 16; 1 Peter ii. 5; Rom. xii. 1). Or if Christ himself giving (or delivering) himself to death for us is called by the apostle an offering and sacri-fice acceptable to God, this ought to be interpreted

of

of an oblation and sacrifice as far as he offered himself to God to be slain for us,—although the offering of Christ himself in heaven might be understood here. And the meaning would be—that Christ delivered himself to death for us, that he might be an acceptable offering and sacrifice to God for our sins. For accusatives added by apposition are wont to have the force of the final cause. See among other places, Acts v. 21; 1 John iv. 10, 14.

What then is the meaning of this passage of Scripture (Heb. i. 3), that Christ " when he had by himself purged our sins sat down on the right hand of the majesty on high ?"

It does not follow from this passage that Christ made his oblation, and his purgation of our sins, by his death; since between his death, and his being seated at the right hand of the throne of the majesty on high, intervened his entrance into the heavenly tabernacle, and his appearance before the presence of God, which began from his offering, whence followed the purgation of our sins; and the power was given to Christ of delivering us for ever from our sins and the punishment of them ; which is meant by his being seated at the right hand of the majesty.

Why does the Scripture (Rom. viii. 34; Heb. vii. 25), when it treats of the priesthood of Christ, state that he maketh intercession for us ? ·

When the Scripture testifies that Christ makes intercession for us, it is not because he literally offers prayers to God for us; for this would not comport with the full authority which God has actually

conferred

conferred upon him, and on account of which he is our king;—but because those things which Christ, by the will of God, does for the remission of our sins, have a certain resemblance to prayers, in so far as they powerfully impell God to grant the remission of our sins, and are the most efficacious means of our reconciliation :—which mode of speaking the Scripture employs the more freely, in order the more thoroughly to impress upon our minds that all the authority which Christ possesses, he possesses not of himself but by the gift of the Father; and that he performs all things, not as if he did them himself, but as if God performed them at his solicitation. This the Holy Spirit does, in order that the prerogative, the pre-eminence, and glory of the Father might be preserved entire and inviolate [m].

---

[m] [The reader ought to be apprized, that few modern Unitarians, if any, will assent to the preceding interpretations respecting the offering and sacrifice of Christ, the death of Christ being regarded by them generally as a sacrifice only in a figurative sense. TRANSL.]

SECTION

SECTION VII.

OF THE KINGLY OFFICE OF CHRIST.

━━◆━━

I WISH now to learn from you what the kingly office of Christ is ?

You shall directly. You must know then that the kingly office of Christ is to be considered in two points of view;—first, as it respects his kingdom; and secondly, as it relates to his people, who are subject to him.

What is to be considered in respect to his kingdom ?

That God, having raised him from the dead, and taken him up to heaven, has placed him at his right hand, having given him all power in heaven and on earth, that he might at his own pleasure govern, protect, and eternally save those who believed in him.

Where are these things written ?

The Scripture is full of them. Concerning the resurrection, among other things, Paul testifies, when he says (Ephes. i. 19, 20) that " God showed the exceeding greatness of his power, which he wrought in Christ, when he raised him from the dead." And in his epistle to the Romans (chap. x. ver. 9), he says, " If thou shalt confess with thy mouth the Lord Jesus, and shalt believe in thine heart that God hath raised him from the dead, thou shalt be saved."

And

And (Acts ii. 36) Peter says, "Let all the house of
Israel know assuredly that God hath made that same
Jesus whom ye have crucified both Lord and Christ,"
which without his resurrection he could not have
done. The same apostle again observes (Acts v. 30,
31), " The God of our fathers raised up Jesus, whom
ye slew and hanged on a tree. Him hath God exalted with his right hand to be a prince and a saviour,
for to give repentance to Israel and forgiveness of
sins."

But some assert that Christ raised himself from the
dead?

They are greatly mistaken; since, as you have
heard, the Scripture plainly asserts in various places
(Acts ii. 32; iii. 13; Gal. i. 1; 1 Thess. i. 10), that
" the God of Abraham, of Isaac and of Jacob," or that
" God," simply, or expressly "God the Father," raised
Christ from the dead, or that God raised his Son.
Which is so true, that the Scriptures of the New Testament sometimes thus describe God without naming
him: "HIM that raised up Jesus from the dead" (Rom.
iv. 24; viii. 11). And the author of the epistle to the
Hebrews (chap. v. ver. 7) testifies that Christ " in
the days of his flesh offered up prayers and supplications, with strong crying and tears, unto him that
was able to save him from death,"—which surely he
never would have done, had he been able to deliver,
and, what is more, had actually delivered, himself
from death.

But why do they hold this opinion?

They conceive that some testimonies of Scripture

R   inculcate

inculcate this opinion :—as when our Saviour says (John ii. 19), " Destroy this temple, and in three days I will raise it up :" and further on (chap. x. ver. 17, 18), " Therefore doth my Father love me, because I lay down my life that I might take it again. No man taketh it from me, but I lay it down of myself. I have power to lay it down, and I have power to take it again." And when the apostle says (1 Peter iii. 18), " Christ also hath once suffered for sins, the just for the unjust, that he might bring us to God, being put to death in the flesh, but quickened by the spirit."

What reply do you make to the first passage ?

I answer, first, that testimonies so few in number, and so obscure, expressed in figurative language, cannot be opposed to so many plain testimonies of Scripture, so that those which are few and obscure should explain those which are so numerous, plain, and perspicuous :—but rather the few and obscure should in all cases be interpreted according to the meaning of those which are the more numerous and clear. In the next place, in respect to the first testimony adduced, the Greek term εγερω, in Latin excitabo or erigam, ' I will raise,' or ' erect,' may be interpreted as if Christ had thus spoken,—" Destroy this temple of my body, and within three days I will set it up or erect it for you alive and entire." Now Christ might with propriety thus speak, although not himself, but God by his own power was to raise him from the dead : because he is not discussing whether he himself was to effect this ; but whether, after death, he was to

show

show himself alive, and thus exhibit an indisputable proof that he had executed every thing which he had done by no other than a divine power. And, indeed, in this figurative mode of speaking, not so much the literal meaning of the terms as the subject is to be attended to ; especially if according to the literal significuation of the words any thing false, or repugnant to other Scriptures, should be affirmed. In a similar manner, Jesus says elsewhere (Luke xvii. 33), " Whosoever shall lose his life shall preserve it." Whence, if any one would contend for the literal interpretation of the words, he must infer that believers also will restore themselves to life, and raise themselves from the dead.

What do you reply to the second passage ?

This mode of speaking does not prove that Christ while he was dead, was alive, and had even power to raise himself ; since we read concerning believers that power was given them to become the sons of God, that is, to become like God in immortality ; although it is certain they were not to render themselves immortal, but that God, in respect to their immortality, would make them his sons. Nor does the word translated POWER, signify here any virtue or efficacious ability, but a right only to something ; and any one may be said λαμβανειν, to receive, that which he obtains through the gift of another ; in which manner also we receive, that is obtain, immortality.

What then is the meaning of this passage ?

It is as if Christ had spoken in this manner :—As it is not in your power to put me to death, but de-

pends

pends upon the will of myself and my Father; so
neither does it rest upon your will that I should continue dead. For this is the will of my Father and of
myself, that having laid down my life I should arise
from the dead and receive from my Father life eternal:—which is intimated by the words following;
" This commandment have I received of my Father:"
where the term COMMANDMENT signifies the requisition to lay down his life with the promise of receiving
it again, as the preceding context requires.

What answer do you make to the third passage?

That it does not any way appear from hence that
Christ raised himself from the dead; since it is not
written here that he quickened himself by the spirit,
but only that he was " quickened by the spirit,"
that is, by God. If any one should contend that this
spirit is spoken of in opposition to the body of Christ,
he ought to consider that at the death of Christ the
spirit returned to God, from whom, consequently, and
not from Christ, at this time dead, it was sent for the
raising of his body. Thus it is said (Romans viii. 11),
according to some editions, God shall quicken us by
his spirit that dwelleth in us :—it does not however
follow that we shall raise ourselves. Whence also the
apostle Paul thus expresses the same sentiment as
that which is comprised in the words of Peter (2 Cor.
xiii. 4), " Christ was crucified through weakness, yet
he liveth by the power of God."

In what body was Christ raised?

In that certainly wherein he was crucified: since
we read that he ate and drank with his disciples after
his

his resurrection, and showed them the wounds in his hands and feet and side (Luke xxiv. 39—43).

Why was Christ raised in such a body?

That he might assure his apostles and disciples of his resurrection. This was also the reason why, after he was raised from the dead, he conversed with them afterwards during forty days, and spoke concerning the kingdom of God.

But was no change made in the body of Christ by his glorification?

There was;—for when he was made a quickening spirit, his body was made incorruptible, glorious, powerful, and spiritual. 1 Cor. xv. 42, 43, 44.

What kind of bodies shall believers have at the resurrection?

Bodies like unto the glorious body of the Lord Jesus Christ. Philipp. iii. 21.

Where does the Scripture testify that Christ was taken up into heaven?

Luke expressly testifies to this fact chap. xxiv. ver. 50, 51, where we read, "And he led them out as far as to Bethany, and he lifted up his hands and blessed them. And it came to pass that while he blessed them, he was parted from them, and carried up to heaven." Concerning which, see also Mark xvi. 19, and Acts i. 9.

Why was he taken up to heaven?

Because heaven is the seat of immortality, and the dwelling-place and commonwealth of all the children of God are there;—whither Christ has gone before

them

them all, as their forerunner, in order to prepare a place for them; and from heaven to rule over all men. 2 Pet. iii. 13; Philipp. iii. 20; Heb. vi. 20; John xiv, 2, 3.

Where does the Scripture assert that Jesus is set down at the right hand of God?

Mark xvi. 19; Rom. viii. 34; Ephes. i. 20, 21, 22; 1 Cor. xv. 27; 1 Peter iii. 22; Heb. i. 3, 13, and elsewhere.

What is meant by Christ's sitting at the right hand of God?

By the seating of Christ at the right hand of God the apostolic writer meant (Ephes. i. 21) his exaltation; whereby he is raised " far above all principality and power, and might and dominion, and every name that is named not only in this world, but also in that which is to come:" together with the subjection of all things under his feet, and his supreme dominion and authority over all men and all things; which excels in this, that Christ has absolute authority over our bodies and our souls, and rules not only over men but also over angels, good and bad, and over death and hell.

Why has Christ this power over the souls and bodies of men?

That he might be able to succour them in all their necessities both spiritual and temporal; and also on the other hand punish the disobedient with both spiritual and corporal penalties; because he is constituted the judge of quick and dead, who must render to every one according to his works. For which

reason

reason also such wisdom is given to him, that he might try the hearts and the reins, and judge all according to the secrets of their hearts [54].

Wherefore

---

[54] That those who disobey the commands of God and Christ, after being raised at the last judgment, will be doomed to punishment, and cast into the fire prepared for the devil and his angels, has always been the opinion of this church. This appears, not to mention other proofs, from the Confession of Faith published in 1642, and afterwards in 1651, in the name of these congregations; and also from the *Brevis Declar. Art. Rel. Christianæ*, published in 1656 under the name of John Simplicius, Art. 22. See also Crellius's Commentary on Matth. iii. 10; 2 Thess. i. 8, 9; Heb. x. 27; Rev. xxi. 8. also Volkelius *De Vera Religione, lib.* iii. *c.* 33: and Schlichtingius on John v. 29; where, among other things bearing on this subject, we read, *Hæc igitur Christi verba*, &c. "These words of Christ therefore manifestly and clearly teach, not only that the good shall be raised to life, but also that the wicked shall be raised to condemnation and punishment. This is one part of the Christian faith, which whoever has not, has not the whole Christian faith." See the same writer on Heb. x. 27; 2 Peter iii. 7. also Wolzogenius on Matth. iii. 12; x. 28; xxv. 41, 46; John v. 29; and A. Wissowatius on Acts xxiv. 15, and[1] on Jude, ver. 6, 15, &c. It is therefore a mere calumny of some persons that these churches, which choose to be called simply Christian, but which by others are commonly styled Ebionite, Samosatenite, Arian, Photinian or Socinian, deny the resurrection and the punishment of the wicked. For it is evident from the cited authorities that they, equally with others, constantly maintain that there will be a resurrection both of the just and of the unjust—and that the latter shall be consigned to everlasting punishment, but the former admitted to everlasting life[n]. B. WISSOWATIUS.

[n] [The doctrine of the proper eternity of hell torments is rejected by most Unitarians of the present day, as, in their opinion, wholly irreconcileable with the divine goodness and unwarranted by the Scriptures. In reference to the future fate of the wicked, some hold that after the resurrection they will be annihilated or consigned to "everlasting destruction," in the literal sense of the words: but most have received the doctrine

trine

Wherefore has he dominion over good and bad angels ?

He rules over the good angels that he may be able to employ their ministry, whereby they may either enlarge the boundaries of his kingdom or succour believers in all their necessities. He has power over bad angels, that he may restrain their endeavours and machinations, which are wholly bent to effect the ruin of all mankind, and especially of believers, who have the way to immortality appointed to them: that he may employ their power at his own pleasure either to punish or restrain men who oppose his honour or the salvation of believers, or in any way, as far as in them lies, are bent on doing injury, or are in any respect enemies, to himself or to believers; and lastly that he may punish them with everlasting fire.

Why has he power over death and hell ?

That he may snatch believers, though they may have been swallowed up by death, from the jaws of death and the mouth of hell, restore them again to life, and make them immortal. Wherefore Christ himself says (Revel. i. 18) that he has the keys of hell and death.

---

trine of universal restoration, which maintains that all men, however depraved their characters may have been in this life, will, by a corrective discipline, suited in the measure of its severity to the nature of each particular case, be brought ultimately to goodness and consequently to happiness. Transl.}

SECTION

SECTION VIII.

OF THE CHURCH OF CHRIST.

I HAVE understood what you have stated respecting the kingdom of Christ;—explain to me now who his people is?

It is the church, or society of Christians; which, as it is distinguished by some, is either visible or invisible.

CHAPTER I.

OF THE VISIBLE CHURCH.

WHAT is the visible church?

It is a society of such men as hold and profess saving doctrine; which society may be considered in general, and in particular:—In general, when all the visible societies of Christ, dispersed over the whole world, are considered as one society or church;—In particular, when every single society, existing in certain places, is taken for a church of Christ.

As at this time all societies in every place claim for themselves the title of the Church of Christ, I wish to learn whether there be any signs whereby the church of Christ may be known?

It is to little purpose to seek the signs of the true church of Christ, since I have explained to you what constitutes a true church, namely, saving doctrine; for every church which holds and professes this, is a true

R 5 church

church of Christ. But no church which has not and professes not the saving doctrine, although it display and pretend to I know not what signs, can be deemed a true church of Christ. And since to hold the saving doctrine is the essence of the church of Christ, it cannot, speaking literally, be the sign of it, since the sign ought to differ from the thing signified.

In order then to know what is a true church of Christ, it is sufficient to know the saving doctrine?

You rightly apprehend the matter: for he who has embraced the saving doctrine knows as far as is needful for him what a true church is. He has therefore no occasion to seek for the signs whereby a church may be known. And what the saving doctrine is, you may have learnt from our discourse and conference.

CHAPTER II.

OF THE GOVERNMENT OF THE CHURCH OF CHRIST.

Since you have stated to me that saving doctrine is essential to the visible church of Christ, I now wish to know from you what order is prescribed to it in this doctrine?

This order is comprised in the offices of the persons of whom the church of Christ is composed, and in diligent watchfulness and care that every person discharges his own duties.

Who are the persons of whom the church is composed?

Of these there are some who govern, and some whose duty it is to obey.

Who

Who are they that govern?

Apostles, prophets, evangelists, teachers, pastors or bishops, elders and deacons [65].

What is the office of those persons who are denominated apostles?

To go forth to the whole world (Matth. xxviii. 19; Mark xvi. 15) to proclaim the gospel of Christ, and particularly to exhibit a testimony of his resurrection; for which purpose they were chosen and sent forth by Christ: whence also they were called apostles; whom likewise Christ endued with the Holy Spirit sent from heaven, and armed with powers suited to so high an office. Acts ii. 4.

What is the office of prophets?

To unfold the secrets of the divine will,—to reveal things hidden, and far removed from human sense,—

---

[65] That these offices, instituted by the Lord Christ through his apostles, were continued and observed in the primitive church, appears evident from the writings of all antiquity: but especially from that very ancient epistle, and so worthy to be read (seeing that among other vestiges of antiquity it contains the orthodox opinion of the primitive church concerning God) of Clement, the disciple of St. Paul, which he addresses to the Corinthians in the name of the Roman Church, whereof he was bishop. For the primitive Christians were above all things careful that the church should not be corrupted by tyranny or disorder. About the year 600 (when also tyranny chiefly entered into the Church) there arose a sect of men who were called ACÉPHALI (that is, without a head). These took away all rule from the church, and endeavoured to introduce disorder into it, if what Nicephorus (*lib.* xviii. *c.* 45) affirms be correct: otherwise, in all times and places, this appointment of Christ and the apostles has been held in respect by Christians, and has continued in uninterrupted succession from their time to our own.—B. WISSOWATIUS.

to

to know and predict things that are to come. 1 Cor. xiv.

What is the duty of evangelists?

To assist the apostles in proclaiming the gospel, and to spread and plant it in different places. Such were Philip, Timothy, and others. Acts xxi. 8; 2 Tim. iv. 5.

What are the offices of teachers, of pastors or bishops, and of elders?

To speak before others in discourse and prayers, and in all things to preserve order in the church of the Lord.

What is the office of deacons?

To minister to the necessities of the church, especially of the poor. Acts vi. 2, 3.

Are all those persons who, you state, are to rule over others, and whose offices you have described, to be found at this day in the church of Christ?

With respect to apostles, and to prophets, (who were nearest to apostles,) it is certain that they are no longer to be found in the church of Christ. For the cause on account of which they were chosen, sent, and given by God, no longer exists; which was, that God designed by them first to announce and establish in the world the doctrine of his Son. Whence they were called also by Paul (Ephes. ii. 20), the foundation of the church of Christ. After, therefore, the doctrine of Christ had, according to the purpose of God, been abundantly revealed and confirmed, the office of these persons in the church ceased.

Why

Why do you call the apostles and prophets the foundation of the church of Christ, when Christ himself is the foundation thereof, 1 Cor. iii. 11 ?

The apostles and prophets are called the foundation of the church of Christ in one sense, Christ is the foundation of his church in another. For the apostles and prophets are called the foundation of the church of Christ in respect of other persons who belong to that church, and rest upon the doctrine and authority of the apostles and prophets. But Christ is considered as something more; that is, as the chief corner-stone of its foundation, as is written Ephes. ii. 20. And Christ is the foundation of the church not only in respect of other men, but also of the apostles themselves, who, as well as all other believers, are built upon the Lord.

What say you respecting the evangelists ?

That they also have ceased, as well as apostles : for they, together with the apostles, were chosen for the promulgation of a new doctrine, which is now the oldest.

What think you of the other persons ?

As the causes, on account of which their offices were appointed, do still altogether remain, I certainly conclude that the persons themselves or their offices do also continue.

What kind of persons ought teachers and bishops to be ?

On this subject the apostle Paul treats at large in writing to Timothy (1 Epist. chap. iii. ver. 2—7), " A bishop must be blameless, the husband of one wife, vigilant, sober, of good behaviour, given to hospitality,

pitality, apt to teach : not given to wine, no striker, not greedy of filthy lucre," that is moderate, " but patient, no brawler," or not contentious, " not covetous, one that ruleth well his own house, having his children in subjection with all gravity. (For if a man know not how to rule his own house, how shall he take care of the church of God?) Not a novice, lest being lifted up with pride, he fall into the condemnation of the devil. Moreover, he must have a good report of them which are without, lest he fall into reproach, and the snare of the devil." In like manner, in writing to Titus, and showing what kind of elders ought to be appointed by him, he says (chap. i. 6—9): " If any be blameless, the husband of one wife, having faithful children, not accused of riot, or unruly. For a bishop must be blameless, as the steward of God; not self-willed, not soon angry, not given to wine, no striker, not given to filthy lucre; but a lover of hospitality, a lover of good men, sober, just, holy, temperate," or chaste, " holding fast the faithful word as he hath been taught, that he may be able by sound doctrine both to exhort and to convince the gainsayers."

Is it not necessary that they who teach in the church, and attend to the support and preservation of order, should be sent by others?

It is not : for they do not now bring any doctrine that is new, or not before promulgated, or not yet sufficiently confirmed; but only propose and inculcate the apostolic doctrine, long since abundantly confirmed, and received by all Christians; and exhort men

to

to regulate their lives conformably to it. Whence
the apostle, in describing at large all that pertained
to such an office, makes no mention of a mission of
this kind. When, however, such persons are ordained
and constituted according to the prescript of the apostolic doctrine, or even when, the affairs of the church
having fallen into disorder, they go forth of their own
accord, excited by a regard for the divine glory and
the salvation of men, for the purpose of regulating
and settling the church, and excel in these two qualifications, innocence of life, and aptness to teach,—they
ought deservedly to have just authority among all men.

What then say you to those words of the apostle
(Romans x. 15), " How shall they preach except they
be sent ?"

That the apostle does not in these words speak of
the preaching of those persons who speak as the disciples of the envoys of God and Christ, and who
rest their declarations on the authority of the latter,
and not on their own ; but of the preaching of those
who profess that they have received what they teach
directly from God himself and Christ, and are commanded to announce it to others, and thus claim for
themselves the authority of envoys from God and
Christ :—Of this kind was the preaching of the apostles, and of some others who were their assistants in
the same work ; and this certainly required a mission.
But as the preaching of the teachers of the present
day is not of this kind, as I have lately shown, no such
mission is in the least necessary for it.

What kind of persons ought deacons to be ?

" The

" The deacons, likewise, must be grave, not double-tongued, not given to much wine, not greedy of filthy lucre, holding the mystery of the faith in a pure conscience."—" Let the deacons be the husbands of one wife, ruling their children and their own houses well. For they that have used the office of a deacon will purchase to themselves a good degree, and great boldness in the faith which is in Christ Jesus." 1 Tim. iii. 8, 9. 12, 13.

You have enumerated the persons who govern; explain now those things which pertain to the hearers?

The duty of the hearers, and of the younger members, is to obey those who govern in all those things which are commanded by the word of God; concerning which we read in the epistle to the Hebrews, (chap. xiii. ver. 17), " Obey them that have the rule over you, and submit yourselves; for they watch for your souls as they that must give account, that they may do it with joy, and not with grief, for that is unprofitable for you." To communicate to those that teach in all good things (Gal. chap. vi. ver. 6). To count them worthy of double honour; and to receive no accusation against them, but before two or three witnesses; which indeed pertains also to the whole church. (1 Tim. v. 17, 19.)

CHAPTER III.

OF THE DISCIPLINE OF THE CHURCH OF CHRIST.

You have explained to me the offices of those persons who compose the church of Christ; state

moreover

moreover the way in which those offices are discharged.

This way relates in part to all; but chiefly to those who rule.

How does it relate to all?

In the manner stated Heb. iii. 12, "Take heed, brethren, lest there be in any of you an evil heart of unbelief, in departing from the living God." And further on (chap. x. ver. 24—26), "Let us consider one another to provoke one another to good works. Not forsaking the assembling of ourselves together, as the manner of some is; but exhorting one another; and so much the more as ye see the day approaching:" and again (chap. xii. ver. 15), "Looking diligently, lest any man fail of the grace of God." And the apostle Paul (1 Thess. v. 11, 14) says, "Wherefore comfort yourselves together, and edify one another." "We exhort you, brethren, warn them that are unruly, comfort the feeble-minded, support the weak, be patient toward all men."

How are those who are unruly to be dealt with?

In two ways;—for they are to be corrected either privately or publicly.

How are they to be corrected in private?

As Christ directs, Matth. xviii. 15, 16, "If thy brother shall trespass against thee, go and tell him his fault between him and thee alone: if he shall hear thee, then thou hast gained thy brother. But if he will not hear thee, then take with thee one or two more, that in the mouth of two or three witnesses every word may be established."

Why

Why are they to be thus corrected?

Because, as may be seen in this passage, they have offended privately against us: and for the same reason, the same thing is to be observed in respect to other private offences, whether against God, or against other men; for so equity itself suggests, and Christian charity requires.

How are they to be publicly corrected?

Either by words or by deeds.

In what manner by words?

In such a way as that they be publicly reproved by all in the church of Christ:—concerning which the apostle writes (1 Tim. v. 20), "Them that sin rebuke before all, that others also may fear:" which is spoken of elders who transgress: to others, who publicly or heavily offend, or refuse to attend to admonition, these words of the apostle (2 Cor. ii. 6) may with propriety be accommodated,—"Sufficient to such a man is this punishment, which was inflicted of many."

In what manner are they to be publicly corrected by deeds?

By our shunning the society and conversation of such a person, and refusing to eat with him; though we do not regard him as an enemy, but admonish him as a brother (as long, that is, as he professedly acts as a brother, and does not become the enemy of truth and piety, or of believers), or at least by shunning him in the holier fellowship of the Lord's table.

Where

Where is any thing written concerning the former mode of correction?

First, in Matthew xviii. 17, "If he neglect to hear the church, let him be unto thee as an heathen-man and a publican." Next, 1 Cor. v. 11, 13, "If any man that is called a brother be a fornicator, or covetous, or an idolater, or a railer, or a drunkard, or an extortioner, with such an one do not eat." "Therefore put away from amongst yourselves that wicked person." And also 2 Thess. iii. 6, "Now we command you, brethren, in the name of our Lord Jesus Christ, that ye withdraw yourselves from every brother that walketh disorderly, and not after the traditions which ye have received of us." And below (ver. 14), "If any man obey not our word by this epistle, note that man, and have no company with him, that he may be ashamed."

Where is any thing written concerning the latter?

There is indeed nothing written concerning this mode of correction: but reason itself and the order of the church seem to require, that those who in such things conduct themselves unworthily be not admitted at least to the holy supper of our Lord; notwithstanding they do not yet deserve to be kept from all fellowship and conversation with us, and to be utterly excommunicated: that by such means a proper respect for the Lord's table may be preserved; and that those persons, seeing themselves already, in a certain degree, placed in a condition of excommunication, may hasten their penitence.

Why

Why is such correction employed in the Christian church?

That the transgressor may be healed, and brought back to the right way; that others may be stricken with fear, and kept uncorrupted by the wicked; that scandal and disorder may be removed from the church of Christ; that the word of the Lord be not evil spoken of; and that thus the name and the glory of the Lord may not be profaned.

What danger threatens such persons?

It is this;—that after being excluded from the church of Christ, and consequently from his kingdom, there remains nothing further for them, while they continue in this state, but destruction : since this ex-communication is no other than the binding of which Christ speaks (Matth. xviii. 18), "Verily I say unto you,Whatsoever ye shall bind on earth shall be bound in heaven, and whatsoever ye shall loose on earth shall be loosed in heaven."

What is the power of binding and loosing which the church possesses?

It is the power of declaring and denouncing, according to the word of God, who is worthy, and who unworthy, of being in the church, or a member of the church.

State now the way of preserving order in the church, which relates chiefly to the elders and those who rule?

Elders and those who rule are bound not only to attend more carefully than others to those duties which pertain to all universally, and to go before all
in

in their example,—on which account also the younger
members, being instructed in their duty, are to submit themselves unto the elder (1 Pet. v. 5),—but are
from time to time to excite others to the discharge of
the same duties, to overlook the church, to watch
each individual, " to be instant in season and out
of season, to reprove, rebuke, exhort with all long-
suffering and doctrine," as the apostle writes (2 Tim.
iv. 2), but yet with that caution which the apostle
prescribes (1 Tim. v. 1, 2), " Rebuke not an elder,
but entreat him as a father, and the younger men as
brethren : the elder women as mothers, the younger
as sisters, with all purity."

CHAPTER IV.

OF THE INVISIBLE CHURCH OF CHRIST.

TELL me now what you think of the invisible
church ?

The Holy Scriptures seems hardly any where to use
the word Church to designate a society of truly pious
men, distinct from that church which is called visible ;
since all who are truly pious either do now belong, or
have formerly belonged, to the visible church also:
though it must be confessed that this visible church
is sometimes considered in such a light, that it is assumed that it discharges its duty, and truly obeys
God ; regard not being had to what it really is, but to
what it ought to be in virtue of its profession, condition, and discipline : as also the same thing is often
taken for granted in respect to individual professors

of

of Christian truth. Nevertheless it is possible to imagine a certain peculiar multitude of people, and their union among themselves, which it might be allowable, on account of some likeness, or metaphorically, to call a church: for the truly pious, dispersed in all directions, or concealed,—if indeed true piety can be concealed,—cannot in literal propriety of speech be designated a church, that is, a congregation assembled in one place.

Who then are the invisible church?

They are those who truly confide in Christ and obey him; and are therefore, in the most perfect sense, his body: an assembly or congregation of whom, so that we may be assured in respect to the real piety of each individual, we shall not, I apprehend, ever find or see except at the coming of Christ.

Why do you call this assembly of men invisible?

Because at present it can only be conceived by the mind; and because those qualities which constitute this church and the members thereof are invisible. For no one is a member of this church who has not true faith in Christ and real piety; for by faith we are grafted into the body of Christ, and by faith and piety we remain in him. But true faith in Christ, and real piety, can in no way be seen by our eyes, since they both lie hidden and concealed in the inmost recesses of the heart.

Can it not be known from the external actions, who is a member of the church of Christ?

From evil external actions any one may easily know that a person is not a member of the church of
Christ;

Christ; that is, that he has not a lively and efficacious faith :—but from external actions having the appearance of virtue, it may be difficult to ascertain where true faith and piety reside.   For it is easy to conceal certain vices ; and those actions which do not proceed from a sincere heart may wear the same appearance as those that do.   In short—he that is evil-disposed may assume the external appearance of a good man ; but it is different with a good man, who never attempts to put on the appearance of a wicked man.

Have you any thing to add, which relates to the knowledge of the saving doctrine ?

I have now explained to you all that I could, in a compendious way, state upon this subject. It belongs to you, after having rightly perceived and understood these things, to imprint them on your mind, and to regulate your life conformably to their directions. May God assist you in this work :—to whom, as he has graciously permitted us to bring our conference to a termination, be praise and glory, through Jesus Christ, for ever and ever.   AMEN.

THE END.

INDEX

INDEX

OF

TEXTS OF SCRIPTURE

Quoted and Explained in this Catechism.

s

GENERAL INDEX.

—————

Printed by R. and A. Taylor, Shoe-Lane.